ENTRANCES & EXITS

A Life In and Out of the Theatre

ENTRANCES
& EXITS

A Life In and Out of the Theatre

NORRIS HOUGHTON

Limelight Editions
NEW YORK

For
Frank

First Limelight Edition February 1991
Copyright © 1991 by Norris Houghton

All rights reserved under international and Pan-American Copyright Conventions.
Published in the United States by Proscenium Publishers Inc., New York, and
simultaneously in Canada by Fitzhenry & Whiteside, Limited, Toronto.

A portion of this book, "The Yalta Conference," originally appeared in *The New
Yorker* in somewhat different form.

Library of Congress Cataloging-in-Publication Data
Houghton, Norris.
Entrances and exits : a life in and out of the theatre /
Norris Houghton. -- 1st Limelight ed.
p. cm.
ISBN 0-87910-144-X
1. Houghton, Norris. 2. Theatre--United States--History--
20th century. 3. Theatrical producers and directors--
United States--Biography. I. Title.
PN2287.H68A3 1990
792'.023'092--dc20   90-40527   CIP
[B]

Contents

Acknowledgments

During the five years I have been at work on this volume, I have racked up a long list of debts of gratitude that I wish to acknowledge. The first helping hands were those of Simon Michael Bessie, who gave me a sort of crash course on how to deal with the problems of autobiographical writing. Following him was Robert Emmett Ginna, Jr., who helped me to fashion my story into form and sequence. Along the way, editorial guidance came from Van der Veer Varner, T. Edward Hambleton freshened my recollections of the Phoenix years, and Mary Houghton Boorman reacquainted me with some of my paternal antecedents. Sophia Yarnall Jacobs, the late Emily Kimbrough, Anna E. Crouse, and Frederica B. Barbour were kind enough to read my manuscript as it moved toward completion and made valuable suggestions. F.L. Dent was of inestimable help in indoctrinating me into the strange new world of the word processor and was of constant aid in turning my yellow legal-sized sheets of handwritten prose into readable form. I much appreciate William F. Draper's kindness in granting permission for the reproduction of my portrait on this book's jacket. Finally, for his indefatigable industry and skill in editing the final draft, I am deeply grateful to my editor and publisher, Mel Zerman.

For their hospitality in providing places to which I could retreat from telephonic and social interruptions for weeks or months at a time I am indebted to Mary and Barry Bingham in Chatham, on Cape Cod; Jean Malahan, also in Chatham; Mercedes and Heath Bowman in Rome; Mary Burke in Hobe Sound; Gertrude Legendre at Medway Plantation in South Carolina; and Margo and John Wilkie in Katonah, New York. Without their kindness this memoir might never have reached completion.

Overture

One gusty March evening in 1954, the lights were burning bright on the marquee of the Phoenix Theatre on the Lower East Side of Manhattan. They guided pedestrians, taxis, and limousines coursing down Second Avenue (not Broadway) to the opening of *The Golden Apple*, the third production of a new stage venture and a debut for T. Edward Hambleton and Norris Houghton as musical comedy impresarios.

After I had installed in her aisle seat my tiny and slightly bewildered seventy-eight-year-old mother, who had come from Ohio for this night, I joined T. Hambleton backstage, where we made the rounds of the dressing rooms, exhorting the leading performers and the ensemble to "break a leg," and shook hands with the stage managers and crew heads. We then proceeded to the lobby, where people were pushing to get out of the wind and into our arms.

Soon the curtain is up and we are in Angel's Roost, state of Washington. It's 1900, and the boys come marching home from the Spanish-American War, boys whose names are Achilles and Patroclus and Ajax and Ulysses. Among their fair greeters are a couple of girls, Penelope and Helen. What's going on? It sounds like the wrong war. Now Paris drops in—literally—from the sky in a marvelous striped gas balloon. Of course, we know when

Paris meets Helen the action will really heat up, especially with her serenading him throatily:

> It's a lazy afternoon
> And the beetle bugs are zoomin'
> And the tulip trees are bloomin'
> And there's not another human   in view
>   but us two . . .

In no time he will carry her off in his balloon.

> Helen! Paris!
> You had better come back!
>   They took the china
>   And the bric-a-brac!
> Helen! Paris!
> You are liable to crash!
>   They also have the jewels
>   And the household cash!

Nothing now but for the boys to take off again, this time to rescue Helen for Menelaus: "Row, boys, row . . ."

And that was enough for the first act. Already there had been one solid show-stopper—Kaye Ballard's crooning of "Lazy Afternoon." There were others in the second. My favorite: Bibi Osterwald in an orange spot, singing her Siren Song, backed by hula-swaying Sirenettes:

> By a goona goona goona
> Goona goona goona lagoon
> We will croona croona croona
> Croona croona real jungle tune.

What an evening it turned out to be: cheers and stomps when the final curtain fell. Off Broadway was upward bound! We had wanted to outcharm Broadway and we did, snatching the New York Drama Critics Circle Award for the best new musical of the season 1953–54.

I have been, I must confess, stagestruck for most of my life. When asked what aspect of the stage struck me hardest, I have been wont to reply, modestly but accurately, "I've done everything in the theatre except the two most important things: I've never written a play, and I've never acted professionally." By the time I was twenty-five I had concluded, bowing to a total absence of popular demand, that I was not to be an actor, and that lacking any discernible impulse toward creative writing, I was unlikely to startle the world as a dramatist.

Furthermore, early on I decided against aiming for vertical advancement. Instead of seeking to rise from the mailroom to the boardroom—the dream of many young men—I would seek to advance horizontally, rather more like the crab than the lark. Without thinking much about it, I guess I was opting to be a generalist, not a specialist. To pursue such a course in America's twentieth century is—let's face it—tantamount to saying goodbye to Success. The specialists run off with the millions.

To myself I said, "I want to become a 'theatre man' in the broad sense of the word," and I began to reach out to fulfill myself in many directions: by designing scenery, and building and painting it, by trying my hand at directing, by writing books and articles about the theatre, by helping edit a theatre magazine, by becoming a producer and even starting a theatre of my own; and, finally, by sharing with a new generation on college campuses what I had learned about the theatre through all of the above.

I encountered not long ago in Daniel Yankelovich's *New Roots* a phrase that threw light on my behavior. He wrote of persons with "a slender incentive toward the acquisition of affluence," a delicate phrase that accurately characterizes myself and accounts for my tendency to flee from specialization and to find self-fulfillment in minimal dependence on the dollar and maximal devotion to my love, the stage.

Early on I also discovered a compensatory *modus vivendi:* to live off the affluence of others. The Guggenheim Foundation staked me to thirteen months in Europe in the 1930s, thus allowing me to escape unharmed the darkest days of the Great Depression; and in the early 1940s, the Rockefeller Foundation funded a seven-month, nineteen-thousand-mile journey around the United States.

True, I returned from both trips without a dime in my pocket, but from my experiences came two books that, while widely remaindered, did not go altogether unnoticed. Better still, I returned with broadened perspectives on foreign cultures, especially their theatres, and on our own regional cultures, including their stages and stage workers. Also, my travels served at least to quadruple the number of my friends and acquaintances, and since I turned insatiably gregarious after a rather solitary childhood, this pleased me enormously.

In later years my experiences abroad paid off in other, unexpected ways. I would never, for instance, have gotten to the Yalta Conference and stood in the same room with Roosevelt, Stalin, and Churchill had it not been for the extended exposure to the USSR that the Guggenheim fellowship had afforded me a decade earlier. I probably would never have latched onto the twin concepts of the decentralization and decommercialization of the American theatre, which became central pillars of my faith, had it not been for the Rockefeller grant.

I made yet another discovery fairly early on: contained within me were two warring impulses—one toward scholarship, the other toward artistic expression. For as long as I can remember, while I was in love with the art in myself (to paraphrase the great Russian Stanislavski), I was equally in love with scholarship and learning. From the time I was in the second grade until I reached the end of my fourth year at Princeton, I ran myself ragged between stages and classrooms, eager first for the applause of an audience and then just as eager for good grades.

After college I turned initially to the theatre, but in a few years I found myself writing the first of six books. From the start, while working as a designer on Broadway with mounting frequency, I was also lecturing at one university or another, not to mention women's clubs and other organizations dedicated to cultural advancement in the hinterlands, and was contributing articles on theatre to national magazines. Then, after a decade with the Phoenix, I spent my next eighteen years as an educator, practicing pedagogy, serving as departmental chairman at a college and dean at a university, becoming a fellow of the American Academy of Arts and Sciences, and, in the end, acquiring three honorary degrees, though with no longer a place to show off the hoods save at Halloween parties.

Whatever I have done has been marked by a struggle between the two lobes of my brain, the affective and the cognitive—the first stimulating my senses, imagination, and emotions, the other impressing on me ideas, language, and information. This may explain other apparently harmless schizoid tendencies. I think, for instance, of my intense preoccupation with reality versus illusion and with personal freedom versus duty (the latter traceable no doubt to staunch adherence to my Presbyterian faith), both as themes of dramatic conflict and as aspects of my attitude toward life. I think of my instinctive craving for stability and security, exhibited in an unattractive penny-pinching streak, wrestling with a strong tendency toward risk-taking, derived from confidence that the Lord's eye is on me as well as on the sparrow.

But if my occasionally frenetic comings and goings, and the thought processes that prompted them, are full of contradictions, there has been one constant in my life: service to the theatre. It is this that has informed all the teaching, the lecturing, the traveling, and of course the designing, the directing, the producing. Should "service to the theatre" smack of duty, I must quickly add that it was performed out of love. And so, while it has not brought me great riches or fame, it has, like a requited love, given me some very special satisfactions . . . and I never grew bored.

ACT ONE

1

Indianapolis to Princeton (1909–31)

*W*hen I was writing the opening
chapter of a panel report on the arts and American education in
the 1970s, I made use in its first paragraph of a quotation from
Alexis de Tocqueville: "We must watch the infant in his mother's
arms; . . . the first occurrences which he witnessed; we must hear
the first words which awaken the sleeping power of thought.
. . . The entire man is, so to speak, to be seen in the cradle of the
child." Tocqueville, of course, was writing, in 1835, about the
infancy of democracy in America (the title of his epochal book);
but I find it a satisfactory rationale for beginning these memoirs
with an account of my birth. The trouble is, of course, that while
I was present, I was in no position to watch myself in my cradle
or hear my first words. But then Tocqueville wasn't even around
when our America lay in its cradle.

I consider I did have a notable nativity: it occurred on Boxing
Day, 1909. My mother was five months pregnant when Halley's
Comet was first sighted over Egypt. By Christmas it was approaching Indianapolis. So was I. But as so often has happened
to me in other circumstances since, I missed it by a hair. What
a blow for my mother: a new Star in the East but no Babe.
However, twenty-four hours later I arrived—in ample time for
the Wise Men, not due until Twelfth Night. (No Wise Men
turned up in Indianapolis then—or, as far as I know, ever thereaf-

ter.) Instead, I have had to be comforted by the knowledge that I was born on the Feast of St. Stephen, the first Martyr. I have never been sure, however, whether he was born on the twenty-sixth or was stoned to death on that day.

My maternal great-grandfather, Thomas Munns, who from his portrait appears to have borne an unexpected resemblance to Jefferson Davis, had become an Ohio settler from Ireland in the 1820s and in 1845 had built the family house in Oxford. My grandfather Norris arrived there in the 1870s to occupy the pulpit of Oxford's Presbyterian church and to marry Thomas's daughter. My grandfather Albert Houghton brought his family down from northern Ohio shortly thereafter to settle in this peaceable kingdom too.

My nineteenth-century progenitors were well educated for those days in the Middle West: most of them had college degrees and several became teachers. Grandfather Norris had been a professor of mathematics at Wabash College before joining the clergy. The only trouble with these forebears of mine was that—like myself—they seemed not to be drawn to occupations (such as glassblowing) that led to fortunes. The pulpit and the classroom, seldom noted for their pecuniary rewards, attracted them, and so by the twentieth century those still alive were highly respected but less than affluent.

Oxford, the little town upon which all these ancestors converged, lay about forty miles from Cincinnati. There Miami University and the Oxford College for Women nestled more or less side by side. The pride of Oxford was its glorious elms, its pale pink brick houses and its white ones with green shutters, built in the 1840s and 1850s. There in the 1890s Charles Houghton, a strapping six-footer, met tiny Grace Norris while he was an undergraduate at Miami and she was living at home and winning prizes for proficiency in Greek at Oxford College. He married her in 1896, when she was nineteen and he twenty-one.

Grace and Charles each had younger sisters, and my father had a brother too, named Henry. Grace Houghton was a painter, Sara Norris a musician. Aunt Sade, the latter, graduated from Oxford College at seventeen and then from the Cincinnati Conservatory of Music, but gave up a performance career in order to take care of her invalid maiden aunt, after whose death Sade spent five years in Chile as a missionary. I had thought it was a Christian country already, but it was apparently not Christian enough to suit the Methodists.

My paternal aunt, Grace Houghton, a truly gifted artist, studied in Paris with the Czech painter Duvanek. She was also truly an oddball. She was addicted to picture hats that very nearly obscured her entire face, and wisely so. She would have been quite pretty had she not had a mouthful of protruding teeth, all of which, however, were removed by an Indianapolis dentist in the course of one day during a visit to us. (I was astonished.) When they had been replaced, she returned to St. Andrews, Tennessee, cast aside the picture hats as now unnecessary, and lived on a mountaintop above Sewanee with the young Anglican priest she had married in 1913. His name was Father Flye. Among the mountain boys whom he taught at St. Andrews was a youngster, James Agee, who would later win fame as a writer and critic. After Jim's death in early middle age, Father Flye acquired some minor renown-by-association when their lifelong correspondence, *The Letters of James Agee to Father Flye*, was published to considerable acclaim.

Aunt Grace in due time passed to her reward, a victim of the rare disease, better known in India and Sri Lanka than here, beriberi, a malady brought on by malnutrition, doubtless owing to her idiosyncratic lifetime diet of cornflakes and chocolate bars.

As for my father's brother, Henry, the only "normal" one of the brood, I saw little of him, his wife or his six children, for they lived in China. He went as a medical missionary first to Wuhu, then on to Shanghai and finally Peking, there to become in 1921 the first director of the Rockefellers' great Peking Union Medical College (known round the world as PUMC) and the most distinguished member of my immediate family.

My mother was tiny: she never weighed more than ninety pounds. She was mild-mannered but tough-minded, for she had lived through many misfortunes and heartaches. She had lost two baby girls before I was born. That may have accounted for the slight look of sadness that her face assumed in repose. She was not an especially demonstrative mother, but she had a roguish Irish sense of humor, a considerable intellect, and an unexpected quiet wit. She was a devout Christian and sought to bring me up as one.

She was also an enthusiastic member of the Anti-Saloon League. I soon became her principal preoccupation and she mine, for before I was twelve she lost her husband and I my father; he, like Tom Wingfield's dad in *The Glass Menagerie,* ran away from home, although less "in love with long distance" than with another woman. That occurred later—in 1921—when I was in the seventh grade.

My earliest recollection is of an evening in August 1914, in Indianapolis, when my father came home with an announcement: the Kaiser had invaded Belgium and war had broken out—"the guns of August." I'm not sure that at four years of age I was ready to appreciate the implications of that news, but my "sleeping powers of thought" had already been thoroughly aroused and my "first words" had been flowing almost nonstop for at least a couple of years. However, I hadn't caught up with Sarajevo and was a bit uncertain as to whether the Kaiser was a person or a place. But I had no reticence about asking questions, so before being packed off to bed, I had the Great War's immediate origins all straightened out and could fall asleep at once.

When America entered the war in 1917 I was seven. That was also the year I discovered the stage. My clergyman Grandfather Norris was responsible for that mind-boggling occurrence. During a visit to us, he took me by the hand one afternoon and escorted me downtown to see E. H. Sothern and Julia Marlowe in *The Taming of the Shrew.* It was the outstanding event of my winter.

Sothern and Marlowe were the principal purveyors of Shakespeare to the provinces then. She was forty-seven and a touch plumper and more matronly than we admire in a Katherina today; he, at fifty-eight, a bit long in the tooth to be a persuasive Petruchio. But never mind. I had no basis for comparison and so thought them awesome and the whole event very jolly, especially when the pots and pans began to fly.

I don't recall who took me on my next theatrical sortie, the following year—to a musical called *Chu Chin Chow,* imported from London by impresario Morris Gest and announced as based on *Ali Baba and the Forty Thieves,* doubtless the reason it was selected for the delectation of an eight-year-old. I recall nothing about thieves, but as clearly as yesterday can call up the sumptuous Near Eastern harem wherein my astonished Hoosier eyes beheld their first belly dance, executed by a voluptuous female, from whom I discovered the provocative value of veils. Together, these productions were no doubt responsible for forming my eclectic taste in theatre.

"The road" in that second decade of this century was the principal source of entertainment in Middle America. Movies were grainy to look at and of course silent to the ear; radio was only approaching the scratch-and-wail era of the crystal set. In my case, we owned no radio, and since I was too young to attend movies alone, and my mother had neither the inclination nor the time to take me to them after school, I grew up with unconcern for the celluloid medium, an unconcern that seems to have deepened with the years. But the traveling troupes called collectively "the road" offered transient glimpses of what the big theatre outside was like, from *Nellie, the Beautiful Cloak Model,* which I did not see, to *Abie's Irish Rose* which I did (though that was early in the twenties).

Back at the end of the summer of 1917, my father, then a captain in the army, received his sailing orders. World War I being much cozier than successor conflicts, my mother and I went east to attend a sort of sailing party—not, I grant, on board the troop transport itself but ashore for a few days prior to its departure from port. We stayed in unaccustomed grandeur at the Hotel Seville on Twenty-ninth Street. Charles looked very noble in his uniform (not unlike Sergius in *Arms and the Man,* I have since decided). His boots were as shiny as his black hair and heavy black eyebrows, of which latter I was both envious and fearful.

On Fifth Avenue around the corner from the hotel were several Japanese curio shops. From one I came back to Indiana with a collection of miniature bridges, bonsai-like trees and shrubs, tiny houses, and a pagoda or two. Acquiring a sizable cardboard carton, I removed its lid and one side, lined the others with florist's green waxed paper, arranged my Orientalia in pleasing configurations, and invited Mother, Grandpa, and Lendora, our extremely homely but beloved Negro cook, to inspect my first stage sets to the background accompaniment of a Victor Red Seal rendition of "Gems from *The Mikado.*" The result was much admired, although Lendora, being a literalist, inquired where the action was.

I had never seen a "puppet show," but when several years later I was given *Tony Sarg's Marionette Book,* I realized that they were the missing element in my admittedly static exhibitions. With the single-minded zeal of an eleven-year-old, which I was then, I set to work on an undertaking that I would repeat over and over again for the next fifty years—I would put on a play. I faced the necessity of finding (or writing) the play, then peopling it with performers, both the marionettes themselves and the manipulators of their strings; the former must be costumed, the stage decorated and lighted (Christmas tree bulbs), and the whole pulled together by an impresario (myself). With an assist from four fellow artists in the eighth grade, my company of puppeteers, the first production, *Snow White and the Dwarfs,* opened on February 2, 1923, and closed on February 3. It was pronounced a triumph. The house—our living room and front hall, facing the dining room double doorway, which accommodated the stage—was sold out for the entire run.

Next I offered a "Festival" of short plays. The company grew from five to nine; we increased our run to three performances. Owing to popular demand, our third season lasted four performances. Now the company consisted of twelve, all in our early teens, including a stage manager, a business manager, and an electrician, who installed saltwater dimmers to control the Christmas tree lights.

The trouble with the whole enterprise was that time was running out. In what seemed no time, its founder was sixteen and a high school junior. It was time, as the Good Book tells us, for me to put away childish things. *Alice in Wonderland,* in which my high school sweetheart, Valentia Meng, manipulated and spoke for Alice, was my swan song to the world of marionettes, in 1926, but not to the wonderland I was now bent on exploring.

From my earliest childhood I had grown up in an atmosphere of fervor and faith. Churchgoing was as accepted an activity as going to school. I rejoiced at Christmas in the angels' voices as much as in reindeers' hooves, loved singing hymns at home on Sunday evenings, joined the church when I was twelve. Deeply troubled by the sins of emission and commission common to most boys emerging from puberty, I prayed for forgiveness with a contrite heart (although, like most of us, I went on committing my small sins). It seems quite natural, therefore, that I was happiest when I could bring together my two loves—the church and the stage.

This became spectacularly possible when I had just turned fifteen and learned by devouring *Theatre Arts Monthly* (while my contemporaries devoured *Boys' Life*) that Max Reinhardt, the great German director, was taking his famous production of *The Miracle* on tour after its New York engagement. Down to Cincinnati I went. The Academy of Music there had been converted by Norman Bel Geddes into a medieval Gothic cathedral: the auditorium became its nave, the stage its apse. Up and down its aisles surged great processionals. Music of organ and orchestra swelled forth from hidden galleries. Candles flickered, banners waved in and out of the beams of light pouring through high stained-glass windows. Overwhelmed, I wept with excitement. I had never sniffed the heady scent of incense before, certainly never seen anyone more beautiful than Lady Diana Manners as the Madonna. It was by far the most exciting theatrical experience of my early years—even more than *Chu Chin Chow.*

My Max Reinhardt period lasted two or three years. It was highlighted by a pair of Christmas pageants I created in blatant imitation of *The Miracle,* directed and designed for my church, the first in 1925.

In this case the real miracle was how I sweet-talked and bamboozled the church fathers into saying "yes" to my grandiose proposals. But there they were—the church treasurer my staunchest supporter; committees of churchwomen sewing away for dear life on garments for angels and shepherds, kings and peasants, altogether one hundred and fifty; the choir and organist earnestly rehearsing unfamiliar excerpts from Monteverdi and Pergolesi, and little Norris racing around, checking costumes and props, and the installation of what lighting equipment there was, rehearsing the crowd scenes, and staging the tableaux. I was infatuated by spectacle.

Tabernacle Presbyterian Church had recently completed a new sanctuary, Gothic in spirit and, judged by the standards of ecclesiastical architecture in Indiana then, worthy of its middle-class congregation's pride. It was a big church, seating five or six hundred worshippers, and on the two Sunday evenings every pew was filled fifteen minutes in advance. A number of foolish virgins, who (naturally) arrived late, had to be turned away. It was, in a word, a howling success. The following autumn the church fathers encouraged me to mount another sacred extravaganza. I obliged with a second crowd-pleaser and might still be at it, I suppose, if I hadn't had better sense.

By the 1920s the road I've talked of was supplemented by local resident commercial stock companies, offering a new bill weekly. Indianapolis had a rather top-drawer company in the twenties. Its producer-director was Stuart Walker, who leased a huge downtown theatre, brought excellent actors from New York like ingenue Ruth Gordon, her husband Gregory Kelly and Alexander Kirkland as juveniles, like Blanche Yurka, and Margery Maude. He treated us locals to marvelously funny farces and comedies— Avery Hopwood's *Fair and Warmer, Dulcy, A Very Good Young Man, Merton of the Movies*—more serious dramas like *Beggar on Horseback, Peter Ibbetson,* even a dramatization of the Book of Job. This was the summertime fare I gobbled up in my high school years.

Church and Stage were my two adolescent loves. But there was a third: School. Having entered the first grade with a slender but recognizable capacity to read and write, I skipped that year and commenced with the second grade. The succeeding semesters passed without great travail, except for playground recesses. There was no sport at which I seemed able to excel, not even marbles, so I came perilously close to being labeled a sissy.

I also dreaded the hours in the woodworking shop. I could never hit a nail with conviction, drive a screw straight, or saw a board cleanly. I managed, however, to distract my peers from my manly insufficiencies by winning at spelling contests in grade school and by acquiring enough merit badges to reach "Life and Star" rank after I joined the Boy Scouts, for I loved the outdoors.

I think back on my childhood as happy. While other boys were out playing ball, I was brushing up on Dickens (my favorite), the mystery novels of Wilkie Collins, *The Count of Monte Cristo, The Prisoner of Zenda.* Who could be unhappy in such exhilarating company?

These joys were mixed with soberer matters, outstandingly the necessity to start contributing to my own livelihood. (Apparently my father provided but meagerly for my support.) So while a seventh grader I acquired a newspaper route and devoted afternoons after school for the next three years to the distribution of information to others and the acquisition of knowledge in business for myself. The high point of that career came about 5:30 A.M. on the second of August, 1923, when a phone call summoned me to my newspaper substation to go forth shouting "Extry! Extry! Harding Dead; Coolidge In!" It was the first time I sensed I was in direct touch with history. The summer before my first high school year, I worked packing lawbooks for Bobbs-Merrill; next I was a draftsman's aide, a blueprinter, in a structural-steel company; the last two summers before college, in a paymaster's office, where my nimble fingers with greenbacks and my nimble wit at addition and multiplication made me a valuable adjunct to the meat-packing business.

In my upper-class high school years I captained one of two debating teams, the only competitive sport I engaged in. I loved it, for it allowed me to appear in public in a major role, next best to acting. Besides, I loved the sound of my own voice. Although I never played on any high school ball team, never ran a track race, never graced the tennis team, never became a Lothario or joined a high school "fraternity"—and so seldom went to a dance—and had to live down the dubious reputation of being about to graduate with a perfect four-year academic record, I was elected the president of my class. In our national elections these days, under fifty percent of America's eligible voters turn out, alas. So was it with the Shortridge High School class of 1927: only 207 out of 475 seniors bothered to cast ballots. Houghton won 114 of them, hardly a landslide. Nor could he claim a firm mandate; but then he had no platform.

2

I entered Princeton on a scholarship in September 1927. I chose it over Harvard, which also offered me one, partly because it was smaller but mainly because I had seen its Triangle Club musical comedy in Indianapolis on its Christmas tour, with its chorus girls drawn largely from the football team.

At the opening of college in September, the Pennsylvania Railroad's Spirit of St. Louis made one of four annual unscheduled stops at Princeton Junction. Along with a noisy bunch of other teenaged and twenty-year-old Middle Westerners, I hauled my suitcases off it and lugged them to the waiting two-car shuttle train that connects junction with borough. I knew nobody, so I sat by myself and looked out the window at the prospect: the big foursquare Gothic tower of the Graduate College against the sky and the smaller tower of Holder Hall dominating the slight ridge on which the university stood. Sixty years ago it was approached across empty fields—an oasis in a desert.

A welcoming letter from the dean of freshmen had told me I would be lodged off campus. A map was enclosed. My destination turned out to be at the foot of a little dead-end alley opening off Nassau Street, called Bank Street. All its houses were small and of white clapboard; all looked alike. No collegiate Gothic on Bank Street. There were four fairly Spartan rooms for freshmen on the second floor of number 37. In one of them I found C. Wadsworth Farnum, already nicknamed "Dusty" in obeisance to a current silent-film star. He, too, was a scholarship student, and together we waited table in Freshman Commons. We might have drifted apart after Bank Street were it not that we both majored in English Literature and four years later reviewed for our comprehensives together and shared highest honors. He was a rather self-effacing little fellow, but he possessed a quiet wit and considerable sagacity. He became an executive vice president and director of the mighty Bankers Trust Company in New York.

Like most great institutions, there are many Princetons. Each of its sons searches to find the one he wants and needs. Shortly before my time, F. Scott Fitzgerald and Edmund Wilson were inhabiting the campus simultaneously. Each brought to, put his stamp on, and took away from his alma mater a quite different and equally authentic image. My Princeton was not either of theirs, although it partook of both.

Henry Adams claimed his education was acquired in spite of Harvard. Contrariwise, much of mine I owe to Princeton. I was in love with learning. I felt at home in the library; I was exhilarated by discovering there was a minute place for me in the stream of Western culture. That excited me more than the discovery of sex or, say, Harlem nightclub life in the twenties.

When it came time to write my senior thesis in 1931, I chose a subject drawn from the stage: "The Artistic Collaboration of Ben Jonson and Inigo Jones in the Production of English Masques of the 17th Century." How was that for a scholarly effort?

As I felt at home in the library, so equally did I feel comfortable in the lecture hall and in the informal "preceptorials," Woodrow Wilson's adaptation of the seminar system. I recall many of my professors with delight, but none more than J. Duncan Spaeth, Walter P. Hall, and Christian Gauss.

Professor Spaeth's Shakespeare course was a one-man show. A figure of Falstaffian girth and the possessor of a mane of long, stringy gray hair worthy of Lear, he had talents as various as Bottom's: he could play Pyramus, "a lover that kills himself most gallant for love"; yet his "chief humour is for a tyrant." But then, "Let me play the lion too. I will roar that I will do any man's heart good to hear me." His performance of Desdemona was tear-jerking; to his summons as Henry V: "Once more into the breach," delivered fortissimo, we responded with huzzahs.

"Buzzer" Hall's moniker derived from his hearing aid, which occasionally ran amok during lectures. Pacing the platform, waving a pointer to punctuate his rapid-fire delivery, intoning in the high pitch of the totally deaf, he made modern European history enthralling. At his annual lecture on Garibaldi, undergraduate auditors turned out in droves to sit breathless on windowsills and stand in the aisles, as he shouted at them about the Italian Unification.

Christian Gauss, dean of the College, was my preceptor as well as lecturer in modern French literature. His preceptorials, held once a week in his study in the yellow house on the front campus that is the dean's residence, allowed me a close-up of one of President Wilson's first preceptor appointees. He was then in his fifties, but to my twenty-year-old eyes he looked prematurely aged: his face cross-hatched with lines and crinkles, his head balding, his body small and rather slight. But he held that head erect, his eyes sparkling, bright blue, now ironic, now compassionate, always wise. Nobody could pull the wool over them. Dean Gauss was one of my academic heroes.

Donald Clive Stuart was Princeton's professor of drama. Naturally, with him I had the closest association, for he was also permanent director of the Triangle Club. Not until my fourth year was I eligible to take his course in the history of dramatic literature. It was the closest thing Princeton had to a survey of my future profession, but was noticeably somniferous despite being delivered in a wing collar. The chief thing I remember from it was Dr. Stuart's oft-repeated aphorism: "Novels are written, plays are rewritten"—neither an accurate nor a remarkable dictum.

Let me return to my assertion that "there are many Princetons." I entered shortly before the coonskin coat era ended, when only about twenty percent of entering freshmen came from public high schools. Princeton was still widely thought of as a country club where young gentlemen of wealth and breeding, mostly WASPS and largely from Philadelphia and points south, gathered to pass four golden years in rollicking fellowship and mirth, accelerated by a more than adequate supply of illegal "bathtub gin." That Princeton was still very much alive, though I qualified in no way except as a WASP.

Alongside it was another Princeton. Less vociferously hedonistic, its adherents came to college, first, to make friends; second, to acquire, as easily as possible, a respectable education, one that might lead to employment after graduation; third, to learn to play bridge or soccer or improve their tennis, to become entertainingly literate dinner partners and qualify as good Ivy League husbands. I'd hazard a guess that in the early thirties the majority belonged to that Princeton.

My own Princeton was another matter. I demanded—and received—from my alma mater serious academic consideration. It sought to satisfy my own—and other like-minded men's—thirst for knowledge, to stimulate our minds and imaginations, answer our questions and provoke more. A humanistic education was the goal of most of us. Our Princeton encouraged us to lap up learning rather than liquor or ladies.

The only problem was the richness and variety of its cupboard. I consider mine an acceptably liberal education. As an English major, I was required to master a reading knowledge of Anglo-Saxon so that I might—I can't say I did—enjoy *Beowulf* in the original. At least it qualified me to join the ranks of the rankest pedants.

I strengthened my acquaintance with the classics—two more years of Greek and one of Latin to add to the three of the former and six of the latter I'd brought with me—and acquired a superficial knowledge of medieval history, Italian painting, the history of architecture, French literature, and one course each in chemistry and biology to "broaden" me, plus, of course, a lot of English literature, especially dramatic. Nonetheless, I wound up my four years with no inkling of philosophy, politics, economics, or sociology, no exposure to either heaven via astronomy or religion, or earth via geology or archaeology. Although I claim I received an excellent education in the liberal arts, the fact is that the principal thing I learned from Princeton was how little I knew. But that, I suppose, is always better than nothing. At least it encourages humility.

For theatrical nourishment I was dependent on the occasional weekend I could afford in New York. Like many other indigent stagestruck students, I rushed via the subway to Gray's Drugstore, hoping to arrive in time to snatch up just before curtain time a half-price two-dollar balcony seat to some Broadway hit. That was how I managed to see my first musical, Rudolf Friml's *Rose Marie*, then in its third year, "The Indian Love Call" you-ou-ouing as longingly as ever. I saw Robert E. Sherwood's *Reunion in Vienna* and S. N. Behrman's *The Second Man*, both starring

the impeccable Lunts, the original productions of *Porgy,* Eugene
O'Neill's *Marco Millions* and *Strange Interlude,* Marc Connelly's
The Green Pastures. I discovered the luminous magic of settings,
lighting, and costumes by Robert Edmond Jones, Norman Bel
Geddes, Lee Simonson.

Back in 1918, George Jean Nathan, scintillating iconoclastic
critic of those days, had referred to Broadway as "the popular
theatre," where, he claimed, "the best in drama and dramatic
literature must inevitably fail." He called it "strident, half-cooked,
credulous, unlearned and egregious, uncouth and shabby and
common," and declared it "the epitome of mob America and of
mob America's view of art and letters."

He was writing in retrospect, at the end of World War I. Ten
years later I made Broadway's acquaintance at first hand—as a
spectator, that is. The old dogs were still up to their old tricks,
so disparagingly limned by Nathan, but the decade between had
wrought incredible changes. In those first years after the war, a
new generation of producers, playwrights, players, and public
had made its entrance. They brought to Broadway new concepts,
new taste, new demands and standards, new ideas. It wasn't that
they ousted the old dogs; they just made them move over.

The result was that Broadway flourished as never before. Its
1927–28 season, which coincided with my freshman year, broke
the all-time record for a season's productions, 264, a peak that has
never been hit since. I've read that seventy theatres were alight
and not enough to go around. (Compare that to the 1988–89
season, with just thirty new productions—but twenty of them
plays—and thirty-six playhouses, including the Vivian Beaumont
at Lincoln Center, to house them.)

Those afternoons spent poring over *Theatre Arts* had prepared
me to expect excellence and to shun Nathan's "uncouth and
shabby and common," still hanging on through the twenties
alongside the new "theatre for adults," as Brooks Atkinson later
dubbed it in his book *Broadway.*

At seventeen I was eager to appear "adult." I was unquestionably an incipient culture snob. I had no avant-garde preten-
sions—I was a follower of the "establishment." That meant being
in favor of drawing rooms rather than custard pies. I preferred

uplifting messages to debauchery. But I did love to laugh, and I caught on to satire rather early.

Not until Princeton's one-thousand-seat McCarter Theatre opened in 1930 were Broadway's luminaries visible locally. Then at last the university had a house to offer to the likes of Ethel Barrymore and Mrs. Fiske. The latter, surely in her seventies, brought *Ghosts* in a farewell touring appearance as Mrs. Alving. President Hibben invited Joshua Logan, president of the Triangle Club, and Houghton, its vice president, to accompany him backstage to be presented to the star after her performance. The tiny old lady emerged, smiled briefly at the timid Houghton, turned with enthusiasm to the more imposing Logan, and unexpectedly announced in her husky baritone, "Young man, I've heard a great deal about you!" Taken aback, Josh swallowed twice, then graciously responded, "And I've heard a great deal about you too, Mrs. Fiske!"

The Christmas 1927 production of the Triangle Club, the bait that had lured me toward Princeton, was already deep in the works; in any case, freshmen were ineligible, so I would have to mark time. I discovered, however, an available alternative outlet for my eager but uncertain talent: Princeton's extracurricular dramatic society, the so-called Theatre Intime. It had in fact been founded only six years earlier—in 1921; thus it was, come to think of it, a contemporary of the famous Provincetown Playhouse in Greenwich Village.

In the Intime was a talented junior named Erik Barnouw, who had written a slight but honest comedy about undergraduate life, *Open Collars,* scheduled to lead off the new season. Among freshmen applying were Joshua Logan, at eighteen a two-hundred-pound genial chap with contagious enthusiasm, a laughing bon vivant, burning with ambition and apparent self-confidence; Myron McCormick and Alfred Dalrymple (of whom more later) and myself. Josh and Mac were accepted as actors, I to design the one set.

When in high school I saw my first Triangle show, I had a premonition that it held some sort of key to my future. I had no such awareness of the Theatre Intime and its possible role. I had acted a good deal on amateur stages in Indianapolis. I made a hit in the title role of Booth Tarkington's farce, *Clarence*, that had elevated Alfred Lunt to stardom in Manhattan. As a septuagenarian bishop in a comedy called *Honor Bright*, I teetered and tottered about the stage, wheezing my lines in what I took to be an appropriate facsimile of an ancient cleric. I persuaded one of my mother's friends, at least, for she announced loudly that at seventeen I reminded her of no one so much as George Arliss, the distinguished graying British character actor, then starring in *Old English*. Where could I go from there?

It didn't take long, however, for me to discover that Princeton did not agree with my mother's friend's enthusiasm. In my freshman year, I auditioned for all the Intime plays but was rewarded only by the three-line role of A Thin-Haired Gentleman in the first act of *The Wild Duck*. It was a shock. In the spring, I was encouraged, however, by the Triangle's president, Charles Arnt, to submit sketches for the scenery for its 1929 musical, *Zuider Zee*. My drawings were accepted, and thereafter no one else designed sets or costumes for the Triangle Club in my time. But I never acted again.

In front of the campus student religious center, Murray-Dodge Hall, stood a larger-than-life bronze statue: "The Christian Student." I think he held a football in one hand and a Bible in the other; however, he certainly did *not* wear a mask and buskins. The Murray wing of the hall was a tiny Victorian chapel; its pews accommodated not more than sixty or seventy. The university, fortunately for us, decided to allow the chapel to alter its mission from the sacred to the profane: it became the Intime's home with very simple architectural alterations. The raised platform for lectern and choir became its stage by the insertion of a picture-frame proscenium to separate it from the pew-filled auditorium. That proscenium was sixteen feet wide and ten feet high, and about eight feet separated it from the back wall.

In that minuscule bandbox our predecessors had presented *Hamlet* and *Doctor Faustus*. We had no qualms about its capacity to accommodate Shaw's five-set *Caesar and Cleopatra*, whose opening scene, you recall, occurs at the foot of the Great Sphinx. It was presented later that freshman season. Nor did we quail two years later before *Othello;* it gave Logan a chance to play the Moor and me to follow my fancy from Venice to Cyprus.

Apropos of *Caesar,* the execution of whose sets required as many hands as were available, I encountered on the shop crew another freshman, Joseph Sloane, who became my most valued classmate. As we hammered and painted away at the Sphinx, we found much to talk about, for we both had the gift of gab and had like senses of humor. Because he was taller and stronger than I, by our senior year I found myself looking up to him as to an older brother.

The Intime did the next season really rather overreach its grasp with *Tsar Fyodor Ivanovich.* Only the more learned of our public knew the name of its author, Alexei Tolstoy, or that it had been the opening production of the Moscow Art Theatre in 1897. We were giddy at the thought of presenting its American premiere.

Much of the play's action, laid in a sixteenth century dominated by Ivan the Terrible, occurred in the Kremlin. The basic set consisted of frescoed cross-vaults springing from massive piers. Since the proscenium was but ten feet high and the overhead stage space added only another twenty-four inches or so, the curving vaults had to start springing at about waist height. All might have been well had the cast not numbered some twenty souls, most of them clad in magnificent heavy costumes (made for the Metropolitan Opera's recently discontinued production of *Prince Igor* and rented from Brooks Costume Company) and, as boyars, wearing high fur hats, rather like British guards regiments' busbies, and long, luxuriant beards. The only way the audience could tell who was speaking in the numerous ensemble scenes was by noting which beard was moving.

Now, under those lowering vaults, against which the busbies were always bumping, and clad in heavy brocade with high fur collars, the actors were well nigh overcome by the heat. Thinking to be helpful and provide a breath of air before everyone suffocated, an assistant stage manager opened the backstage door, which faced directly onto the stage. The temperature immediately dropped five degrees, but the draft set all the beards simultaneously waving. Unable any longer to identify the speakers, the audience collapsed in a wave of hilarity.

The Intime was almost unique among American college dramatic societies of the day in that it had no faculty adviser or mentor. Hours put into production were rewarded by no academic credits. The university provided no subsidy beyond giving us the space rent-free and paying our utility bills. The Intime's founding fathers had willed it thus. We successors faithfully guarded their spirit of independence.

Managerial functions rested in an undergraduate board of directors that decided everything—choice of plays, who would direct and design—supervised casting, dealt with matters of finance, and in case of losses, determined how to recoup them. It was a great experience for anyone planning to make the stage his profession, an idea I began to conjure with as I approached the end of my senior year and of my Intime presidency.

That year (1931), the Intime turned ten years old—an excuse to do something on an even larger scale than the extravaganzas I have described. It would be the first production to be staged by undergraduates in the newly completed McCarter Theatre. I would direct, as my Princeton swan song. The largest-scale play I unearthed was called *Masse Mensch (Man and the Masses)*; it was by the young contemporary left-wing German poet-dramatist Ernst Toller, an early Expressionist.

Princeton had never been subjected to anything like it. It had been seen on only two stages in America: the Theatre Guild's in New York, the Vassar Experimental Theatre's at Poughkeepsie. Lee Simonson designed and directed the Guild production (it was a flop). Hallie Flanagan staged the Vassar production. I invited them to our anniversary, and both accepted.

What they saw was an elaborate cubist system of platforms, a bridge, steps, all painted battleship gray, locked together and backed by an empty cyclorama whose color changed under light. Like most Expressionistic European dramas of the late 1920s, its message was a bold call to the proletariat (the *Masse*) to rise up against plutocracy, to "strike" *en principe*—it was seldom clear why or on behalf of what, save a vaguely perceived sense of "humanity." Its characters—The Woman, The Man, The Nameless One—were all exhorting the mob to side with them. The Man, I seem to recall, symbolized the State; The Woman, Humanity; The Nameless One, Revolution. It's not hard to see why it was a Broadway flop.

I doubt I was attracted to *Man and the Masses* because of its subject matter; it was rather for the chance to play around on a big stage with lots of performers, to experiment in an unfamiliar theatrical form just becoming the rage of the international avant-garde. It was well received in New Jersey, largely because the faculty reviewer for *The Daily Princetonian* told his readers it was "an event" and they'd seen nothing to which they could compare it.

In our senior year, Josh had "discovered" a junior majoring in architecture named James Stewart, who also played a mean accordion. Josh, at work in the fall of 1930 on the book for our farewell Triangle show, *The Tiger Smiles*, wrote in a part for Jimmy and his accordion—the romantic lead, in fact. It was not obvious typecasting: Jim was tall and gangling and not notably handsome. He spoke with a kind of hesitant twang. But in spite of—or because of—his patent insecurity, he was, as Josh had discovered, immensely winning.

Overwhelmed by Josh's enthusiasm, which was formidable, Jim succumbed and accepted the role. Once he was hooked on the footlights, his dedication to architecture gradually faded. It was not too hard, therefore, to persuade him to try out in the spring for the juicy role of the butler, Dvornitchek, in the Intime production of Molnár's *The Play's the Thing*; it was a character not unlike the wondrous waiter in Shaw's *You Never Can Tell*. Stewart lost his gangling stance, acquired unexpected urbanity, delivered his lines with deadpan suavity, and ran away with the show. It was his first appearance on the legitimate stage. By the end of the following year he abandoned architecture for acting, and our stage and screen have been ever after enriched.

Over the intervening years, the 1926–34 era of the Intime and the Triangle Club has become something of a Princeton legend, a golden age, and perhaps justifiably. By sheer happenstance, an unusually gifted generation of theatrical talents flowered simultaneously, beginning with Bretaigne Windust and ending with José Ferrer and designer Lemuel Ayers.

Windust, for instance, was never drawn to musicals then (the rest of us were ambidextrous), but he was a great power in the

Intime, where he acted, directed, and was president in 1929. A slight, wiry young man with a rather foxlike face and limp, skimpy, blond hair that kept falling into it when he became excited, Windy seemed a born professional; we others were struggling amateurs alongside him. He fed that image by his sublime self-confidence. He once confided that if one wanted to be an effective stage director, one must always have an answer for every question. "Never say 'I don't know' to an actor," he warned.

Windy also possessed incredible energy. When a set for an Intime play he was staging turned out the wrong color, he stayed up all the night before the dress rehearsal, himself repainting the set.

None of us in that Princeton golden age approached the theatre intellectually. We had no theories or artistic principles, but, perhaps paradoxically, we had very high standards. We depended on instinct and taste and our talents—and each other. Not surprisingly, Windust made a distinguished name for himself on Broadway in the relatively few years before his untimely death. He directed the Lunts in *The Taming of the Shrew* and *Idiot's Delight*; he staged the original productions of *Life with Father*, *Arsenic and Old Lace*, and *State of the Union*. I suspect he was so successful with the Lunts, Howard Lindsay and Dorothy Stickney, Josephine Hull and Boris Karloff, because they did not really approach the theatre intellectually either. Mastery of their craft was more important to them than principles of psychological truth, which they grasped without thinking about them.

Myron McCormick was a fellow Hoosier, short, with sandy hair and a face almost, but not quite, a mug: his ears stuck out at right angles to the rest of his face, like wings. He was one of those Phi Betes who wouldn't be caught dead wearing his key but whose vigorous articulation (when he was sober) betrayed superior intelligence. He, too, died young, but not before he left us with the unforgettable memory of his belly-dancing sailor, Luther Billis, in *South Pacific* eighteen years later on Broadway.

One unseasonably warm afternoon in late April 1931, I sat with my visiting mother in the garden of a borrowed Turtle Bay apartment in New York, a quiet spot in which to speculate for an hour about the future, for commencement was close in the offing.

Although the country was moving toward the depths of the Great Depression, I found myself isolated from the widespread anxiety and desperation that assailed many of my contemporaries and their fathers. This was partly because we had no money to lose, partly because I faced no specter of unemployment: two opportunities offered themselves. One was a full fellowship to the Princeton Graduate College to pursue English literature, the other an urgent invitation to join a summer theatre at West Falmouth on Cape Cod, the University Players Guild, which looked forward to becoming a year-round venture.

The U.P.G. had been founded three years before by Bretaigne Windust with Charles Leatherbee, Harvard '29. Josh Logan had been involved in it too. Windy, now a production stage manager for the Theatre Guild, had only a few weeks earlier invited me to come to New York to talk about joining the company after graduation.

All this I explained to my mother, ending up, "So you see, here I am with two options. Which fork in the road do you think I should follow?"

"I think, since you ask me," she replied after a moment, "that you must travel the one you believe will make you happier, that will most fulfill you."

That was the trouble, I responded. I believed that either one would make me happy, that either way I could fulfill myself. But I added I felt surer about the academic one. About the stage I wasn't so certain. "I think, then, that that's the one I should choose first. If I take the academic road, I'll never know whether or not I could have made it in the theatre. If I opt for the stage, and find in a couple of years or so that I can't make it, it won't be too late to pursue the scholarly path; but once in academia, I'll almost surely find it harder to break out in order to prove myself in the theatre."

Mother agreed, although I daresay that as a professor's daughter she wished in her heart that I had chosen the other road. Mine was indeed "the road less travelled" (only four of us out of five hundred classmates chose it) that led into the perilous, uncertain, alluring realm of the theatre. I wonder whether I would have had the courage to choose it had it not been for the University Players.

When I sat down the next week with Windust and with Logan, just returned from spending his last semester abroad with Leatherbee, which included meetings with Stanislavski in Moscow, they outlined my duties.

"We want you to more or less alternate between stage managing and designing," Windy said.

"How will I know how to stage-manage?" I asked.

"It will be no different from Princeton," replied Windy. And it wasn't. "And no different from Broadway either," he added. And that turned out to be true too. So the big plunge became but a small smooth step into familiar waters.

2

University Players (1931–32)

*J*une 1931 was a month of commencements in my life. The Princeton one came first. Next came my introduction to a 1931 cocktail racily known as a Sidecar, to mark my full-time transformation into an alumnus faring forth into what Princeton seniors ironically sang about in a traditional "step song": "safe now in the wide, wide world." I met it—the Sidecar—in a speakeasy on West Forty-sixth Street favored by Old Nassau undergraduates. My classmate Alfred Dalrymple introduced us as we killed an hour waiting until time to board the New Bedford boat for the overnight voyage to Cape Cod, my first night on the bounding main. Dal had been a character actor the previous summer so knew the ropes and could be a competent guide through unknown shoals.

On a bleak and windswept stretch of dunes and sand called Old Silver Beach stood the ungainly structure that was our destination. We reached it the next morning via Woods Hole. We passed under a flimsy wooden arch announcing THE UNIVERSITY PLAYERS and drove across a wide expanse of empty parking lot.

As I passed under that arch, I doubt that I realized this was—next to Princeton—the most significant commencement I'd ever experienced: I was about to enter upon my first full-time professional theatre job. I don't even remember the date.

We dismounted onto a sort of brick terrace, passed the box

office, and entered a lobby. Seated on the floor, clad only in a pair of dirty white ducks and a little mechanic's felt cap with holes cut in it in geometrical designs, a black-haired, barefooted young man with stooped shoulders was carefully lettering a sign that said NEXT WEEK, followed by a tantalizing blank. The youth was about twenty-five, and his two-day stubble of beard did not altogether conceal a sensitive, almost pretty face. He was introduced as Henry Fonda. I thought his sign painting looked very professional.

From a door marked DIRECTORS' ROOM emerged another young man. With a flashing smile, he held out his hand. "You must be Norrie Houghton. I'm Charles Leatherbee. Welcome!"

He was tall and rather handsome, though his face was a little too long, his dark hair thinning slightly; but he had strongly, deeply set eyes, a fine brow. He was twenty-three years old. He wore a French sailor's T-shirt of blue and white horizontal stripes. As it turned out, he had picked up enough of them in Marseilles to provide each of the boys of the company with one that summer; around the theatre, we looked like a musical comedy chain gang.

Leatherbee led me into the theatre. The auditorium, seating four hundred, had a simple, serviceable Celotex air about it. As we clambered over the footlights my enthusiasm grew. The Old Silver Beach theatre in 1931 was one of the best-equipped summer playhouses in the country. The stage was large, had a full counterweight system for the hoisting and lowering of scenery, an excellent lighting system. The floor was completely trapped. Behind the stage, separated by a twenty-foot-high fire curtain, was the shop.

About that young fellow Fonda. It happened that the first summer the U.P.G. settled on the Cape, at Falmouth, he had made his first trip east of the Mississippi. (He'd grown up in Omaha and attended the University of Minnesota.) He headed for the Cape Playhouse, at neighboring Dennis, where he was to play walk-ons. A fellow Omahan named Hanighen, also a classmate of the University Players contingent from Harvard, heard Fonda was nearby and brought him over to see them perform that summer at the movie house in Falmouth.

The play was *The Torchbearers,* a farce-comedy about amateur theatricals. The first awareness the company had of Henry Fonda was the sound of his laughter as the performance progressed. It was not just a laugh; it was a high, choking sob that exploded and overflowed, shaking the old ladies for rows around. Josh Logan and John Swope (another Harvard undergraduate), playing torchbearers Mr. Hossefrosse and Mr. Twiller, had only to walk onto the stage, and Fonda erupted. They were the funniest men he had ever seen, and when half of Swope's mustache unintentionally fell off and he was unable to get it back on, Fonda, choking with sobs, fell into the aisle.

If Hank was captivated by the performance, the actors were equally enchanted by this unseen but not unheard presence. So when Hanighen brought Fonda backstage, he had already fallen in love with them and they with him. By the end of the evening, their tall, good-looking visitor in white linen knickers and black stockings was invited to leave Dennis and join them. Back he went, packed his bags the next morning, and came right over.

They had a part for him at once. The play was Sam Benelli's sardonic comedy, *The Jest*, made famous by John and Lionel Barrymore, and the cast was so large that Logan was assigned two parts. One of these he generously offered to his new admirer—the role of Tornaquinci, an elderly Italian with long white beard and heavy wig. Josh was not sure he would have been very good in it anyhow.

If Logan would have been poor, Fonda was worse. Local critics kindly overlooked his effort and made no mention of his hirsute performance. Not so Windust. The Players had made a disastrous error, he felt, in inviting this boy on first sight to become a member of the company. It was embarrassing, but they would have to send him back to Dennis. But Windy was overruled, and Fonda stayed, for four summers.

The Jest was an elaborate undertaking, with three sets and heavy Italian Renaissance costumes. At its dress rehearsal, the celebrated New York producer Winthrop Ames paid an unexpected call. That evening was more chaotic than usual, or perhaps it just seemed so because the Broadway celebrity made everyone self-conscious. About one o'clock in the morning they completed the third of the four acts—the dungeon scene—in which Harvard undergraduate Kent Smith, in the Lionel Barrymore role, stripped to the waist, was chained to a huge pillar, which, being four feet in diameter, provided a massive background. It had been put together over seats in the auditorium, and now that the scene was completed, the stagehands pushed it through the curtain and carried it up the aisle.

"What are you going to do about the pillar tomorrow night, when you have an audience?" inquired Mr. Ames. No one had thought of that. They had no answer. No room offstage. Perhaps they could fly it? Too tall, the grid too low to get it out of sight overhead. Possibly it could be swung around and hung on its side? They tried it. It worked. So they discovered how to "trip" scenery—the technical name for that process. That was the way they learned everything—good old trial and error.

The second bill of the 1931 season, the first to utilize my budding talents, was *Interference*, a British melodrama of indifferent quality. It gave the cast a chance to exercise and improve their prowess with English accents; it gave me my initial whack at being a stage manager. At the first rehearsal, on Tuesday morning, I sat in the circle with the cast as we read the play aloud. Some stock companies, having only six days to stage a play, don't allow themselves the luxury of a first reading, but we did.

In the afternoon, however, Windust (directing) began to "put the show on its feet." He worked slowly, with great care for detail. He was particularly articulate at explaining the "why" of every direction he gave. When an act had been gone through once, it consequently had body and was not just sketched in.

The principal problem in stock is time: no time to experiment, to let a performance emerge gradually. Lines must be learned in three or four days, business and action set and held to; tempo and pace, which come only through repetition and after familiarity with the play has been acquired, are elements to be superimposed arbitrarily. It is wonderful exercise but otherwise really inexcusable.

On Thursday I didn't see how the play would conceivably be ready for Monday, but on Friday and Saturday the miracle began to take place. Windust spent little time on run-throughs; he continued to interrupt and develop points. But even as he did so, the actors showed signs of greater sureness and there was impressive self-confidence in their attack.

The play that followed *Interference, Mr. Pim Passes By,* a popular comedy of the twenties by A. A. Milne, had special importance for me: it marked my debut as a designer. I poured great care into fashioning the English country house's morning room, the play's one setting. The walls' panels were built of real molding, not painted; in the long windows opening onto a sunny, ivy-covered brick terrace I hung draperies of faded olive green flecked with gold, and I found some good, appropriate Queen Anne furniture in the community, of which I made use.

For the designer in a stock company time is again the all-important factor: there's not enough to prepare detailed drawings. He must improvise and adjust to the exigencies of his stage and the limitations of the stockpile of used scenery. With no color sketches, he is guided by the look of the paint as he mixes it in buckets. I have searched my files in vain for drawings of University Players productions. I guess I never made any.

Margaret Sullavan arrived in West Falmouth two weeks after the season opened, just in time to rehearse the ingenue role in *Mr. Pim Passes By,* and the company, especially our press department of one, was in a twitter of excitement. Here was our own Broadway star—she had succeeded Margaret Perry in *Strictly Dishonorable* on Broadway that spring—somebody to be really proud of, something momentous to advertise. However, the University Players did not then, or ever afterward, officially star Margaret Sullavan. We didn't believe in stars.

But we believed in Peggy. (It was not until later, in Hollywood, that she became known as Maggie.) She had joined the company in its second season, lured by Leatherbee and Windust away from a job at the Harvard Coop. She was sweet and twenty now when I first met her, with a husky voice and a Virginia accent. She was not exactly beautiful—but she had undefinable magic. When she walked on, you looked at nobody else. I guess nowadays we'd call it "charisma"; James Barrie called it "charm."

I never saw Helen Hayes play Norma Besant in *Coquette,* a role she created, but Sullavan's performance that summer was good enough for me. She blended gaiety with deep emotion and heart-rending pathos; it was hard to believe there ever could have been a better. This authentic jasmine-scented tearjerker followed *Mr. Pim*, so again I stage-managed. Josh directed, and he allowed Mary Lee, his younger sister, still in college, to play Norma's gangling next-door neighbor, a comic relief. At the first reading, Mary Lee wept so inconsolably that she was unable to speak her lines; and, indeed, at the dress rehearsal all the company wept. *Coquette* provided our summer's great sentimental catharsis.

At the second performance, Mary Lee sat in the wings opposite my prompt corner, awaiting her entrance as the unsuspecting and eager little friend who was to tell of a jolly house party. Her gaiety, after the scene of impending tragedy that preceded it, was intended to be almost unbearably poignant to the audience.

As Mary Lee listened, the Sullavan magic started to work, and she began to cry. Never had she heard anything so deliciously sad. Norma Besant's heart was breaking, and so was Mary Lee's. She had to stuff her handkerchief into her mouth to prevent her sobs from reaching the audience's ears. Now the scene grew sadder; she heard words spoken that she had never heard before; it was almost more than she could bear. Suddenly, deep in her sub-conscious, she became aware that the words of her entrance cue had come and gone some time before, that these new sorrows were ad libs as Peggy and Charlie Leatherbee, playing opposite her, stalled, waiting for Mary Lee's entrance. Horror-struck (for this was her debut role), Mary Lee rushed to the door, threw it open, and entered, tears streaming down her face. Her voice choked with sobs, she went through her gay—and now baf-fling—little scene as best she could.

It was after the last performance of *Coquette*, I think, that George Fedoroff, also a staff designer that summer, sitting in the company room over cocoa with Sullavan, asked amiably, "Peggy, why do you always point your toe so affectedly on stage? You look as though you were about to execute a pirouette." Before she could reply, he went on: "And why do you always lift your right foot backward when anybody kisses you on stage? Because you think it looks cute?"

Peggy was hotheaded, and George's observant criticism in-furiated her. She jumped up from the army cot that served as a sofa and ran down to the fogbound beach to cool off. But she remembered his words and never again was guilty of those clichés.

That is what I mean when I say that the company learned from one another. Windy taught his actors a good deal, but probably their principal source of training came from observations of each other's work and from the great variety of roles in which they were able to try out newly discovered techniques. Often these were things they never should have tried, but their colleagues were quick to take note and tell them. For as a company they were immensely self-critical. Nobody could get away with anything phony or affected. And that's why so many extraordinary actors emerged from the University Players.

The Players had a firm policy that no one was to be consistently exploited at the expense of the ensemble. The variety and prodigality of the company's talent and the way it functioned was never better demonstrated than in two productions rehearsing simultaneously toward summer's end. While Kent Smith and Elizabeth Fenner from Vassar were preparing Molnár's *The Guardsman*, made famous by the Lunts, O'Casey's *Juno and the Paycock* went into rehearsal, with Frieda Altman as Juno and Josh Logan as the Paycock, and with strong support from Charles Arnt as Joxer. None of these three was in *The Guardsman*, although Smith, like Fonda, had a walk-on in *Juno*. Hank didn't even appear in *The Guardsman*.

The University Players delighted in carrying their current onstage preoccupation into their collective offstage life. During *Coquette*, the dining porch and company room sounded as though invaded by cotton pickers from the Deep South; for *Juno*, by refugees from the potato famine.

The company were great ones, too, for a song. That summer, Windy had taught us the old English madrigal "Come follow, follow me," which at the drop of a hat we offered lustily as a round. Now we added to our musical repertoire "The Sacred Heart of Jesus," a hymn sung offstage in the last scene of *Juno and the Paycock*. We were much smitten by its mournful air and sang it frequently in four-part harmony. It gave us special delight to congregate in a corner at a cocktail party with an impromptu and somewhat anachronistic but deeply felt rendition of "The

Sacred Heart of Jesus." If the stage had failed us, we could quickly have turned into a glee club.

Next the University Players turned to a thriller, *The Silent House.* Thrillers were much favored in my youth. There were *The Bat* and *The Cat and the Canary* in the twenties, both running for years, to the shivers and screams of packed houses. Our company had already chilled its summertime audiences with renditions of *In the Next Room, The 13th Chair, The Last Warning, The Donovan Affair, The Trial of Mary Dugan, The Wooden Kimono.* No one ever claimed we were an "art theatre." The 1920s public delighted in these knife-in-the-dark whodunits, and our predilection, I fear, was to give the public what it wanted.

To put it another way, we took pleasure in facing the pressures of commercialism and bowing to them, like willows in the wind, by providing out-and-out theatrical fare—mindless farces, mystery thrillers, wild melodramas, lush costume plays. Nothing of Chekhov or Ibsen was ever seen on our boards. We relished external action, romance, and laughter enormously for their own sake. Were we perhaps clutching onto our childhood?

Because Windust, Logan, and Leatherbee were busily occupied with some long-range planning, I was at last allowed to try my hand at directing. *The Silent House,* no-holds-barred thriller, had exotic new ingredients mingled with familiar clichés: an evil Chinese doctor with hypnotic influence; a fair maiden named T'mala [*sic*], in his power; hidden treasure; a strange will with its legacy of trouble; secret hiding places; a band of conspirators, including a black-fedoraed knife-thrower, played by Said Riza, our Turkish member; and a liberal assortment of such odds and ends as snakebite, poison gas in a lethal chamber, sliding panels, and plenty of pistol shots.

Fonda was my leading man, George, the young chap who inherited the Silent House and its millions, but the show—if not the millions—was stolen away from him by Princetonians Myron McCormick and Charles Arnt, who played good and bad Chinese respectively. Both boys were never so happy as in front of their makeup mirrors, and Ho-Fang and Doctor Chan-Fu turned out to be more Chinese than any "Chinamen." There were two sets:

a shadowy library with a fireplace large enough to contain within its secret panels a body or two; and Dr. Chan-Fu's ominously exotic hideaway, in black and gold and lacquer red with elaborate dragons sprawling across it.

There was no call for the kind of pseudo-psychological motivation of today's whodunits, like *Deathtrap* or *Sleuth*. The characters in these old twenties and thirties mysteries were as simplistic as a Punch and Judy show. Startling and spine-tingling effects were already prescribed in the script, so the director's job was insignificant: all he really had to do was to see that the shocks occurred in proper order.

Most of them worked in our production: iron shutters clanged down to cut off egress; the idol's human hand holding a revolver was in place; poisoned smoke poured out of the idol's mouth on cue. McCormick successfully slid down the rope that descended through a trapdoor in the ceiling in time to rescue George and his T'mala from the Chinese doctor's lethal chamber.

The only mishap occurred on the evening when Fonda, supposed to swing at one point from a chandelier in his echoing mansion—don't ask me why—bore the misfortune of having the fixture give way and come down with him to the floor. It's always a nuisance to play a scene holding a chandelier in both hands, with no really suitable place to put it, just when evil men are bursting in with revolvers drawn. (He stowed it in a corner.)

By the time I joined the company, in 1931, it was three summers old. In the first two seasons there was apparently a good deal of irresponsibility; nobody, save Charlie and Windy, thought much about goals. It was a wonderful way for stagestruck youngsters with talent to spend summer vacations, and even for those who had already graduated, the University Players offered a respite from wintertime job-hunting. However, by the fourth season all the members were out of college, and if the group was to achieve any kind of continuity, this was the time to firm it up.

Charlie had taken Josh to Europe that spring (Windy was too involved with the Theatre Guild to take time off), to expose him to permanent repertory theatre, instilling in him Charlie's own fervor for the idea of theatre artists working together over a long period of time, subordinating themselves to the whole and finding therein a satisfaction beyond that accruing from individual glory. Josh was persuaded. Windy already understood; a militant crusade was his meat. Consequently, the company assembled for the summer season of 1931 was an eagerly dedicated group of young people, no one more so than I.

As the summer waned, two events occurred that had far-reaching consequences, one for the Players, one for me. First, a social item in our local paper mentioned that Mrs. Frances Crane, Charlie's mother, was entertaining Mrs. W. Stuart Symington, a social leader of Baltimore, and a gentleman named Leonard McLaughlin, who, it turned out, was manager of the Maryland Theatre there. The company thought nothing of it, for we were frequently being visited by outlanders as our individual and collective notoriety spread. But a week later the three directors called us together and shocked us all by announcing, "The University Players are going to Baltimore in the fall for a season of repertory!" The company was jubilant. At last they would be a "Theatre"; no longer would each as an individual be exposed to the vicissitudes of commercial Broadway.

As for the second event, I received a telegram from the Theatre Guild, inquiring whether I would be available to serve as assistant stage manager of *Mourning Becomes Electra*, rehearsals to commence in four weeks. In 1931 the Guild was the ace theatrical producing company in the country, and O'Neill's play would undoubtedly be the most important event of the forthcoming season. It was the kind of break that comes to one beginner in a hundred. I consulted Charlie Leatherbee. To him one took dilemmas like this. He appreciated the chance it was for me personally. But he said, "Stick with the company."

Charles had a clear vision of what a permanent stage group could accomplish jointly. Not by accident, he asserted, had he and Windust assembled this present aggregation of talent. He believed in each one of us and in the power that could be ours if we stuck together. It might require sacrifice, but Charlie made even that seem desirable. He pointed out that the exciting days to have been part of the Theatre Guild were in the 1920s, when it was aborning. Now the birth was ours. "Don't ally yourself with the past, no matter how distinguished," Charlie urged in effect. "Join hands with us and walk into a future of our own creation." After weighing my choices for only twenty-four hours, I declined the Guild's invitation. I never regretted it.

The plan was to end the summer season on Labor Day and then start to work. We would rehearse and build five productions on the Cape, take them to the Maryland Theatre in Baltimore, there to set up and dress-rehearse for ten days, opening in mid-November. Meanwhile, we would hunker down in our Silver Beach theatre.

Those weeks were as exhilarating as any I'd ever spent. Cape Cod is at its best in September and October. At night the stars came down within hand's reach. The pinpoint dots of New Bedford across the bay seemed to advance over the water like tiny candles on some faraway, bobbing birthday cake. The days' blue skies were even more unforgettable.

It grew cold toward the end of October; save for the kitchen stove, the only heat came from a big stone fireplace in the "company room." Around it we gathered before and after every meal and for an hour or so after evening rehearsals before going to bed. Everyone worked both day and night, toward the end in sweaters, overcoats, and gloves.

The crew in the scene shop labored with the ferocious zeal of Dutchmen mending a dike, and well we might, with twelve sets to build and paint. Those Cape Cod days sped by as they only can when you are absorbed in the work you love, surrounded by people you love.

One morning in early November, we found that two baggage cars had been dropped during the night onto the siding beside the West Falmouth railroad station—our own cars! Rehearsals suspended, and everyone lent a hand to help the crew load and unload the company's truck, carrying scenery, lighting equipment, the costume shop's sewing machines and dye vats, prop boxes, actors' trunks. It was late, even by our private double-daylight-saving time, when the cars were loaded and sealed. Everyone returned to Old Silver Beach exhausted but greatly excited. At last it had arrived—the D day for which the last nine weeks had been mobilizing. Forth we were setting as a theatre into a world waiting, we hoped, for us to conquer it.

2

Out of our Cape Cod never-never land we were yanked into the chill of the outside world, to be reminded that in the winter of '31–32 the country was approaching the depths of the Great Depression—mortgage foreclosures, breadlines of unemployed, gray despair. The Depression brought forth a new set of values. Gone was faith in the "get-rich-quick" philosophy of the 1920s; the dream of the leftists to reorder our economic structure was alluring, especially to artists, for both are insecure and susceptible to dreams. The cult of the individual, so encouraged in the twenties, was being replaced by the idea of collective security, as applicable to persons as to nations. It was a propitious time for a theatre collective to spring up, and it may have strengthened our belief in "All for One," which became the title of our theme song.

The only reason we'd acquired the Maryland Theatre on a four-wall lease for the season was that the road was in shambles, and with no bookings at the Maryland for the foreseeable future, the local union stagehands would doubtless join the long lines of the unemployed.

Then we hove into view, a nonunion company. Their own jobs again at stake, the locals were understandably upset by our arrival. They vented their disapproval and frustration first by snarling all the ropes of their antiquated backstage sandbag counterweight system and then by donning sandwich boards and picketing in front of the theatre, urging the public to boycott us. Since there was no public in evidence, their march was an exercise in futility, but the snarled sandbags did put a crimp in our carefully planned and exceedingly tight schedule.

We had intended to hang the scenery for all five plays before the first one opened, set up each play and light it. However, all hands repaired to the grid and fly gallery to help disentangle the ropes and sandbags, an operation about which none of us knew anything. By the time this was done, we had only two days to prepare for our entire opening week. Now, the University Players were dedicated, you understand, to orthodox repertory. We were self-committed to presenting five plays in eight days.

Our debut Monday night would be *The Devil in the Cheese*,

about which the less said the better. It was full of complicated effects that took the place of action. We chose it for sentiment's sake: it had opened our Falmouth playhouse.

With the help of most of the acting company, the show was assembled in time for the dress rehearsal on the day of the opening, but nothing had been done toward setting up the succeeding four plays. When the opening night curtain fell, we must consequently strike the sets and start on the next show, to open twenty-one hours later, *The Silent House.* Then in rapid succession we unveiled a revival of *Mr. Pim Passes By, Hell Bent fer Heaven,* and *The Constant Nymph,* the latter requiring four sets. Happily, Margaret Sullavan arrived from New York to assume the role in it she'd played at the Cape two years before.

By the end of the second week, the Baltimore public, hitherto innocent of the workings of repertory, was so confused by what was going on at the Maryland Theatre—and we, equally innocent, were so confused—that with chagrin and disappointment, but with ill-concealed relief, we abandoned repertory and returned to stock, with consecutive presentations replacing concurrent ones, a system in which we and the Baltimoreans felt equally at home.

The Maryland Theatre was a late-nineteenth-century anachronism. The lobby's marble walls and sweeping staircases reminded you of the Paris Opera in miniature; but the brass spittoons set at decent intervals brought you back to the U.S.A., where grandeur used to be so reassuringly mated to convenience.

Inside was a horseshoe tier of mezzanine boxes, a balcony above that, and topping all a "peanut" gallery, which always smelled of disinfectant and stale popcorn. Altogether, the auditorium, bottle-green velvet and faded gold leaf, could seat over a thousand spectators. The stage was correspondingly capacious.

Next door was the Kernan Hotel, manifestly a commercial hostelry, where not infrequently guys and dolls arrived without luggage and were asked to pay for their rooms in advance. I remember that once we were enchanted when we encountered a troupe of midgets in the hotel lobby. Hotel and theatre were under joint ownership; a door from the hotel's entrance lobby led directly into the foyer of the theatre, and from one corner of the hotel's ballroom a stairway descended to a passage that led to the basement under the stage. This our company found useful as a shortcut from dinner table to dressing rooms.

For five months these umbilically bound buildings were our home. The hotel's main dining room, of the McKinley period, was our combined dining room, company room, and kitchen. (We had brought our own cook from the Cape.) Here we ate, relaxed, and officially entertained. In the basement was a low-ceilinged, rather frowsy nightclub, empty by day, which we utilized for rehearsals. Upstairs, behind red-mahogany-transomed doors, we roomed in twos and threes.

At one end of the top floor was a large suite. Frances Crane took it and installed Charlie, Windy, and Josh there with her. Her sitting room became the new Directors' Room—a kind of sanctum sanctorum to which certain favorites were invited for breakfast in dressing gown from time to time.

"Miss Frances," Charles Leatherbee's mother, was born a (plumbing) Crane in Chicago, where she grew up. She spent her summers at Woods Hole, in the family's mansion, and there she was wooed and won by a Mr. Leatherbee. By him she had three sons, our Charles the eldest, and from him she was later divorced, to marry Jan Masaryk, the son of Tomáš, founder of Czechoslovakia.

For some years, as Madame Masaryk, she lived abroad, and in the mid-twenties she presided over the Czech embassy in London, where her husband was his country's ambassador. However, she always maintained her summer home at Woods Hole, overlooking Buzzards Bay. When in due time she and Masaryk separated, the Czech government required her to renounce the historic name. Not wanting to revert to Mrs. Leatherbee, she became Mrs. Crane and, to the University Players, "Miss Frances."

She was tall, of regal mien, very much the grande dame. Strikingly beautiful, with deep-set dark eyes, and soft, wavy graying hair, she seemed quite remote from all mundane concerns. She affected long strands of pearls and pastel chiffon Empire gowns that swept the floor. Miss Frances had a keen mind, a delicious sense of humor, and an indomitable will. She made our actresses exceedingly nervous; the young men were in awe of her, but most succumbed to her charm. I became very fond of her, and she in a sense became my first patroness.

She idolized her son, and because the University Players was his brainchild, it became her obsession: quite logical, therefore, that she should turn up to winter in Baltimore, although the sixth floor of a fleabag hotel provided an incongruous environment for so grande a dame. Through all our ups and downs, her presence provided our one truly civilizing influence. It also led to our social acceptance in Baltimore.

Margaret Sullavan's Baltimore debut in *The Constant Nymph,* opposite Fonda, didn't do what we'd hoped to change our cash flow. There were acres of empty seats. We reduced our ticket prices, hoping in that way to offset the snobbish carriage-trade label the press had—with some justification—stuck on us. But lowering our top from $1.50 to one dollar and selling our matinees for fifty cents didn't do the trick.

Then, four weeks after the bold beginning, the company presented *Death Takes a Holiday,* a Broadway hit of two seasons back, which had not yet been seen in Baltimore. Kent Smith and Sullavan played the leads. I designed the setting, using the Old World charm of Alice Foote MacDougall's chain of Gotham restaurants as my inspiration. I was much smitten by her use of fake Moorish, Spanish, and Sicilian wrought iron and tiles.

We won. The reviews were all raves. For the first time, there was a line at the box office.

"Today this department arises to full, dignified height and bows low in the direction of the University Repertory Theatre," wrote the *Baltimore News* critic a bit flippantly.

He was echoed in the *Baltimore Sun:* "It is gratifying to report that the University Players, striking their full stride at last, have given *Death Takes a Holiday* a production which compares favorably in every respect with that given in New York."

We celebrated Christmas with *The Ghost Train,* another spine-tingler. Mildred Natwick, Henry Fonda, Frieda Altman, and Myron McCormick shared honors, but their combined efforts did not suffice to persuade Baltimoreans to put aside their Christmas shopping.

Our company Christmas, however, was a joyous occasion. That morning, word was passed that we were to assemble in our dining room at noon. At a quarter past the hour, Henry Fonda and Margaret Sullavan entered. With them were Kent Smith as Hank's best man and Julia Dorr (mother-to-be of actress Jill Clayburgh) as Peggy's maid of honor; Horace Donegan (later bishop of New York) officiated.

Behind a screen, Dalrymple made a good deal of noise mixing a bowl of combined wedding and Christmas cheer; the long spoon clattered against the glass in the silence. Instead of the perfume of orange blossoms, the room was heavy with the odor of cauliflower, boiling on the stove at the other end.

Windust played "Lohengrin" on the piano. The company stood in a semicircle. As Dr. Donegan began to read the service, Windy switched to the love song from *The Constant Nymph*, the song that the character performed by Fonda, a musician, had composed for the girl played by Sullavan. It was their favorite, and nobody at the time thought anything about the inapropos and frighteningly prophetic words to the song: "Ah, say not so! Another love will cheer thee."

Everybody cried, for everybody was deliciously sentimental; besides, we had watched the ups and downs of this romance for a long time, and its culmination seemed wonderful. Then, too, we cried because we loved them both and because it was Christmas.

As soon as the groom had watched his bride cut the first piece of cake, he bolted, for he had a special Christmas Day matinee at three o'clock. The bride, having nothing else to do, viewed the performance from a back row.

3

At the beginning of the 1930s, despite the Depression, two significant theatre companies appeared on the American scene. One was ours, but its disappearance crowded hard on its appearance. It quickly became a legend, however, because of the emergence of Henry Fonda and Margaret Sullavan as Hollywood stars and of Bretaigne Windust and Joshua Logan in the front line of Broadway directors.

The other company was the Group Theatre, which came to New York in 1932 and played a distinguished role on the Broadway scene throughout the 1930s. Then it, too, became a legend. Toward the middle of January 1932, the two theatres collided in Baltimore. The Group brought its first production, *The House of Connelly*, to Ford's Theatre in Baltimore en route to Broadway. The company was of immense interest to us because at several points its objectives paralleled our own; furthermore, it, too, was young and on its way. That it should be headed for New York aroused in us secret envy.

The Group was much more mature than we. Its members and its directors—Cheryl Crawford, Harold Clurman, Lee Strasberg—had vastly more professional experience than any University Player. If the Group's average age was only half a dozen years older than ours, those few years nevertheless made a decade's difference. Their revolt against the commercial theatre—and it was a self-conscious revolt—was predicated on an actually experienced clash with its circumstances. Ours was a temperamental assumption of incompatibility, for few of us had any actual Broadway experience to judge by.

Like the University Players, the Group had no use for the star system and intended to build a collective ensemble. Like us, it had been impressed with the work of the Moscow Art Theatre and was seeking in some degree to emulate it. Like us, it had an enthusiasm and a dedication that had carried it through a summer of preparation and would take it forward for another eight years.*

---

*Together the University Players and the Group would in subsequent time, after the formal demise of both organizations, bequeath to the American theatre, through the genius of their original creators, an incredible legacy. It was Windust's directoral talent that guided to the stage *Amphitryon 38, The Hasty Heart, Idiot's Delight, Life with Father, Arsenic and Old Lace, State of the Union, Finian's Rainbow;* Logan performed the same office for *I Married an Angel, Annie Get Your Gun, Happy Birthday, John Loves Mary, Mister Roberts, South Pacific;* to Harold Clurman it was indebted for *Waltz of the Toreadors, The Member of the Wedding, The Autumn Garden, Men in White;* to Elia Kazan (a Group Theatre charter member) for *The Glass Menagerie, All My Sons, A Streetcar Named Desire, Death of a Salesman, The Skin of Our Teeth, Cat on a Hot Tin Roof, Sweet Bird of Youth;* to Lee Strasberg, Robert Lewis, and Cheryl Crawford (plus Kazan, another Group founder), the American theatre was also indebted for the creation in 1947 of the Actors' Studio, which became another legend in its own right. And while the Group yet lived, we all were in debt to it for William Saroyan's first play, *My Heart's in the Highlands,* and the creations

But there the similarities ended. Spurning the intuitive creative approach native to our American theatre, the Group undertook a self-conscious examination of the elements of creativity in acting, far beyond anything our company had thought of, desired, or taken time to have an opinion about. Having formulated these elements, the Group put them into constant practice. Their results were eminently gratifying.

It is generally conceded in the theatre that any ongoing company takes on the character of its leadership. The University Players as a whole, and to a lesser degree perhaps as individuals, were profoundly affected by the personalities, temperaments, and prejudices of Leatherbee, Windust, and Logan (WASPs all, incidentally).

The Group, I suggest, derived its color from its directorate, especially Strasberg and Clurman, who were Jewish intellectuals with strong political convictions and social consciousness, possessed of artistic purpose. We had no thought of spearheading theatrical revolt. If we were "longhairs," it was literally rather than figuratively: we had neither time nor money to go to the barbershop.

We had enormous respect for the best that the contemporary professional theatre offered. Modestly we sought to perfect our tools. But the University Players were, I suspect, less conscious of social, economic, and political trends than any other educated group of youngsters in America. Not so the Group. Whereas we believed the theatre was an end that justified itself, the Group was convinced that any theatre's value lay in its service to society.

Harold Clurman announced, for instance, on the eve of its arrival in Baltimore:

> What the Group Theatre proposes to do is to give the most expert and complete dramatic expression it can to the living forces of our day. . . . The Group Theatre holds that it will justify its existence only by undertaking to give voice to the essential moral and social preoccupations of our time, to

---

of Clifford Odets: *Awake and Sing, Golden Boy,* and the others. The University Players never found such a voice. But then, like the Duchess of Malfi, we died young.

make its work bear a clear, cogent, inescapable relation to the public for whom it is presented.

We were a little awed when we read that. We weren't sure that we had any very accurate idea of what "the living forces of our day" were, nor "the essential moral and social preoccupations of our time." All we knew was that there would be inevitable comparisons made locally between this other young group and ourselves, and that although they were just passing through, we meant to stay on, so it was essential that we not come out second best.

Gilbert Seldes's version of Aristophanes' *Lysistrata* seemed a formidable piece of artillery with which to protect our embattled turf. It was without doubt the biggest and also most successful production the University Players ever mounted. That it was done with five days' rehearsal seems miraculous.

There were sixty-six performers on the stage, at least fifty of them culled from among the city's admirers of Thespis. Four choruses, designated as "young men," "young women," "old men," "old women," played an integral part. Even I was recruited to play an "old man."

For the concluding bacchanalia, director Windust was assisted by a choreographer from the Denishawn School in Washington. Her bacchantes, whirling to Stravinsky's *Sacre du Printemps*, brought to a wild orgiastic climax a performance that was notable for its broad, rowdy, honest farce. Windy wisely insisted that this ancient Greek sex comedy be played frankly and gaily, without leers or innuendos, and with touches of bold caricature.

This last quality was best epitomized in Josh Logan's characterization of the president of the Senate. Shrouded in delicatessenham pink, laurel wreath tipped over one eye, his already bulky frame padded to double its size, Josh, with assumed nearsightedness, plowed across the stage and over the footlights and, to the delighted screams of the public, was rescued at the last second from plunging into the orchestra pit.

We had a smash hit on our hands at last. With the rest of the week sold out, we decided to hold *Lysistrata* over for a second week. That was sold out before it began.

Whether via *Lysistrata* we were giving voice to "the essential moral and social preoccupations" of the day might be questioned, but we (and Aristophanes) had hit upon the public's appetite. At any rate, with the SRO sign at our box office and the grapevine report that the Group Theatre had taken in only three hundred dollars on opening night, we felt we could afford to be gracious to the visitors, so we invited them to lunch that Thursday in our drafty marble hall.

It was not an overwhelming success. The herd instinct, so strong in us, apparently seized the actors of the other company in as great degree, with the result that the hosts talked principally to each other with the intense air of old friends reunited after years of separation, and the guests—Clurman, Strasberg, Crawford, and the rest—congregated at the opposite end of the room, equally preoccupied with themselves. We thought them overly earnest and humorless; they thought us light-minded dilettantes. Both were right and both were wrong.

It was a strange winter. Isolated from the world, we lived, slept, and worked in those twin drab buildings on Franklin Street. From time to time we emerged in white tie and tails to show up at some Baltimore ball. But mostly we were as marooned as though we had emigrated to Easter Island. The shadow of America's Depression deepened, but being already as depressed, economically, as we could be, we avoided reading the newspapers and functioned all but oblivious to the surrounding gloom. At least we weren't unemployed, like so many of our contemporaries—far from it; the thirteen-hour day was usual with us—and although close to penniless (we received room and board and fifteen dollars a week), we were cheerful and full of hope.

We were able to continue *Lysistrata* for a third week, which, we were told, made it Baltimore's longest legitimate theatre engagement in anybody's memory. But after those three fat weeks came seven lean ones. Nothing seemed to draw the reluctant populace. We were again inching toward bankruptcy.

At the end of the seventh lean week, on the Saturday night

between Good Friday and Easter, we folded. Of course, the Depression played a part. In Baltimore, as elsewhere in America, the theatre is an acquired taste, a luxury that can quickly be dispensed with if times are hard. And in any case, Baltimore was commonly conceded to be one of the worst theatre towns in America! The wonder is that we survived the winter.

On the Sunday after our departure—we closed on March 27, 1932—the most eloquent and thoughtful of our obituaries appeared in the *Baltimore Sun* under the byline of its critic, Donald Kirkley:

> Baltimore did well by the University Players but not nearly as well as it deserved. We were perhaps too close to the Maryland Theatre to realize the significance of the experiment going on there. It is doubtful whether anything quite like it has been done before. For a group of young persons to come into a town supposedly as indifferent to new things as Baltimore, open under a series of heartbreaking mishaps and then fight their way through a season of eighteen weeks was an achievement which means more than appears on the surface.
>
> In producing 19 plays, building the sets and making the costumes with their own hands and wits, getting each out on schedule, sometimes with only a week of preparation, the University Players did more than offer a series of plays for sale. They learned things that can be learned in no other way. When they came here in November they were a band of rather frightened, uncertain semi-professionals and they made many of the slips and blunders commonly associated with amateurs.
>
> When they left they were like a regiment that has been through its first tough campaign. Slips and blunders were few and far between. Scarcely a member of the company failed to show marked improvement and several, the writer is sure, laid the foundations of creditable stage careers. The profits of their season here cannot be measured in dollars.

4

The first summer on Cape Cod (1931) had been magical. But the battle of Baltimore had produced in us a disheartening awakening to the facts of theatrical life. Despite the Kirkley envoi, it must be acknowledged that not only financially but in another important way we had failed: we had been forced to abandon the idea of "repertory," which had a challenging ring but was not accomplishable in our country—at least not then or by us. Eighteen weeks of stock were, to be sure, vastly easier, but even they were a grind: a new act of creation every eighth day outstripped even Jehovah's long-standing record.

As for myself, I felt I'd acquired a journeyman's expertise but few creative insights. The future looked uncertain, too, and a bit frightening. What if the University Players collapsed? All of us were soberer in May than we had been in September. We were certainly wiser.

The directors would not let us down. In June, Charlie, Windy, and Josh went down to New York from Falmouth, where those of us with nowhere to go had taken refuge to recover from our labors; having had no vacation in eleven months, we were "bone tired."

We were saddened that Margaret Sullavan, Henry Fonda, Kent Smith, and Elizabeth Fenner would not return. The Princetonians among us were heartened, though, that Josh had successfully recruited James Stewart, just graduating from Princeton. We weren't certain how good an actor he was, nor was he. But he was drawn to the stage and thought it would do no harm to try it for a summer; he could always continue in architecture. As for us, the prospect of being serenaded by an accordionist when we felt blue was enough to assure Jim a warm welcome.

There was no part for him in the early summer, so he contented himself with giving a helping hand backstage and sweeping the floor and, of course, playing the accordion in our nightclub/tearoom until, as Jim puts it today, he was "let go because people in the tearoom complained that my playing interfered with their digestion."

During the fourth week, however, use for his histrionic talent was at last found in the part of Cool Kelly in *It's a Wise Child.* (In Baltimore, Fonda had played it.) In this revival of one of our winter's lighter-weight successes, Stewart impersonated the ice-man who wants the girl he marries to be "one hundred percent pure." It was clear to Old Silver Beach audiences on that night in July 1932 that in him they were discovering a comedian with special gifts—an all-American drawl, a lanky good humor, an air of bemused naturalness, an infectious charm.

The biggest news the directors brought back was of a connection they had established with Broadway. The "sleeper" that spring on West Forty-fifth Street was Rose Franken's *Another Language,* starring Dorothy Stickney, Glenn Anders, and a new-comer, John Beal. Its producer, a young man named Arthur J. Beckhard, hitherto unknown on Broadway, had been a concert manager and summer-theatre entrepreneur. He was much impressed by Windy, Josh, and Charlie's dreams and their company's past accomplishments. They, in turn, were flattered by his interest. Their congeniality of outlook was strengthened by their common love of laughter, by their optimism and offhandedness in coping with finance.

The boys arranged with Beckhard to present at Falmouth three or four new plays, on which Arthur would take options. If something worthwhile was uncovered, we would participate jointly in its subsequent life and thus enhance our professional position, perhaps even acquire a toehold on the Broadway ladder. For Beckhard, nothing could be lost by making an association with a tryout theatre that would foot the production bills.

In midsummer, for a repeat of *Death Takes a Holiday*—the company's sixty-ninth production in five years—I designed my twenty-third and last play for the U.P.G. In it Windust, Logan, and Leatherbee performed for the first time together in more than two seasons, and for them, too, the last time ever. Thereafter, the association with Beckhard was formally acknowledged in the masthead of every program: he was now our producer.

The last weeks of August were strange ones at Falmouth. We felt we didn't belong in our own house. Beckhard brought the road company of *Another Language* to open prior to a pre-Chicago engagement. The first Monday, while our actors lay on the beach, a cast of strangers began a week of rehearsals. Then followed a new play Arthur wanted to try out, *Goodbye Again,* a comedy by Allan Scott and George Haight, which would turn into a Broadway hit that fall. This time there was a happier blend of the newly wedded forces: Windust directed, and McCormick, Stewart, Mildred Natwick, and Barbara O'Neil joined Beckhard's cast, supporting Howard Lindsay, its Falmouth star.

Simultaneously, the rest of the company were at work on another Beckhard tryout, *Carry Nation,* by Frank McGrath. With it the 1932 Falmouth season would end. Arthur chose an old friend and associate, the actress Blanche Yurka, to direct. Josh was appointed to "assist" her, although neither he nor she knew quite what that meant. Josh was not by nature an assister, nor, if it came to that, was Blanche a director. Mrs. Beckhard, whose stage name was Esther Dale, played the militant old window-smashing prohibitionist upon whose life story, from 1846 to 1910, the drama was based.

I designed the sixteen settings, a task that took two weeks instead of the usual one and required the use of more than the back of an envelope. Indeed, this time I made a full set of color sketches and proper working drawings, which, with three rolling wagon stages in constant use, were truly essential.

Carry Nation was one of the most complicated, bizarre, and lugubrious plays anyone ever attempted. Its dress rehearsal lasted all night and elicited from McCormick the observation: "Time this rehearsal not with a watch but with a calendar!"

On opening night the first company curtain call was to be followed by a solo call for Esther Dale. The large cast had to clear the stage in seconds. Mildred Natwick chose to exit downstage left, between the scenery and the curtain. When she reached that corner she discovered there was no way to get off stage and also that the space was narrower than she had anticipated. Just then the curtain started up on Miss Dale's call, and as it did so, the pipe along the bottom of the curtain caught Millie's skirt and started up with it. Unable to release her dress and realizing it would soon be around her ears, Millie jumped on the pipe, seated herself, and ascended with the curtain, her feet dangling in space.

Ken Berry, who was raising the curtain, caught sight of her, suspended head high. "Come down from there!" he admonished sharply, as though she had playfully chosen this means of egress.

"How can I?" piped Millie, holding on for dear life. So Ken gently lowered the curtain and Miss Natwick was extricated from her corner, while Miss Dale waited to take her bow.

On September 10, 1932, the curtain fell on *Carry Nation,* the last performance of the University Players' last summer as a troupe. After the show, the entire company lined up for our photograph, a kind of passport picture into the future.

Arthur Beckhard decided to bring *Carry Nation* into New York. To do so cost five thousand dollars. It opened on the night of October 29 at the Biltmore Theatre on West Forty-seventh Street, the week before FDR was elected President. And on that night Joshua Logan, James Stewart, Myron McCormick, Mildred Natwick, and the twenty-odd rest of us made our respective Broadway debuts—a memorable occasion in retrospect but not a particularly auspicious one.

If the die had been cast and there was no going back, there was no going forward either. The play was a flop that ran for only four weeks. There were no more funds. This time we couldn't return to the Cape, for it was the beginning of December. We could not immediately sustain ourselves in New York as an organization. Anyhow, we were no longer a group in the complete sense that had characterized our communality of spirit the year before. We were a bunch of uncertain, bewildered, broke youngsters, like all the others trudging the pavements of Manhattan. No, not quite like the others. For we had friends—each other; and we had the memory of a dream that was not yet really proved vain. It had been a glorious prelude to a life in the theatre.

3

Young Man on Broadway
(1932–34)

"New York—New York!" It was the *only* city in 1932 for a twenty-two-year-old professional stage hopeful to assault. There were no regional theatres, no winter stock companies. No reason, then, to return to Indianapolis. After only a year and a half, no incentive yet to return to Princeton. For as a Broadway designer, I already had a sixteen-set play to my credit, rather obliquely noted on a program as: "After the drawings of Norris Houghton," since I was not yet a union man.

The United Scenic Artists, Local 829, which has always controlled Broadway's working conditions for scenic artists, would allow no nonunion designer to ply his trade there. I would have been glad to join, but membership required passing an entrance examination, and in the Depression it temporarily ceased to be given. Too many brothers were already unemployed.

If I'd been accepted, it wouldn't have helped much: I had no portfolio to show producers. After each of the twenty-three productions I'd designed in Baltimore and Falmouth, the envelopes on whose backs I had sketched my plans in pencil were gathered up with the rest of the scene-shop trash and thrown out.

New York—New York! Now I was a resident! The summer before, Harold Bassage, another young hopeful, a few years my senior, had come to the Cape as alternate stage manager. He was now hired by Arthur Beckhard to stage-manage *Goodbye Again* on Broadway that fall. We took a ground-floor apartment together in Greenwich Village. Through a glass door was a view of a dreary little plot of ground called a garden. Of course, we were burgled in short order, but because we had little of value, it was no great calamity, and probably more a disappointment for the burglar than a nuisance for us. The rent was sixty dollars a month, which Hal put up entirely until I could get a job and reimburse him for my half.

One day I ran into Ken Berry at Walgreen's drugstore in the Paramount Building. In those days young unemployed actors spent much time there with a five-cent Coke, "resting between engagements" and exchanging gossip about the Rialto.

"Hey, Norrie," cried Ken. "Have you heard about the beer party?" No, I hadn't. So Ken explained that it was going to be on Wednesday after the theatre at a hall on West Forty-seventh Street. John Swope and Kent Smith were arranging it, and Falmouth alumni were summoned to appear. Almost everyone did. Swope and Smith presided over the beer kegs. We sang "Come follow, follow me," which Windy conducted, and "Sacred Heart of Jesus," which Josh led, and "Ah, Say Not So" from *The Constant Nymph*. We drank oceans of beer and ate pretzels until two—or maybe three.

"Let's do this every Wednesday," someone cried, and everybody shouted "Hurray!" So a minor Broadway legend came into being, initiated by that noisy and gregarious crew from Falmouth.

Old-timers like Aleta Freel and Ross Alexander, Peggy and Hank, would of course show up, and as word got around, other young actors would tag along: Burgess Meredith, Broderick Crawford, John Beal, Karl Malden became regulars. At ten cents a glass (or for free if you had to save your money for the subway), it was a cheap place to bring your date; mostly the dates paid their own way. Soon everybody knew everybody else. The beer parties continued through that winter and spring of 1932–33—so long ago. I wonder if anything like it goes on today.

Robert Edmond Jones was a name to be reckoned with, the most influential scene designer the American theatre has ever produced. I had pored over his illustrations for the book *Conti-*

nental Stagecraft and his frequently reproduced sketches in *Theatre Arts*—for Lionel Barrymore's *Macbeth* and *Richard III,* for *Desire Under the Elms,* and *Anna Christie,* for John Barrymore's *Hamlet,* for *The Green Pastures.* So when a pleasant youngish man of about forty named Ben Webster leaned across the lunch table one day and asked if I would like to meet Bobby Jones, I almost choked on the sweetbreads.

"You know him?" I gulped.

Webster replied that they were working together on the same project—Radio City Music Hall. What on earth had Robert Edmond Jones to do with Radio City? I wondered.

"He's the artistic director," explained Webster. "Roxy" Rothafel, its impresario, had wanted someone with a wide-ranging theatre imagination to participate in program planning and execution at his new showplace. He had approached Jones, who accepted.

This exchange occurred in the sunlit dining room of Olivia and Ridgely Torrence; he was a well-known minor dramatist and poet, a friend of my aunt Sara Norris, out in Oxford. She had written to tell them proudly of her nephew, recently arrived in Manhattan to seek fame and fortune. By the end of lunch Ben Webster had offered to arrange an appointment for me with Robert Edmond Jones.

Three mornings later I presented myself at the latter's apartment in the East Fifties, my little portfolio containing the sixteen *Carry Nation* sketches (the only things I had) tucked under my arm. I was very nervous and not a little awestruck to be there. Mr. Jones did little to reassure me. He was very busy, he said, and could spare only half an hour, that and a cup of coffee.

While he looked at my drawings, I looked at him. He was forty-five years old in 1932, tall and slender. What you noticed first were his eyebrows—black and bushy, they reminded me of my father's; then his thick black hair and long white fingers. He wore a thin mustache. He had been born in New Hampshire, and his New England accent had never left him. His speech was rapid and his tone brusque. He wore horn-rimmed glasses, then something of a novelty.

Saying nothing, Robert Edmond Jones studied my tempera drawings of Kansas saloons and parlors and street corners and hotel rooms of the 1880s and 1890s—Carry Nation's habitat. He returned them to me. "I like them," he stated matter-of-factly. "They are simple and forthright. Yes, I like them," he said again.

After a pause he asked if I would care to come and work in his office. He needed someone to run errands. The Music Hall was due to open in seven weeks. His secretary, Rose Bogdanoff, was trying to run the office, answer the phone, and do all the shopping, and he'd concluded it was too much for her. "It'll be getting worse, too, from now on," he added ominously.

I accepted on the spot.

"Good," he said abruptly, handing back my portfolio. "I must be going. Can I drop you off somewhere?"

In the cab as we crossed town, his voice acquired a warmer timbre when he spoke of the Radio City theatres. They could be "dwelling places of wonder—the most glorious stage works the imagination can devise." That was the way he talked.

At ten the next morning, I presented myself, as instructed, at the Palace Theatre's Forty-seventh Street entrance and climbed to a nondescript gray-green door with a milk-glass panel, on which I read his name. It was clearly a temporary, makeshift space. He had been careful, I recalled, to call it an office, not a studio. Nevertheless, two draftsmen were already at work at huge drafting tables. Although they looked like English bank clerks, they were the cream of the crop of New York stage draftsmen, I would later discover.

Rose Bogdanoff, small and frail-looking, with wispy black locks and a sallow complexion that set off her huge black eyes, wore cotton batik smocks under several strands of waist-length glass beads, which were forever getting caught on door handles as she wandered about the office suite. She spoke in a sad, whiny voice. Rose worshipped Bobby, even as we all did. And he couldn't have gotten along without her. For behind those sad eyes was an orderly brain that forgot nothing, not even telephone numbers. And she had the strength of a piano mover.

I combined the job of office boy and Wall Street runner—except that the running took me all over town. When Mr. Jones had mentioned shopping, I'd wondered why, with all there was to do, he was already preparing for Christmas. I found out quickly. Yuletide had nothing to do with it. There were samples of fringes and tassels for *Carmen* to be collected, all sorts of breakaway props for the comics, samples of material for veils, smart little tapping canes for the chorus girls, and on and on.

Christmas was indeed coming apace. Soon the scenery began to be hauled into the Music Hall; costumes and props were delivered a week later. Christmas arrived and departed. The final dress rehearsal was scheduled for nine o'clock on the morning after Christmas. I reported at eight. Mr. Jones was already there; so was Rose, trailing behind him with a notepad. With no more shopping to do, I just sat there, available for emergencies. I don't remember when the run-through began, but I recall vividly when it ended—at eight o'clock the next morning.

At eight o'clock the following night, December 28, 1932, Radio City Music Hall opened. The curtain came down well after midnight. Sixty-two hundred people filled the hall; sixty thousand had applied for tickets.

Percy Hammond, respected drama critic of the *New York Herald Tribune,* was moved to describe what occurred between eight and twelve-thirty thus:

> . . . The least important item in last evening's event was the show itself, a long program of song, dance and tomfoolery presented in the spacious manner of Mr. Roxy, the Director-General. As was to be expected the mountain labored and gave forth a mouse. However, it was a very large and magnificent mouse. . . . The show is extravagant and cumbersome, but has occasional moments of beauty and alacrity.

(I would have said one of the principal things it lacked was alacrity.)

The program began with a rendition of Rimsky-Korsakov's "Hymn to the Rising Sun," selected, I feel sure, to show off the Music Hall's dimmer boards. It was followed by the Flying Wallendas mated with a Japanese acrobatic team, the Kikutas. Among the evening's highlights: a tabloid version of *Carmen,* with an orchestra of ninety and a chorus of one hundred; the Tuskegee Choir of one hundred ten voices; comedians Weber and Fields; DeWolf Hopper, Dr. Rockwell, and Ray Bolger, interspersed at suitable intervals, as were various dance companies: the Harald

Kreutzberg ballet, Florence Rogge's huge ballet corps, Martha Graham and her troupe, and Russell Markert's forty-eight "Roxyettes" (before they dropped a syllable from their collective name).

I thought sadly of Robert Edmond Jones's dreams of dwelling places of wonder and how they had been betrayed. I suppose Roxy understood what the public wanted better than Bobby, but then I hated to think so. Jones resigned the day after the opening. The office boy wasn't required to resign. All he had to do was quit, and he did. It had been quite a short engagement.

In January, I presented myself at the Theatre Guild's new playhouse, on Fifty-second Street. That production of *Mourning Becomes Electra* I'd flirted with the year before was still running. Lee Simonson may have been a bit miffed that I spurned its assistant stage managership, but he appeared ready to forgive and forget when I told him I was out of a job after Jones had resigned from Roxy's Gargantua. Simonson instructed me to get myself over to the Guild and see Margaret Linley, who had replaced Cheryl Crawford as the casting director—"since Cheryl has taken it into her head to be a producer herself," he added rather sourly.

The Guild's executive offices were approached through a door adjacent to the stage door. I found Miss Linley on the third floor.

"Mr. Simonson has talked to me about you," she announced, and went on to explain that the Guild was going into rehearsal shortly with Maxwell Anderson's new play, *Both Your Houses*. Worthington Miner would direct; Leonard Loan, on leave from the Lunts' company, would stage-manage, but they had no one yet to be his assistant. Would I like that job?

"Yes, please," I replied. I began to doubt the stories I'd heard about unemployment in the theatre. The University Players job I had been wooed for; then came Jones's offer, now the Guild's. I began to realize how lucky I was. I'm even more amazed as I look back on it today.

"Before you leave, go upstairs and see Mr. Simonson. You'll find him with Bud Wicks, our technical director. He knows you're here." I had no doubt he did.

Simonson was one of the founders of the Theatre Guild and

its principal designer, one of New York's finest. He provided the Guild with many of its most beautiful settings: *Marco Millions, Liliom, The Tidings Brought to Mary, Peer Gynt, The Adding Machine, Roar, China!* He did more than anyone else to further my career during its early days.

The thing I remember best about Lee was his voice; it was a nasal, rasping drawl. He spoke loudly most of the time. When he was excited or angry, which was the rest of the time, he shouted fortissimo. He was a creature of moods. He could affect an innocent child's smile when he wanted to;' he could wither someone with sarcasm with equal relish. He was, I guess, a witty man and certainly well educated. He was widely traveled, a true cosmopolite. He was also arrogant and vain and given to loud neckties. Physically, he was not tall and, by the time I knew him, growing a little bulky. He had a hooked nose of sizable proportion and flashing black eyes. He wore his black hair in a slick pompadour.

For reasons I never discovered, he decided from the start he would be my mentor. (He never said as much—I gleaned it from his actions.) I was always a little afraid of him, but I liked him— grudgingly—very much.

The day for the first reading of *Both Your Houses* arrived. I reported to Mr. Loan, a tall, distinguished Englishman, the Guild's number one stage manager. We arranged chairs around a long table for the author, director, and cast. More chairs were set against the wall for the board of managers, who regularly attended a play's first reading to assess its chances: Theresa Helburn, Lawrence Langner, Philip Moeller, Helen Westley, Maurice Wertheim, and my friend Simonson.

Worthington Miner, the director, bustled in, out of breath. He was short, bald, rotund, with an infectious laugh and twinkling eyes. I sensed at once that he was very bright, self-confident, and that we would get along well. Maxwell Anderson, then in his early forties, was a lumbering bear of a chap with thinning sandy hair, large features on a broad, amusing face, a friendly grin, and a pipe. He had the traditional appearance of a college professor— baggy tweeds, steel-rimmed glasses, and that pipe.

The play was a political comedy. It lacked most of the boisterous profanity of Anderson's *What Price Glory?* (written with Laurence Stallings), but it was both funny and hard-bitten. Its title was, of course, taken from Mercutio's "A plague o' both your houses!" The two houses of Max Anderson's world were the Senate and the House of Representatives, and his title signaled his cynical view of the body politic. The play read well at that first hearing, and I went home much elated.

I was in for a shock. Just before supper the phone rang. It was Margaret Linley. "I've some bad news for you, Norris," she began. "The management has decided this must be our economy production. With only one set, no special effects, no supers, an assistant stage manager seems like an unnecessary luxury. So you're out. I'm terribly sorry." I don't recall what I said then. But she went on: "We even must sacrifice Mr. Loan, because the stage manager must understudy Oscar Polk, and being British, Loan could never have a persuasive Southern Negro accent."

"Well," said I, quick as a rabbit, "if you're having to replace the stage manager, why don't you let me take over?"

There was a very long pause. "You've never stage-managed on Broadway before, have you?"

"No, but I'm sure I can do it. And I'm not British," I added, thinking of the great Oscar Polk. (I remembered Windust: "Stage-managing for the University Players is just like for the Intime; just like for Broadway too, for that matter.")

Obviously unprepared for this new "opportunity," Miss Linley said, "Let me consult Tony Miner. I can't imagine what he'll say. I'll call you back."

What Miner said was "O.K. Let's give him the chance." So it turned out that instead of being fired, I was promoted! Just turned twenty-three, never having seen the backstage of a Broadway house, save for *Carry Nation*'s, I was now a full stage manager for the Theatre Guild. My luck was holding.

Both Your Houses opened in March and played for seventy-two performances. Along the way it won the Pulitzer Prize for 1932–33. But political satire—as I would reconfirm when I had my own theatre, the Phoenix—is not what American audiences flock to. Even the prize could not carry it through the summer.

I then designed a couple of other Broadway plays, for which, like *Carry Nation*, union reasons mandated that the settings be "after the drawings of Norris Houghton." Both of them were produced by our recent so-distant benefactor, Arthur Beckhard.

One, a play from the Spanish called *Spring in Autumn,* starred his old friend Blanche Yurka. She was by now my old friend too: hadn't she been at Falmouth directing *Carry Nation* and then come with us to New York? Blanche was a fine figure of a woman: almost six feet tall, blond, high-cheekboned. She possessed a most euphonious voice and at the age of thirteen had sung the role of the Grailbearer in *Parsifal* at the Metropolitan (not very taxing, as I remember it, but a harbinger of what was to come in *Spring in Autumn*). What most people recall about Blanche are the knitting needles she plied as Madame Defarge in the 1935 film version of *A Tale of Two Cities.*

Spring in Autumn concerned an opera singer whose major claim to fame was an ability to sing an aria while standing on her head, a considerable feat for a diva of any age. What with her *Parsifal* background, Blanche Yurka was well cast. Accomplish the headstand she did, and I was very impressed. But since that flamboyant display occupied only five minutes of a long evening, it was not sufficient to save an otherwise ho-hum comedy, which proceeded to close in no time. As for my scenery, who could look at it when the majestic spectacle of Miss Yurka upside down held center stage?

The following season I returned to the Theatre Guild to work on *They Shall Not Die,* a play about the Scottsboro case, by John Wexley. He had had success with *The Last Mile,* laid on death row, the play that had launched the career of Spencer Tracy and that even we had triumphed with in Baltimore. The Theatre Guild produced Wexley's latest, hoping that since its action was set first in an Alabama jail, then on death row, and finally in the country courthouse where the Scottsboro Nine were on trial for their lives, the shock value of the earlier play would be repeated.

They Shall Not Die was a semidocumentary about the recent notorious murder trial of the "Scottsboro Boys," which involved a serious miscarriage of justice. In March 1931, nine black youths were falsely accused of raping two prostitutes on a freight train; as a result of collusion between the ladies, their lawyer, and the judge, the defendants appeared to be headed for the gallows.

However, Samuel Liebowitz, the noted trial lawyer, intervened to take their case, and their conviction was later set aside by the Supreme Court. In Wexley's reenactment, the two prostitutes were played by Linda Watkins and Ruth Gordon, the defendants' lawyer by Claude Rains. Philip Moeller, the Guild's most celebrated director—he was a founder of the Guild and a dramatist in his own right—staged it. I was one of two assistant stage managers, coping with a cast of forty, including many extras in the courtroom scenes, and five sets.

I didn't mind my demotion from full stage manager to assistant. The first time had been by a fluke, and I could learn much from a big show like this. There was, first of all, Moeller to watch. He was close to being an eccentric; at least, he was an easy figure to caricature. His trademark was the same kind of long cigarette holder that FDR affected. He kept it clenched in his teeth except while talking to his actors, when he absentmindedly waved it in circles. He seemed to move about the rehearsal room on tiptoe; perhaps he wanted not to distract the cast from their concentration, but I think it was because he was naturally light on his feet. He also wore a shawl in all weather. Since the hall did not seem drafty to any of the rest of us, possibly Moeller had a Linus complex and felt safer when partially hidden beneath his wrap. Or was he seeking to emulate the Great Emancipator?

The headliners, Miss Gordon and Mr. Rains, Moeller treated with special old-world courtesy, as befitted their station. After all, he knew how to handle stars if anybody did—a long line of them had worked with him, not least Alfred Lunt and Lynn Fontanne.

I was particularly interested in Moeller's dealings with Ruth Gordon. For the first ten days she seemed to make no effort to master her part. She was almost inaudible much of the time, held on to her script, asked few questions. If she had been a new young actress she'd have been fired. But she didn't seem to faze Moeller. He told her where to move and when to sit down; sometimes she did as told, sometimes not. He never pressed her in any way. It became difficult for the other actors. While they had learned their lines, played in full voice, and grew with their characters, Gordon was still just walking through.

Then one day, after almost two weeks, the miracle occurred.

Ruth woke up. She threw aside her script; she was letter perfect. She began to act. The character was there, fully conceived. She made every point: wrung from us our laughter and tears just when she should. I could only think of a hen who patiently sits on her egg, instinctively knowing when it will be ready to hatch. I wondered if this was the way Ruth always nested, but I never discovered; we never worked together again.

Claude Rains was rather aloof, which didn't surprise me; after all, he was an Englishman. He had some difficulty with memorization, and well he might. His big scene was his final summation: "May it please Your Honor," and he started in. It lasted fifteen minutes. The jury box was on stage, the focus of his attention, whether he stood still, paced up and down, or turned his back on it. That soliloquy he developed into a virtuoso performance, and it was fascinating to see the speech emerge in all its nuances— now blistering sarcasm, now full-blown indignation, now quietly confidential, finally eloquently impassioned.

"Keep close on the book, old boy," he said to me when I was prompting in rehearsals. "Don't be afraid to stop me if I go off. That's the only way I'll ever learn the damned thing."

The summation ended with Rains reciting the Lord's Prayer. "This must be printed out in boldface and placed on this lectern," he commanded. "This is one speech I can't improvise if I forget; that will make me so nervous I'll be sure to blow the prayer some night without it."

Sad to say, at the first trial the Scottsboro case was lost. So was the play.

2.

The preceding fall, during the brief run of *Spring in Autumn*, I had dined one evening with the Torrences and bemoaned my plight: in New York almost a year and still with no chance to design under my own name. Stage-managing was all very well— good training and small-income producing—but still impeded by the United Scenic Artists, I was unable to get on with my true career.

Mr. Torrence had a proposal: I should apply for a Guggenheim Fellowship to study abroad the next year; if I succeeded, by the following year the Depression should have abated, the union would open up, and I could get going.

I was fired by the idea. "Move fast, though," said Mr. Torrence. "I think the application deadline is October fifteenth."

I moved fast. I listed a dozen people to solicit letters from. I composed the required "Plans for Study," basing it on a conversation I had with Bobby Jones when I went to seek his support.

He'd be glad to write for me, he said, but first wanted to give me some words of caution. Don't spend my time running from theatre to theatre across Europe. I'd only come back with a hodgepodge of other people's creative ideas, which I'd then likely try to imitate. This year must open *me* up. The best way to do that would be for me to go to Scandinavia, for example, to look at the little red houses clustered in villages at the mouths of Norwegian fjords. Note the juxtaposition of the great pine forests and walls of rock isolating one village from another. Someday I would work on an Ibsen play or a Strindberg. Then I could rouse my memory to create an authentic atmosphere and better understand and interpret their worlds.

"When you go to Venice," he continued, "don't rush to the Teatro Fenice; wander instead along the canals and note how the sun striking the water throws moving iridescent reflections on the walls of the palazzi so that they seem to be hanging tremulously in the air. Someday you'll be called on to provide a background for *Othello* or *The Merchant of Venice* or a Goldoni play, and you can evoke that image too."

To me every word coming from the mouth of Robert Edmond Jones was gospel. Thus, I framed a poetic-prose piece fashioned after his advice and sent off my application.

Three months passed; *They Shall Not Die* was about to begin rehearsals. One morning the phone rang. It was Henry Allen Moe, director-general of the Guggenheim Foundation. He asked whether I could come in to see him someday soon. The next morning I appeared at his office.

"Mr. Houghton," began Dr. Moe slowly, in a rather high-pitched voice, "we're in something of a predicament about your application." I stirred anxiously. "We have received very warm recommendations from your excellent references. You sound like the kind of young man we'd like to support. The problem is with your study plans. It looks to us as though you were asking to be staked to the 'Grand Tour'! That's not our business. As far as we can see, you really have no plan of study, have you?"

Those little red houses and Venetian reflections hadn't gone over well. "Perhaps I don't," I conceded. The chance for a Guggenheim began to recede.

"Now let's see what's to be done about this," continued Dr. Moe. "Can't you think of a project abroad you'd like to explore?" My mind was a blank, and I told him so.

"Well, I have a suggestion; it comes from Lee Simonson. He says there is a job that badly needs to be done: a study of methods of production in the Soviet theatre. We hear the Russian theatre is the world's finest. How has that come about? Would you like to go to Russia and find the answers? Simonson thinks they could fill a book and that maybe you could write it."

I was taken aback. Obviously, what he was suggesting went against everything Robert Edmond Jones had advised. Besides, I knew nothing about Russia and little about its theatre; Stanislavski and Meierhold were little more than names. I told Moe as much.

"Exactly," was his rejoinder. "Neither does anybody else. That's why it's a good project."

"What about the language problem?" I asked.

"Learn Russian," said Moe. "And if you can't afford a crash course at Berlitz, we can stake you to it. Think it over. Let me know when you decide. The award won't be made for another couple of months."

After wide consultation and deep soul-searching, I called Dr. Moe, who was delighted to have me accept.

"Shall I put it in writing?"

"No, that's unnecessary. I take your word for it."

When the fellowships were announced late in March, Houghton's name was there. His broad and ambiguous subject: "Studies in the field of the arts of the theatre abroad." And that—to answer a question I am still asked frequently more than fifty years later—is how it came about that I learned to speak Russian.

After *They Shall Not Die* closed in April, I leapt into preparations for my travels. I was scheduled to design for a summer theatre for six weeks, then leave in mid-August for the USSR via Scandinavia, arriving in time for the opening of the Second International Theatre Festival in Moscow, on September 1.

When I wasn't attending my Russian classes at Berlitz five days a week, I was scurrying about town following up leads to old Russian hands in New York, who could proffer advice, or to other people going to the Soviet Union, whom I might encounter there. I was also collecting letters of introduction to folk throughout Europe, in case Moscow didn't work out.

Russia was a mysterious, somewhat fearsome destination in 1934—seventeen years after the Bolshevik Revolution. The United States had only that spring granted it diplomatic recognition, and our first ambassador, William C. Bullitt, was just setting up shop.

Frances Crane was particularly helpful; she knew many persons of consequence throughout Europe, to whom she addressed cards of introduction. I never had the nerve to present the one to Eduard Beneš, then foreign minister of Czechoslovakia, and Sir Ronald Storrs was in Jerusalem, but I did use the others.

Also preeminent among my travel advisers was Elizabeth Reynolds Hapgood, the wife of Norman Hapgood, author, editor, and drama critic, who was a dozen years her senior (just as she was a dozen years mine). They were well matched nonetheless: he tall, lean, angular, gray, with a fine proboscis, a man of erudition and wit; she beautiful, cultivated, and gracious, with lovely hair and violet eyes, well-read and multilingual.

Aside from her husband, Elizabeth was subject to crushes (I suspect usually platonic), on other older gentlemen, of whom an outstanding exemplar was Konstantin Stanislavski. They had met when the Moscow Art Theatre came to New York in 1923 and subsequently in the south of France later in the 1920s; they kept up a warm correspondence, and he thereafter entrusted his three volumes on the art of acting to her to translate.

It was at a Hapgood reception honoring Max Reinhardt that Charles Leatherbee and Bretaigne Windust met in 1929. Some years later Elizabeth gave a reception for Maurice Maeterlinck, to which I was invited. He was the only man I have ever encountered who wore a hair net to a tea party.

It was through Windy and Charlie that I had entered the Hapgood ménage, for she had helped plan the Leatherbee-Logan trip to Moscow in 1931. The boys asked her to assist me in preparing for my Russian days ahead, and she did so graciously.

Of equal importance at that time was Henry Wadsworth Longfellow Dana. It was Dr. Moe who advised me to go to Boston to pick Dana's brains. "Harry Dana," Moe told me, "is generally conceded to be the leading American authority on the Russian stage. He's made, I understand, at least half a dozen trips to the Soviet Union, for he's preparing a definitive monumental history of the Soviet drama since 1917."

Since H.W.L. Dana was a man for a neophyte researcher like me to cultivate, up I journeyed to Boston. He lived on Brattle Street, in Cambridge, and as I walked up the front steps I realized I was about to enter Craigie House, once the poet Longfellow's home, now the residence of this descendant who bore his name.

Being twenty-four, I thought Harry Dana an elderly man, but he was probably in his early fifties. He was of medium height, like myself, but twice my weight (I would have hesitated to call him pudgy), and his sandy hair was thinning. He was most hospitable, and I felt quickly at ease. I had been invited to lunch, but his collection of Russian theatrical memorabilia was so vast and for me so engrossing that before I knew it the afternoon was over and I would have had to scamper to catch the train back to New York. This he warmly discouraged, insisting that I stay for dinner and spend the night.

I was boyishly thrilled at the thought of being put up at Longfellow's house—a literary monument, complete with visiting hours when it was open to the public. Naturally, I accepted, and I was provided with a small hall bedroom. Next morning my host appeared in flapping slippers and dressing gown, bearing a breakfast tray. I was surprised when he sat down on the edge of the bed, and I had just time to slip out the other side to avoid a friendly embrace. It was my first experience of learning how to have my cake without being eaten.

As I got to know Harry Dana better I discovered that he was, alas, a procrastinator and a dilettante. All that ever got written of his "definitive monumental history" was a five-page preface, the table of contents, lists of productions, and a bibliography, which was published as a "Handbook" shortly before his death. It totaled 148 pages. His encyclopedic reach, I regret to say, exceeded his flaccid grasp.

One of the most memorable Moscow-bound characters I was advised to seek out was Muriel Draper, whom all the world but me seemed to know. The widow of Paul, an eminent lieder singer, who died young, she had two sons: "Smudge," who was beautiful, and Paul, who was talented—an accomplished tap dancer of about my age. Muriel was the sister-in-law of Ruth Draper, the unique and world-famous "diseuse."

Mrs. Draper lived in a tiny three-story white clapboard house in the East Fifties of Manhattan. On Thursdays after four o'clock, she was "at home" to her friends, one of whom wangled me an invitation, my first appearance at a social "salon."

Mrs. Draper received her guests while seated on an oversized gilt armchair. She was a small woman, and the seat was half again too large for her. It could have done service as a throne in some grand ducal palace. It was almost, but not quite, late-seventeenth-century Venetian.

The hostess herself looked almost, but not quite, late-seventeenth-century too. The gown she affected was a flowing, smoke-colored garment that seemed too large for her rather bony frame but helped fill the empty space around her on the throne. It was the face that was arresting: long and lean, it looked like a horse's, with a strong protruding jaw; her stringy, blondish hair suggested a mane more than a lady's coiffure. In front it was cut in a bang and in back gathered into a bun, like that of Grant Wood's farm wife. Her skin was pale and beautiful. She had a broad slash of a mouth, with carmined lips. Her eyes were lively and full of humor.

I looked around the smallish room. There were a dozen or more people, none of whom I had ever met, although I had seen several in theatre lobbies or at gallery openings. The majority were young men, slightly older than I (what a difference five to ten years make when one is twenty-four). Mrs. Draper didn't bother to introduce her guests; most of them were known to each other anyhow. The insecure youth from Indiana was ignored by some, viewed by others with curiosity; surprisingly, I found that many were actually not unapproachable. There was a dark, dour, well-built young man with very short hair named Lincoln Kirstein; another with a like haircut, Glenway Wescott. With him was a small, intense young man, Monroe Wheeler, who worked at the Museum of Modern Art. There were several young composers: Virgil Thomson; George Antheil, who claimed to be "futurist-terrible" and had startled Paris with his *Ballet Mécanique* a few years earlier; Aaron Copland, who at first glance seemed almost as homely as our hostess and who was accompanied by a beautiful boy named Victor. There were Kirk and Constance Askew and Edward Warburg and several whom I can no longer remember. Nor can I recall what, if anything, we were served. This was principally a feast of reason and a flow of soul, led with wit and laughter by Mrs. Draper, who, in her husky voice, never stopped talking.

I must have made a better impression on the lady that day than I thought, for a week later she called and invited me to tag along with her to the corner of Fifty-ninth Street and Madison Avenue, where she was to meet Lincoln Kirstein. He would show us a class at a school of the dance he had just established with a strange, thin young man no one had ever heard of, someone named George Balanchine. There we watched a flock of ten-year-olds swooping about and learning *pas des deux* and *entrechats*. The School of the American Ballet, in its first year, seemed like a good way to get in the mood for Russia.

"I'll see you in Moscow in September," Mrs. Draper said, pressing my hand as we parted.

4

Moscow (1934–35)

A bout five o'clock in the after-
noon, I went up on deck; we had sighted land. It was a gray, still
day, and the coastline looked deserted. The water churned up was
an olive-brown color, adding to the strangeness of the picture.
We sailed past three or four huge, low-lying round fortresses
built on islands at the mouth of Leningrad's harbor. Beyond them
half a dozen ships of the Soviet fleet lay at anchor. Just before we
approached them, the largest fired a five-gun salute—not for us,
I'm sure—and as we passed, a band was playing, the ship's solid
red standard was flying, and all her crew were lined up on deck.
Some official must have been paying a visit.

The sky served to contribute to the dramatic effect: heavy
clouds were piled up over the smokestacks and spires and domes
of Leningrad to the east, but behind us over the water the sun had
broken through and sent long rays in under the lowering clouds
to pick up highlights on the land and the water.

I arrived in Leningrad on August 31, 1934. I had landed in
Hamburg, gone on to Stockholm, then to Helsingfors, as Hel-
sinki was called then, and up the Gulf of Finland, to this spot and
this moment.

It was after nine when, after all the formalities, we finally left
the pier. We drove very fast, with the driver honking practically
all the way, for we were to catch the Red Arrow Express train

to Moscow at ten o'clock. That ride I shall never forget. It was
my first realization of what Russia was, and a tremendously moving experience.

For what seemed miles we drove through the outskirts and
then through the streets of the city.

At first I thought I was passing through the slums of a tenement district, the buildings water-stained shells. But the surroundings didn't change, and gradually, for me, the people came
to dominate their environment. They overflowed the streets, and
I suddenly suspected that there weren't any residents other than
these tenement dwellers: all so dreadfully poor-looking—dressed
not in rags but in well-worn work clothes, blue denim, no neckties. Almost no automobiles were to be seen anywhere, but there
were lots of overcrowded streetcars.

The train trip down from Leningrad was memorable too. The
"soft" third-class car I rode in was divided into compartments,
with four bunks in each—two men and a woman shared mine.
We were each given a mattress, blanket, pillow, and clean sheet,
but of course we slept in our clothes. Though the berth was
narrow and rather hard, I managed to get six hours' sleep, which
I thought splendid. Professor Dana, my friend from Cambridge,
and his party, also en route to the International Theatre Festival,
were in a second-class sleeper; I had spent the evening with them
in the restaurant car, drinking beer and nibbling caviar, the large,
gray kind. On our way there, we had passed through half a dozen
"hard" third-class coaches, where people were sleeping on narrow wooden shelves, all piled up together. When I returned to
my own car about midnight, I stood at the corridor window for
about an hour, gazing at the moon and the endless flat countryside.

At ten o'clock the next morning we reached Moscow, exactly
on time. I registered at Intourist's second-class New Moscow
Hotel, across the river from Red Square; from the upstairs dining
room one could see the Kremlin. My single room was graced by
a washbasin, with running hot and cold water, and a bed that was
not uncomfortable. It could have been worse!

In 1934 Moscow at first glance looked as disreputable as Leningrad: again everywhere water-stained plaster peeling off the faces
of buildings; shopwindows empty because there was nothing to

display behind the paint-splattered glass; grass in the parks seemingly uncut for years. I had the impression these people were so busy with important things that they gave no thought to grass-mowing. (Later I discovered the real reason—Russians like high grass waving in the breeze: it reminds them of the steppes.) But those streets that were paved were immaculate, and throughout the center of the city, large buildings were in various stages of construction. It was a most paradoxical place.

During my first ten days in Moscow, the Theatre Festival was in full swing and we visitors from a dozen countries were kept on the move day and night. Many of the sights I ogled at then are still on the itinerary of visiting theatre specialists today—a trip, for example, to the fabulous Bakhrushin Theatre Museum, where room after room is filled with stage models, sketches, portraits, and photographs of artists. After seeing it, I noted in a letter home: "What's the use of doing anything? Everything's been done already and so perfectly. Oh, to be able to do work like that!"

A dozen productions were scheduled for the festival visitors—plus backstage meetings, colloquiums, interviews with appropriate government officials, and informal get-togethers over dinners or drinks at the hotels, whereat we compared notes among ourselves.

I have never forgotten my first night at a Moscow theatre, the Vakhtangov, one of its most important: no gilt, no cherubs, no velvet curtain, no upholstered seats or carpets, none of the trappings of playhouses in New York or even in Indianapolis in the twenties and thirties. Plain, plastered walls were without ornamentation. A heavy, mouse-colored flannel curtain separated stage from auditorium. Unmasked spotlights hung a few feet in front of the proscenium. Seats had no cushion padding; their wooden backs, like undertakers' folding chairs, kept the audience bolt upright.

My fellow spectators were as unornamented as their surroundings. Most appeared to have come straight from work. It seemed that about every tenth man was in military uniform, and almost half the audience looked under thirty. No middle-aged, well-groomed Broadway-like audience was this. I scanned the hall and found not an empty seat.

For almost four hours the crowd sat on the edges of those hard seats, enjoying three breaks to stretch their legs, promenade, or buy a sausage-and-black-bread sandwich and a bottle of kvass. When the show was over, they stamped and cheered; flowers came floating toward the footlights. The play—*Intervention*, a rather crude drama about the Civil War in the 1920s—had been in the repertory for a year, but that ovation was like a first night's.

The afternoon after we had seen Vsevolod Meierhold's four-and-a-half-hour production of *Camille*, Harry Dana took a dozen of us to interview the great revolutionary director. He sat at a table, a lean figure, his slightly stooped shoulders giving to his head something of a forward thrust, which added prominence to a large and stately nose. His thinning gray hair seemed to stand on end. He gestured a good deal, and his movements were rapid; so was his speech. He talked about his new theatre—which would never be built—and about his theories of a "theatre theatrical," based on outward form. When he concluded after an hour and a half, I presented him with a letter of introduction from Herbert Biberman, a Broadway director, and was in return patted on the head and invited, when he learned I would be staying on, to visit his theatre whenever I liked.

Two days later, at the Moscow Art Theatre, during an intermission of *The Marriage of Figaro* (the Beaumarchais play, not the opera), several of the foreign visitors, I among them, were taken backstage and introduced to the distinguished actress Mme. Knipper-Chekhova, Anton Chekhov's widow, a plump, elderly woman with a Mona Lisa smile.

Suddenly Stanislavski himself emerged from the wings, the most leonine figure I had ever seen, well over six feet tall, perfectly erect, with a fringe of snow-white hair and heavy white eyebrows. Mr. Dana presented me in French—Stanislavski spoke no English—and we shook hands, a kind, friendly smile on his face as he said, in Russian, "We shall see each other often."

Equally exciting was the final curtain call, when Stanislavski came out before the festival audience. While he stood there waving, everyone rose and cheered for about five minutes. Most of them no doubt realized they might never see him again.

There were three world figures of the Russian stage in the fourth decade of this century. All headed theatres in Moscow:

Konstantin Stanislavski, Vsevolod Meierhold, and Alexander Tairov. Thanks to the festival, I had been presented to the first two by the time I had been there a week. Then, on the eighth day, Intourist gave a huge supper party at the Metropole Hotel for all foreign visitors to the festival, and there I was presented to the third master, Alexander Tairov, a short man, his hair combed carefully across his balding pate, wearing a well-fitting Western suit.

During the festival days I also encountered several old acquaintances and friends, like Blanche Yurka and George Freedley, curator of the Theatre Collection of the New York Public Library. With him (at the time, I thought they were together) I met a young man who reminded one vaguely of an exotic moth— or perhaps of movie glamour girl Mae Murray. His name was Thomas Quinn Curtiss. I don't know where home was for him in 1934—I suppose New York—but today he lives in Paris, the respected drama and film critic of the *International Herald Tribune,* who doubles as a stringer for *Variety.* He's one of the few persons I've mentioned thus far who is still alive.

At Tairov's Kamerny Theatre the next night I saw *The Optimistic Tragedy,* a new play about the navy in the Revolution, which I liked very much. During the intermission I ran into Muriel Draper. Since she had not come for the Theatre Festival, I was only now crossing her path. With her were her friends Gifford Cochran and Lincoln Kirstein. They invited me back to supper with them at the National Hotel, then Moscow's most chic. We consumed great quantities of caviar and ham and eggs, wine, vodka, and champagne, and afterward I felt very unwell and lost, alas, my taste for caviar. I should instead have lost it for the Russian champagne, which was abominable.

2

For the past fifty or more years, the Soviets have offered foreign travelers no alternative to Intourist hotels. But before the Stalin purges of 1936–37, the majority of transient aliens spending three months or more in Moscow were permitted to live in apartments or furnished rooms if they could manage to find them. You simply registered with the militia in the district where you took residence. Consequently, as the festival ended, I started my search for quarters not too far from the center of the city.

Luckily I found a place quickly, and ten days after I'd arrived I left the hotel and moved into my own room. It had at one time been occupied by a young under secretary at the British embassy, Alexander Wainman, and then by Ambassador Bullitt's personal secretary, Charles Thayer, until he was moved to Spaso House, our embassy residence. That room was now up for grabs, and I grabbed it.

It was in a small two-story house on a little back street near the Arbat, in a modestly respectable residential quarter about a twenty-minute walk from the city center and accessible by a streetcar line and bus. The exterior was unattractive in the ways of most old Muscovite houses: planted in a sea of mud with no surrounding vegetation, its walls marked by the usual peeling paint and chipped plaster, the entire two-story house looked as if it were about to collapse.

Here lived a family named Gan. The father had been a distinguished Russian scientist. When he died, a grateful state allowed his wife and two daughters to live on in the house it had bestowed upon him. In return they spent most of their time bitterly reviling the government.

Mother Gan was otherwise a cheerful, well-upholstered lady, monolingual, a schoolteacher; her older daughter, Zinaida (Zina for short), about four or five years younger than I, had just graduated from the foreign-language school and thus was proficient in English. In addition, there was a youthful maid-of-all-work, Dunya, who slept in a hall passageway and who Charlie Thayer claimed was an illegitimate niece. She always addressed me at the top of her voice, attributing my incapacity to follow her conversation to deafness!

Zina, inclined to plumpness and shyness, was a sweet girl and engaged to a distant cousin, an architect. The week before Christmas she married him in a ceremony in which I served as one of four best men. We spelled one another at holding golden crowns steadily in place over the bride's and groom's heads, with devices that looked rather like forceps, while the Russian Orthodox wedding ceremony went on for its customary seventy-five minutes or so.

There were various relics of past cultivation chez Gan: a big, square, black ebony piano, some fine Russian Empire furniture, heavy blue damask draperies. My small room had one window, facing south, on its sill a thriving asparagus fern; walls of green and gray wallpaper; a lovely blue-glass Russian chandelier with crystal pendants. A small table stood by my narrow but comfortable bed. The bureau was of satinwood and matched two armchairs and a straight chair, all upholstered in yellow-green satin. The room was a little overstuffed, but that couldn't be helped because there was no more space. Heating was provided by a tile stove.

As for the rest of the Gans' apartment (they shared the house with a barber and his wife, who lived on the ground floor), the dining room was the general congregating area: in it were the grand piano, a huge grandfather's clock, an immense sideboard, a desk, a couch, and half a dozen chairs surrounding the dining table. Another boarder occupied the parlor. Mother and both daughters slept in one bedroom, the other having been turned over to me. In the kitchen was the bathtub. When using it, you drew a curtain around it, so as not to splash soap into the porridge. The other facilities were in a closet down a passageway.

Everyone thought me very lucky to live in such style. For the room and three meals a day I paid thirty-one dollars a month, and I enjoyed the further advantage of help in learning the language, which living with a family abroad usually provides.

But I needed more help with my Russian than meals with the Gans and thirty Berlitz lessons could supply. So I acquired a Russian grammar teacher, one Mme. Alexandra Vasilevna Rostovtseva, who lived about ten minutes from my house. An hour a day, five days a week, I spent with Mme. Rostovtseva. Plump as a capon, she lived in a one-room apartment and shared a communal kitchen with three other families. Many of the hours when she was not teaching uses of the dative she must have spent over the hot stove, for not a lesson went by that she didn't woo me with some exotic concoction. This she would bring forth steaming, halfway through the hour, accompanying it by clucking sounds and admonitions that I was losing weight and working too hard. She was correct on both counts. "Eat! Eat!" she would cry. And she taught me a great deal.

Four weeks passed before the formidable wall that constitutes the language barrier collapsed for me. I had been told this would eventually occur—your self-conscious inhibitions would be released, and you would realize that you had nothing to fear. It happened at Zina's engagement party, to which I was invited. Festivities began about half past nine. There were fifteen or sixteen young people, only half a dozen of us Westerners—Alec Wainman and a toothy English girl, whom I disliked, Charlie Thayer, whom I did like, an Australian with a Russian wife. The others were mostly young Russian intellectuals: one an assistant at the Tretyakov Gallery of Russian Art, another a critic of Western literature, a third Zina's co-worker in a foreign-language library. Three or four spoke faltering English; one spoke it quite well, the others not at all.

The evening was a scene out of Chekhov. There was dancing to a phonograph, a good deal of singing, parlor games, an excellent supper, a lot of laughter. Wine and vodka flowed, and champagne was uncorked to honor the occasion. The bridegroom-to-be, a fine pianist, played Chopin; several people delivered recitations, mostly of Pushkin's poetry. There was a call for me to follow suit in English. The Russians were horrified that I couldn't even recite "To be or not to be" past the first eight lines, and I was ashamed of my limitations. But feeling obliged to make some contribution, I began to recite "with expression," in English, "Oh, say can you see by the dawn's early light," and continued all the way to "the land of the free and the home of the brave." Only two Russians and the five Westerners could understand my outpouring and my odd choice, but they were outnumbered two to one and I received an ovation.

Toward the end of the evening I suddenly realized that I was babbling away effortlessly in Russian. The moment had arrived—helped along by strong drink, I've no doubt. I had overcome the language barrier.

Not anticipating this breakthrough, I had just engaged the

services of Professor Dana's interpreter, one Luba Imkhanitskaya (the good professor had departed). Luba was so homely a female that I was sure she was able. Her English was indeed faultless and her Russian native. She was available four hours a day, for which I paid her twenty-five cents an hour. Since Dana had already taught her the theatre ropes, with Luba at my side I could show stage bigwigs I was not the innocent young man they thought but a chap who knew his way around.

Our first joint sally occurred shortly after Zina's party, when Luba accompanied me to the Commissariat of Education to present my credentials to the chief of its Theatre Section—the stage then functioned under its aegis—and to receive in exchange a document requesting directors of all state theatres in the USSR to grant me entrée. I never purchased a single ticket to a stage performance during the next five months, and I attended the theatre ninety times.

The United States had extended diplomatic recognition to the USSR the winter before I arrived. Ambassador Bullitt was supported by a group of young secretaries specially trained in Riga. Their caliber was extraordinary; one need mention only three: Loy Henderson, George Kennan, and Charles Bohlen, the latter two subsequently distinguished ambassadors to Moscow. It was stimulating to rub minds and elbows with such young men, even if they, especially Kennan, didn't spend much time in theatres.

With the ambassador's private secretary, Charlie Thayer, who was nearer my age and, like me, a lover of laughter and an extrovert, I hit it off at once. He seemed, too, to have more time for the theatre than secretaries in the political section. Charlie distinguished himself by his ingenious use of the language. Commanding a broad vocabulary, he could talk Russian to a collective farmer and a ballerina with equal ease. What was unique was that he used the first person singular in the present tense for all verbs and the nominative case for all nouns—and everyone understood!

Charlie's prowess reminds me now of an experience I had at the Gans' less than a month after I moved in. Well past midnight, I was awakened by a sound within my small room. I sat up with a start, and the beam of a flashlight hit me in the eyes, so that I could barely see that the intruder had one foot on the windowsill, the other on the table near it. He whispered a stream of sibilant Russian. Of course, I didn't know whether he was saying, "Your money or your life," "Give me your typewriter and I'll go," or "Excuse me, I must have the wrong window."

I wanted to call for help but couldn't think of the word. Suddenly I recalled a verb Alexandra Vasilevna had just the day before added to my vocabulary—*pomogat,* a rather formal word, best translated as "lend assistance." I could not remember the imperative, but the infinitive would do, so I cried loudly in Russian, "To lend assistance! To lend assistance!" The robber was apparently so startled by my choice and grammatical usage that, getting my message and muttering something to himself, he backed out the window and down the wall, taking nothing.

When the next morning I told the family about the intruder, Mrs. Gan said, "I've told you that you should never leave your window open at night."

Zina said, "I heard you, but I thought you were practicing your verbs!"

I understood then why Charlie Thayer was such a successful conversationalist—any word form would do in a pinch.

I had put into Thayer's hands two letters of introduction to the ambassador. He responded a week later with an invitation to call at the chancery. Bullitt was much attracted to the performing arts and reasonably knowledgeable about Moscow's stages.

I explained my game plan. Since there were so many theatres there, I proposed to focus in depth on only four: the Moscow Art, Meierhold's, the Vakhtangov, and Tairov's Kamerny. The ambassador agreed with my choices but urged me to add a fifth: the Moscow Theatre for Children—there was nothing like it is America. Natalia Sats, its director, was lunching with him the next day. "Come along, too, and meet her."

Spaso House, the embassy residence, was a handsome nineteenth-century mansion, one of the untouched old ones, with gorgeous chandeliers and handsome gilt furniture. The library was painted light blue. Its furniture—Chippendale and early American—was brought most likely from Philadelphia, the ambassador's hometown.

There were only six of us. Though a small group, we spoke

four languages—English, French, German, and Russian. Once more I felt inhibited, for I considered it safe to speak only in English, which Miss Sats did not know. She chose German, which the ambassador in turn translated! It was all casual and informal, although, of course, the surroundings were quite otherwise. As for Miss Sats herself, she was in her early thirties, had bobbed hair, was pretty, charming, vivacious, and enthusiastic, ideally cast to run a children's theatre.

I returned to Spaso House a couple of weeks later, invited to come in after dinner to hear a string quartet. Donning my dinner jacket, I appeared at nine-thirty, to mingle with foreign diplomats and their spouses, a few Russian artists, and such secretaries as Henderson, Kennan, and Bohlen, and under secretaries as Durbrow and Thayer. After the diplomats left, Bullitt urged me to stay on, to tell him how I was getting along. So I drank his good French champagne until two and told him of my principal problem.

I'd been in Moscow a month and had made no progress toward being admitted to rehearsals at the Moscow Art Theatre (MXAT, its Russian acronym). I couldn't seem to get to Stanislavski, without whose approval no one dared move. True, his theatre was world-famous and didn't need to be written about, but for my part, I couldn't write a book about the Russian theatre and omit it.

The ambassador replied that he thought he could help. He knew a man in the Kremlin named Schteiger, whose job seemed to be principally to deal with the problems of the diplomatic corps and those introduced by it. He would call him, and Charlie Thayer would then let me know when and how to reach him.

Such things moved slowly through the Moscow apparatus. Ten days later Thayer called. "Meet Mr. Schteiger in the lobby of the National Hotel at five o'clock this afternoon." We met and I told him of my frustration with the Art Theatre. Schteiger reassured me: he would speak to Stanislavski directly about me. I would know the outcome shortly.

Six days later the road was cleared: the maestro had agreed to receive and welcome me into his theatre. I was instructed to go at two o'clock, with my interpreter, to 6 Leontevski Lane, off Gorki Street. A big yellow house, it was large enough to contain both rehearsal space for Stanislavski's Opera Studio and his living quarters. His secretary came over from the theatre and met us in a large entrance hall.

From there we passed through a cloakroom, at whose far end was a little door where, after ringing a bell, she ushered us into the director's study. Since Stanislavski spoke no English, we talked through my interpreter, or rather Luba talked, because I was so excited that for once I could think of nothing to say. She, not being so afflicted, managed to supplement my stammerings with a little biographical data, although Stanislavski knew who I was, for Elizabeth Hapgood had written to him.

He talked with me for about half an hour, explaining what he expected to do with the rehearsal of *Carmen* we were about to attend. The company had been working on it for ten months, since he had first outlined their objectives. But this was the first time he would see the second act. We crossed a hall and entered the Opera Studio, where the company was assembled, about a hundred strong, with the entire chorus present. When he walked in they stopped talking and rose. He shook hands with the prima donna and the conductor and then advanced to the center of the room, where he presented me to the company. Then he sat down and invited me to sit at his side.

When they completed the first scene, he talked with the company about parts of it for some time, a stenographer recording everything he said. After about two hours he was tired, so they took a recess. He brought me back to his study, where we had tea and strawberry jam and little cookies and talked some more.

I asked if he remembered Charlie Leatherbee and Josh Logan, and he said he did, quite well, and asked if the company was still together. After tea the principals came into the study, where there was a piano and it was cooler and more comfortable. Then, following about another hour, the rehearsal ended and I retired, as exhausted as the old man by the nervous strain of trying to fix in my memory the whole experience as it unfolded.

There is a postscript to this story. It concerns that mysterious but apparently powerful figure who succeeded in getting me into Leontevski 6 when all else had failed—the so-called "Baron"

Schteiger. Before I left Moscow, I was told that he was the chief of that bureau of the OGPU (now the KGB) assigned to diplomats and their protégés. That explained why, for several weeks after we parted, I kept running into him on street corners, in hotel lobbies, even occasionally outside a theatre. I have often been asked whether I felt I was ever "tailed" as I scampered around Moscow. I tell the Schteiger story, for it fits: after a few weeks—when he was satisfied that I was doing what I said I was doing—he disappeared from my life.

And let me explain now about the six-day hiatus after Schteiger undertook my cause. It apparently occurred because of the death of Sobinov, one of the mighty bassos of the Bolshoi Opera and the last in a line that went back to Chaliapin. Sobinov was a lifelong friend of Stanislavski, who, much moved by his death, went into seclusion for several days.

My understanding of the difference between Soviet and American attitudes toward the arts was underlined by an experience I had that week.

On my way home after the theatre one evening, I approached Sverdlov Square, which the Bolshoi Opera faces, and observed a line of people standing in the rain. I crossed the street to see what was happening. For eight blocks, in the dark and drizzle, the line stretched to the side doors of the Bolshoi. Within, the body of Sobinov was lying in state. I was told people had been in line all day. And I could see they were not curiosity-seekers. Many were wearing the shabby clothes and shawls of working men and women; many were young people. Here was spontaneous expression of grief.

The funeral was set for the next day. Everyone said I should attend, but admission was by invitation only and I didn't know how to get a pass. Luba and I decided to go to the Bolshoi anyway. Its facade was draped in black; fastened to its columns were clusters of red flags banded in black, and flanking its big doors were potted cypress trees and silvered palm leaves. The square was kept clear by two lines of militia; directly before the theatre a line of cavalry was drawn up.

Luba was a most intrepid female: she worked her way through the ranks, with me tagging behind, up to a side door—and more guards. Finally, by showing all my papers, she was allowed to enter to see if she could find anyone who would admit us. She returned in a few minutes, and we were ushered into a box!

The ceremony had already begun, and the secretary of the Central Executive Committee was delivering a eulogy. Then the combined choruses of the Bolshoi and Stanislavski operas sang Mozart's *Lacrimosa,* after which Kachalov, the Art Theatre's greatest actor, read Pushkin, as only he could do. The orchestra played the finale from Tchaikovsky's *Pathetique* Symphony, Bach, and Beethoven, and the ceremony was over. The opera house was filled with the great of the USSR, and throughout the service four of them came forward every five minutes to stand in tribute at the corners of the catafalque. I recognized the faces of many of these artists and political leaders.

Afterward we went out into a side street. Unable to pass because of the crowd watching the procession, we could hear two bands playing Chopin's "Funeral March" in unison. I was told this was the most impressive occasion since the death of Lenin. When I asked who else's death, outside of Stalin's and President Kalinin's, would earn such a demonstration, I was told probably only Gorki's and Stanislavski's.

Looking back over more than half a century, I can recall only President Kennedy's funeral as having provided such a moving display in our country. Certainly the death of no performing artist ever has or ever could.

3

In 1934 the American community in Moscow was very small, not more than fifty people, as against the five hundred I read constitute it today, and almost everyone knew everyone else. That was why I had put Mrs. Draper on a back burner at first, for I knew we would sooner or later connect. We did indeed.

The Metropole Hotel then, as today, did not possess the ancien régime grandeur of the smaller National Hotel, where some suites were endowed with grand pianos and all had heavily carved cornices, red-plush- or brocade-covered sofas, gilded wall sconces with amber silk shades, and fin de siécle chandeliers. The Metropole, on the other hand, was a worldlier hostelry, in favor with the foreign press, with those rare Western traveling salesmen who ventured to the Soviet capital in the thirties, and with a few daring young Muscovite couples. The latter were especially drawn to its restaurant by a blaring jazz band, from one of the Balkan countries, which played loudly until two in the morning, and by a large pool with a fountain and goldfish that unexpectedly occupied the center of the dance floor. As the hour waned and inebriation waxed, several couples regularly fell into the fish pond, to the delighted screams of all present.

Although Mrs. Draper lived at the National, she preferred the knockabout hilarity of the Metropole's restaurant, where she could frequently be found after the theatre. She chose a corner table not too close to the music—for she loved talk—but with a clear view of the dance floor and the fish pond, for she also couldn't bear to miss anything. This would become her *coin* for the next several months. If you could not find her elsewhere, you would head for that little table, where she would be, holding court to Alec Wainman or Charlie Thayer, or to Tom Curtiss, who had left Moscow for a while and gotten as far as Amsterdam, only to come back when faced with the alternative of returning to America. I found myself joining them after the theatre far oftener than was good for my digestion or my head. But Muriel was magnetic.

Not everyone liked her; she was too bright and perceptive; for some, she was too inquisitive. Women especially were uneasy in her company, for they sensed, I believe, that she cared less for them. She had lived abroad a good deal, especially in Florence and London, and seldom a week passed without some distinguished artist, diplomat, scholar, or journalist from her past coming to seek her out. She could discourse in French, German, or Italian. To my envy, she could make jokes in whichever was the prevailing language of the evening.

As September and October came and went, Muriel began to dig herself in for the winter. What she was really up to in Moscow I couldn't figure out. Indeed, I never have discovered. She was still there in February, when I left. She had known Ambassador Bullitt well in Philadelphia in "the old days," but I got the impression that he kept some distance between them in Moscow. Was she perhaps somebody's secret agent? A crypto-Communist?

She was very interested in the lives of those who piqued her
curiosity, and apparently I was one such. When McNeill Lowry
asked Lincoln Kirstein in a *New Yorker* interview not long ago
why Muriel had taken an interest in him, Lincoln replied: "She
liked young animals. I mean she had lots of young animals
around. She had been all over the world, she had a considerable
reputation; she was the mistress of Bernard Baruch at one time.
She was a considerable person."

This young animal would frequently take Muriel to the
theatre, after which we might return to her table, to occupy it
à deux. By November she had decided that Tom Curtiss was
developing a secret passion for me, and leaning across the table,
she insisted that I be "kind" to him. She was sure that I recip-
rocated his feelings, whether I knew it or not; indeed, she demanded that I allow him to come and share my quarters.

I remonstrated that I was in Moscow to do a job of major
theatre research, that I found it absorbed all my days, most of my
evenings, and much of my energy and thoughts; I wasn't interested in having a liaison with Tom, her, or anybody else—anyhow, I didn't think Curtiss was my cup of tea. But such were her
powers of suggestion, not to mention of will, that I agreed to
increase my cordiality.

I had decided that I must visit Leningrad for ten days or so just
to see its sights, and the beginning of December seemed a good
time for a break. I had been working terribly hard for three
months, and Leningrad and its environs were said to be beautiful
in the snow. So I booked space on the Red Arrow and invited
Tom to come along.

Leningrad was indeed a change of scene: how beautiful the city
was! After I saw Vienna the following spring, I would bracket
the two as the most "imperial" cities in Europe. The snow had
a marvelous way of covering many of the eyesores of both Leningrad and Moscow.

To be sure, I didn't get exactly the break I needed, for what
with sightseeing, theatregoing, and meetings with stage folk who
had been alerted by their Moscow colleagues to welcome me, I
returned as exhausted as when I set forth.

Looking back, the high point of the ten days came the afternoon of our visit to Tsarskoe Selo (then still called that) to see

the Catherine Palace—the most beautiful in Europe, I still say, remembering it as it was before the thousand-day siege of Leningrad by the Germans.

It was midafternoon when we moved on from it to the Alexander Palace, not far off. This was the one being occupied by Alexander's son, Nicholas II, and his family when, only seventeen years earlier, they were taken off to Ekaterinburg to be executed. It begins to get dark by three o'clock in December that far north, so we were taken through much of the palace at dusk by lamplight, which added to an extraordinary pervading sense of intimacy. We were paying a personal call on the occupants, who were out for the afternoon; they would return home soon for dinner.

The drawing room was lovely—a soft pink, the Tsarina's favorite color, as you discovered when you passed into her personal quarters, pastel and comfortable: her Red Cross sewing basket on a table, postcards stuck into the frame of her dressing table mirror, a volume of Chesterton on her chaise longue. The Tsar's apartments were tasteless by contrast: his bottle-green private study with its daily calendar still open at the fateful day, July 31, 1917; his larger study, containing a billiard table on which maps of the war front were spread out; his swimming pool. When the royal family were carried off, the Bolsheviks sealed up the palace, and only two years before my visit had it been opened; they left it just as they found it, and put it on public display. I was much moved by my hour among the shadows of the Romanovs.

The playwright Alexander Afinogenov and his American wife were visiting Leningrad, and one evening after the opera, we returned to the hotel for supper together. He was then at the peak of his fame as a dramatist: *Fear,* his latest work, then playing throughout the country, was in the repertoire of the MXAT, where I had seen it. One of the fair-haired boys of Soviet drama in the thirties, both figuratively and literally, Afinogenov looked more like a young Scandinavian than a Slav and was, I thought, a bit impressed by his fame. When we first met, in Moscow, I had found him serious, rather quiet, and a bit shy. This evening he was more open. Interesting, I thought, that Russians were more relaxed the farther away from Moscow they found themselves. By the time I got to the Caucasus that winter, they were as unreserved and straightforward as children. The same was true forty years later, when I spent four days on the Trans-Siberian Express crossing into the heart of Siberia.

That night, over Georgian red wine and chicken *tabaka*, Afinogenov discoursed for an hour on modern Russian drama and theatre. Naturally, he spoke in Russian, with his wife helping out in English.

He began with the MXAT, the progressive mouthpiece of liberalism before 1905, he observed. It exposed Russians to Ibsen and his social concerns—the emancipation of women, for instance; to Chekhov, of course, showing them the feckless irresponsibility of the bourgeoisie; to the German writer Hauptmann; and to Gorki, introducing them to the proletariat, as well as to the men and women of the sharp, money-minded business world.

After 1905 the MXAT began to turn reactionary, he went on. They drew veils of mysticism around themselves and became preoccupied with symbolism: Maeterlinck and Andreyev, Ibsen's late plays, Dostoyevski. That's where they had hidden as 1914's storm clouds threatened.

Afinogenov next turned to the 1920s, when he was growing up. Meierhold, he pointed out, was inevitably popular in the early twenties, for several reasons: his was almost the only new theatre open in Moscow or Leningrad; further, by discarding scenery and stage costumes, he made the people feel he was more akin to their own denuded state; and, finally, he played upon their emotions inspired by the Revolution. Said Afinogenov, "His audiences were never interested in his theories of biomechanics or any of the rest of his aesthetic."

"And today?" I asked.

Today, he claimed, Soviet drama was studying problems of life and death, morality, human relationships, because it had to serve the function of church as well as theatre. "People go to learn about those things. And if not about them," he added with a grin, "then about clothes or interior decoration. In any case, the trend must be toward more realistic psychological drama and away from formalism." He was indicting Meierhold three years before the latter would be indicted by the same word—"formalism"— and liquidated by the Party.

These snippets from a conversation over supper in Leningrad, one of so many I had with various Russian theatre people, suggest one of the primary ways I managed to increase my knowledge and understanding. Although certain nuances no doubt escaped me, such talks nurtured my feeling that a book, after all, might emerge. I must write home and report.

4

Before I left for Leningrad, Spencer Williams, Moscow representative of the American-Russian Chamber of Commerce, had asked if I'd care to sublet his apartment for the remainder of my stay—until early February. He was going home for the holidays. After inspecting it and the live-in housekeeper-cook who came with it, I accepted gladly.

The Leningrad trip with Tom Curtiss had been more a trial run than a honeymoon, and because we got along reasonably well, when we returned to Moscow I moved out of the Gans' and into the Williamses' four-room flat with Curtiss. I think we made each other miserable much of the time. He had no visible occupation; I was working harder than I ever had. He was an omnivorous reader; the only book I had time for was my Russian grammar. He had a motley assortment of idols: Ernst Lubitsch and Emil Jannings in Hollywood, Sean O'Casey in Dublin, George Jean Nathan in New York, all of whom he talked about incessantly. None were comparable objects of my veneration. He adored movies; I was wedded to the living stage and snobbishly considered the cinema in those days infra dig.

Tom loved to weep; I loved to laugh. But we both had Irish blood, and whenever he got tired of crying, he, too, loved to laugh. So I guess it could have been worse. Fifty years later I find him marvelous company—no tears, just laughter. In Moscow he was a boy who may indeed have looked like Mae Murray. But in many ways he was older than I. He is now an urbane, witty, erudite citizen of the world.

Muriel Draper, then, did not skew up my personal life forever. Certainly she wrought permanent good in my artistic and critical growth. I had come to Moscow with preconceptions about the theatre, largely based on what I had experienced in my still brief stage career. The American theatre then practiced what it called "realism" in acting, writing, and staging. It was post-Belasco, pre-Strasberg realism, of course; it thought box sets, which imitated the looks of rooms with one wall inexplicably removed, provided the environments necessary for actors to play at being "real" people in exaggerated situations. *Tobacco Road* was the longest-running play to date largely because it had *real dirt* on the stage floor.

To be exposed to what realism could actually be profoundly expanded my theatrical horizon. Stanislavski became my god and his Art Theatre a latter-day blessed company of Holy Apostles. "Truth to life" became my Confession of Faith. Seeking to grasp and experience this revelation became a full-time preoccupation.

Muriel saw it otherwise. Realism, no matter how accurately it revealed people and places, remained bourgeois, she claimed. Art was *not* life, and the harder it tried to become like life, the worse it became as art. The more she saw of his creations, the more she was persuaded that the true Russian genius of those times was Meierhold. His was a theatre theatrical, and the farther away he moved from the look and smell and sound of the everyday world (which the Stanislavski artists worked so hard to recreate on-stage), the louder she cheered.

Consider, for example, Meierhold's famous production of Cromelynck's *The Magnificent Cuckold*. It had been in his theatre's repertoire since the 1920s but still drew audiences a decade later. You entered his theatre to find not a curtain but the brick rear wall as the background. In front of it was an arrangement of platforms whose scaffoldings were completely unmasked. Its bare boards and cross-bracings were visible to the audience. There were ladders and slides and, hanging above the highest platform, three wheels of different sizes which were later to revolve, apparently at will. No furniture onstage, nothing that *looked like* anything! It appeared to be a structural representation of Coney Island thriller equipment, stripped of its painted externals. A fairly large cast was dressed alike in blue jumpers, as though a group of airplane mechanics or gas station attendants had gathered together to put on a play.

The plot was the old triangle situation, a man, his wife, and her lover, given by Meierhold what they called in Russia "social meaning." This was apparently accomplished by the introduction of acrobatics. The cast raced and tumbled about the stage, turned somersaults and cartwheels—all for a purpose. I can suggest this purpose by describing the entrance of the lover. At another theatre there would be a knock at the door, he would enter, see his girl, move toward her eagerly, smile, and take her in his arms. They would both "register" joy at the meeting. Meierhold, however, placed the lady at the foot of a playground tin slide, had the lover climb the ladder to its top, then zoom down the slide, feet first, knocking the lady onto the floor and shouting something that sounded like Russian for "Whee!" Thus did Meierhold express the effect of an eager lover meeting his mistress. Of course, he knew that lovers don't come down slides in real life, but he believed that the abandonment and joy that filled the man could be much more accurately conveyed if he catapulted himself down a ten-foot S-curve to meet his lady than if he followed the dictates of conventional movement. And believe me, it really worked.

For the most part, however, I could not figure out what Meierhold was up to with his "biomechanics" in acting, his futuristic and constructivist sets, his elimination of the stage curtain, his unmasked lighting sources, his use of exaggerated commedia dell'arte–like makeups, and his insistence that the spectators must never forget where they were—in a theatre. Some of it was exciting, I granted, but what did it all have to do with reality?

"Everything!" Muriel would shout. "Never think realism and reality are synonymous. The reality of great art has little to do with the way things *look.* "

Muriel Draper would never let go. She wasn't satisfied until she managed to get Tom Curtiss under my roof. She wouldn't be satisfied until I understood what Meierhold's theatre was about. If Muriel were alive today, she, too, would be an urbane, witty, erudite citizen of the world. She would have outlived Baruch and her friends Norman Douglas and Pablo Casals and Lady Cunard and Lady Colefax and Chaliapin and Nijinsky and Diaghilev and Gertrude Stein—all of whom people her delightful volume of memoirs, *Music at Midnight.* Indeed, "she was a considerable person."

Christmas was coming. There was so much yet to do. Lee Simonson's response to my message from Moscow—that if I stayed six months I would have collected enough material for a book—was in the form of an announcement that he had lined up a publisher for me. I should expect to hear from Harcourt, Brace shortly.

Once again, I am astounded by what I then accepted as a matter of course: Why shouldn't one of America's top publishing houses offer to publish, sight unseen, my first book, of which not even the opening sentence had yet been written? As I had told Margaret Linley at the Theatre Guild about stage-managing, I was sure I could do it. Among my weaknesses, lack of self-confidence could hardly have been included in those days. How I wish I were still twenty-five!

December 25 came. It certainly didn't seem much like Christmas in the West. In the morning, as on any other day, I went to the Vakhtangov Theatre to observe a technical rehearsal, watching scenery being set up and lighted, very much as at home. At two I went to Alexandra Vasilevna for my Russian lesson and a bite of lunch, and later to interview a man at the Palace of Labor for an hour and a half about workers' theatrical clubs and their activities.

I hurried home after dark through a snowstorm to prepare for dinner. Muriel Draper was coming; we had imported sherry, excellent roast goose with vegetables and cranberries, and a mince pie I tried to teach our housekeeper to make, though not knowing how myself. We enjoyed a merry Christmas, aided by Russian wines and spirits, and afterward went out on the town.

Twelve days later the Russian faithful celebrated their orthodox Christmas. My diary (the only year I ever kept one) records: "I went to the Gans, arriving at supper time. They had a Christmas tree, played some music and danced, but it wasn't very exciting. So I was home at 2:30." I wonder what time I'd have gotten to bed if it *had* been "very exciting."

Tairov's Kamerny Theatre celebrated its twentieth anniversary on January 4. There were many speeches; Tairov and his wife (and leading lady), Alice Koonen, were made People's Artists of the USSR; skits were performed by several theatres, gifts were presented, certificates of honor were awarded to senior members of the company. Indeed, I was asked to bring greetings from the American theatre but never got the chance because, as you can see, the program went on too long. "It seemed like Christmas and Commencement Day rolled into one," my diary noted. "By the time that part of the evening was over I had a headache from the klieglites." I made my way to the theatre's foyer, where a huge banquet was laid out.

I was particularly impressed at the way the government showed up on such occasions. It was represented that evening by Foreign Minister Maxim Litvinov, Bubnov, the commissar of education, Marshal Voroshilov, et al. By now I had become acquainted with many of Moscow's theatrical leaders, so we chatted as old friends. Most of them were fifteen to forty years my senior, but they treated me without condescension, with courtesy and good humor as though I were their contemporary—indeed, almost as if I were as celebrated as they. "Home to bed at three. It was very cold today—about thirty-five degrees below zero by the Russian count."

January's thirty-one days were too few for me to wrap up my mission, especially when faced with the Russians' obstinate tendency to procrastinate just when pressure of time is strongest. I had kept to my early decision to focus my study on the MXAT, the Vakhtangov, Meierhold's and Tairov's theatres, and added to them the Realistic Theatre of Okhlopkov. At each I followed through the preparation of a single play, entering the production process as close to its beginning as possible and trying to carry on to the opening. I had been reasonably successful, observing at the Art Theatre a new production of Gorki's *Enemies,* directed by Mikhail Kedrov, who after Stanislavski's death would become his successor; at Meierhold's, an evening of three Chekhov farces, directed by the master himself; at the Vakhtangov, a slight contemporary play staged by Reuben Simonov; at Okhlopkov's, a production of Pogodin's latest play, *Aristocrats;* and at Tairov's, an extravaganza called *Egyptian Nights,* which tried to combine Shakespeare's *Antony and Cleopatra* and Shaw's *Caesar and Cleo-*

patra into one grand production that turned out, not surprisingly, to be more grandiose than grand. I was able to see public performances of the last three plays, all of which opened before I left.

The memory of one of my final evenings of theatregoing I shall always cherish: the Moscow Art Theatre's jubilee performance, on January 30, 1935, of *The Cherry Orchard*, in honor of Chekhov's seventy-fifth birthday anniversary. All the great actors of the company who were still alive and able to get there played their original roles—among them Kachalov, Moskvin, Knipper-Chekhova, Leonidov; Stanislavski, the original Gaev, was, alas, among the absent. All of them were, of course, thirty years older, but it made no difference.

And the audience! Admission was by invitation only. It consisted almost entirely of contemporaries of the author and actors, men and women who had attended that opening night in 1904. The clock had stopped. These aging Muscovites, who had lived through war and revolution, brought out for the first time in the new era their ancient finery: women wore gowns of taffeta with high net-and-whalebone collars, men rusty black dress coats, clipped beards, and pince-nez à la Chekhov himself. They gave themselves up to the play completely: one minute they were rocking with uncontrollable laughter, the next minute they were dissolved in tears. The great dramatist and this public were as one—in perfect communion.

I had saved for the last week my farewell visit to Leontevski 6. I brought along my copy of Stanislavski's autobiography, *My Life in Art*, and a clipping, just received from New York, that announced the reassembling of the University Players. I asked if I might read it to him and return with a message to inspire them anew. Stanislavski sat back and removed his glasses.

The newspaper reported "the formation of a new and permanent organization of comparatively young people, all experienced in the theatre, for the purpose of producing new plays." After describing our seasons in Falmouth and our winter in Baltimore and listing the membership, the article wound up with a statement of policy, designed, I suppose, largely to stress distinctions between us and the Group Theatre:

The intention is forthright. It is not founded upon any dogma, is devoted to no particular set of aesthetic principles, has no program of propaganda for or against anything, no revolutionary message for mankind and has, in fact, no other aim than that of presenting stimulating plays in the most professionally competent manner and with the most efficiency.

When I finished reading, there was a long pause. Stanislavski's pince-nez swung back and forth on their black ribbon. Then he spoke.

"I don't know what that statement means. I don't think it means anything. It adds up to saying that all you want is to do good plays well. Well, I never heard of anybody wanting to start a theatre in order to do bad plays badly." He paused. "To start a theatre you must be revolutionary. Oh, I don't mean politically. I mean you must be motivated by dissatisfaction in some way with the status quo. Either you must want to produce plays different from those being done around you, or to present them in a different style, or in a different form of theatrical space, or for a different audience."

As I pondered this, Stanislavski went into an adjoining room for a moment. He returned with a copy of the Russian edition of *My Life in Art.* He'd like me to have the original text, he said; perhaps by now I could read Russian. Well, I could at least read the inscription he'd written on the flyleaf, a few lines familiar, I've no doubt, to some of my readers, for they encapsulate his credo: "To Charles Norris Houghton, my dear comrade in art, with this friendly advice: love the art in yourself and not yourself in art. This leads to success in our work. K. Stanislavski."

From my meetings with that towering figure, I acquired two objectives to guide me through the decades ahead: the never-ending search for creativity—upset the status quo; and the virtue of humility—learn to serve your art, not to expect it to serve you.

On Saturday the ninth of February I left Moscow by the night train for Kiev and Kharkov in the Ukraine, thence by the Trans-Persian Express to Baku; then to spend a week in the Caucasus in Georgia. It was snowing a little in the morning. I stayed at home finishing up my packing until three o'clock, when I went to say goodbye to Alexandra Vasilevna. During the six months, she had formed a romantic attachment to me, twenty years her junior, in the best Turgenev tradition. It was a sentimental, tearful farewell. From her I went to the post office to send a cable home, and to Intourist to pick up my travel tickets, then back home for an early dinner with Tom, after which Muriel and a half-dozen other cronies appeared. We drank a final vodka toast and set forth for the railway station. There Zina Gan and a couple of other friends were waiting to fill my arms with fruit and candy. It was all very Russian and very dear, and everybody wept and waved.

5

On February 24, 1935, I took leave of the Soviet Union. I sailed from Batum—overnight by train from Tiflis (now Tbilisi)—at the eastern end of the Black Sea, on an Italian steamer, my destination Istanbul. The ship was primarily a freighter; I was its only passenger, except, of course, for a constant flow of deck passengers, who came aboard with their bundles and their goats and chickens, shouting and chattering together in Turkish or Bulgarian, sleeping on the lower deck and disembarking at the next port of call.

Five days on the Black Sea—alone; rest and relaxation, a chance for reckoning and reflection on the extraordinary six months I had just experienced. I hadn't realized how exhausted I had become. Each day in the Soviet Union had brought new assaults on mind and spirit. I had lived at fever pitch. I felt during the last days like a swimmer heading for a distant shore, knowing I must somehow keep afloat until I reached it.

In six months I had aged years, or so it seemed. The eager young chap who had sailed into Leningrad at the end of August seemed a far cry from this weary fellow now outward bound across the Black Sea.

There were quite a few things to sort out: matters artistic, political, personal. But since I had no one to talk to, I thought that perhaps by the end of the five days at sea I'd have acquired some

perspective on both the Russians and myself. I didn't quite
achieve that, but I did make a stab at it.

To begin with, in 1934 and '35, the Russian air vibrated with
enthusiasm and confidence. Granted, there were many among
the bourgeoisie who hadn't been as adept as the aristocracy at
mastering the art of flight. The upper class recognized at once
the fragility of their plight and fled in all directions. The middle
class didn't feel the same urgency; like Gorki's merchant Yegor
Bulichev, they would wait and see how the Bolsheviks made out.
The proletariat, who made up the vast majority, as they always
had, were euphoric, for they were innocents and believed all the
infectious slogans and the plays and movies of which they were
unfailingly the heroes. This revolution, they were told, was for
them—workers and peasants.

Neither a worker nor a peasant, I was nevertheless young and
swept along by the exhilaration of the times. As the Russian
people were urged to overlook present deprivations and to take
fierce pride in the miracle of having thrown off the grinding
burden of the tsarist system, as they were admonished to focus on
the future and have confidence in tomorrow, my heart sang with
theirs.

I had no serious run-ins with the secret police; government
officials treated me, for the most part, with consideration, were
in fact cooperative. Even the burglar at my windowsill had taken
nothing as he fled. No one had sought to convert me to commu-
nism. Indeed, I could count on the fingers of one hand the serious
political debates I had engaged in, and those were more often
with fellow Americans or Britons than with Russians.

Why, then, did this country still strike me as a paradoxical
place, even as it had in September? I suppose because there was
such a disparity between the glowing dreams and the bleak reality. The Red Arrow, for instance, ran exactly on schedule, but
it was the only passenger express train to connect the two principal cities of the Union. There were oranges in the bowls on the
stage, but none in the grocery stores. My memories of Moscow
are vivid with dancing till dawn in hotels, caviar and champagne,
sparkling snow, plays, ballets, concerts, opera. I have invented

none of that. At the same time, I have not forgotten my first shocked confrontation with the drab desolation of decaying buildings, unpaved streets, vast holes in the ground betokening slow-motion labor on the subway or on the foundations of sky-scrapers; they, too, were very much part of the scene. I have been back to Moscow and seen the metro and the skyscrapers—they did appear, but in 1935 they had to be taken on faith.

And although the government officials were cooperative, as I've said, the daily encounters with queues, postponements ("Come back tomorrow"), and red tape, with the frustrations of shopping, with the petty deceptions and prevarications, could not be ignored.

After a few months there were nights when I'd go to bed thinking this was the worst place imaginable, and other nights when I thought it the most wonderful. More of the latter, no doubt of that, but the negative couldn't be pushed aside. Odd that judgment always came down to best or worst, nothing in between.

As for the Russian people, I liked them very much indeed. Almost from the outset I discovered they were truly on our American wavelength, their sense of humor more compatible with mine than was, say, the British. They also loved to tease. They were garrulous, warmhearted, sentimental.

Russians in my day have had a reputation for being devious, taciturn, dour. Granted, I've never had friends in the Politburo, where such adjectives may have been deserved. But the people I met in 1934 were mostly theatre folk, artists, intellectuals. While many of them may have been impatient with the party line them-selves in those days, they were hospitable, friendly, openhearted. When I left I was sure I would go back, and I have, eight times over the intervening fifty years. I've found them always the same.

About the theatre I naturally thought a good deal on that Black Sea crossing, about both theirs and ours. The latter didn't hold up well in the comparison. Most of my fellow artists seemed to have limited vision—just as I had had. Their conceptions of style were imprecise, based on intuition, arrived at by chance. They accepted realism (the only style they felt comfortable with) but couldn't define it, couldn't say *why* they accepted it or what the alternatives were. They wore blinders, like horses. To be sure, I had to admit that I'd seen Broadway for only seven seasons, worked in it but two, and I, too, had taken it as I found it.

I wondered uneasily whether it was capable of change; indeed, whether I was myself capable; or, finally, whether change was desirable or necessary. In Broadway rehearsals I'd never heard phrases like "psychological truth" or "inner motivation," nor talk among my contemporaries about "emphasis on the rational" or "appeals to the subconscious" or "search for the subtext." Did it make any difference anyhow? Were these perhaps things my colleagues were practicing without using the jargon of the Russians? I doubted it; otherwise why were our performances too often such pallid imitations of nature, of the real? Most of this I hadn't worried about before I went to Moscow. And maybe there wasn't any point in worrying now, in 1935, since American theatregoers in general seemed satisfied with the stage as they found it.

If I was, however, troubled about style in the theatre, I was even more alive to "the degenerating and deadening effect of commercialism in it." (Strong words, those, but I wrote them— and stronger ones—in *Moscow Rehearsals.*)

On the Black Sea I was, in fact, in the process of forming a conviction that would govern much of my future life: belief in nonprofit professional theatre. That would be demonstrated subsequently in the creation of Theatre Incorporated, then in the Phoenix Theatre. It would become a thesis of my second book, *Advance from Broadway.*

As for myself, I've said that I'm not given to introspection, but I gave it a whirl as the five days at sea drew to a close. I had arrived in the USSR an innocent, I decided, and I was leaving with a good deal of my innocence intact, which didn't upset me at all. In a self-congratulatory mood, I sensed, too, that my faculties of perception, appreciation, and critical judgment had deepened. My self-assurance had also received a boost. I decided that I was more interested in other people than in myself. I also found that in Russia I was more attracted to the men than to the women. Was that a reasonably common appraisal, or was that the way my life was going to turn out? What I was sure of was that I had a lively curiosity about everybody and everything. Now I was anxious to debark from that Italian ship, for I was rested and ready to discover Europe.

5

European Grand Tour (1935)

I had approached the USSR from the north, through Sweden. I returned to Europe by heading south to the Mediterranean. I was starting on my Grand Tour. I felt that having dedicated six of my eight-month fellowship to the Russians, I had earned the right to take the kind of look at Europe that I had proposed in the first place. When I received word in early April in Sicily that my Guggenheim had been extended, I decided to add a third month for travel and then settle down someplace for the additional three to write.

Forthwith I became a dedicated sightseer. I have never recovered: awake with the birds, rushing up one street and down another, looking into every church I pass, seeking out every vantage point for a view, examining noted graveyards, racing through as many galleries and museums in a week, guidebook in hand, as most tourists visit in a month. My curiosity is apparently insatiable. And on that first three-month tour, for me everything was new.

I traveled alone. I could linger when I became engrossed or encountered interesting people; I could hurry on if I became bored, though that hardly ever happened. I spent little time shopping, for I had to save my pennies. I rarely ate in dining cars or took a sleeper; of course, I had no automobile and never boarded an airplane. Occasionally, I would be given a lift in a car, but by an acquaintance, never a stranger; in other words, I did not hitch my way across Europe.

Respites came at the beginning of my travels, when I took short sea voyages: two nights on the Aegean from Istanbul to Piraeus; three days and nights from Athens to Naples; overnight to and from Sicily. I struck up interesting connections with fellow passengers—not many Americans, but whatever their language, these travelers were usually friendly and worth knowing.

Other breathers, briefer but more frequent, which I grew to cherish, occurred toward dusk when the weather was propitious. As other tourists were seeking out a hotel bar or sidewalk café, I would head for an open meadow or a ridge or a rocky promontory that commanded a view toward the west and the setting sun. There I would allow myself an hour listening to the silence, looking out over hills or the sea or a smoking volcano or a town or an acropolis. I became quite an authority on sunsets. If I had a companion, well and good; if not, so much the better.

Don't think I was turning into a loner. I came down from these habitual retreats braced for whatever evening activity might seem tempting. But I have always been shy about wandering into a strange bar or nightspot alone. Many an evening I preferred to take refuge in my hotel or pension with a book. (I managed to read a good deal that spring. That was before I gave up literature.)

My habits developed as I moved unhurriedly through Greece—Athens, really, where, except for a trip to the clean white temple at Cape Sounion and a short bus ride to Eleusis, I remained for eight days. The weather was mostly foul and thus inhospitable to junkets, so I spent a few evenings in my little hotel bedroom, with a view of the Parthenon from its window, for which I paid eighty cents a day (including breakfast).

I allowed myself to linger in Taormina for twelve days. It was the most beautiful spot I'd ever seen. In early April, the Sicilian weather was blue and gold, and the flowers were profuse. My small hotel, its terrace hanging a thousand feet above the sea, its food and service impeccable, its clientele charming, seemed close to perfection. Under the lemon and orange trees in the garden I started to write my Russian book, thereby soothing my conscience as I luxuriated in this sybaritic spot.

I spent Easter in Rome with Frances Crane's brother John,

whom I had met often on Cape Cod, and his wife, an Italian principessa. From their handsome fresco-ceilinged apartment in the Palazzo Rospigliosi they introduced me to Rome's glories. Teresa, John's wife, invited me to go with her one afternoon to the Palazzo Ruspoli, which belonged to cousins, to attend a lecture by the great dramatist Luigi Pirandello. It was followed by the performance of a one-act play of his, after which Teresa introduced me to the now-aging dramatist, with his neat gray beard and almost bald pate. When I recount this vignette in college seminars, to impress upon my students what remarkable theatrical connections I've had, they ask with awe: "What did you talk about?"

"Nothing," I have to reply. "We just smiled and shook hands." That's the truth, for he spoke no English and I no Italian.

The Cranes had procured for me a ticket to the Papal High Mass at St. Peter's on Easter morning; I arrived before eight-thirty and was shocked that what I had thought would be a very sacred and solemn occasion turned out to resemble a football rally, with the crowd cheering wildly for their favorite quarter-back—"Viva Papa! Viva Papa!"—and a delegation of Austrian youths in Tyrolean garb shouting in German, "Prosit! Prosit!" or something that sounded like that.

After leaving Rome, I was indeed on the way to Austria, but first I had to inspect Italian hill towns and of course stop in Florence, Siena, and Venice. I felt it essential to visit Venice, so that upon my return I could tell Robert Edmond Jones that I had happily noted the reflections of the water on its walls. Like everyone else, I found it, and still find it, one of the earth's greatest jewels.

I did take leave of the Quattrocento in Florence for an evening with Norman Douglas, to whom Muriel Draper had given me a letter. I had read *South Wind* in Sicily, in anticipation of the encounter. I loved the book and eagerly looked forward to our meeting. I recorded it succinctly in my diary, in an entry almost as brief as the handshake with Pirandello: "Then I went out for dinner with Norman Douglas, a good meal in a little restaurant; but he was rather a disappointment—a dirty-minded pervert, not very scintilling though with a rather amusing way of talking. A friend of his joined us. I left them at 9:30."

It was already the second week in May when I reached Vienna. I knew at the end of the first day that I adored it. Indeed, everything I had seen of Austria—that is, from the train window, as we rode from the Brenner to Innsbruck to Salzburg to the capital—enchanted me: the Tyrolean Alps, the churches with their onion-shaped domes, dark evergreen forests, splashing mountain streams. And then magnificent Vienna. Five days was too short a time, of course, but I had vowed to be in London before the end of the month, and Budapest and Prague still remained to be seen before I left Central Europe.

The day after I arrived I went to the National Library to present Lee Simonson's letter to Joseph Gregor, the world-renowned stage historian, a bulky man with heavy spectacles who presided over the library's Theatre Department. He had only a few minutes for me, but it was enough to impart an important piece of news: Gordon Craig was in Vienna. When he learned we had never met, Dr. Gregor said he would call Craig and arrange an appointment.

What a coincidence! Here was a man who had long preceded Stanislavski as an icon of mine. I had pored over Craig's drawings ever since I was twelve; I had read *On the Art of the Theatre, Towards a New Theatre,* and *The Theatre Advancing* while still in high school. I considered them great seminal works, just as I thought his sketches, though unrealizable, the inspiration and the fulfillment of all that could be dreamed of for the modern theatre.

I went back to the hotel, to find a message from Herr Dr. Gregor: "Be at Mr. Craig's hotel at 8:30 tomorrow morning." I went out again and walked about in the gardens of the Hofburg, thinking only about Edward Gordon Craig: the son of the great actress Ellen Terry, an actor in the company of Sir Henry Irving, the lover of Isadora Duncan. I knew nobody to match such credentials. How old must he be? I thought he was born about 1870, so he'd be in his mid-sixties, almost ten years younger than Stanislavski, forty years my senior. I recalled that the two had collaborated once: Stanislavski had invited Craig to design and direct *Hamlet* at the Moscow Art Theatre around 1911. It had been a fiasco: his scenery fell down!

Craig, a tall, gray-maned Englishman with a fine brow and keen eyes, was already breakfasting at a table in the dining room.

He waved me to a seat, offered me rolls and coffee. Cordial and charming, he impressed me as an active person, not at all as the stage's greatest dreamer. We talked, of course, about Russia. He was en route home from a brief state visit to Moscow. He thought Russia hadn't really changed much since 1911! Stanislavski hadn't carried his stage realization through to its final conclusion; he had been sidetracked, Craig asserted, just as Stanislavski had in turn sidetracked Vakhtangov from his intention to create a theatre theatrical. It was a conversation of high-level stage gossip.

Had I ever seen the Italian actor Petrolini? he asked. No? What a genius—one of the really great actors. He was at that moment in Vienna. I must go and see him perform the day after tomorrow. Craig would be there too. He would look for me.

The breakfast hour over, I left, vaguely disturbed, I didn't know why. Gordon Craig hadn't seemed to rise to the stature I had expected of him, as Stanislavski had so fully done. Perhaps it was my fault; perhaps I had overidealized him. But no. He hadn't talked about the theatre at all, only about theatre folk, and I had hoped for more.

I would encounter him again. First, two days later at the Vienna playhouse, where I saw for myself that Petrolini was indeed a remarkable performer. He was best, I thought, in comedy; his burlesque of the grand style as Hamlet was hilarious.

But my next exchange with Gordon Craig was by mail. I sent him a copy of *Moscow Rehearsals* when it was published and received a four-page handwritten letter in return. Since he wrote such heartwarming lines as "I hope that some day we may speak together more about these things, for I come across too few younger minds who are worth listening to or reading . . . You are blessed in a nature which is receptive," and a slew of other flattering remarks, I decided to frame the letter and keep it under glass. And here it remains, rather reminiscent of Treplev's seagull in Chekhov's play.

I have never forgotten my encounters with those two of the world's greatest theatre artists alive in my century, Konstantin Stanislavski and Gordon Craig, nor do I prize any mementos more highly than the one's autobiography with its holograph inscription, the other's letters in his tiny hand.

I traveled from Vienna to Budapest by bus, a six-hour ride through a flat, boring countryside. I stayed two and a half days in that great city, for it was such before the war, then set out for Prague, which was even more lovely. There I found a note at the hotel from the Princess Lobkowicz, a close friend of Frances Crane, telling me she was at their country place and inviting me to "come for lunch and spend the night." I was intrigued: did they go to bed immediately after lunch and remain there until morning? I could hardly wait until the day after next to find out.

Meanwhile, however, I presented myself to other people to whom Miss Frances had given me cards, among them Alphonse Mucha, the great painter and a leader of the Art Nouveau movement. He turned me over to his son, George (Jiri, in Czech), a chap about my age, who became my guide and companion during my five-day stay. He took me to see a remarkable team, Voskovec and Werech, who were captivating Czech audiences with their satiric *Vest Pocket Revue.* Nineteen years later, George Voskovec would appear in New York under my direction in *The Seagull* at the Phoenix Theatre, which says something about the indestructibility of his spirit as well as his talent.

Young Mucha and I hit it off beautifully and formed a friendship that continues despite increasingly infrequent encounters. The last time I was in Prague, in 1964, with Mary Leatherbee and Van Varner, Van and I stayed at the Mucha house, which faced the old palace across Hradčanske Namesti. Part of the house is a museum containing many of Mucha *père*'s paintings.

One day during that visit, George took us to St. Vitus's Cathedral. "I want to show you the westernmost stained-glass window to the left of the nave." He pointed it out. "It was designed by my father. It's called the Wenceslas window. Look closely, for I posed as young King Wenceslas."

We were mightily surprised. None of us had ever gazed at a window in a European cathedral wherein the likeness of a personal friend was enshrined forever in stained glass.

The day came for the Lobkowicz date. I was driven to Roudnice, the Lobkowiczes' country place in Bohemia. It was early-eighteenth-century Baroque, with three hundred rooms. Most of them were closed, but before lunch I was shown the museum, the library, which housed 100,000 volumes, and paintings hung in some of the state apartments in an open wing. Ever since my discovery of Vienna (where, incidentally, another Lobkowicz palace stands, almost diagonally opposite the Hofburg), I had been increasingly drawn to Central European architecture. At Roudnice the palace's exterior was a soft terra-cotta color, with copper roofs that had turned a deep green, altogether a stunning sight.

Lillian Lobkowicz, my hostess, Irish by birth, welcomed me warmly.

"I'm so sorry my husband, Max, isn't here to meet you. Unfortunately, he's gone to London to see his dentist." I was awed: a man who crossed half of Europe to have a tooth pulled.

It was a lovely day, warm and sunny. Guests at lunch conversed mostly in English, to oblige the visiting American, with occasional lapses into French, German, and Serbo-Croatian that kept him high and dry and, as always, annoyed by his linguistic inadequacy. After lunch we spent much of an idle afternoon in the garden under a huge spreading tree, as in Act II of *The Seagull*, and had a fine Irish tea there. The absent Max, I learned, had been chargé d'affaires in the Czech embassy to the Court of St. James's when the Jan Masaryks had been presiding over it. I learned, too, that the Lobkowicz family had been princes of Bohemia in Hapsburg times.

After dinner Mme. Lobkowicz suggested a short drive to a wood on the estate where nested a nightingale. I had admitted to never having heard one. We went and we waited and we waited. The bird did not oblige. In fairy stories, nightingales always sing for princesses. I was deeply disillusioned.

At six-thirty the next morning I was awakened by a footman, who arrived to light a frightening-looking object—a geyser—that was to provide hot water for a bath, if it didn't explode first. Then he returned with my breakfast. I was driven to the railway station and was back in Prague before nine o'clock. The princess, I presumed, was still dreaming of the nightingale.

2

I bypassed Paris—imagine spending a year in Europe and never setting foot in Paris!—traveling to London by way of Ostend instead. On May 24 I arrived. After all those street signs and notices in Hungarian and Czech, it was a relief to encounter English. I knew at once I had made a wise decision to settle down in England to work, though it almost didn't turn out to be so.

First, I sought a suitable place to live. Setting forth alone, I found a semidetached house with a "Bed and Breakfast" sign in the window. It was just off the Edgware Road, behind Marble Arch, not on the way to or from anywhere that I would want to go, except Paddington Station and out of town. I leased for two weeks a little hall bedroom up two flights. There was a table under the window on which I could write, and it was quiet. The loo was at the end of a dark passage. From a public telephone in the downstairs hall, I could make calls to the gentry on Frances Crane's and Muriel Draper's lists and to a few others whose names I had picked up in Moscow and intermediate points.

Among them most notably—for it became a long-term relationship—was Mrs. Leonard Elmhirst, on whom I called armed with one of Frances Crane's little visiting cards. She was tall, slender, erect, with slightly graying hair; she rarely wore makeup; she had a soft voice and a tentative manner of speaking that somehow turned statements into questions. She invited me to weekend at her historic castle in Devon, Dartington Hall; I accepted.

I was met on a Friday afternoon at the Totnes railway station and taken to a charming old farmhouse on the estate, called the Parsonage. It housed eight or ten persons, all involved in the life of a remarkably multifaceted enterprise.

Mrs. Elmhirst had been born to great wealth in New York. The daughter of William C. Whitney and christened Dorothy Payne Whitney, she had married Willard Straight, by whom she had three children: Whitney, Beatrice, and Michael. From her youth she was an espouser of liberal causes: she bought the *New Republic* for her husband, who became its publisher, she founded

Theatre Arts and the *Antiquarian,* not for their politics (they had none) but to satisfy her own arts interests.

When Willard Straight died, she was in early middle age; in due season Dorothy met and married a young, lean, redheaded Englishman sporting a fine mustache, Leonard Elmhirst, who was an agricultural specialist at Cornell. Dorothy acquired a somewhat derelict thirteenth-century castle in Devonshire, Dartington Hall. Although the rumor that Richard II had given it as a present to John of Gaunt is quite untrue, I'm told, there is no question that Dorothy gave it as a present to Leonard. After renovating and restoring the Great Hall and surrounding buildings, they brought into being the unique operation I was to see that weekend (as well as my hostess).

Leonard's major objective was to create a center for the revival of rural industries: textile weaving, chicken and dairy farming, sheep grazing, cider pressing, woodworking, pottery making. A second concern at Dartington was educational: the Elmhirsts established there one of the first and most widely known "Progressive" schools in England or America. And, finally, to reflect Mrs. Elmhirst's interest in the arts, she invited young painters, composers, and artists of all kinds to take up residence at Dartington. Among those accommodated were the entire company of the Joos Ballet, fleeing from the harassments of Hitler, and in 1936 the diminutive genius Michael Chekhov, nephew of the great playwright, who crossed the Channel from Paris to set up a studio-school of acting at Dartington.

The next day I saw many of these sights and met some key people, but my hostess was not among them. I was somewhat bewildered, and was even more bemused when I was called to the telephone at the Parsonage after tea on Saturday.

It was Mrs. Elmhirst, who hoped I was having a good time. I assured her I was. Would I be free to come up to the Hall for luncheon tomorrow? She was eager to show me the house and the gardens and tilting yard. I gave her my word that I had no conflicting engagement. At lunch I sat next to her son Michael Straight, then a Cambridge undergraduate, a brilliant, articulate young man of nineteen. Years later he would follow in his father's footsteps to become editor of the *New Republic* for a time. We are still friends. I then joined my hostess and Julian Huxley, also a house guest but on a level both more intimate and more exalted than mine, for a walk before tea.

The second week after my arrival in London I reached a sort of social pinnacle when I received an invitation from Lady Sybil Colefax to dine at Argyll House, her stately mansion in the King's Road, Chelsea. I had presented myself the week before, armed with Muriel Draper's introduction.

"I thought she was awful," I wrote tersely in my diary then, adding, "though her house is very grand. Perhaps I disliked her because I thought she wasn't impressed with me."

It took a lot to impress Lady Colefax. I wasn't aware of it at first, but I soon learned she was one of London's great lion-hunters—and I was certainly no prize trophy. She was close to the Prince of Wales and Mrs. Simpson. Later (for her suspicions of me gradually faded) I would meet a galaxy of legendary men and women in the little drawing room of the house to which she moved in Lord North Street when war was imminent: Desmond MacCarthy, David Cecil, Mrs. Wellington Koo, Rex Whistler, Diana Duff-Cooper, Cyril Connolly, Harley Granville-Barker; glamorous theatre folk like Noel Coward, Gertrude Lawrence, J. B. Priestley, Terence Rattigan, the Lunts, Katharine Cornell, Guthrie McClintic, Thornton Wilder. She was a most successful collector. (I believe I caught my propensity for name dropping from her.)

Sybil Colefax was small and not overly prepossessing. She was round-shouldered, which, as she grew older and her condition grew worse, caused her to address many of her remarks to the carpet. Since I never lay at her feet, I consequently missed some of her conversation. But she was bright-eyed and sufficiently adept at keeping talk going to satisfy her guests, many of whom possessed the great wit that she herself may not have had.

She was, I would eventually find, extremely kind and considerate, a loyal friend, and I ended up devoted to her, as was everyone else (except those she snubbed). I once complained about her illegible handwriting, to which she replied, "I don't worry. Everybody seems able to decipher my scrawl well enough to read my invitations and show up at the right time. That's all that matters—to them or to me!"

That first dinner party was a typical Lady Colefax evening.

Among the guests were Mrs. Somerset Maugham, at whose right I found myself; Bruce Lockhart, the military expert and writer, seated beside Ruth Draper; and on my right her young niece, Diana Draper; Ivor Novello, prince of the London musical comedy world; Oliver Messel, a leading stage designer; and Lord David Herbert, a younger and apparently footloose, fancy-free, and unemployed son of the Earl of Pembroke. Aided by an ample supply of champagne, I relaxed and had a dandy time, especially with Diana Draper, whom I found most attractive. When the party broke up, David Herbert and Oliver Messel invited me to accompany them to Le Fiacre, a fashionable London after-hours nightspot. Much later, Herbert drove me back to the Edgware Road in his low-slung red sports car. It was a night to remember.

Oliver Messel invited me to lunch the next day. I went first to his studio, where we had a drink and he showed me some of his work. He then took me to a posh restaurant, the San Marco, which he had been commissioned to decorate in the rather chichi style the *haute monde* favored in those days. At cocktail time I turned up at David Herbert's, where I was charmed to find Diana Draper again. Two evenings later I escorted her to see Diana Wynyard in *Sweet Aloes*. I took her back to her aunt's house for a nightcap, whence I was sternly evicted by Aunt Ruth on the stroke of midnight. She obviously distrusted any young man of cousin-in-law Muriel's acquaintance.

My saga of wanderings about Western Europe has contained but rare mention of theatregoing—only in Vienna, Prague, now London (with but this single reference to Diana Wynyard). I seemed, in fact, to have resolutely turned away from the stage for those four months. Why?

To tell the truth, the theatre in Turkey, Greece, Italy, and Hungary was in the doldrums during that 1935 season, or so the natives sadly reported, and my itinerary excluded France and Germany. But I think another reason was that the Russian theatre's vitality and creativity had so profoundly affected me that I was disinclined to expose myself to what by comparison sounded bland and insipid. I felt, too, that it was important not to dilute or confuse my Soviet impressions, at least until they could be recorded in my book.

The next night in London I was invited to a party for Mei

Lan-Fang, the greatest Chinese actor of his generation. Marie Seton, a good friend in Moscow, was the hostess, and Essie and Paul Robeson were among the guests. I had gotten to know the Robesons pretty well when they visited Moscow in December and thought them a wonderful couple.

I am always much intrigued by unlikely juxtapositions. One was the sight of the yellow Mr. Mei, five feet four inches tall, in animated conversation with the black Mr. Robeson, six feet three. Neither color nor height appeared to bar their compatibility.

At the end of a week of that kind of high life, I knew London was no place for me if I expected to complete a rough draft of my book by the end of the summer. While I most certainly enjoyed being taken up by these Mayfair charmers, it was too rich a diet to sustain day after day: two-hour lunch parties, nights out on the town that ended at dawn, waking at noon with a hangover. I must flee London, I said to myself, and I did so, being careful, however, to leave my forwarding address just in case. I ventured into Surrey, to a country inn at the edge of Farnham called Bourne Mill, reputedly built shortly after 1066. But it looked stable—and was but an hour from Waterloo Station. Despite that, by September the first draft of *Moscow Rehearsals* was completed.

6

Back to Broadway (1935–39)

"*M* r. Houghton, this is Gilbert Miller," a high-pitched, somewhat whiny voice announced on the phone one October day in 1935. I had never met Gilbert Miller, but like everybody on Broadway, I knew that his was a gilt-edged name. At that moment he had two great hits running— *The Petrified Forest,* starring Leslie Howard, supported by Humphrey Bogart, and *Victoria Regina,* starring Helen Hayes, with Vincent Price. Simultaneously in London was another Miller hit I'd seen that summer: Eugenie Leontovich and Sir Cedric Hardwicke in *Tovarich.* But how in heaven's name had Gilbert Miller ever heard of me?

I didn't exactly say, "And what can I do for you?" Struck dumb, I just held the receiver, transfixed. I wondered whether Sybil Colefax or some other titled acquaintance in London had dropped my name in passing. For you see, Mr. Miller was one of the great transatlantic snobs of his day. He seemed aware I had been in Moscow and London, but he hadn't, I felt sure, been informed of my stay in the bed-sitter on the Edgware Road.

"What are you doing?" he inquired, as though it were any of his business. I replied that I was at work completing a book on the Soviet theatre.

"Come in and see me at Henry Miller's Theatre tomorrow,"

he commanded imperiously. "I have a job for you. It won't start for another month, so it shouldn't interrupt your writing."

So I went to the theatre he owned on Forty-third Street, one of New York's loveliest, reminiscent of London's Haymarket. I entered through a door marked "Offices of Gilbert Miller," climbed a flight, and was ushered into the inner sanctum.

Rachel Kempson, Lady Redgrave, in her memoirs described Mr. Miller's appearance with great accuracy. "He was," she wrote, "a repulsive mountain of flesh with his beady eyes sunk in his puffy face." She was recalling a time when he had just turned her down for a role, and of course there is no fury like an actress scorned. Nevertheless, I must say that although he was offering, not refusing, me a job, I can find no more fitting description than hers for the man seated behind the huge Chippendale desk, selected no doubt because it was scaled to his size.

After a cozy chat about foreign capitals and his titled friends, Mr. Miller got around to explaining that he was about to produce a play called *Libel!* He was bringing over a Viennese director to stage it—Otto Preminger. He asked if I'd ever heard of him.

"Oh, yes," I replied, "I saw his production of *Der König mit den Regenschirm* at the Theater in der Josefstadt last spring." I thought a cosmopolitan touch on my part would help cement our relations. "It was delightful," I added. Miller nodded.

He wanted me to be stage manager. Preminger had never been to America, and he would need someone to show him around as well as guide him through our rehearsal process. From what Miller had heard, I seemed the right man for the job.

I agreed, but I thought it best to protect myself by saying, "I don't really speak German, Mr. Miller." I didn't savor another crash course at Berlitz.

"He speaks enough English to get by," Miller reassured me. He would arrive in mid-November, and *Libel!* was to open the week before Christmas.

"Go finish your book, and be ready to take care of Preminger. By the way, he's addressed as Doctor, not Mister." With a wave of what Rachel would call his puffy hand, he dismissed me.

The interview relieved me of a great weight: how to support myself during the weeks I was finishing *Moscow Rehearsals.* Actually, the book did not need much rewriting, save for a recast of the opening chapter. The completed manuscript went to press just as the German director was stepping off the boat and onto Ellis Island, where I had been sent to meet him.

Alongside Rachel's "mountain of flesh," Dr. Preminger seemed perfectly proportioned, although he was, in fact, rather hulking, his large head totally bald. He was but three years my senior, but he comported himself like a man in his late thirties. His accent was certainly thick and his vocabulary limited; I hoped Miller was right and that he knew enough English to get by. He proved affable, and I grew to enjoy my dual role as his mentor as well as his stage manager. I took him to Brooks Brothers and Altman's and Sardi's. (I left introductions to Bergdorf's and "21" to my boss.)

The cast of *Libel!* contained a number of Britishers, which was certainly appropriate since all the action took place in a London courtroom. Colin Clive was starred, but the plum in this legal pudding belonged to Wilfrid Lawson, who played Counsel for the Defense.

Lawson was an extraordinary artist, here making his New York debut. He had cut his teeth on Shaw, having appeared in the West End in *Man and Superman, The Doctor's Dilemma, Mrs. Warren's Profession, The Philanderer, Misalliance, Fanny's First Play,* and always in juicy roles, like Alfred Doolittle in *Pygmalion* and Mangan in *Heartbreak House.*

Lawson was by no means handsome. In *Libel!* he chose to wear his barrister's wig askew much of the time, which added to his odd appearance. He was of medium height, with shaggy dark hair atop a large head; his face was pockmarked; he possessed the gravelly voice of a Yorkshireman, which he was, and a gift that he shared with only two other actors of whom I'm aware, Laurence Olivier and Eleanora Duse. He could turn purple with fury onstage like Larry and blush with embarrassment to the roots of his hair, as Shaw claimed Duse could, and—like them—he could do it exactly on cue. However Olivier may have accomplished it (in *The Dance of Death,* wherein I observed it), Lawson's complexion altered, I am convinced, as a result of overwhelming inner psychological tension of almost apoplectic power. When the scene was over, from my place in the wings I could see him wipe the sweat from his brow as he sank onto the bench facing me. It was awe-inspiring.

Offstage—and sometimes on, as well—Wilfrid was an undisciplined man. He drank more than was good for him, and when under the influence he could be rude and gruff, almost boorish. The rest of the company avoided him, or possibly it was the other way around. In any case, as stage manager, I lived in constant fear that some night he would not show up or blow his lines or fall down. Miraculously, Wilfred never missed a performance, a cue, or a line. But when he was in the mood, he could drag out a pause unconscionably, blow his nose majestically, and race through a cross-examination so fast that the actor opposite was hard put to keep up with him. Yet everything he did, every line he uttered, rang absolutely true. Of course, I never uncovered his mystery, any more than I could understand what Laurette Taylor was up to when onstage. Wilfrid Lawson was of Miss Taylor's caliber, and I mean that as highest praise.

Libel! was still running when publication date of *Moscow Rehearsals* finally arrived—February 25, 1936. To celebrate the event, Messrs. Brace and Harcourt entertained in their offices: as I recall, there were three other guests—Lee Simonson, Lewis Mumford, and Louis Untermeyer, the latter two, I suspect, just passing by.

The reviews of the book, I must say, were extraordinary. Of course, the subject was newsworthy—everything about Russia was then—and no American had previously written at length about the backstage world of the Soviets. But though it was easy for me to appear the authority, I was nonetheless amazed when Lee Strasberg, who had been to the USSR, wrote in *New Theatre* magazine: "No other book I know of succeeds so well in depicting what one perceives and experiences in a Russian theatre." And when John Mason Brown wrote two columns in the *New York Post,* I was taken aback.

> "Mr. Houghton's book," Brown wrote in part, "is not only the best book on the Soviet stage that I have seen. . . . It is a volume that ought to be devoured by every director, manager, actor and critic in our theatre, and that should be

pushed by its publishers until it has had a chance to burn its way into the consciousness of every so-called drama lover in these United States."

I didn't know whether it was according to protocol, but I wrote Mr. Brown a note saying how much I appreciated his review and how much more he had found in my writing than I was aware I had written. He responded quickly.

"A thousand thanks for your letter and even more thanks for your book. . . . Would you do me a favor? Would you give me a ring any morning at your convenience and let me know when you are free for lunch?"

Over the Harvard Club's popovers, a lifelong friendship was sealed on sight. John and his wife, Catherine, known as Cassie, became my mentors, my most cherished confreres. John was nine years my senior, Cassie close to my own age. I never knew a more delightful woman nor a more gracious or witty man.

I found it a touch ironic but most pleasing that *Moscow Rehearsals* was hailed by both the *New York Times* and the *Daily Worker*, that I was commissioned by both *Harper's Bazaar* and *The American Scholar* to do follow-up feature articles on the Soviet theatre.

I had as many invitations to speak that spring as my *Libel!* schedule would allow. I was amused, incidentally, more than once when I arrived at the hall, or was met at the station by the committee chairman. "I'm Norris Houghton," I would say. "Yes, how nice to see you. But where is your father?"

I went to see Robert Edmond Jones to present him with a copy of *Moscow Rehearsals.* It was a wonderful afternoon. I told him of the discoveries I'd made and the dreams I'd built in my year abroad. As I left, Bobby said, "Norris, never forget what you've told me today, nor the enthusiasm and way you feel about the theatre at this moment. There will be many times over the years when you'll find it hard to sustain them. Just remember that what you feel today is right, and the trials and disappointments hereafter are wrong and must be overcome. Hold on to this present!" I've tried hard to follow his advice over the years; it hasn't always been easy.

It seems to me mysterious that after I returned, no effort was made to recruit me into the left-wing theatre movement of the mid-thirties, then at the peak of its power. The Theatre Union on Fourteenth Street was capturing as many headlines as the Theatre Guild on Fifty-second Street. Fellow travelers surged all around me. They held meetings constantly, usually after 11 P.M. I attended some of them, but often I was sleepy and anxious to get to bed. Occasionally, I was asked to sit on the stage at a rally and did. The New Theatre League invited me to write for their periodical; I accepted. I was invited to share my meager savings with the Spanish Loyalists and did so. But that was as far as it went. I suspect Gilbert Miller was in part responsible. He was as capitalist-minded as any producer on Broadway. I was another case of guilt by association.

What's more, if I'd been asked to throw my hat into the Left's ring, I would have desisted. I was as ardent a supporter of the Soviet theatre as anyone, but my enthusiasm was for its artistic excellence, not its message. Those Black Sea meditations had firmed my resolution to seek to change—to improve, if I could— our American theatre. That was the revolution I sought to bring to pass: the stage as an end in itself, not as a means to any other end, political or economic. I had become very socially con-scious—but I was unwilling to allow that to alter my artistic objectives. I insisted, if you will, on retaining my innocence.

2

In the fall of 1936 a job offer came from Guthrie McClintic. He was the opposite of Miller—a slight man with a mobile face, thin mustache, limber wrists, and a quick laugh. He smoked inces-santly. Whenever possible he wore a navy blue polo shirt to the office, as well as to rehearsals, and even to his own opening nights. In addition to propelling Katharine Cornell, his wife, into a series of triumphs—most recently *The Barretts of Wimpole Street*—he had the season before produced and directed Maxwell Anderson's *Winterset* and in it had made Burgess Meredith a star.

The Cornell-McClintic team was more than a twosome. It was a closely knit group of loyal and congenial ladies and gentlemen that included Gertrude Macy, Kit's general manager, Stanley Gilkey, who was Guthrie's, Ray Henderson, their in-house wizard of a press agent and public relations counsel, and two or three personable young stage managers. It was a sometimes tempestuous but mostly happy family, with just enough tension to keep everyone on his toes.

Jo Mielziner had long been one in my pantheon of designer heroes; he, too, was a frequent member of the Cornell-McClintic team. He had designed *The Barretts of Wimpole Street* and *Winterset,* Miss Cornell's *Romeo and Juliet* and *Saint Joan,* McClintic's production of *Hamlet* starring John Gielgud, and others. Now he was to design Anderson's *High Tor,* and I was to be its stage manager. Burgess Meredith, for whom Anderson had written the lead, again would star.

High Tor was to open on the January 8, 1937, at the Martin Beck Theatre. Rehearsals started in November and were followed by an out-of-town tryout tour. We would spend Christmas week in Philadelphia. Those old pre-Broadway tours were wonderful. Not only did they allow the director and cast to gauge audience responses and to tighten up and smooth out the performances; they also helped to strengthen company spirit. By the time we got back to New York, we were an ensemble—and in this instance we had spent Christmas together. What matter that we celebrated in Philly's old St. James Hotel (shades of Baltimore's Kernan in 1932), where troupes had lodged and Christmases been celebrated for decades?

McClintic, an idiosyncratic fellow, followed an unusual rehearsal pattern. Each morning began with about a half hour's warm-up—for him. During it Guthrie gathered his cast around him on the bare stage and told anecdotes, stage lore he had picked up, backstage jokes. He had an apparently limitless supply. Just when you began to wonder if he had forgotten why we were gathered, he would break off, saying, "Well, let's get to work." One day he interrupted a scene and announced that we must stop and listen to the radio. "The King—he's to deliver his abdication speech in five minutes. It's an historic moment we mustn't miss." We gathered around the portable shortwave he had brought. Several actors wept, because it *was* a dramatic moment. I must say it wasn't easy to move from Edward VIII back into the scene in the steam shovel with the bandits.

Recalling that incident reminds me of our English cast member, Peggy Ashcroft. She was persuaded to come to New York for the first time to play opposite Burgess Meredith, but she didn't arrive until the end of the first week of rehearsal. Everyone promptly fell in love with her—so modest, so self-effacing, so anxious to please, yet so totally serene, so wonderful a young actress. We both celebrated our birthdays on the pre-Broadway tour, she on December 22, I four days later and two years younger. She would return to the New York stage but once again: eleven years later, in *Edward, My Son.* In Peggy I feel I have a lifetime friend for whom I have great respect. I'm only sad that we meet in London only every year or so.

Jo Mielziner always insisted on lighting his own shows. In *High Tor* he used for the sky a translucent backdrop hung far upstage; I had never seen one before. All the way downstage, he used a seamless dark blue gauze drop, even persuading McClintic to stage comedy scenes behind it. The setting depicted a point high above the Palisades, looking down on the Hudson. It mattered not at all that at dawn and sunset the sky turned exquisite pink and orange through rifts of mist over the river as it flowed southward!

To watch Jo light *High Tor* was as good training as any course in stage lighting; to watch Guthrie conduct its rehearsals was better than any course in directing. Thus did I prepare for my professional career: on the stages of the Martin Beck, the Royale, the Henry Miller, the Guild. To become a designer or a director, being a stage manager gave you the grounding.

In the spring of 1937, during the run of *High Tor,* I was at last allowed to present myself for admission to the United Scenic Artists, Local 829, offering myself to the furtherance of art and my standard of living, which I hoped would go hand in hand. I passed the examination and thereafter could be addressed as Brother Houghton. I also had to pay an initiation fee of five hundred dollars, which I could not rustle up without severe embarrassment to my cash flow. Generously (and typically), McClintic came forward with a loan to cover the fee.

Over the summer I lined up a couple of productions to design in the fall. I found that the "old boy network" functioned smoothly on Broadway. My first commission was to design a minuscule comedy, *In Clover,* by Allan Scott and George Haight, whose *Goodbye Again* I had designed in Falmouth that last summer for Beckhard; it was directed by Bretaigne Windust. The second was called *Stop-Over* and was directed by Worthington Miner, who had staged *Both Your Houses.* Both plays required only one-set interiors. Each closed, alas, in a very few weeks.

After Christmas, McClintic put into rehearsal *How to Get Tough About It,* a play by Robert Ardrey, and commissioned me to design it. The production was full of "old boys": Kent Smith, Myron McCormick, and José Ferrer, all playing leading roles. That was what made Broadway seem a homey place! Old college and University Players buddies working together under the now familiar banner of Guthrie McClintic. But even we could not fortify the play to survive mediocre notices. I began to suspect I was jinxed: my work was on view for such a short time that I feared people who mattered would never get around to seeing and marveling at my prowess.

By the end of my first season designing, I had chalked up four Broadway shows: even before the Ardrey play opened, I was at work on *Whiteoaks,* starring Ethel Barrymore, scheduled to open in March.

I served as my own draftsman, but I needed studio space, which I found in an excellent scene shop, Studio Alliance, on West Thirty-ninth Street. A small room on a balcony overlooking the paint floor was leased to me. In September, a tall, fresh-faced young man named Oliver Smith, just out of Penn State and not yet in the union, climbed the stairs to my "studio" and asked to be an office boy, just as I had done not so many years before. From his portfolio I could tell he was obviously talented, and I took him on. I think it was his first job in New York.

For *Whiteoaks* I had another one-set interior. I also was to design Miss Barrymore's wardrobe, which consisted of a single gown. The actress, not yet sixty, was playing an aged Canadian matriarch born in the British raj. She made an entrance, of course; no Barrymore would appear in a play that did not afford an entrance. I therefore provided the drawing room with massive mahogany double doors upstage center and saw that the pink spot was carefully focused on it when she appeared. After pausing for the expected welcoming applause, the actress would cross to a great armchair near the fireplace but, of course, placed at right angles to it, so that she could face the audience. There she remained.

As the dress rehearsal was about to begin, the star came onstage in costume to inspect my room and its furnishings. In a moment she advanced to the footlights, shaded her eyes from the balcony spotlights, and called out in her thrilling Barrymore baritone: "Young man!" I knew whom she meant.

I hurled myself down the aisle and over the foots to her side.

"What have you done to me?" she demanded.

"I don't know what you mean," I quavered.

"Look at this dress; look at that chair. They are both the same color. I shall be obliterated."

It was true. To stand out against the gray-green walls, I had chosen to upholster her armchair in plum-colored damask, which I thought a very pretty contrast. For her gown I had selected a fairly close approximation of the upholstery, though, of course, in silk.

"That was the idea," I said in as warmly enthusiastic a tone as I could summon. "That is your character's favorite color—burgundy." (I changed it from "plum" to make it sound more regal.) "That's why she wears it; that's why her one favorite chair is covered in it."

Miss Barrymore was not mollified by my feeble pseudopsychological justification. "Either the gown or the chair must be replaced."

By this time the director, Stephen Haggard, a fine young English actor who was trying his hand at directing as well as performing in *Whiteoaks*, was drawn to us by the electricity in the air. The problem having been put to him, he asked mildly what I proposed to do, though his voice was edged with anxiety. It was no moment to stick to my guns. I may have felt I had good justification for my view, but then so did Ethel.

"How would it be," I said slowly, improvising as I went along, "if we got some tulle or chiffon—shell pink or ecru, perhaps,—and made a light scarf to fall softly around her neck and shoulders? It would be a good character touch and also frame her face."

Haggard thought it a satisfactory solution; surprisingly, Miss

Barrymore did too. So I kept my gown and my upholstery as they were, and proved that compromise can work.

The following season, 1938–39, would turn out to be my second and last as a Broadway designer. I'd designed seven plays by then and had worked for some top managements: Gilbert Miller, Guthrie McClintic, the Theatre Guild, and Arthur Hopkins.

I very much wished to be associated with Mr. Hopkins, for he was another of my idols. That winter of 1938–39 he turned sixty. During earlier years he had made numerous major contributions to the American theatre. He had brought Eugene O'Neill up from Greenwich Village in 1921 and produced his first Broadway play, *Beyond the Horizon*. He had formed an artistic collaboration with Robert Edmond Jones later in that decade: together they were responsible for John Barrymore's *Hamlet*, Lionel's *Macbeth*, and *The Jest*, in which the brothers appeared together. He had written two wise little books about the theatre: *How's Your Second Act* and *To a Lonely Boy*.

Arthur Hopkins owned the Plymouth Theatre, on Forty-fifth Street. There, in a dark cubbyhole of an office off the mezzanine, I went to see him, carrying my portfolio. He was seated before a rolltop desk, wearing his derby hat and the bow tie he was never without. He was short and plump, with a round, red face enlivened by bright, searching eyes. He looked at my sketches without comment. I sat down and waited. I would have been very uncomfortable had I not been warned he was a man of few words. Finally he leaned back in his swivel chair and told me the name of the play he was about to do: *Waltz in Goosestep*. It called for two sets: one yet another drawing room, the other composed of two adjacent compartments on Hitler's private train.

Mr. Hopkins gave me a copy of the script, told me his terms and the timing of his production schedule. He never offered me the job, so I never had the chance to accept. I left assuming I had it. Mr. Hopkins then accepted my sketches without asking for alterations. He never invited me to have lunch with him or go out for a drink. He never commended my work, never criticized it. When I had read the play, I feared another short run. I was right.

It was a strange experience. The most I could say was that I had worked for Arthur Hopkins. But I've never forgotten him.

Even though most of my friends never got around to seeing what I was doing, it was agreeable to be constantly working. Still, in time it does become depressing to be associated exclusively with flops. Even Ethel Barrymore had been unable to turn *Whiteoaks* into a solid hit. And *Dame Nature,* the play I designed for the Theatre Guild that season, fulfilled its five-week subscription (introducing Montgomery Clift to its subscribers) and folded. Because I regularly got good notices, I refused to believe my scenery was in any way responsible for an unbroken record of failures and near failures.

If my professional life was not completely rewarding, my personal life throve. After *Moscow Rehearsals'* critical success, I found I was a step or two higher up the social ladder. Not that many people ever read the book, but its title and my name began to ring small bells. The John Mason Browns were largely responsible. They usually entertained one evening a week at small black-tie dinners. I became a regularly summoned extra man, sharing that honor with others whose names ran from Auchincloss to Zerbe.

A frequent after-dinner feature of those evenings was a round of games, such as "Who Am I?" in which the literati, and those who considered themselves such, like Phyllis and Bennett Cerf, tried to stump each other in identifying characters of literature, history, and the arts. My favorite personage was Marc Connelly's "dentist who helped the Empress Eugenie escape from the Tuileries." Needless to say, I couldn't compete with such esoterica.

Years later, Dorothy and Richard Rodgers invited me to posh dinner parties once or twice a year. Each was an event, largely because of the glamour of the guests of honor, such as the John Lindsays, then living in Gracie Mansion, Mr. and Mrs. John D. Rockefeller 3rd, Arthur Rubinstein. After dinner, Dick would frequently sit down at the piano and play and sing old tunes of his own, usually dating back to Rodgers and Hart days.

I recall with special relish one evening when I was seated next to Edna Ferber at one of several small tables seating six. Suddenly in midmeal Miss Ferber leaned across the table, fixed a stern eye on Alfred Gwynne Vanderbilt, seated opposite, and asked slowly and earnestly, "Mr. Vanderbilt, are you happy?" I wished for a camera to record his startled look. "I—well—uh,—I guess so, Miss Ferber," he gulped. I wonder if they ever met again.

I was rising in theatrical social circles too. One spring Sunday evening, Theresa Helburn, chairman of the Theatre Guild board, invited me to dinner. Punctuality being one of my vices, I was the first guest to arrive. The second was Katharine Hepburn, then starring for the Guild in *The Philadelphia Story*. Bringing me to her, our hostess asked, "Kate, do you know Norrie Houghton?"

"Houghton? Houghton?" said she.

"Yes, Miss Hepburn," I replied. "I do believe we are related." (Her mother's maiden name was Houghton.)

Without missing a beat, she leaned forward. "You know, I've always wondered!" Of course, she had never heard of me, but how charming of her to say that.

Several weeks later I was invited to an after-theatre supper party at Kit Cornell's and Guthrie's on Beekman Place. Katharine Hepburn was there. "Hello, long-lost cousin!" she cried when she spied me. We had a jolly conversation, but since that evening I've never seen her again, to my infinite regret. I couldn't think how to effect a reunion. I am not often accused of shyness, but to myself I frequently seem a timid violet.

While my personal life may indeed have been flourishing, my private life (if one can make such a distinction) had its ups and downs. I considered myself adequately passionate in those days, but one object of my passion, after a few weeks into an affair, said regretfully, "Norrie, I don't think this is going to work. You're really only in love with the theatre, and I'm not interested in playing second best." And another, the only lady I ever proposed marriage to, responded gently but firmly, "I don't think you know what you're talking about." This may—or may not—explain how it is that I approach the grave a bachelor.

For two summer seasons, 1939 and 1940, I went to St. Louis to serve as art director of the St. Louis Municipal Opera in Forest Park. The "Muny," as it was referred to locally, was an opera in name only. Its repertoire was principally made up of revivals of wonderful old musicals, plus some rather tired, now unremembered song-and-dance hackwork.

The Muny Opera had to be seen to be believed. It held eleven thousand people seated in rows on a sloping hillside. The stage, which was ten feet wider than that of the Radio City Music Hall, had a huge turntable and two things even Radio City couldn't boast of: a pair of live gigantic oak trees that rose through the stage floor, about fifty feet apart and fifty feet high, twenty feet upstage of the footlights. They were the pride of the Opera and of all St. Louisans, I was told. But they caused incredible aesthetic pains to designers challenged by a ballroom set, or a revival of *Anything Goes,* in which most of the action takes place on the deck of a liner crossing the Atlantic. At such times it was well to recall Coleridge's famous phrase about the "willing suspension of disbelief."

Old favorites like *Rio Rita, Naughty Marietta, Rose Marie,* and *The Chocolate Soldier* were heavy with scenery, and there were but six days to build and paint the multiple sets, for the bill changed weekly. I would arrive in St. Louis four weeks in advance of the opening in order to get a flying start, but by the time the season was half over, the pace had caught up with me; like Alice's Red Queen, I had to run for my life just to keep in place. It was a marvelously rigorous experience; I lost ten pounds each summer.

To add to the torture, there was, obviously, no air-conditioning. St. Louis has one of the most spectacularly torrid climates in our heartland. Days when it reaches 100 degrees and above march past in an endless procession from Flag Day to Labor Day. My office-studio was endurable only between five and nine in the morning and after nine at night. Much of the time I was forced to turn myself into a one-man nightshift, returning for a few hours' rest in the middle of the day to my hotel room, which was, thankfully, air-cooled.

Despite my odd schedule, I found time to meet a number of St. Louisans. Those I encountered were, for the most part, cosmopolitan, great fun, and quite sophisticated. From William Bernoudy, for instance, who was just starting what would be a distinguished architectural career, I learned a lot about his teacher,

Frank Lloyd Wright, about life at Taliesin, and, on the side, about Rachmaninoff's piano concertos; from "Dojean" Sayman, what dangerous distraction an amusing girl with money and sex appeal can exert if one was not careful; from Joseph Pulitzer, something about contemporary art, which he was just beginning to collect, and from his wife, Lulu, how many gin-and-tonics one could safely consume beside a swimming pool in the sizzle of a Missouri prewar Sunday noon.

Although invited, I never returned for a third season, for I had acquired other occupations, which led me away from stage design for the next few years, as you will eventually learn.

ENTR'ACTE
Unexpected Interlude—The War Years

7

To London (1942–44)

*T*he years between autumn 1939 and the end of 1941, a dark interlude that began with war clouds breaking over Europe and ended with the infamy of Pearl Harbor, were for me a period that in the context of this book seems more pertinent to a later time in my life. So permit me to "flash forward" now to my entry into the Second World War and, several chapters hence, to "flash back" to 1939.

I entered Harvard at the age of thirty-three, enrolled in neither graduate school nor the College; I was a tenderfoot lieutenant (jg), USNR, assigned to a five-month course in naval communications that began on February 1, 1943. The Harvard Yard was our parade ground. When in and around the Yard, we were "afloat." When we were allowed to take the subway into Boston, we went on "shore leave."

I was top man in the typing class of 120: I could click off 86 words a minute. I was less spectacular at Morse code or signal flags. The course in codes and ciphers was vastly more exciting—a whiff of cloak-and-dagger. I considered the operation of the ECM, claimed to be an unbreakable-cipher machine, the most remarkable thing since the invention of the Model T Ford.

In late May, we were summoned one by one to be interviewed as to our choice of sea duty versus shore duty, not that it made any difference: the navy would send you wherever it chose. But

I did tell the interviewing officer that I had a fairly fluent knowledge of Russian. Having done so, I thought I would surely be sent to sea duty in the Philippines. My orders on the eve of graduation were consequently most unexpected: to report to Camp Crowder, in Neosho, Missouri. "Curiouser and curiouser," as Alice remarked of her trip down the rabbit hole.

I arrived there a bit too late to celebrate Independence Day. Neosho, in the southwest corner of Missouri, was enjoying a temperature of 98 degrees. Since no sea was in sight, only the distant Ozarks, I was apparently not headed for sea duty. In fact, Camp Crowder was an army post, where twenty thousand GIs were undergoing basic training. I reported, however, to a navy commander, who was off in a corner taking charge of some two hundred naval personnel, all of whom turned out to be communicators.

After receiving our barracks assignments and unpacking our gear, which should have included a pith helmet but didn't, we were assembled to be briefed and then found out we were a secret—indeed, a top-secret—outfit. We were divided into a collection of teams—army and navy—six officers and fourteen men on each, called Combined Communications Teams. Each team was proficient at a particular foreign language, except for half its enlisted men, who as radio technicians required no linguistic prowess. There were several French teams, and perhaps more than one Italian, Spanish, Portuguese, Greek, Turkish, Dutch, German team, but only one Russian team—Combined Communications Team Five. I would be a member of it for the duration.

When American forces had swept into Casablanca the year before, all telephone and telegraph services there had been manned, naturally, by French-speaking Moroccans. Our communicators couldn't communicate with the native operators— clearly a snafu—and time had been lost in trying to locate the needed French-speaking Americans. Never again. We had to be prepared for everything: Churchill's "soft underbelly," a landing in the Azores, parachute drops anywhere in occupied Europe. Furthermore, army and navy specialists would probably have to work together—hence, the "Combined." Hence, also, our exposure to army basic training.

We learned close-order drill and creeping and crawling, sought to qualify on the rifle range. This last would be my undoing, I felt sure. I had never handled a firearm of any kind and hated the whole idea. The day came when we marched out to the range. Lying on our bellies, we aimed in the general direction of the targets. When I rose to my feet an hour later, I discovered I had miraculously qualified as a "marksman" or a "sharpshooter," I forget which. After the war I joined Handgun Control.

The senior officer of Team Five was a senior-grade lieutenant, ten years older than I (I was five years older than anyone else). His name was George Scherbatoff. Born a Russian prince, he had a great fund of stories, all of which we believed. He had emigrated to America fleeing the Revolution. He was a bachelor and wanted to enlist, but never having become an American citizen, he had a problem, one that was solved with the help of a friend, Winthrop Aldrich, chairman of the Chase Bank. Even so, George said he had had to abdicate his titles to become one of us. His princely title came from his father's family, the Scherbatoffs; from his mother, a Stroganoff, he inherited the title of Count. The Stroganoffs were the older, richer, and more powerful. It seems that in the seventeenth century the Stroganoffs got together and one day, being fond of the reigning tsar, they decided to give him a present. After much consultation, they agreed on Siberia, which they happened to own at the time. Or so George told us.

George spoke fluent English, but he wasn't very good at spelling, which created some hazards for him and for national security. He was not, however, involved in any incident like one we heard about, where a communications watch officer in Washington had to decipher a top-secret message received shortly before the Yalta Conference. He had heard of Malta, but he'd never heard of Yalta, so he figured a typographical error had been made and changed the *Y* to *M*. He was immediately sent out to sea.

After three months spent perfecting the creep and the crawl and, in my case, Russian irregular verbs, the teams were sent forth. We Russians, which is to say, five officers of Russian descent and one of Irish (myself), found ourselves embarked on the new *Queen Elizabeth,* bound for the United Kingdom, along with fifteen thousand other troops. There were no usual eating hours, for the galleys cooked round the clock, serving forty-five thousand meals daily.

The *Queen Elizabeth* sailed without naval escort. She could outdistance the navy ships, and although her course was a constant zigzag, to throw submarines off her scent, she arrived in Glasgow six days after leaving New York. It was the end of November when we sailed up the Clyde and put into Gourock, Glasgow's port.

London in wartime that December 1943 took some adjusting to. It had survived the big Battle of Britain, had seen the troops evacuated from Dunkirk. When we arrived from Scotland, another raw, blacked-out winter was settling in amid the desolation of bomb-cratered buildings. We reported to the great mansion in Grosvenor Square that was headquarters of COMNAVEU, acronym for Commander, U.S. Naval Forces in Europe. Our Russian team never had a proper home; there weren't any Russians to speak to, and nobody knew what to do with us. The idea was that we should be assigned to the high command geographically closest to the USSR, and presumably this was it.

That we had no Russians to talk to didn't mean we weren't doing our bit to help the war effort. Trained in naval communications, we could take our places on eight-hour watches. Our coderoom was situated in a subbasement under the annex to Selfridge's department store in Oxford Street, far from outside sights and sounds. We handled no messages between the White House and Downing Street (a disappointment), but for some reason the atomic energy people used our naval systems, and many dispatches were exchanged between "Urey" and "Teller" and their opposite numbers in London. When deciphered, they still made no sense to us laymen. I was just as unprepared as the next fellow for Hiroshima.

On arrival we were put up in a temporary bachelor officers quarters not far from Soho Square, until we could find permanent billeting. Luckily I had friends who still remembered me from 1935, and Mrs. Harold Bowen solved my problem. Friends of hers—Air Commodore Walter Runciman, who was serving in the Middle East, and his wife, who had taken their children to America—had not closed their spacious house in Sussex Square. His secretary continued to live there, to keep things in order, and

Mrs. Bowen was sure there'd be room for me. So I lived in Bayswater, in considerable high-ceilinged elegance, from December until late May of 1944.

Other friends were even more hospitable than in 1935. The capital was a "full-dress command," which meant that navy dress-blue uniforms with starched white collar were required at all times. Outfitted thus, we did cut dashing figures. Lady Colefax was now safely ensconced in Westminster and entertained as constantly as ever, although with rationing, food coupons, and shortages, some of her larger luncheons and dinners had to be transferred to the Connaught Hotel, close by Grosvenor Square. She loved Americans, and plenty of us were around those wartime days.

In the spring, I was bidden to one of her cocktail parties, where, at the bar, I encountered a handsome, tall, blond young lieutenant of the Royal Navy. He was standing alone for the moment, when Sybil came up to us.

"You must know each other: let me introduce you. Norris Houghton—Prince Philip of Greece" (or maybe it was the other way around). The two of us had a long and lively conversation, for I found him most congenial. I saw him next three years later when he appeared not at a bar but at the balcony railing of Buckingham Palace—the bridegroom!

A little club behind Shaftesbury Avenue called The White Room—really a piano bar—was a favorite of several of my naval cronies. One evening, after cheering Hermione Gingold in her revue *Sweet and Low*, I stopped in with a couple of fellow naval officers. Again, a tall, blond young man, this one in mufti, stood at the bar. When I went to replenish my drink, we fell into conversation. He looked vaguely familiar. Finally we introduced ourselves.

"My name is Norris Houghton," I said.

"It can't be!" exclaimed the blond young man.

"But it is," I replied.

"You're the author of *Moscow Rehearsals!* It's a marvelous book—one of the best. Norris Houghton—well, well!"

"Who are you?" I asked.

"My name is Michael Redgrave."

"I can't believe it," I exclaimed. "Why, you're a great star. I've never seen you or any of your movies, but I know all about you! I've seen your picture; that's why I thought you looked familiar."

We became instant friends. During the months that followed our chance meeting, we were together as often as our schedules permitted. I attended a matinee of *Uncle Harry*, in which he was then playing opposite Beatrix Lehmann. He introduced me to her and, as the weeks passed, to half the theatre folk of London. He and his young family lived then in a comfortable flat at Rivermead Court, overlooking the gardens of the Ranelagh Club in Hammersmith. Rachel, his wife, welcomed me there cordially. Their close friends became mine: Diana Gould (who would later marry Yehudi Menuhin), Michael Gough, a fine young actor, and his wife, Diana Gray, who was Robert Graves's niece, among them. Vanessa, his elder daughter, then about seven, offered her hand gravely, Corin, aged five, bowed, and Lynn gurgled in her cradle.

Michael Redgrave was unlike most actors I have known. A Cambridge graduate, he was more than literate, he was erudite. Deeply versed in history and literature and in theatre lore, he was also a linguist. He talked easily and wittily. Myself not given to reticence, I never wearied of listening to him. Having started as a schoolmaster, Michael loved to make pronouncements, albeit he was less than two years my senior. And he was avid to hear from me about the Russian theatre. He showed me articles he had written about Stanislavski and his theories; in one of them he had quoted from me! He told me about his love affair with the great Edith Evans, who had played Rosalind to his Orlando.

Redgrave opened London to me. He took me to galleries and museums, showed me his favorite paintings and sketches; he took me to grand restaurants, where he was ushered to the best table, and to little holes-in-the-wall, like The Prospect of Whitby, hanging over the Thames, where he described their specialties. As spring blossomed, he showed me out-of-the-way little squares and favorite mews and small hidden public gardens.

One afternoon Redgrave appeared in a great War Relief matinee at the Royal Albert Hall, along with Laurence Olivier, John Mills, Ralph Richardson, and other stage stars. Rachel invited me to join her in her box. Its little door opened just as the program was about to begin. Framed in the doorway was the most exquisite creature I'd ever seen. She was wearing a Russian fur hat at a slightly rakish angle and had a bunch of violets pinned to her coat. It was Vivien Leigh.

Nor, to digress, shall I ever forget my last sight of Vivien, three months before she died, in 1967. I was lunching in London with old friends, Yvonne and Hamish ("Jamie") Hamilton, the publisher, when the telephone interrupted. Jamie returned to the table after a few moments.

"It's Vivien," he said, addressing me. "She wants you to come to see her. Go and speak to her."

It had been ages since I had last seen her, and I was taken aback by her apparent eagerness to lay eye on me again. I had never felt close to her, although in 1946 she and Larry Olivier had come to a party at my house in New York for the Old Vic. That was long ago, but of course I went to see her.

She lived in Belgravia, in a small, exquisite flat that suited her perfectly. An old friend, that excellent actor Alan Webb, was with her when I arrived. Another actor, John Merivale, her lover at the end, came in just before I left. In between she talked eagerly and easily; she showed me her dining room, cantaloupe-colored, contrasting beautifully with the little drawing room's walls of violet, to match her eyes. (I remembered the bunch of violets at the Royal Albert Hall.) She seemed lonely, despite the presence of us three men, one after another, within an hour. I was sad as I left her and not really surprised when I heard she was gone. But I was happy she had wanted me to come and say goodbye.

The Hamiltons—Jamie and Yvonne—have lived among the "beautiful people" and in beautiful surroundings as long as I've known them (we met during the war), and they've been happy to share their homes with friends: I have slept under their Hamilton Terrace roof in St. John's Wood, their Cumberland Terrace flat in Regent's Park. Yvonne has welcomed me to their house in Corfu.

Hamish Hamilton, who died in 1988, and I were, in fact, both born in Indianapolis, Indiana, I about a decade after him, although he escaped, unscathed, at a much earlier age than did I. His glittering career as a publisher was made in London. He was a governor of the Old Vic, and the Hamilton's circle of friends,

which was enormous, contained almost as many stage stars as
literary lights. They gave Sybil Colefax a run for her money
when they all were younger.

During that winter of 1943–44, wartime Londoners sought
hard to carry on their accustomed pattern of life as best they
could. The theatres were open and jammed. The Lunts were
starring in Robert E. Sherwood's *There Shall Be No Night* at the
Lyric; that bravehearted couple chose blacked-out London over
glittering Broadway as their base. I saw them there again in
Terence Rattigan's *Love in Idleness.* At the Old Vic, going
proudly full tilt, were Ralph Richardson and Laurence Olivier in
Peer Gynt, Arms and the Man, Uncle Vanya, Richard III—stupen-
dous performances all.

2

By the end of February 1944, the officers of Combined Communications Team Five began to use their Russian. The Soviets had
a military mission to London to coordinate war plans with the
Combined Chiefs of Staff (that is, British and American) and with
SHAEF (General Eisenhower's Allied Command, which included also the Free French and the other occupied countries).
Stalin and the Russians were unhappy about that second front
Churchill and Roosevelt kept promising but not delivering. It
finally became important to convince Stalin that we were not
stalling: such a huge logistical operation took time. We were in
fact moving at breakneck speed. Almost a million Americans
were already in the United Kingdom scattered throughout the
country.

To raise Slavic spirits, if for no other reason, the Americans
arranged a few little trips for the Soviet mission. They were first
to be taken down to Devon, to inspect one of our Assault Training Centers on the south coast, and in March to Londonderry, to
see with their own eyes the huge aggregation of landing craft
assembling at our base in North Ireland. To provide liaison
(which really meant to interpret) was our team's raison d'être.

One night we gathered at Paddington Station, about a dozen
or fifteen Soviet naval officers, a like number of Americans, and

the Camp Crowder Six. On a siding toward the black-out forward end of Paddington was a short, sleek train of three or four cars. When we boarded, we learned we were on General Eisenhower's private train, code name "The Alive," a courtesy to our ally's injured sensibilities. (The general was, of course, elsewhere.)

In peacetime the trip from London to Exeter takes only a few hours. In wartime in the south of England, much of the rail line's activity was at night. "The Alive," when the general wasn't aboard, had to be sandwiched between freight and food trains, so it took ten hours to make the run. We reached the coast of Devon in early morning.

I hoped the Russians were as impressed by the sights and the briefing they saw and heard as I was. As smoke screens were laid down, as the roar of artillery shook the usually quiet Devon coast, as LCTs and LCVPs and other types of landing craft rehearsed their roles in the invasion, the pleasant evenings in London drawing rooms I'd just left faded into insignificance. This was the war we'd come here to be a part of.

Following the trip to Londonderry with our Russky allies, a third expedition, in late March, took us away for almost a month. We started off, again at night, outfitted with foul-weather gear, leather sheepskin-lined coats, as though we were headed for the North Pole. This time our fourteen enlisted men came along, but no Russians, all of us to spend four weeks within the Arctic Circle.

We descended from the night train at Rosyth, a naval base in Scotland, where our astonished eyes beheld the USS *Milwaukee*, a heavy cruiser. We became her passengers and that night sailed down the Firth of Forth, then north to Scapa Flow, the great British naval base. We were about to deliver our cruiser to the Russians' doorstep under the Lend-Lease program. Many other vessels, British and American, filled Scapa Bay—an aircraft carrier, destroyers, minesweepers, "Liberty" ships—the convoy and its escort.

Under gray, scudding clouds the *Milwaukee* and the others weighed anchor and headed north. The Norwegian coast lay to starboard, invisible beyond the horizon. We were well out of range of any shore batteries. We were not, however, out of range of German submarines, but they, too, were invisible. There was an outer screen of destroyers, destroyer escorts, and frigates, and an inner screen that included the carrier and its attack and reconnaissance planes.

The toll of lost ships on the Murmansk run had been severe, up to fifty percent a couple of years earlier, but German strength was flagging by April 1944. Although we could sail only at the speed of the freighters, we made it safely in about six days. From Murmansk half our ship's company returned by the next southbound convoy. The other half, I among them, remained aboard for about seven days. The departed crew was replaced by Soviet sailors; about two hundred Americans and a like number of Russians were thus living side by side below decks, as we prepared them to take over.

Assigned as liaison officer attached to the Navigation Department, I was involved with the bridge and its operation. I dreaded the inadequacy of my vocabulary when the time would come for me to detail the parts of the gyrocompass, the loran, the sonar. I had no knowledge of the words needed to explain them in English, let alone in Russian. Fortunately, I was spared: the Soviet officers knew all about everything. One of them even tried to explain the loran to me, recognizing as he did that here was an armchair sailor.

Murmansk was a dreary place, still snow-covered in early April. There was tremendous activity, however, for it was the headquarters of the Soviet White Sea Fleet, with many sailors and workers on the naval base and airmen from an air base nearby, but nothing that much resembled a city.

Our principal haven ashore was the Sailors Club, a huge temporary building not unlike our USO centers, with a big dance hall and a theatre. With not nearly enough girls to go around, naturally, most of the Russian sailors danced with each other. One evening I went with some of the Russian officers to the theatre. The hall was jammed. A freckle-faced youngster of about twelve sat next to me. He remarked that he'd seen this play twice before. He wore his fur hat throughout the performance but seemed able to hear through its earflaps, for he missed not a laugh.

And the play? Lope da Vega's sixteenth-century Spanish comedy *The Gardener's Dog*, a truly esoteric piece by American standards—I've never yet seen a Lope play in New York—but in fact it was a very amusing work. It was performed by the Northern Fleet Theatre, a professional sailor-and-civilian troupe, with gusto and swashbuckling humor. You could hear a pin drop during the three and a half hours of the performance, except when deep-throated laughs rumbled through the hall. It was a good evening of theatre.

In about two weeks the *Milwaukee* was ready to be turned over to the USSR. It was done with considerable formality. Ambassador Averell Harriman arrived from Moscow and was piped aboard. Soviet naval dignitaries followed. The two ship's companies, Russian and American (the former now at full complement), were drawn up on deck facing each other. Orders were read first in English and then in Russian. Responses followed. The band played the national anthems. The Stars and Stripes was slowly lowered, folded, and removed; the red standard, with its hammer and sickle, was raised and replaced it. It was a lump-in-the-throat moment.

At the end of the afternoon, Combined Communication Team Five boarded HMS *Beagle,* the British destroyer escort assigned to return us to the U.K. We were warmly welcomed and initiated forthwith into the joys of "Simon Says . . . ," a simple drinking game intended to encourage speedy inebriation. The officers were wearing heavy turtleneck sweaters and corduroy pants, their uniform of the day (and night).

This Murmansk run had been their life and the *Beagle* their home for the past three years; a grim life it was, protecting the Allied northern lifeline. In the officers' mess was a large table surrounded by chairs and covered with what had once been a white cloth. By the time we sat down to it, it looked more like a sheet of brown and gold marble, so splashed, splotched, and spotted was it with the remains of overturned mustard pots, tea mugs, and gravy, as the little *Beagle* had plowed her way through North Atlantic swells.

We weighed anchor at dawn and everything settled down, the booze consumed or secured. Only one incident occurred. On the third evening and not yet dark, as we sat in that officers' mess at supper, we were startled by the harsh clanging of the ship's bell: General Quarters. We grabbed our life preservers and rushed on deck. As passengers we had no battle stations, so we tried simply to keep out of the way. Ten miles away, an empty cargo ship had been torpedoed and was sinking. *Beagle* altered course and raced full steam toward the center of action.

A German submarine had penetrated our screen. The damage was done, but the sub had to be liquidated. For several hours we followed a predetermined pattern, dropping depth charges. An oil slick finally appeared. But that might be a ruse, the oil released by the submarine to make it appear to have been hit and thus escape. Only after, I heard that HMS *Beagle* was credited by the Admiralty with a hit. For us it was very exciting; for the Limeys it was all in the day's work.

By the end of the first week in May, the Russian team was back in London. Spring had arrived during our absence, as gloriously blossom-strewn as any peacetime spring; so had the buzz bombs, a new Nazi infernal machine. Before I could get used to them (not that one could), our team received orders to repack our gear and again head out of London, this time to Plymouth. There was the headquarters of Task Force 122, the designation given to the mighty fleet commanded by Rear Admiral Alan Kirk, the U.S. naval component in the invasion of Normandy; Kirk's flagship, the USS *Augusta*, lay at anchor in the harbor. (It was a historic vessel—the one on which Roosevelt and Churchill had signed the Atlantic Charter.)

My orders, however, were to report to another "flag"—Comlancrabuthphib. (What mother's son would not be proud of such an affiliation?) In translation it meant "Commander, Landing Craft and Bases, 11th Amphibious Force (Rear Admiral John Wilkes)." His headquarters were in Hamoaze House, a fine Georgian mansion set on a promontory at the edge of the city, with a sweeping view of the English Channel. Plymouth itself had been horribly mauled, but our Quonset hut, adjacent to the mansion and facing a bright green cricket field, seemed isolated from harm. We were even more isolated—or perhaps insulated—when we went to work, for the Communications Center was eighty-three steps (I counted them) beneath the surface of the Hamoaze lawn.

Cricket field, sweeping lawn, handsome house—who could imagine that this was one of the command seats of an invasion task force being assembled to liberate a continent? The unceasing activity gave it away, officers hastening back and forth with brief-cases and manila folders, cars driving up to disgorge their loads of gold braid, petty officers scurrying in all directions on urgent missions, and over all, the nervous tension hanging in the air. We arrived on the eleventh of May. No one at our level knew exactly when D day would occur, but from these manifold telltale signs we could see it would now be but a matter of weeks.

At last I felt the war I had come to fight was at hand. The excursions with the Russians, the big trip to Murmansk—despite their value, they seemed like curtain raisers before the star's big turn.

The first week passed uneventfully, as we focused on getting to know our newly acquired comrades-in-codes. A weekend pass was even available, which I used to pay an overnight visit to Dartington Hall in nearby Totnes. Dorothy Elmhirst, whom I had last seen in the Ridgefield, Connecticut, retreat of the Michael Chekhov Studio a couple of years earlier, was now back in residence in Devon.

Had I yet encountered Nancy Astor in Plymouth? Dorothy inquired. When I said I hadn't, she replied that I must; Lady Astor was still quite remarkable. She had come back to live on The Hoe, for her husband was Lord Mayor of Plymouth, and as Lady Mayoress, she felt her place was at his side and among its citizens. Dorothy said she'd call and arrange a meeting. "It will do you both good!"

She did call, and Lady Astor and I did meet—first at tea at the Lord Mayor's mansion on The Hoe and again when she invited me to join her on a tour of one of the working quarters of the port city, which she took every afternoon just to "show the flag." Everyone in Plymouth recognized Lady Astor as she stepped from her car and walked down block after block of fire-blackened, bomb-damaged small dwellings, from which old women and children would emerge to grasp her hand and be cheered by her lively quips.

"I'll invite you to dinner some evening, if you can bring a ham from your navy stores," said the Lady Mayoress. "I'm reduced to issuing that stipulation to my military guests, and they usually seem able to produce." (She didn't mention that her guests were usually admirals.) "If they didn't, it would be a pretty frugal meal." I procured one, called her, and was promptly rewarded with an invitation. After dinner, fellow guest Admiral Wilkes drove me back to Hamoaze House in his car, with the two-star flag flying.

Halfway through the second week, the pace began to accelerate: radio traffic and land-line telex messages between bases increased severalfold. By the third week we were serving watches eight-on, eight-off—that is, we manned the coderoom sixteen hours out of every twenty-four. Then an interesting thing happened. While the outpouring of messages never slackened (as a task force headquarters, we received all messages for "Info" if not for "Action"), ninety-five percent of them, when deciphered, turned out to be fakes. It was essential that the Germans, who monitored our air even if they could not decipher our messages, not become aware that there was a major slackening of traffic, for that would have tipped them off that all orders had now been issued and the fleet was on the move.

That was indeed the case. The big battleships—the *Arkansas,* the *Texas,* the *Nevada*—were beginning to steam down from their safe havens in the north. The cruisers and destroyers—the *Tuscaloosa,* the *Quincy*—were moving into their support areas, all under cover of radio silence.

By this time we knew it must be D minus 4 or 3. After lunch on Saturday, the third of June, scuttlebutt had it that the *Augusta* had weighed anchor and was moving out. Aboard her would be Admiral Kirk and General Omar Bradley, commander of the First Army—and my old friend Lieutenant John Mason Brown. Via the intercom from the bridge, Brown had the task of reporting what was going on to the ship's company—to all those below decks, who could see nothing but who were as much a part of the action as those on the bridge itself, and on deck, in lookout positions.

It was another gray day with a stiff wind and heavy overcast. The sea was running high; we could see that from the seawall beyond our lawn. Then we saw *them*—far away where the gray of the sea met the gray of the sky—a line of ships that stretched across the whole horizon. They seemed to be moving from west to east. Slowly, oh, so slowly. Look at the map and you'll see they had a long way to go from Plymouth to the Cherbourg peninsula. Goose bumps rose on the backs of our necks. This was it. But no, it wasn't.

We communicators returned to our cave. The afternoon was quiet—more fake traffic. Probably in the early evening (it's hard to keep track of time's passage when you're underground), half a dozen high-ranking naval brass burst into our coderoom. Eisenhower had decided to postpone the invasion. The weather—winds and tides—held too many risks to add to the risks of the great assault. So out to the big battle wagons and cruisers, to the destroyers and destroyer escorts, to the landing craft—the LCTs, the LSTs, the LCI(L)s, the LCVPs—to the PT boats and the minesweepers, to the tiny craft that had no codebooks at all, altogether some four thousand vessels—out to them all went the signal from our communications center, in plain English, agreed upon in advance if required, "POST MARK 2": Stop where you are! Turn around wherever you are! Proceed to the place you were told to go in case of emergency. Post Mark 2: Postpone 48 hours.

Those hours were agony for all the million men—their adrenaline at work, their minds and spirits set—who had to sit them out afloat and ashore. "In port after port along England's southern coast, in ports in Wales, in ports to the north in Scotland and in Ireland, vessels large and small, freighted with arms and men, with history and with hopes, are waiting more tightly clustered than the grapes of wrath." So wrote John Mason Brown.

But there was no help for it. We all trusted Eisenhower and his weather experts—and so on June 5 we waited all day.

When we came on duty at twelve, we were told that all had been quiet on the four-to-midnight watch. Two or three of us had brought paperbacks to pass the hours, but nobody could concentrate on them. We drank coffee and waited for dispatches that didn't come. Finally, at about 6 A.M., the first report of the invasion arrived from the "Far Shore." It was in plain language, terse and ungrammatical: "*Corry* has sank." Our navy's first casualty.

Combined Communications Team Five was not sent back to London and Selfridge's basement until the middle of July, and there we remained as the summer wound down. The weather was surprisingly lovely. I cannot recall why I couldn't return to the Runcimans' house in Sussex Square, but I found acceptable accommodations nearby in Cleveland Square, where one or two fellow American naval officers lived. The owner was a Mrs. Eyre, who, believe it or not, had a daughter named Jane.

The Germans continued to lob buzz bombs and V-2s, a new carnage carrier, into London; there were firebomb raids too. Now, Mrs. Eyre was an unusual character, owing to both her infirmity and her philosophy. She was stone deaf, and she believed that when the sirens sounded, the thing to do was to head for the roof, not the cellar.

"If we receive a direct hit from a V-2, it won't matter where we are. If we are struck by a fire bomb and are in the basement, we won't know that the house is burning up over our heads. But if we are on the roof, we have a chance of squelching the damage before it gets out of hand."

She had a point, and since she retired early, at which time she removed her hearing aid, she saved herself many midnight trips to the roof in any case. I was at home one evening, however, when the sirens sounded about nine, before the good lady had retired; so, hearing them that time, she shepherded her family and tenants upward.

As I stepped into the acrid night air, I looked out across the usually blacked-out city, now illuminated like the gates to hell by the pulsing orange and red glow of a dozen fires, large and small, some nearby, others—the bigger ones, apparently—farther off, creating macabre silhouettes of the familiar spires and domes that lay between me and the flames. Although many of the fires still blazed after the all clear sounded, we took that as a signal to relinquish our vigil. At last I knew what a firebomb raid looked, sounded, and smelled like: a terrifying panorama of infernos, accompanied by an awesome sound track—the drone of planes overhead, the sharp ack-ack rattle of the antiaircraft guns, the deep-bass roaring echo of direct hits—and the stench of burning. In all, a prophecy of Armageddon, and a great and fearsome spectacle!

8

To Paris (1944–45)

*T*he euphoria had not yet worn off. After all, Paris had been liberated only three weeks earlier, on August 25, 1944. An unfamiliar beatific expression suffused Parisians' faces. The euphoria also took a most un-Parisian form in the bars we dropped into: no man or boy in an American or a British uniform was allowed to pay for a drink. Strangers lined up to stand treat. *"Une fine à l'eau?"* or *"Un coup de champagne?"* Paris had seen no imported whiskey or gin for the past four years, but plenty of cognac and champagne was available to welcome the Allies. I never thought I'd live to see the day! Of course, it didn't last forever: by the first frost the French were back in form, and we paid for what we ordered. Still, those late-September days and evenings hold cherished memories for those of us who arrived in time to share in the universal rapture.

Team Five's orders to leave London after nine months were dated September 14. We presented them at the headquarters of the Commander, U.S. Naval Forces in France, a stone's throw from the Étoile. A marine was on guard, and inside, a confused duty officer and a yeoman received us. The marine's presence signaled that the premises were presided over by an admiral; the reception committee's confusion signaled that things were snafu, as might be expected only a couple of days after the command had been set up. Our job now was not to minister to Russians but to help the communications center become operational as quickly as possible.

A ten-minute walk down Avenue Hoche took us to the U.S. naval officers' BOQ, the Hôtel Royal Monceau. This chic prewar hostelry was well staffed and in good condition, for a German high command had inhabited it during the occupation. With Vice Admiral Alan Kirk in a top-floor suite, the French service staff knew that the style of their establishment had to be maintained, insofar as wartime conditions allowed. Waiters and other attendants did dispense with white gloves, but the potted palms continued to be watered in the main dining room, and if we didn't always have hot water for shaving, we officers at least had private baths and rooms with twin beds, good carpets and choice prints over the mantelpieces.

September and October were a succession of golden days in that autumn of 1944. Since our duties were no more onerous than in London, there were enough free hours to enjoy the weather and the city, to encounter old friends, like Josh Logan and Tom Curtiss, and to acquire new Parisian ones.

Charles de Noailles possessed an old and illustrious name. He and his comtesse, Marie-Laure, dwelt in a huge *hôtel* in the Place des États-Unis. I was taken to call one October afternoon by a young and not-yet-famous cellist, Maurice Gendron, who appeared to be Mme. de Noailles's "favorite," in the classical French sense and in keeping with family tradition. (I have in mind her mother-in-law's famous patronage of Marcel Proust.) Marie-Laure was an Amsterdam Jew, I was told, enormously wealthy and enormously interested in arts and artists.

I was received informally in a small, wood-paneled octagonal library on whose walls hung appropriately small drawings and paintings by Rubens, El Greco, Goya, Fragonard, Corot. My hostess, then probably about fifty, spoke three or four languages in a sort of languishing drawl, punctuated by deep, throaty laughs. She slightly resembled a pouter pigeon, with, in lieu of a top knot, usually disheveled shoulder-length black hair; in contrast, her husband, his hair gray, his garb impeccable, and his stance erect, epitomized my image of an aristocrat. The countess, however, was the glittering center of the household. She loved people and was pleased to have the company of American and British officers.

Once a week Marie-Laure was "at home" to a small circle of friends—usually a dozen or more regulars: Jean Cocteau, the heavily bearded Christian Bérard, known (rather whimsically, I thought) as Bébé, Boris Kochno, my friend Gendron, and others. Like Muriel Draper, Marie-Laure seemed to prefer the company of male artists, although several tall ladies with long necks, whose names were unfamiliar to me, were also among the weekly gatherings.

Those late afternoons invited me to fantasize: Jean Cocteau and Boris Kochno, especially, recalled the early days of the 1920s. Diaghilev's spirit, if not his presence, dominated the room. Kochno, small, slight, his head now a billiard ball, had become the impresario's personal secretary in 1921; Cocteau, now gray, bright-eyed, lean-faced, sharp-nosed like a clever rat, was creating mise-en-scènes for the Ballet Russe in 1917 and, in 1924, *Le Train Bleu, Parade, Oedipe Rex*. The spirits of Nijinsky, Karsavina, Lifar, of Bakst, Benois, Soudeikine, of José María and Misia Sert and Juan Gris, of Matisse and Prokofiev, moved in the shadows of the Noailles drawing room, beckoning to one another. Many of the painters' finer canvases hung in the adjacent salon, along with Rouaults and Braques.

For me the trouble with those afternoons was that the guests insisted on speaking in French as rapidly as possible. I'm sure they were all multilingual, with the possible exception of Cocteau, with whom I played the same conversational gambit each time we met. After greeting each other effusively:

Houghton: *"Je suis triste que je parle français si mal."*

Cocteau: *"Ah oui—mais vous parlez avec l'accent russe—c'est charmant, ça."* (Pause) *"Et c'est dommage que je ne parle pas anglais."* (*Finis* until the next time.)

The others doubtless felt that speaking English wasn't worth the effort. I concluded, perhaps unjustly, that they were a self-centered lot. Perhaps the truth was that their shared memories of two or three decades allowed little or no room for the encroachment of a contemporary unknown American sailor.

There were two great occasions chez Noailles that season: first, a musical afternoon at which about forty guests (mostly Parisians) gathered to honor the poet Paul Éluard and the composer Francis Poulenc, who was himself at the piano. The latter had just completed a song cycle based on poems by the former, and this was its first hearing. Among those assembled in the music room were many old friends of theirs, of whom, in addition to the usual habitués, I recognized only Pablo Picasso and the composer Georges Auric. The music was lovely—quite civilized and French—and again my thoughts were drawn back to 1920, when they were all in their youthful prime and I was a ten-year-old in Indiana.

The other memorable afternoon was the reception Mme. de Noailles gave just after V-E Day to welcome T. S. Eliot back to Paris for the first time since 1939. The great upstairs salon, its walls hung with the avant-gardists of the early Post-Impressionist era, was filled: two hundred people at least. The high points for me came when I was presented to Eliot and to an elderly little Frenchman, with a white mustache and a friendly mien, whose name was André Gide. I had thought he was dead! Indeed, he was then past seventy-five.

As I write of Marie-Laure de Noailles, I think again of Muriel Draper. I have admitted to great curiosity about Muriel's long months in Moscow. Her presence there always seemed mysterious. She did not appear to be writing; in fact, she did not seem to be doing anything. She never became really proficient in Russian. So why did she choose such a benighted spot in which to hibernate? Did the answer lie in the political arena? I was told she returned an ardent Communist. Did she actually join the Party there and become covertly responsive to its needs? Was she already a clandestine member when she arrived? Or had she acquired a secret lover? Because she was so closely a part of my life for almost six months, the mystery still haunts me.

Marie-Laure's mystery also derived from the times. How had she, a prominent Jew, remained untouched during the four years of Paris's occupation? In the face of Göring's unquenchable acquisitiveness, how had her great painting collection remained intact? Was it to scotch any rumor that she had been a collaborator that she was so eager to be seen in the company of Allied officers? Granted that she had been basically apolitical, how could she have so determinedly remained so? Her mystery still haunts me too.

As I think of it now, insofar as I could follow conversations chez Noailles, I never heard serious talk about the war that was still going on. Marie-Laure's whole coterie appeared to live, like her, in a self-created vacuum, where art and gossip about artists were all that counted. Perhaps that was the way it had to be for some who lived in Paris between 1940 and 1945.

The week after Thanksgiving, I was ordered to take up residence in a small château at Louveciennes, a suburb on the outskirts of Paris. There Admiral Kirk chose to set up housekeeping; he would be closer to SHAEF at Versailles and to the British naval high command in nearby St. Germain; and besides, a hotel suite did not suit his style. I was not really certain how I came to join his personal staff, but I suspected once again the hand of John Mason Brown, who had become quite close to Admiral Kirk during the invasions of Sicily and Normandy. John was now detached from Kirk's staff and back in America, but before he left he may well have spoken a good word to the Admiral.

So there I was that first evening, a little abashed by my surroundings. Brown wrote in *Many a Watchful Night* of the "palace atmosphere" of high command headquarters, where I now was and for which I was not exactly prepared. About eighteen of us assembled in the library for cocktails before going in to dinner. I knew most of my confreres scarcely at all, and I'm not sure how well they knew each other, but the excellent whiskey quickly remedied that.

A naval flag officer's mess is not one of your run-of-the-mill military chow lines—at least A. G. Kirk's wasn't. Mess boys in white coats served. The admiral was flanked by his flag lieutenant and his flag secretary, both wearing on their shoulders gold aiguillettes, and by his military aide, a young army captain named McGeorge Bundy. The ruler in this "palace" was indisputably the admiral. He was not tall; he might be overlooked in a crowd were it not for the air of authority that he could exercise, as Brown put it, "with flourishes . . . He was a fighter, gruff, imperious, dogged and willful, as one look at him made clear. But he was much more than that." John, who had longer to observe him, noted his "gaiety (which was genuine), his alertness (which was unflagging), his displeasure (which was authoritative), his anger (which, at those dark moments when it was released, could outdo Conrad introducing a landlubber to a typhoon)." Happily, I never caught him in one of "those dark moments."

That first evening at Louveciennes he was all charm. His twenty-five-year-old military aide, Captain Bundy, was, I discovered, runner-up to the admiral conversationally and intellectually, as his subsequent career—dean of the faculty of Harvard College, national security adviser to Presidents Kennedy and Johnson, president of the Ford Foundation—has given evidence. That mess was, I'm confident, considerably above the average high command's in wit and mental agility.

The enemy decided, however, to spoil our holiday frivolity if at all possible. Ten days before Christmas, the Germans launched the Battle of the Bulge, a surprise heavy counterattack through the Low Countries. It was up to the army to contain it; we landlocked sailors could do nothing to help and were, in fact, merely sitting ducks. On the third night, scuttlebutt circulated that the Nazis were to make parachute attacks on various high command headquarters in the Paris area.

At dinner, Captain Bundy took charge. We were to adjourn after dinner to the rather spacious snow-covered gardens and terraces surrounding our château. We would bundle up, it being a cold night; we would carry side arms; we would go forth in twos. He himself would remain in the château, posting himself at the foot of the staircase with a shotgun to protect the admiral's person in case any German parachutist should slip past us into the house. The admiral he respectfully ordered to his bedroom. It was a nascent dean speaking—and the admiral meekly obeyed.

The moon was down; for about three hours we patrolled the grounds. Our principal fear was that in our zeal we might shoot each other. Indeed, three or four times I heard the crack of revolver shots from behind distant hedges. My partner and I encountered no one. Eventually we were summoned back. The next morning we noted the previous night's casualties: among the marble statuary with which French formal gardens are frequently adorned, three were found headless. The shots from behind the hedges were sheepishly acknowledged by the more trigger-happy

Mother (Grace N. Houghton) and I, 1917. (I was seven. I am always a decade younger than the year.)

With Grandpa Norris, Indianapolis, 1912.

With Father, Major Charles Houghton, Indianapolis, 1918.

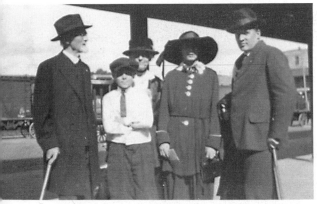

The Houghtons in Florida, 1920: Grandfather with wife, Myra; daughter Grace (in picture hat); son Henry; grandson Norris (with arms crossed).

With Aunt Sara ("Sadie") Norris, my mother's sister, Oxford, 1912.

The Strings Cr Theatre Comp with producer Norris in the top row, left, Indianapolis, 1925.

The class president in his high school graduation picture, Indianapolis, 1927.

Princeton Triangle Club bigwigs, 1929: (left to right) A.M. Wade, president and actor; Robert Hedges, composer; Joshua Logan, author; Houghton, designer.

In New York, 1933.

Two University Players: Henry Fonda, Falmouth, 1931, and James Stewart, with accordion, Falmouth, 1932.

Our theatre on Cape Cod at Old Silver Beach, 1929–32.

Two of my idols: Robert Edmond
Jones and Konstantin Stanislavski.

Thomas Quinn Curtiss, Moscow, 1934; Backstage after a performance of *How to Get Tough About It*, 1938: Myron McCormick and José Ferrer.

Setting for *White Oaks*, 1938, which starred Ethel Barrymore.

Three country places: (above) my hideaway on Apple Hill in Vermont, 1947–67; (right) the house in Chappaqua, 1968–75; (below) Pond Cottage on the Astor estate, Rhinebeck, 1962–64

Robert Woods, my Apple Hill neighbor from 1948 to 1968 and, from 1935 until his death in 1978, my colleague and friend.

Armchair sailor puts to sea:
en route to Murmansk, 1944.

The Redgraves, London, 1945: Michael, Rachel, Vanessa.

Livadia Palace at Yalta, site of "Argonaut" Conference, 1945.

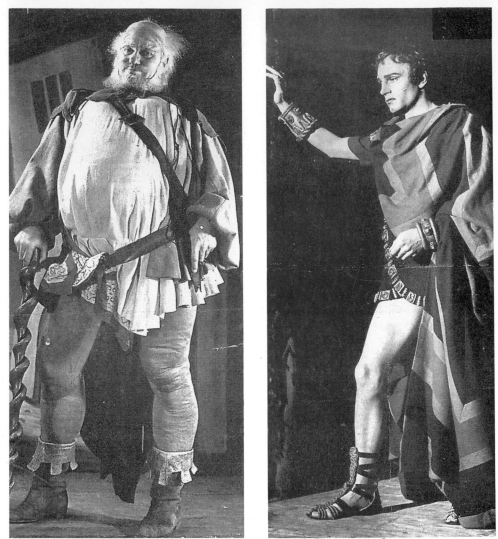

From the historic 1946 Old Vic engagement in New York, produced by Theatre Inc.: Ralph Richardson as Falstaff in *Henry IV,* Part One; Laurence Olivier as Oedipus.

A Theatre Inc. reading rehearsal of Synge's *The Playboy of the Western World,* 1946: (seated, left to right) director Guthrie McClintic, actors Eithne Dunn, Burgess Meredith, and (in white blouse) Mildred Natwick, board members Beatrice Straight, Houghton, and (standing) Penelope Sack and Robert Woods.

of our number. "Better safe than sorry" was their motto for the evening.

At Louveciennes on Christmas Day the admiral gave a lunch party; each of us was allowed to invite a guest. Mine was a charmer, Marina Vorontsov. Like my colleague George Scherbatoff, Marina was born into a princely Russian family. She also married a prince, who was currently absent. Marina was about my age, in her mid-thirties, blond, chic, fun-loving, an accomplished dancer, and extremely pretty. She was interested in the arts and spoke English and French with an adorable Russian accent. Needless to say, the admiral and his staff admired my choice. Our slender romance, like most wartime encounters, has not weathered the years. Let's hope the prince returned to his premises.

9

The Yalta Conference (1945)

*W*hen top-secret orders arrived from Washington on January 12, 1945, directing Combined Communications Team Five to report for temporary duty to the Commander of the Eighth Fleet in Naples, it was McGeorge Bundy who delivered them. He remarked with apparent prescience that "you Russians seem to be heading for a Big Three conference somewhere in the Mediterranean. You will doubtless be useful at last," he added hopefully but, I thought, gratuitously.

Forty-eight hours later we were headed for Naples. On arrival I was summoned to a telephone at the airport. I was told by a voice identifying itself as Communications Headquarters, Eighth Fleet that there was a special plane on the other side of the field waiting to fly us to Sicily. The weather, however, was bad in Palermo, and if it didn't start clearing in an hour, we were to come into town, whence we would sail out that night on the admiral's flagship.

Those were considerably more impressive alternatives than our outfit was accustomed to. Indeed, Bundy might prove to be right. The weather did not improve, so the USS *Memphis* sailed for Sicily with all of us nineteen "Russians" and their Scotch-Irish comrade-in-arms aboard. (I've always liked to believe that that heavy cruiser undertook the overnight voyage solely to deliver us to Sicily on time.) In Palermo, we were passed along to the USS

Catoctin, a communications and command ship, which forthwith weighed anchor and headed eastward toward Scylla and Charybdis.

Once at sea, all passenger naval and army officers were summoned to a large conference cabin, where, the passage locked, a moon-faced young lieutenant (the Bundy of the *Catoctin,* apparently) addressed us.

"We are headed to a Big Three conference," he said, trying to sound matter-of-fact and blasé. "It will take place somewhere in the Black Sea area—we sail under sealed orders. President Roosevelt is presently also at sea, aboard the *Quincy*, heading for Malta to rendezvous with Prime Minister Churchill and the British. Our Secretary of State and Joint Chiefs of Staff will join them there by air. The code name for the conference is 'Argonaut.'"

We had no clue as to our final destination, no clue about our role in the elaborate communications plan for the operation, which was then described. Clearly, however, whatever communications responsibility we were to have would be principally oral: interpreters would certainly be needed. So, as the *Catoctin* steamed through the Aegean in company with four minesweepers and a "Liberty" ship, I devoted more time to my dictionary than any man since Noah Webster.

Five days later we reached Istanbul and, accompanied by snow flurries, our little flotilla steamed slowly through the Bosporus. We encountered no interference from the neutral Turks and proceeded toward Sevastopol. We were the first Western warships to enter its harbor since the war began, and when we were abreast of the lighthouse a shore battery boomed a salute.

The next afternoon our Russian team set foot on Soviet soil at last. In a convoy of jeeps we set out across the snow-covered Crimean peninsula for our final destination—Yalta. Following in the wake of the Light Brigade, we traversed the Valley of Death, but came out without casualties: no cannon there to volley and thunder. Well after dark, the convoy turned through massive gates and finally drew up in front of a large three-story building that looked like a dormitory. We later discovered that in effect that was what it had originally been: housing for the imperial retinue of Tsar Nicholas II, whose Livadia Palace stood behind trees three hundred yards or so away.

Like a busload of schoolboys returning from Christmas holidays, we piled out of the jeeps with our luggage, to be welcomed in the front hall by a portly Pickwickian headmaster, Colonel Donald Lowry. He was liaison officer for the Joint Chiefs of Staff, and we "Russians" were to be part of the liaison.

"You must be hungry," observed the colonel. "Come and have dinner, and then we'll arrange your billeting." The dining room departed from the school image, for it looked more like a restaurant, filled as it was with a dozen or more tables. Only one was at the moment occupied, in this instance by the Secret Service, a half dozen of whom filled the table. They'd already been studying the terrain for a week, we learned. Thus, the imminence of the White House was palpable that very first evening.

A waiter wearing a tailcoat, shiny with use, and a white tie served each of us a mound of beluga caviar. With it we downed a couple of vodkas. Lowry explained that we were the guests of the Kremlin, which accounted for the Muscovite waiters in tailcoats, the excellent caviar, vodka, and bottles of red and white Georgian wine, and the old-fashioned cut-glass wine goblets, not to mention the menu: soup, fish, meat, dessert (champagne offered with it), tea. The Kremlin's towers seemed golden that night.

None of the Russians, we learned, spoke English, and we were there chiefly to help the colonel and his staff keep house. A great burden was lifted. I wouldn't have to try to pass myself off as an interpreter at a diplomatic level. Surely I should be able to tell the Russian officer in charge of the car pool that General Marshall would need a car at ten o'clock to go to the British headquarters, and the maître d'hôtel that Admiral King, Chief of Naval Operations, liked three-minute eggs. If the Yalta Conference failed, it would not be at our level—Colonel Lowry's and mine. I asked the waiter for some *russky konyak* to celebrate the news.

After dinner we were briefed on the overall situation. The brass would arrive on Saturday (this was Monday night). We could expect about 275 in our delegation. There would probably be about the same number of British, quartered some ten miles away, in the Vorontsov Palace. Stalin and his staff, much the largest, would be at the Yusupov Palace, in between. All told, there would be about a thousand souls involved in this Big Three conference. And I had expected a small special event! Special, yes. Small, no.

Between Tuesday and Saturday the liaison staff was as busy as a gaggle of one-armed paperhangers. Livadia Palace itself proved to be a three-story mansion of honey-colored plaster trimmed with white marble, perched five hundred feet above the Black Sea. It contained about fifty rooms, including the President's three-room suite, the ballroom (where Argonaut's plenary sessions would be held), the state dining room, which became a restaurant for the top brass, and parlors turned into offices.

The problem was how to squeeze in the 101 men and two women who had to be under that roof. (The women, incidentally, were the daughters of the President and of Ambassador Averell Harriman.) The delegation was naturally top-heavy with senior officials, civilian and military—seventeen generals and admirals, not counting the five-star chiefs, Leahy, Marshall, and King. The presidential Secret Service detail of eighteen had to be housed there too.

Disposition of the bathrooms—nine of them—was crucial. In 1911 they doubtless seemed sufficient for the Tsar, his family, and some visiting grand dukes, but in 1945 they caused us a good deal of head-scratching. It seemed ungracious not to give those ladies one bath to themselves, and then the President had to have one. That meant that the Secretary of State would share his with seven others, and that various personages, like Harry Hopkins and James Byrnes and Ed Flynn, the President's celebrated cronies, would have to enjoy potluck (pardon the pun) with the Joint Chiefs and others. In short, it meant about ten to a bathroom, which required us to schedule early-morning traffic in the way once followed by tourist-class passengers on ocean liners.

Saturday was at last upon us. By that time I felt that Livadia belonged to me, and I looked forward to playing host and welcoming the distinguished guests. Late in the afternoon, word came that the VIPs were approaching. My teammates and I were among those assigned to help settle them in. Their luggage having preceded them, suitcases and musette bags were spread over the lobby. Then the Chiefs of Staff entered.

I particularly liked the look of General Marshall, who was wearing a fur-lined, fur-collared khaki overcoat, so I offered him my assistance. He identified his bags. A yeoman seized them. In my excitement, I led him up the wrong staircase, down the wrong corridor, and in no time was completely lost. Although I had myself thumbtacked his name to his door, I realized with cold panic that I had no idea where that door was. If our embassy's naval attaché hadn't rounded a corner just then and taken charge of the general, we'd no doubt have roamed the palace until they sent out the St. Bernards.

Next morning, we were told that the President would meet with high-ranking members of his delegation at noon; our team was dispatched to set up the props—ashtrays, pads, pencils, water carafes, glasses—in the big ballroom. It was this sort of activity that largely justified our Yalta presence. We went to work at about eleven and had just finished when word came that since the weather was bright and sunny, the President would prefer to confer with his staff in the sun room, overlooking the sea. That being at the other end of the building, it called for a quick change to get the props transferred in time.

Eager to see the President, all of us hung around in the corridor outside the sun room. Presently, two Secret Service men came down the hall, Roosevelt following about thirty seconds behind them, his aluminum wheelchair flanked by another half-dozen Secret Service men. I had never seen him before, and at six-foot range he was considerably slighter and gaunter than I'd expected. His face was drawn and lined. To be sure, there was no need for the famous Roosevelt smile, for this was no public appearance, and there were no cheers to acknowledge. Indeed, during the few times I was in his presence at Yalta, I never saw him smile. He was, as we now know, soon to die.

Once the conference was in full swing, the easygoing atmosphere of the week before vanished, and everything tightened up. History was in the air.

My special daily contribution was to compile each morning a list of all persons who had been at Livadia during the previous twenty-four hours, noting arrival and departure times. This was required by the Soviet general in charge of security in the special area set aside for the conference. The Americans moved around a good deal, shuttling between Yalta and Sevastopol or Saki, the airport for Yalta, a hundred and forty miles away. Couriers arrived daily from Washington, from SHAEF, from Naples, London, and Paris. One, incidentally, brought copies of the *New York Herald Tribune* every day.

The Russians kept close track of all this activity and maintained a most efficient security cordon around the whole district. Within the palace grounds, we had our own guards, as well—white-capped sailors from the *Catoctin,* who stood watch at the gates to the grounds, at every entrance to every building, and on every stairway landing. In the palace itself, they shared this duty with Russian secret police, who stood, their hands in the bulging pockets of their plain clothes, in every corridor except those adjoining the President's quarters; there our Secret Service was in charge and mounted a day-and-night guard inside and on the lawn outside the President's windows. Whenever the Big Three were meeting in plenary session, Soviet militiamen with tommy guns were stationed on the roof, while others patrolled the grounds. At the front gates were two details, one consisting of American sailors, the other of Russian soldiers, and still other Soviet sentinels were posted at fifty-yard intervals around the two miles of fence that enclosed Livadia. I had never seen or dreamed of such security.

Friday was the day Signal Corps cameramen had been waiting for—official photographs of the conference and its participants; by three o'clock their tripods were set up in the big ballroom. A funereal hush pervaded the lobby, where now some sixty people were assembled, all speaking in whispers. I stood in a doorway watching Foreign Minister Molotov and his advisers, a little group gathered in front of a long mirror. On the other side of the hall, Anthony Eden was in sotto voce conversation with other Foreign Office officials. Secretary of State Stettinius was talking quietly with some of his staff. The rest of the crowd consisted of secretaries, Secret Service, Scotland Yard, NKVD, and a handful of sightseers like myself.

As I stood there, someone came up behind me and politely asked me to let him enter. I turned to see a bulky figure in a British colonel's uniform. It was Winston Churchill, coming from the Secretary of State's bedroom, where he had been taking a nap after lunching with the President. I flattened myself against the doorjamb, and he marched into the lobby, turned left, and entered the President's library. The door closed after him. My closest encounter with one of the great.

His passage through the crowded hall caused only a small flurry. Obviously, Stalin was the quarry the lion hunters were stalking, and all eyes kept turning toward the front door. When he did arrive, he came through a small side door, beneath the marble stairs, crossed to a garderobe unnoticed. As he emerged and started toward the President's library, several chesty men, heavy with medals, formed a crescent around him. He was no more than ten feet away. I was shocked to see how old he looked. The black, bushy mustache of the cartoons was iron gray, and his hair was practically white. He was also shorter and heavier than I had expected—not more than five feet seven, I judged, and weighing nearly two hundred pounds. He moved slowly, a trace of a smile on his lips. He looked to neither right nor left, and his eyes were cast down, almost shyly.

For ten minutes, the Big Three were closeted together, along with Chip Bohlen, the President's interpreter. Then the library door opened and, one by one, they proceeded across the lobby to the ballroom. It was quite a procession: the President first (as head of state, he outranked the other two), his valet pushing the wheelchair. The Secret Service moved forward instantly and formed a circle around them. Next came Marshal Stalin, whose bemedaled guard fell in ahead of him just as quickly. And last came Churchill. No one offered protection, and he puffed along, looking slightly amused by the historic spectacle.

When the principals and a half-dozen advisers to each had taken their places around the huge circular conference table, the cameramen and sightseers like us pressed in. The cameras had been set up facing Roosevelt. Pretending unawareness of the flashing bulbs, he gravely turned his memorable profile first one way and then the other as he conversed with Stettinius on his right, Bohlen on his left, and Harry Hopkins, leaning over his shoulder. Churchill, finding his back to the cameras, swung around in his armchair beaming and full face, in the glare of the flashbulbs. I half expected him to make his V for Victory sign. Stalin stared glumly ahead, waiting for all this imperialistic nonsense to be over. After five minutes or so, it was, and we hangers-on were herded out.

The military conversations ended the next day, Saturday, February 8, one day before the political discussions concluded. Then it was I made my unique contribution to Argonaut. The Joint Chiefs and the military planners were anxious to be on their way—after all, there was also a war in the Pacific. General Marshall and his staff would be flying to Caserta, the Allied Mediterranean headquarters, outside Naples; Admiral King and his staff, directly to Washington via Casablanca. Since it was considered essential that their flights terminate before dark (airports were blacked out at night, you must remember), their big Constellations and accompanying fighter plane escorts would have to take off from Saki, the Crimean air base, at first light.

Because Saki was a five-hour drive from Yalta over a difficult and dangerous mountain road, instead of leaving at 2 A.M. and covering the 140 miles in the dark, the Joint Chiefs and their parties, totaling about thirty, would set forth Saturday afternoon and drive only to Simferopol, the nearest railhead; there they could board a special train to transport them to Saki while they slept, and so be ready to take flight at dawn.

Colonel Lowry called me to his office the night before and ordered me to leave in the morning, to make sure everything was in order and to act as interpreter. About eleven o'clock that bright February morning, Lieutenant Commander Benjamin Griswold, USNR, a Joint Chiefs staffer from Washington, and I set out in a jeep. The roadway from Yalta to Simferopol resembled the Riviera's Grand Corniche, with glorious views, but unspoiled and untrafficked. We arrived in midafternoon.

We easily found the railway station and identified the train drawn up on the first track awaiting our VIPs. Its last car, built in Finland, was a combination dining and club car, finished in pale polished birch. There were three additional sleeping cars. An inspection quickly persuaded us that things were shipshape, the Russian steward friendly and obliging. Again, as at Yalta, there was the delicate task of assigning compartments and berths. That club car had one drawing room suite; a second, smaller suite was in the adjacent car. Who should occupy the larger space? I turned to Commander Griswold to resolve such a tricky protocol dilemma. He was prepared.

"General Marshall must occupy the first suite," he said with assurance. My problem, as I saw it, lay in the fact that both men had been awarded five-star rank by a single act of Congress on the same date.

"Certainly," I said as I fixed a nameplate to the door. "But why, since their date of rank is identical? And isn't the navy the senior service?"

Griswold explained. It was simply that General Marshall's date of commission preceded Admiral King's by one year: he graduated from VMI the year before King graduated from Annapolis.

"Does it really make that much difference?" I asked.

Griswold assured me it did: at meetings of the Joint Chiefs in Washington, Marshall and King always rose when the chairman, Admiral Leahy (also five stars), entered, because his date of commission preceded both of theirs.

Protocol details thus settled, I bethought me of another potential problem. I disappeared to make a tour through the cars and, returning, announced that there was no toilet paper on the train. Past experience of Russian rail trips had forewarned me just in time. This, to me, was an even more critical matter than who slept where. What to do?

I went into the stationmaster's office and asked (in Russian, of course) to use his phone to call the American headquarters at Livadia. He explained that it was on a special trunk line to which his phones had no access. This was understandable, but I had an idea. I pointed out that a long train on the far track, with militia guarding along the platform, had telephone wires stretching from it. Might they perhaps connect with the special trunk line? I asked innocently. The station master eyed me admiringly. Yes, he believed they did. (It was clearly Stalin's private train.)

I bolted out the door, crossed the tracks, and scanned the platform until I spotted a Russian officer. To him I explained that an emergency required me to call the United States headquarters at Livadia at once. Did one of those telephone lines connect with the palace? If so, might I use it?

The captain was sympathetic to my obvious anxiety. He led me down about five cars to the one where the wires originated, ushered me into an office car (Stalin's, perhaps?), and handed me the receiver. The connection was made. Admiral Olsen, our Moscow naval attaché, answered.

Had Admiral King's party left Livadia yet? I inquired urgently. About ten minutes before, I was told. Had General Marshall left too? He was about to leave. "For God's sake, what's the matter?"

"There's no toilet paper on the train. It's urgent, sir!"

"Right you are, Houghton," he replied, and hung up.

Now there was nothing to do but await the arrival of the VIPs. We drove to the edge of town to escort them to the train. After an hour or so, three or four big command cars were seen moving down the winding road out of the hills. We revved up our jeep, fell in ahead of the first car, and led the procession to the station, where their cars could drive directly onto the platform and stop opposite the door of the coach. Admiral King descended with his entourage, which included the Soviet marine minister or some such bigwig.

We returned to our lookout. Soon the action was repeated. When we arrived on the station platform, the American sailor who was driving jumped out, saluted, and opened the rear door. General Marshall descended. We all stood at attention and saluted. The general shook the driver's hand, congratulated him on his handling of a difficult road, then mounted the steps into the railway car. I made a dive for the back seat, where I discovered twenty rolls of toilet paper. The Chief of Staff of the U.S. Army had driven sixty miles up to his knees in the precious stuff.

I might add that I received a Commendation Ribbon—for my quick thinking, I guess. In the cumbersome manner of the U.S. Navy, all our team's commendations were forwarded, with an endorsement by the admiral commanding the Eighth Fleet, to our boss, Admiral Kirk, Commander U.S. Naval Forces, France, "with the added expression of my appreciation of the efficient performance of their assigned duties by those officers which contributed materially to the success of the Argonaut Conference." So much for hearsay. Do you suppose he heard about the toilet-paper crisis? He was a thousand miles away.

Back in Paris on February 26, after an absence of almost six weeks, we were welcomed as local heroes; with becoming modesty we discounted our contribution to the war effort but were careful not to convey too many actual details of the scullery nature of our duties. In fact, as far as we were concerned, the war was as good as over. Nothing could top Yalta.

But when V-E Day finally arrived, on May 8, 1945, it did indeed surpass the Big Three conference in emotional wallop. Paris was the place to be. I came off duty at four o'clock, went to the Royal Monceau, and, as prearranged, found my old friend Robert Chapman, Lieutenant USNR. After a celebratory drink at the hotel, we sallied forth toward the Place de la Concorde. As had a million Parisians.

Already under way was the mighty spontaneous procession that began there. The people, a hundred abreast, filled the Champs Élysées across its vast span from one side to the other. Slowly they moved up the great avenue toward the Arc de Triomphe, the Eternal Flame beneath it, the setting sun behind it. Little children rode on their fathers' shoulders. No shouting, no bands playing, the clomp of a million feet on the pavement the only sound. At the Étoile the marchers broke apart, heading down the avenues that lead like spokes away from the hub. There was still a great quiet—a thousand times more moving than shouts, cheers, or whistles—as the people went of one accord on a wave of solemnity to salute their Arch of Triumph. The war in Europe was over.

ACT TWO

10

Home Again (1945–52)

"*H*ow I wish I knew where you are!" Rosamond Gilder wrote to me in early September 1945. She had just succeeded Edith J.R. Isaacs as editor of *Theatre Arts*, she continued, and if only I were around, she'd try to recruit me as an associate editor. Her epistle arrived the day after I came out of the navy, facing a civilian future with no idea in my head as to how to proceed or which way to turn.

Without allowing time for cogitation, I replied to Miss Gilder that I was very much around and hoped that she hadn't yet filled the post. She hadn't, so everything fell into place: on October first I would start work as an associate editor.

In the intervening weeks, I manufactured an ex post facto rationale to explain the hasty decision. I had not been in the professional theatre in New York since 1939. After six years I wasn't sure I could quickly pick up where I had left off as a stage designer, or whether I wanted to if I could.

From the perspective I then applied to my short-lived scene-design career, it seemed to me that my Broadway productions had afforded little chance to expand my visual imagination in stage terms. Did I even have the ability to do anything more than acceptable imitations of Robert Edmond Jones and Jo Mielziner? Furthermore, most of the plays I had been offered called merely for interior decoration—choosing the color of the walls, carpet, and draperies, and adding a few idiosyncratic touches to differentiate one household from another.

I had lost confidence, I suppose, in my talent for design, and I was unwilling to be a mediocre designer: if I didn't have it in me to be one of the best, I'd rather not play. Besides, I felt I had more to say in the theatre than could be expressed in decor alone. Perhaps I should consider whether directing might not be more fulfilling.

The idea of working for *Theatre Arts*, the finest theatrical periodical in the United States and one of the finest in the world, appealed to me as providing an observation post from which I could view the New York theatrical scene for the next couple of years and could reestablish valuable connections I had enjoyed there in the mid-thirties. Perhaps I could also resolve the conflict in my own mind between nonprofit theatre and Broadway's drive for commercial success, and I could consider once again whether whatever gifts I had belonged in the critical and academic side of the theatrical world or in the creative.

Rosamond Gilder herself was continuing to serve as reviewer of current productions for *Theatre Arts;* she assigned me to do a monthly feature article (a long interview with that luminous actress Laurette Taylor during her run in *The Glass Menagerie* was one of my most cherished experiences), to write captions and to perform other unsung editorial chores.

I lasted at the magazine for two years, during which time, my Laurette Taylor interview aside, I had two unforgettable experiences. One morning in 1946 Roz said to me, "I hope you're free for lunch today. I've invited Jean-Paul Sartre, and it would be nice for you to come along."

If I'd not been free, I would have made myself so, for Sartre had become one of the most talked of literary figures in Europe. I tagged along to a little bistro down Fifty-sixth Street from our offices and became the third at a small table in the rear. M. Sartre was nearly as unprepossessing in appearance as Mlle. Gilder, his hostess. He was short, and his round, sallow face was almost concealed behind enormous heavy-lensed spectacles with horn rims. He looked very owl-like and seldom smiled.

Roz spoke immaculate French. As I've said, I spoke only haltingly. But while my tongue couldn't deliver, my ears could absorb. The lunch conversation had mainly to do with an article Roz had been trying to pry from Sartre for the magazine. Eventually she succeeded when he produced a valuable essay on Existentialism in the theatre, one of the best I'd read.

I was also indebted to Rosamond for the afternoon she took me to a rare press conference with Eugene O'Neill, held shortly before the premiere, in October 1946, of *The Iceman Cometh*, his first new play to be unveiled in twelve seasons. It took placed in the boardroom of the Theatre Guild, which was jammed to capacity. I pressed forward for a good view. America's only Nobel Prize winner in drama was then but fifty-eight years old. Tall, a bit stooped, slender to the point of gauntness, his black hair and mustache now gray and thinning a little, O'Neill looked like the ill man he was. He spoke rather softly, and we all leaned forward to catch every word. The only statement of his I can recall (for, not called upon to take notes, I didn't have the wit to bring a pad) was his reply to some question about America's contribution to the arts.

"The most beautiful thing our country has ever created was the clipper ship," he asserted.

Coincidentally, the same week I started work at *Theatre Arts*, I was invited to dinner by Beatrice Straight, Robert Woods, and Penelope Sack to hear about plans they were hatching. Shortly after Pearl Harbor, they explained, the Michael Chekhov Studio disbanded. (It had been created, you will recall, by Dorothy Elmhirst and her daughter, Beatrice; the other two had been members of it.) However, the not-for-profit, tax-exempt charter that had been issued to the Chekhov Studio in 1940 as an educational and performance institution still existed. Such charters were a rarity in those days.

"Biddy" Straight, "Penny" Sack, and Bobby were now planning to take over the charter and create a new theatre organization, one in which they hoped to interest me. They succeeded with very little trouble. It sounded like just the sort of idealistic, unrealizable charade that inevitably roused my sympathies.

During my seven years on Broadway, I had never found it personally profitmaking: I had earned just enough to keep going from one play to the next, and that had sufficed. If a charitable principle of operation was now to be crowned with new legitimacy, if a whole theatre was about to be brought into being with a purpose of not making money, of course I must be a part. So I pledged the three my troth and joined the board of directors they were forming. I could, I figured, earn a sustaining wage from the magazine and simultaneously be back in the theatre at no salary and however indirectly.

Our agenda called, first, for the selection of a managing director. Acutely aware of our entrepreneurial inexperience, we agreed that a single responsible operating head was essential. Second, in order for the project to materialize before the end of the year, only three months away, we had to draft a statement of purposes, consonant with the existing Chekhov charter, that would furnish evidence for the IRS of our continuing nonprofit status. And, of course, we had to give ourselves a name.

We disposed of these matters with incredible speed. Richard Aldrich was a seasoned and respected Broadway producer just emerging, like myself, from the navy with no plans. A Harvard graduate, tall, handsome, with an aristocratic air and a proper Boston accent, Aldrich was in his mid-forties. His attraction for us was that he provided both know-how and cachet. Our attraction for him rested in the opportunity we offered to return to Broadway producing without having to raise any capital. (Biddy and Penny were to take care of that.) He agreed to become our managing director.

Our manifesto contained the usual high-sounding phrases. We were

aware that the hazards of experimentation in commercial productions are so great that new creative forces in theatre arts have little chance of finding their way to the stage. In an effort to remedy a critical situation, the founders are developing a constructive program:

1. To provide entertainment . . . classics, revivals, new plays . . . on the highest professional level, in its *repertory theatre.*

2. To provide a showcase, in which new ideas and new talents may develop, in its *experimental theatre.*

3. To stimulate a creative fresh approach to drama for youth in establishing a *children's theatre*.

4. To foster and encourage a vigorous drama throughout the country by means of playwriting and acting *contests and auditions,* fellowships and statewide conferences. . . .

For those purposes we proposed to establish a repertory theatre that would ultimately stage "at least four productions each season for limited engagements: with different guest artists playing leading roles, each with a different director, but with members of a permanent acting company."

A succeeding paragraph mentioned an "initial revolving fund of $200,000." (Remember, those were 1945 dollars.) As for a name, we seemed unable to come up with anything better than "Theatre Incorporated," as uninspired and meaningless a cognomen as could have been invented.

The fortuitous, happy joker in our deck was that Dick Aldrich was married to Gertrude Lawrence, that quintessence of glamour, talent, and charm. Gertrude, it appeared, wanted nothing more than to play Eliza Doolittle in Shaw's *Pygmalion* in New York. Her last appearance had been in 1941, in *Lady in the Dark* with Danny Kaye. Would we like *Pygmalion* as our opening production? the managing director asked the board. It would have taken a pretty dumb crew to say no.

The production we assembled in less than four weeks was top-drawer: Sir Cedric Hardwicke to direct, Raymond Massey to play Henry Higgins, that wonderful English comedian Melville Cooper to play Alfred Doolittle, Donald Oenslager to design the settings, the young English team of "Motley" to do the costumes. The Shuberts smelled a hit, and when Beatrice Straight (carefully chosen for her sparkling blue-green eyes and flaming hair to be our emissary) called upon Lee Shubert to seek reasonable terms for a Broadway house, "Mr. Lee"'s hatchet face lighted up with an unfamiliar glow, and he offered her one of his best, the Ethel Barrymore.

On the night after Christmas, 1945, Theatre Incorporated opened its first production. *Pygmalion* ran for twenty weeks on Broadway; its 181 performances set a world record for it in the thirty-four years since it had been written. Miss Lawrence being agreeable, we sent it out the following season, with Dennis King replacing Massey, on a cross-country tour that also included Canada and Mexico City.

"Gertie" Lawrence—who had decided, now that she was the wife of a Harvard man, that she preferred to be called "Gertrude"—was a dream of a star: outgoing, fun, attentive to her six young producers, and easy to deal with by the staff. I think it was because she was happy at that juncture of her tempest-tossed career. We didn't mind that most of the box office take wound up in her pocket. After all, just because *we* were nonprofit didn't mean *she* had to be!

Our first season ended with a second coup. We invited the Old Vic to present a six-week season under our management, and the English company accepted. Again Biddy Straight pretty much engineered the engagement. Her mother, who owned the Globe and Queen's theatres in London, made the contacts there. Biddy herself asked her cousin Cornelius Vanderbilt Whitney to help organize a committee of guarantors. "Sonny" turned to Julius Fleischmann of Cincinnati, a wartime buddy of Dick Aldrich; William S. Paley, chairman of CBS; Joseph Verner Reed of Greenwich, Connecticut, an erstwhile New York producer; and to Alfred G. Vanderbilt. He invited them to join him in putting up $25,000 apiece to underwrite the Old Vic's historic six-week transatlantic visit.

Forty-five actors and staff, headed by Laurence Olivier, Ralph Richardson, and John Burrell (the Old Vic's ruling triumvirate), Sybil Thorndike, Lewis Casson, Margaret Leighton, and Joyce Redman, flew to New York; the sets and costumes for five plays arrived on the *Queen Mary*. The Century Theatre, at Seventh Avenue and Fifty-ninth Street, was made ready to receive them.

Their repertory consisted of the two parts of *Henry IV*, Chekhov's *Uncle Vanya*, and a double bill of *Oedipus* and Sheridan's *The Critic*. They opened on May 6, 1946, with *Henry IV, Part I*, Olivier playing Hotspur and Richardson Falstaff, both definitive, unforgettable performances. Then came Olivier's historic, breathtaking tour de force: he followed a truly titanic interpretation of Oedipus with his Mr. Puff, the farcical eighteenth-century hero of *The Critic*, only a twenty-minute intermission between them, and astounded all who saw him. I myself have never witnessed its equal.

We had discussed plans for an opening-night party with the Vic's advance-planning team. They pointed out that since *Henry IV, Part II* would open twenty-four hours after *Part I*, an elaborate celebration would not really be appreciated. We all agreed, however, that immediately after the premiere everyone would be too keyed up to go off to bed. We settled then on a sort of private family welcome and chose the little Coffee House Club as the appropriate milieu.

About two weeks before the opening, we got a call from the British delegation to the infant United Nations, asking if the ambassador, Sir Alexander Cadogan, might purchase twenty-six seats for the opening night to entertain his fellow members of the Security Council. Furthermore, he wished to invite the Old Vic Company to supper afterward. Some hasty conferring ensued, our hands cupped over the phone; we replied that we would be delighted to provide the tickets, but since we ourselves were having a small after-theatre party for the company, we would be honored to have the ambassador and his guests join us. He accepted.

The little clubhouse has rarely seen a more motley assemblage than on that May night in 1946: Theatre Incorporated's board, staff, advisory committee, guarantors; the entire Old Vic Company; Gertrude Lawrence and her *Pygmalion* cast; and the twenty-six members of the United Nations Security Council, including Soviet Ambassador Andrei Gromyko, who rarely went out. Hardly the cozy gathering we had envisioned.

As might have been expected, the actors all congregated at one end of the room, the diplomats at the other, with Miss Lawrence, alone among us accustomed to such a gathering, serving as liaison between the two factions. After the Security Council departed, the artistes focused on the supper and the bar. In no time they gulped through everything in sight, so it turned out to be a comparatively early evening after all. The only thing that confounded the Theatre Incorporated people was how some of the raspberry trifle got inside the grand piano, where the Coffee House manager reported next day she had found it.

From the substantial number of telephone calls and letters we received during the Old Vic's run, it appeared that many in our audience were unable to hear the performers. We decided finally that we had to bring the matter to their attention. I was deputized to approach Laurence Olivier with the problem. The Century Theatre, I pointed out, was larger and its acoustics perhaps poorer than their New Theatre in London; I wondered whether he would please ask the company to speak up.

He would do nothing of the sort, he replied. The audience could hear perfectly well. It was just that they didn't listen, he explained sternly, adding that it would "destroy the performance if we all began to shout, you must agree." I did.

But the complaints continued. I sought out Olivier once more. "I hate to bring it up again," I began, "but people are still upset. Perhaps it's the fast tempo you play at; they're not used to your accents and your lilt. Would it help if you slowed down the pace a bit?"

Indeed, it would not help if they turned their speeches into dirges; he could assure me of that. I pursued the matter one final step. "Then would you mind if we put microphones in the footlights?" (Now standard operating procedure on Broadway, amplification was then all but unheard of.)

Yes, indeed, they would mind that too—very much, Larry indicated. "You must understand, old cock," he said, putting a soothing arm around my shoulders, "that even if they *could* hear and *would* listen, they still wouldn't understand what we are saying. Why, much of the time we don't understand it ourselves!"

The Old Vic season was a transatlantic smash—not an empty seat throughout the entire six-weeks run, with standees at every performance. Mr. Whitney and his fellow guarantors were never called on for their money: the undertaking paid for itself.

Theatre Incorporated (we now all referred to it simply as "Theatre Inc.") entered its second season (1946–47) on the crest of the wave, and no wonder. Our first production was Synge's ironic Irish classic comedy. *The Playboy of the Western World.* Guthrie McClintic directed, and Burgess Meredith played Christy Mahon, the title role. The director had seen in Dublin an

Irish actress, Eithne Dunn, whom we brought over for Pegeen
Mike; Guthrie cast Mildred Natwick, an old McClintic favorite—
she had twice appeared as Prossie to Katharine Cornell's Candida—as the Widow Quinn, a perfect role for her.

The previous spring, Theatre Inc. had decided to offer "open
auditions" to actors who wished to present five-minute samples
of their talents. We considered this a service due young performers, who often and justifiably complained (and still do), "How
can a newcomer ever break into this vicious circle if the only way
he or she can be cast is by having already been seen?" Altogether
we heard some eight hundred young aspirants.

One day a slight, shy, rather frail-looking girl took the stage.
She seemed not yet eighteen. She announced she would do scenes
from *This Property Is Condemned*, Tennessee Williams's two-
character, one-act play. We three in the auditorium were transfixed: a real talent, indefinable but true. When she finished we
asked her what experience she'd had and where she went to
school.

"I'm finishing at Miss Hewitt's Classes this June," she told us.
"My only experience has been acting in school plays there."

"And your name?"

"Julie Harris."

Before the season was over, Julie was given a walk-on as a
handmaiden to Sybil Thorndike in *Oedipus*. We took her to
McClintic: he cast her as a young lassie in *Playboy*, along with a
"find" of his own, Maureen Stapleton. That *Playboy* had an
extraordinarily talented cast, even down to the bit parts. But it
didn't click. I never understood why not.

The preceding summer, after the Old Vic's triumphant departure, I journeyed to London, Ontario, to lecture at the University
of Western Ontario and direct a play of my choice at the local
theatre. I selected Thomas Middleton's Jacobean tragedy, *The
Changeling*. I assured them that by excising the entire subplot,
which takes place in a madhouse and provided comic relief to
seventeenth-century audiences, I could deliver a short, powerful
melodrama with tragic overtones.

My enthusiasm for *The Changeling* derived from reading T. S. Eliot's essay on Jacobean dramatists, parts of which I read to the cast at the first rehearsal.

> The heroine is a young woman who, in order to dispose of a fiancé to whom she is indifferent, so that she may marry the man she loves, accepts the offer of an adventurer to murder the affianced, at the price (as she discovers in due course) of becoming the murderer's mistress. . . . The tragedy of *The Changeling* is an eternal tragedy, as permanent as *Oedipus* or *Antony and Cleopatra;* it is the tragedy of the not naturally bad but irresponsible and undeveloped nature, caught in the consequences of its own action. . . .

Eliot emphasizes the heroine's *habituation* to her sin, likening it to Macbeth and his habituation to crime. "In some respects in which Elizabethan tragedy can be compared to French or to Greek tragedy *The Changeling* stands above every tragic play of its time, except those of Shakespeare."

The production succeeded in conveying much of the power Eliot discerned, and my Theatre Inc. colleagues who flew up to see it, and Lincoln Kirstein, likewise moved to attend owing probably to his predilection for Renaissance sin, thought it worth a New York revival. As a result, the board voted to put it on our agenda, provided I could organize a production. However, though I made a quick trip to England to find the right actors—I had Marius Goring in mind to play DeFlores, the "adventurer"—and persuaded Boris Aronson to design the sets and David Diamond to write a score, alas, the production in New York never materialized.

My Canadian success convinced me that the time had come to move from designing to directing. So one day after returning from Ontario I invited Theresa Helburn to lunch. The chairman of the Theatre Guild's board of managers now tinted her hair blue, which startled me but didn't alter my warm regard for her. I asked her if the Guild would consider giving me a production to direct.

No, Terry replied. They knew my work as a stage manager; they knew and admired my work as a designer. But frankly, she had no idea whether I could direct; it would be folly to put me in a position where I could injure a play for them—and myself—if I failed. The thing for me to do, she continued, was to find something I'd like to stage, take an option on it, then either find a producer who'd let me direct it or else raise the backing and produce it myself. If it turned out well, then the Guild and other managers would be glad to offer me a play. Although not what I wanted to hear, this was good advice, and I tried to follow it.

The first script that caught my fancy was a new play by Peter Ustinov, *Paris Not So Gay,* which I took an option on with Nancy Stern. I had known Nancy during a brief stint at USO Camp Shows in 1942 while I waited for my naval commission to materialize. Now she was executive secretary of Theatre Inc. but eager to become a Broadway producer. Peter, unknown in America, was at twenty-one already considered an *enfant prodige* in London. His *Paris Not So Gay* was not about the glittering city on the Seine but about the abductor of Helen of Troy. It turned legend upside down, provided a new set of shenanigans to explain the causes of the Trojan War, had the wittiest dialogue I had read since Saki, offered luscious parts for Helen and Paris and an even more succulent one for Thersites—an ideal role for José Ferrer or Rex Harrison.

I offered it to both actors in turn, and each said, in effect, "If Ustinov can figure out how to end his play, I'll be delighted: otherwise not." The third act, it was true, fell apart. What we had to do was persuade Peter to put it together. To that end, Nancy and I invited him to make his first visit to New York.

Peter was a chubby young man with a big head, a winsome smile, and as quick a mind as I've ever encountered. He could speak in many tongues, and could offer good imitations of those he hadn't mastered; in fact, his gift for mimicry was already famous. He was, however, completely lacking in self-discipline. I put him up at my apartment on Madison Avenue, and he proceeded to entertain everyone wherever he went. But instead of working, Peter spent his time writing verse parodies of *The Changeling* and accomplished nothing on *Paris*. He promised he'd rewrite that third act as soon as he got home, but he didn't, and when, at the end of the summer, I went to London to apply pressure in person, I found he'd lost all interest in our play and was engrossed in two others he was working on simultaneously.

I look back upon *The Changeling* and *Paris Not So Gay* as critical to my maturing in the theatre. Although both were abortive efforts, for me they typified the kind of theatre I was drawn to: plays with style and literacy, tending dangerously toward the elitist. Indeed, they might possibly be considered caviar to the general.

In futile pursuit of their realization, I gained considerable awareness of how the London–New York axis functioned. I got to know major West End agents—Aubrey Blackburn, Cecil Tennent, Margaret Ramsay; London managers—Henry Sherek, Hugh Beaumont, Stephen Mitchell (the latter I particularly liked), and such key figures as George Devine, Glen Byam Shaw, and Michel St. Denis, who were already changing the London theatrical landscape. In New York, too, I was learning practices that would stand me in good stead for as long as I would remain on Broadway.

2

What I just referred to as the "London–New York axis" was coming to dominate one of the major periods of my theatrical career. Its beginnings are traceable to the end of the war years, when among the subjects Michael Redgrave and I talked about on country walks was his desire to play Macbeth.

As I grew to know Redgrave better, he seemed to me ideal for the role. Tall, broad-shouldered, powerfully built, he conveyed the image of the medieval warrior, capable of besting any man in hand-to-hand combat with broadswords. But behind this facade of strength, I became aware of a vulnerability and nervous instability that from time to time shook his psyche to its foundation. Not only was this combination of power and weakness one of the fascinations of Michael's personality; it precisely coincided, in my view, with the inner clash that made Macbeth so complex a figure. I urged him to pursue the idea after the war. It was then that he said, "Why not do it together someday before I lose my brawn— and you your wits?"

Later we talked of it again, still more or less casually, when I was in London on *Changeling* business. Then, in January 1947, Redgrave went to Hollywood to star in *The Secret Beyond the Door* and stayed on to play Orin Mannon in the film of *Mourning Becomes Electra.* He would be finished on the Coast by midsummer, and at last ready to tackle *Macbeth* in London in the autumn. It would be produced, he wrote me, by Hugh Beaumont for Tennent Productions, the nonprofit, tax-exempt wing of H. M. Tennent Ltd., London's most prestigious commercial management, in association with the Arts Council of Great Britain.

"Binkie" Beaumont, the head of Tennent, was the "czar" of the West End theatre, and Tennent held long-term leases on several prime playhouses—the Haymarket, Globe, Lyric, Queen's, among them. A small, fastidious young man, Beaumont naturally knew everyone in the worlds of English theatre and film; and everyone, from Peggy Ashcroft, John Gielgud, and Noel Coward to Terence Rattigan and Thornton Wilder, longed to work with him. Personally he was a cool, smooth, entertaining operator, as comfortable in Lady Colefax's drawing room as in his small office atop the Globe Theatre, reached by the tiniest elevator on either side of the Atlantic. Broadway has never in my time had a man quite like him. He combined something of the personalities of Roger L. Stevens, Gerald Schoenfeld of the Shubert Organization, Alfred de Liagre, and Elizabeth McCann, coproducer of *Amadeus, Nicholas Nickleby,* and *Les Liaisons Dangereuses.*

During Redgrave's six months in Hollywood we corresponded frequently. In April I received a six-page letter, which I recently reread with avidity.

> . . . Now, about *Macbeth.* The first time I discussed the idea with Binkie he was anxious that I should either direct myself or co-direct with a good stooge who would carry out my general ideas and take the physical burden off my shoulders. This, for the reason that I had planned to do Macbeth for so long now (if you remember, the Vic asked me to do it in 1939 . . .). Then we discussed it again during *Uncle Harry,* with Ena [Burrill] in mind, or possibly Bea [Beatrix Lehmann]. Then, a year ago I was to do it in Germany. The

result of all these abortive attempts is that I have certain very definite ideas about casting and interpretation of which he fully approved.

There followed a page setting forth some of them: the "gradual disintegration of Lady Macbeth" theory, with which he did *not* agree, the treatment of the witches, the casting of Banquo and Macduff, "about which I feel strongly."

So. It was agreed that I would direct and have a stooge co-direct. The more I thought about Macbeth himself the more I would like to be able to concentrate all my attention and strength on playing him. The idea of a stooge co-director does not please me. I do not think I should ease my own burden, and also I should not profit in my own performance by the lack of an original mind watching and directing. So I ask you.

I had waited long for this proposal in writing. When it came, I experienced understandable hesitancy. This would be the first time I'd tackled Shakespeare; indeed, it would be my first full-scale professional directorial assignment ever. How would the English public and critics react to an unknown American director's temerity in staging a major Shakespearean tragedy in their midst? Michael seemed to have confidence in me, but could I count on it from the others, especially Binkie Beaumont? What if I blew it? Was I, in sum, biting off more than I could chew? I answered myself that I probably was, but here was the chance of a lifetime, and I must dare all. So I did.

Through the summer I exposed myself in depth to the Variorum and absorbed what Dover Wilson, A. C. Bradley, Mark Van Doren, G. Wilson Knight, and others had written about *Macbeth*. Redgrave was, as I've said, a scholar/artist, and I wished not to be caught out by him. I carefully examined the preliminary sketches and ground plans of the designer, Paul Sheriff. He had been responsible for the scenery for Olivier's triumphant film of *Henry V*, for John Gielgud's *Crime and Punishment*, for Elisabeth Bergner's *Duchess of Malfi*. We were in good hands.

He devised a basic unit set of ramps, platforms, and steps,

backed up by stunning boldly painted translucent backdrops: misty heaths; dark, heavy passages, courtyards, and banquet hall; rough parapets, crenellated battlements; lowering skies that suggested Christ's blood streaming in the firmament.

In mid-August, I went to London for preliminary conferences with Binkie and Tennent's marvelously capable technical staff, took Ena Burrill, who was to play Lady Macbeth, out to a long lunch, met frequently with Michael, just back from Hollywood. I returned to New York for a fortnight, then at the beginning of September once again took off across the Atlantic. I settled in a borrowed flat in Albany, Piccadilly (where Wilde laid the first act of *The Importance of Being Earnest*). Final auditions for the supporting cast were held and, of course, more urgent discussions with Redgrave.

Michael and I were in agreement that the world of this play was primitive and violent, that Inverness, Glamis, Cawdor, Dunsinane were illumined by smoky torches and peopled by Scots who had no access to barbers and slept in their clothes; that with Duncan's first line of the play (after the Weird Sisters' prelude "through the fog and filthy air")—with thunder, lightning, rain in the offing—"What bloody man is that?" Shakespeare led us at once into a world of blood, turbulence, and fury, where "darkness does the face of earth entomb." We agreed that supernatural forces—and they not benign—were omnipresent, sometimes visible, sometimes not. And we determined that the opening moments should create awe and unease in the spectators, not self-conscious, amused disbelief in the reality of three hags stirring a pot of haggis in their backyard. "Out, out, damned pot!" we cried.

Those Weird Sisters, I claimed, should fulfill two functions: as the familiar fortune-tellers in whom the Elizabethans put their trust and whom some of us still visit on occasion; and, beyond that, as considered outward manifestations of those metaphysical forces constantly at work to undo good in the world, then as now, now as then.

I consequently proposed that the witches not stir their cauldron, but that three nine-foot-tall, darkly robed figures, their gaunt, specterlike masked faces almost hidden under cowls, speak the opening lines with the voices of men, not women; and that not until the drum announces "Macbeth doth come," would three small hags, "so withered and so wild," emerge from the folds of the dark robes to confront Macbeth and Banquo, as the Three Fates, towering above them, melt into the mist. Macbeth would never see the latter until the apparition scene, when he returns to the witches and commands: "Answer me / To what I ask you." Then comes their question:

> Say if th' hadst rather hear it from our mouths
> Or from our masters'.

And his reply: "Call 'em. Let me see 'em!"

At that, they would turn and point upward; Macbeth would wheel in the direction they indicate, confront in the swirling mists the nine-foot figures, and become aware at last that he was defying awesome unearthly forces. It is they who then would take over and summon the apparitions; the hags would have vanished.

One or another of these gaunt specters appeared from time to time throughout the action, as in the moment before the slaying of Banquo, when the Two Murderers were joined out of nowhere by an unexpected Third.

> *1st Murderer:* But who did bid thee join with us?
> *3rd Murderer:*   Macbeth . . .
> *1st Murderer:* Then stand with   us . . .

By the light of Banquo's torch this unexpected third murderer revealed his spectral face. The same cloaked visage appeared as one of the murderers of Lady Macduff and her little son. Wherever there was violence afoot, at least one of them would be present.

It's hard enough to make witches believable today, but ghosts are even more problematic. However, there can be no banquet scene without Banquo's: invisible to the court and the queen, he must be visible to Macbeth and surely to the audience. After experimenting with various complex but ineffective devices to present the Ghost, we decided to follow the Bard's direction and timing: "Enter the ghost of Banquo, and sits in Macbeth's place," eight speeches before Macbeth sees it. Unnoticed in the movement of servants and with all eyes on Macbeth, the Ghost entered on Shakespeare's cue and sat with back to audience while Macbeth moved toward his place; thereupon Banquo rose and faced the audience. They gasped.

A critic describing the scene wrote:

> No less stirring is the way in which Mr. Houghton introduces Banquo's Ghost. Instead of attending the banquet as a spotlight or as a figure sprung into place by a trap, Mr. Houghton's Banquo is a walking cadaver. . . . His chest is bare. A green light may follow him, but dark red blood shines over the expanses of his cut throat and on the beaten fringes of his forehead.

When this *Macbeth* opened, in December 1947, at the Aldwych Theatre in London, it received mixed notices. The one that best caught our intent was by T. C. Worsley, the respected and thoughtful critic of the *New Statesman*, who wrote:

> Here we have a designed production, an attempt to give a considered and rounded version of a play, instead of a series of virtuoso performances of parts. The company might well be anonymous. They play as a group, subordinated to the overriding pressure of an idea which they all appear to share, an idea of the play as a whole. And this sustains the production on an extraordinarily high level . . . and gives to the whole a unity unlike anything we have seen in London for some years.
>
> A bit Moscow Arts? Certainly, and what a welcome infusion. And how exciting the result. The skies lower or flare out blood red, the great bell booms in the murky hall, the cavern smokes and the cauldron bubbles and from it the apparitions ghoulishly rise. Yet with what admirable art the resources of stagecraft are subordinated to the needs of the story. . . . For this, of course, we have to thank not only the producer [i.e., director], but also Mr. Michael Redgrave. He is perfectly capable of giving a virtuoso performance which we might then argue over and compare

with that of the other disputants for our local Oscars. He chooses not to. He chooses to plot his course beautifully within the proportions of the whole.

That "idea of the play as a whole," as Worsley put it, was identified by another critic in his review.

What is contemporary in the ancient agonies of Shakespeare's tragedy is its picture of the horrors and wounds of a land in a dictator's grip. It is this sense of pillage and bloodspilling, and of the sorry price a people must pay for one merciless man's ambition, that Mr. Houghton has emphasized more clearly in his *Macbeth* than in any other production of the tragedy that I have ever seen.

When next I was in London, Peggy Ashcroft asked me how I found working with Redgrave. I replied that Michael at one time or other was superb in every aspect of his role. The trouble was that he never seemed able to reveal all of them at any one performance. I remembered a night on tour, watching the dagger scene and feeling the hair rising on top of my head. I had gone back at the intermission and told Michael so. He smiled and said, "You liked it? I thought it went well." But never had he been able to repeat it.

Peggy paused and then said, in effect, "Norrie, I've played many of the great parts. I've played opposite John [Gielgud] and Larry [Olivier]. I've discovered in my own work and in theirs that there are some great roles—mostly in Shakespeare's tragedies—which no one can play at full strength from beginning to end. It's just not possible. One simply hopes that one can hit the peaks as often as one has the strength."

Our production of *Macbeth* gave 134 performances in England before being transferred by Theatre Incorporated to New York, in the spring of 1948. Needless to say, in the U.K. and the U.S., I read every review (unlike Michael, who claimed he never read his critics, which is hard to believe) and was confounded by the mixed press. Some critics praised Redgrave's performance and those of his ladies—Ena Burrill in London, Flora Robson in America. Others felt cheated by his lack of virtuosity, the very element for which Worsley commended him. When the production opened on Broadway, Brooks Atkinson wrote as close to a rave as it received in New York, and he reiterated his enthusiasm in a Sunday *Times* follow-up.

"The current *Macbeth* is the most stirring we have had," he began. After praising the two principals he continued:

> Although the effectiveness of *Macbeth* rests on the acting of the two great parts, the current performance is no vehicle. Under Norris Houghton's direction, it gives us, for the first time in my memory, the sweep and excitement of the drama as a whole. Not played for the big scenes alone, it is a unified work of the theatre.

3

Robert Chapman, fellow Princetonian and sea dog, dispatched to me in the autumn of 1948 the manuscript of a play he and Louis Coxe had just completed, a dramatization of Herman Melville's *Billy Budd, Foretopman.* They entitled it, somewhat pretentiously, I thought, *Uniform of Flesh.* Coxe was a poet, and he had written his dialogue in blank verse. The play was thus almost Shakespearean in form, with the lower orders growling Chapman's muscular prose in the vernacular and the tragic passages rising to quite fine lyricism.

Never having encountered Melville's short novel, I was unprepared for the power and beauty of their manuscript and, subsequently, of the novella itself, the story of a handsome and innocent young sailor serving aboard a British man-of-war during the Napoleonic era, and his eventual death by hanging at the yardarm.

I have been much drawn to two themes in drama—the conflict of moral absolutes, as between good and evil, present in *Billy Budd* as it is in *Macbeth* and in *The Changeling,* and, indeed, as it is in all great tragedies; and the conflict between conscience and duty, as in *Antigone, Saint Joan, A Man for All Seasons,* and, obviously, again in *Billy Budd,* save that in it, the tragic hero—who, incidentally, is not, in my opinion, Billy but Captain Vere—

places duty before conscience. This was, I felt, no ordinary drama: it spoke to me powerfully, and I resolved that it must reach the stage, with myself, I hoped, directing and, if necessary, producing.

I turned to the Experimental Theatre of ANTA, the American National Theatre and Academy's adjunct, created to provide a hearing for new talent in playwriting, directing, and acting. I was a member of its production committee as the voice of Theatre Incorporated.

I presented the script to George Freedley, head of the play-reading subcommittee, who gave it a green light. The Experimental Theatre provided the playhouse, the Lenox Hill, for five performances. Although the all-male cast was large, twenty-five in all, costumes could be borrowed, sets could be built by volunteers, and of course the actors were inspired not by love of gold but by the chance any showcase offers to exhibit what they can do.

Uniform of Flesh went into rehearsal a few days before Christmas, paused for a brief observance of the holidays, and opened toward the end of January 1949.

The Lenox Hill Playhouse seated only ninety-nine, so at most not more than five hundred people saw the play, but their enthusiasm was heartwarming; Brooks Atkinson and Richard Watts, critic of the *New York Post*, found their way to East Seventy-first Street and wrote glowing reports.

There followed many months of negotiation with producers, potential backers, and major actors on both sides of the Atlantic. From the start I neither wished nor felt competent to serve as both producer and director; it was the latter I wanted to be. I was following Theresa Helburn's advice on how to launch a directorial career: find a play and someone to produce it or coproduce it, with myself as director. During the ensuing year, I lured one coproducer after another into a series of deals, all of which sank with depressing splashes.

I found, for example, a young man, Lasser Grosberg, with money and enthusiasm, who insisted that the play be done first in London. (He was British-pounds-heavy.) The idea attracted me: *Billy Budd* was set in the resoundingly British environment of a man-of-war flying the Union Jack; its severity of theme might be more appealing to the English than to Americans; production costs would be only about half of Broadway's; the characters of Vere and Claggart could doubtless be more effectively cast with English stars than American. But Grosberg eventually withdrew, to be replaced by a shyster lawyer/crook, in league with a well-meaning idiot, who together managed to destroy any possibility of a London production. I was back to square one, with my able lawyer, Arnold Weissberger, once again the only person I could depend on.

Throughout 1950 I sought the interest of a number of major actors in starring as either Vere or Claggart. I felt that with a star committed, I could return to producer Stephen Mitchell in London or Gilbert Miller or the Theatre Guild in New York—each of whom had expressed some interest, but only that, in the play. Laurence Olivier, Alec Guinness, Jack Hawkins, Robert Harris, and Louis Calhern were all receptive, some more than others.

Not until the autumn of 1950, after I had made another trip to London and one to California, both on behalf of *Billy Budd*, did a producer finally crash through, Chandler Cowles, his crash facilitated by multimillionaire Anthony Brady Farrell, who put up much of Cowles's backing. (By now the cost of production had risen from $65,000 to $100,000.) Chandler was a young charmer who'd made a name for himself by producing Gian Carlo Menotti's *The Medium* and *The Telephone* and *The Consul*, among other works. (I've heard he's now withdrawn from stage production and breeds Lippizaner horses—less chancy than Broadway, I hope.)

Within a month a cast was set: Dennis King as Captain Vere, Torin Thatcher, also of English extraction, as the antagonist, Claggart, the Master-at-Arms, and Charles Nolte as Billy Budd, the part he had created in the ANTA tryout and in which he could not be bettered.

We spent the two tryout weeks prior to opening in Philadelphia. From there I called Josh Logan and asked him to come down and see the play, for I sensed it was not achieving all of its potential impact. Josh appeared on the second Monday night. Following the performance, he conferred with Chapman, Coxe, and me for an hour and proposed a couple of major alterations, which, he told me afterward, he had no idea we would be able to accomplish.

Josh observed that the opening scene contained scarcely any action. Played on the open main deck and marked by the arrival of the newly impressed sailor, Billy Budd, it may have established a generalized seagoing mood and served to introduce the principal characters, especially Claggart, but theatrically it was time wasted. Why not begin, Josh suggested, with the second scene, laid belowdecks, where the seamen ate, slept, and brawled? Take whatever action there was in Scene One—namely the arrival of Billy—and blend it into his first encounter with his new shipmates, with Claggart, and with Captain "Starry" Vere, to create a new beginning, in a scene crowded with action, color, and noise. In other words, assault the audience *in medias res.* It would make considerable difference, Josh was certain.

Louis and Bob sat up all night rewriting, and when the company assembled next day, the authors read them the changes. They were put into rehearsal at once, and the reorganized sequence was tried out at the Wednesday matinee. Josh's suggestions made for a great improvement. By the end of the week, we were in full swing and ready to face the upcoming previews in New York, to be capped by a Saturday night opening at the Biltmore Theatre on Broadway on February 10, 1951.

The New York critics took the play and production seriously. Those whom I particularly hoped would be favorably impressed—the *Times, Herald Tribune, Post, World-Telegram & Sun,* the weeklies, especially the *Saturday Review* and *Cue*—all responded with full-fledged endorsements. But ironically and, I suppose, understandably, their well-intentioned support did not help at the box office. Consider this from Richard Watts's opening paragraph in *The Post:* "*Billy Budd* is basically a stern and tragic philosophical contemplation of the plight of goodness in an evil world. . . . There is certainly no relieving gleam of optimism." And his final sentence: "It is a challenge to intelligent playgoers."

If so, it was a challenge intelligent playgoers didn't seem to take up with any great celerity. They weren't buying "a stern and tragic philosophical contemplation" of anyone's plight, not even their own. If they'd been told loudly enough that the play featured a murder, a court-martial, and a hanging, they—or perhaps less "intelligent playgoers"—might have had their curiosity piqued.

Brooks Atkinson was following our success, or lack of it, with concern: he sought to help with one Sunday piece and then with another. And each time he wrote of this "profound, philosophical tragedy," business fell off another notch.

As we entered our third week, the closing notice had to be posted. Word of our imminent demise got about, and at midweek two ads that we had not paid for appeared in the morning paper. Those, too, were unprecedented in my memory.

The afternoon after our Saturday night closing (at which there had been standees and cheers), we called the company together. Would they, from stars to walk-ons, take salary cuts for a while? Would the authors and the director waive royalties temporarily? Everyone said yes. They really cared.

So we announced a reopening twenty-four hours later. Business built. I'm confident that John Mason Brown's *Saturday Review* piece, written before the closing but appearing just as we reopened, had significant effect. Brown wrote:

> . . . Just what it was that kept ticket buyers away from *Billy Budd* is impossible to determine with any precision. . . . Who knows? who can say?

But this I do know and this I can say. Those who did not see *Billy Budd* did their bit to discourage the theatre from doing its best. They turned their backs on courage and distinction. They helped the cause of cheapness and mediocrity, of the third-rate and the silly, a cause which, Heaven knows, has its overnumerous champions and needs no new recruits. Worst of all, however, they denied themselves an engrossing adventure. . . .

Louis O. Coxe and Robert Chapman succeeded in turning *Billy Budd* into an enthralling play. . . . They did not cheapen or compromise. They did not try to combine the easy sadism of *Mutiny on the Bounty* with the rough-and-tumble talk of *Mister Roberts*. Instead they wrote and wrote skillfully, as men who understood Melville at the same time that they understood and respected the stage. . . .

For eight more weeks *Billy Budd* kept its head above water. Then, in mid-April, I was invited by Columbia professor Maurice Valency to lunch at Sardi's. He confided to me that he was a member of the three-man jury that nominated plays to the Pulitzer Prize board at Columbia University and that the panel had selected the Coxe-Chapman drama. He told me this, he explained, to encourage us to hang on for another few weeks, until the award was announced, for it would be a pity if the play closed before the Pulitzer Prize could help us.

I was grateful for the tip. But it turned out otherwise: for the first time of only twice in its history, if my memory serves, the board repudiated its jury (the second victim was *Who's Afraid of Virginia Woolf?*) and in 1951 gave the coveted award to Sidney Kingsley's dramatization of Arthur Koestler's *Darkness at Noon*. The Drama Critics' Circle had already made the same choice. So it was doubly heartwarming to read *Cue* magazine's anonymous critic's comment on that decision:

I'm not minimizing the spectacular smash of it [*Darkness at Noon*]. I realize its propagandistic usefulness. But I'll be blowed if it's art—and the prize-giving occasion is the critic's only annual chance to ask of his choice that it anyway be an effort toward genuine art.

Several of 1950–51's plays have made such an effort ... and certainly the ten times more thoughtful, more feelingful, more distinguished dramatization of Melville's *Billy Budd*. It was *Billy Budd* I did vote for. About a third of us did, I'd say. We weren't quite numerous enough. We weren't sunk, however, and hope that *Billy* won't be either.

But *Billy* did sink the following Saturday night, after eking out a twelve-week run. But by no means did I consider the more than two years I had devoted to it to have been wasted. Despite the woes and frustrations and disappointments its young authors and I had suffered, I was proud of the endeavor. And I was a wiser man, at any rate. I was not certain, however, that Broadway was for me; after all, clearly its values clashed with mine with alarming frequency.

4

I never worked in Hollywood. While many of my friends were signing seven-year contracts, guaranteed by their agents to ensure their security and enhance their chances for fame, I was unwilling to sell myself into bondage for that long a stretch, no matter how rich the mess of pottage, unless I could dictate the terms. Obviously, I never was invited to dictate terms—but once I came close.

Just as *Billy Budd* was going through its death throes, in May 1951, a phone call came from David O. Selznick's New York office saying that the wonder boy was in town and would like me to call upon him. *Billy Budd* may have been a Broadway flop, but it appeared to have brought me considerable if fleeting kudos. For a brief time—quite brief—I was "hot." I knew it must be so: otherwise why would Selznick call?

I ambled over to 444 Madison Avenue and was ushered into the presence. I had persuaded myself that he was thinking about the film possibilities of the Melville-Coxe-Chapman piece, but no. In fact, I don't recall whether he had even seen the play—I rather think not. What Mr. Selznick wanted to discuss was a movie production of *Romeo and Juliet* to be filmed in Verona and starring—who else?—his wife, Jennifer Jones. Would I be interested in directing?

"You know Jennifer's work, I presume?" I heard him ask.

"Oh, yes," I replied, but with sufficient vagueness to put him on guard.

"She has enormous potential range, don't you agree?" he went on.

I nodded. "She was excellent in *The Song of Bernadette*," I said.

I thought it would be rude to add that that was the only film of hers I'd ever seen. He saw through me at once, I felt certain. "How did you like her in *Portrait of Jenny?* As Madame Bovary?" I mumbled that I'd missed them both.

"Well," said Mr. Selznick, "the first thing to do is to have you see them and perhaps others. Can you take some time tomorrow or the next day? I'll tell them to book you a screening room."

I appeared at the proper place and time, to be shown five Jennifer Jones movies in rapid succession. To be accurate, I was shown about thirty minutes' worth of each, after which time I would clap my hands, signifying "Enough—next!" It was sufficient to persuade me that Miss Jones's "enormous" range might not easily encompass Shakespeare.

After recovering from the experience, I allowed twenty-four hours to elapse while I tried to figure out what to do. Then I called Selznick's office. His secretary said that he had already returned to the Coast; he would call from there, or when he came back to New York. He never called. I never called. He never made *Romeo and Juliet*. I never went to Hollywood—or Verona. And I never saw another Jennifer Jones movie.

I was not yet through with Hollywood stars, though. That summer, two more movie queens came my way. One was Constance Bennett, whom I directed in Samson Raphaelson's *Skylark*, a charming comedy. She was a pleasant lady, surprisingly unpretentious. We opened in Matunuck, Rhode Island, on Bastille Day, after rehearsing for ten days, and enjoyed reasonably good success.

Two weeks of rehearsal preceded the opening of Shaw's *Candida* in Westport, Connecticut, later that summer. It starred Olivia De Havilland, who, I guess, was really a superstar. Again, the assignment to direct, I decided, had almost certainly come out of *Billy Budd:* Miss De Havilland's husband, Marcus Aurelius

Goodrich, had written a humdinger of a novel about a destroyer named *Delilah*, which—naturally—also took place at sea. So Marcus felt that he, Melville, and I (ex-USNR) had something in common, and his hunch weighed with his wife.

I had seen the production of *Romeo and Juliet* in which Miss De Havilland had appeared on Broadway two seasons or so earlier; it was not an evening I cherished among my souvenirs. However, after spending an afternoon with Mr. and Mrs. Goodrich, I concluded that she would probably be a fine Candida, and I was happy and excited to undertake the project.

The experience turned out not unhappily. I use the double negative to suggest less than complete satisfaction. Olivia suffered from those two ailments to which film actors lacking much stage experience are regularly subject. She did not know how to project; she had not developed the stamina necessary to play all the scenes sequentially without running out of steam. So my principal tasks were to encourage her to speak up with enough voice to hit the gallery, and to help her to allocate her forces, so that passages of relative relaxation might pay off in enough reserve strength for her to hit the climactic scenes when they arrived. She was a very hard worker and a bright woman as well as a talented one, and she did learn to speak up.

The fly in the *Candida* ointment, and a very buzzing one, was husband Marcus A. He insisted on sitting in at all rehearsals and taking notes, mostly about his wife but from time to time commenting on the other actors' work, as well. These notes he usually passed on to me via the telephone after rehearsal, making me suspect that perhaps some had emanated from the star herself, whose mouthpiece he might have become. In this fashion she could free herself to remain serene and possessed of gracious bonhomie at all times. Of course, I may have been wrong, but I felt that Marcus was in fact Olivia's worst enemy, unless possibly she herself was. Despite these tensions, the production worked well. The public thronged to the summer playhouses the superstar graced with her presence.

"Do you see it?" asked the slender, sallow, rather haggard middle-aged man who ushered me into his office and into a seat.

It was a corner office with windows that faced up Madison Avenue and across it, so I knew that, despite his ashen look, he must be powerful. His name was Hubbell Robinson, and I discovered that he was head of television programming for the Columbia Broadcasting System. No wonder he looked exhausted.

"Do I see what?" I countered cautiously as I looked about the room.

"Television," he said.

"Oh. Well—not any oftener than I can help," I replied truthfully, but hoping not to give offense.

I imagine it was not the answer he expected. Thoughtful, he paused for a moment before venturing on. "Would you be interested in becoming a producer-director for CBS?" It was my turn to pause.

"That would depend," I answered carefully.

"Depend on what?"

"On what kind of thing I was asked to produce or direct. You see, I've worked hard in the theatre to build a reputation for being associated with worthwhile, challenging projects. So I wouldn't be particularly interested if you meant doing daytime soaps—even to learn the medium," I said.

Mr. Robinson assumed as much. The job he was talking about would, however, be highbrow enough to satisfy me, he thought.

He had a matter-of-fact manner of speaking; his story was a good one. CBS, it appeared, had decided to revive for TV its prestigious "Columbia Workshop" of radio fame, the program for which Orson Welles had produced his famous Martian broadcast and Archibald MacLeish had written *The Fall of the City,* and through which Norman Corwin and Arthur Laurents had achieved early fame. In effect, this TV "Workshop" was intended, Robinson said, to "carry forward into television the pioneering spirit" of the earlier one on radio, to be a "proving ground for experiments in techniques, new writers, and artists." It would start by being a proving ground for Houghton, who knew next to nothing about TV techniques but could provide a "fresh look." I accepted the job and went to work in mid-November 1951.

From what was really an on-the-job, crash course in television production, I absorbed just enough to get me to the series' permiere, on Sunday afternoon, January 13, 1952, from four to four-thirty (just preceding Edward R. Murrow, whose hour always topped whatever we did, however well we did it).

In my infinite ignorance, I had acquiesced in the bizarre notion of doing a thirty-minute version of nothing less than Cervantes' monumental *Don Quixote*. Although we had the talents of Boris Karloff in the title role, the great comic Jimmy Savo as his Sancho Panza, and the beauty of Grace Kelly as Dulcinea, plus the skill and energy of a coming young director, Sidney Lumet, to mount the piece, it received—and no wonder—rather less than resounding huzzahs.

Once an enterprise like the "CBS Television Workshop" has been launched, however, there is no drawing back. I never worked so hard in my life: every Sunday afternoon for a long succession of Sabbaths, the "Workshop" offered a potpourri of oddments, but none odder than that twenty-eight-minute *Don Quixote*. There was a semidocumentary on jungle warfare based on John Hersey's short *Into the Valley*, with James Dean as one of the dogfaces; a fantasy on a theme of Dixieland jazz called *Careless Love;* a glimpse of *The Beggars' Opera;* a Roald Dahl original (adapted from his *New Yorker* story), *The Sound Machine;* Synge's tragic miniature, *Riders to the Sea*, with that wonderful old British actress Cathleen Nesbitt; a dramatization by Samuel Grafton of Freud's famous case of Anna O. At the very least we were eclectic.

All of this was "live": it was long before the day of tape. For actors, cameramen, sound engineers, effects people, director and assistant, and producer, whether on the floor or in the control room, the tension of that half hour was electric, for everything had to be totally controlled: nothing could go wrong while on air, although so many things might. It took strong nerves.

I was lucky in my staff, especially in the young man who directed all shows for which no guest director had been chosen, Robert Mulligan (who subsequently distinguished himself as a movie director), and in my floor manager, another young man headed upward, Joseph Papp. CBS provided the "Workshop" with top cameramen, for everyone wanted the project to succeed.

During its first ten weeks, the Twentieth Floor (where the bosses held forth) hoped for a sponsor. Of course, the "Columbia

Workshop" of radio never had one, and the network was proud of that fact. But TV was vastly more costly than radio, and the ratings for our half hour were disappointing. We were not exciting enough, not experimental enough to justify the staggering expense. When we finally expired, our time slot was taken over by a fine program called "Omnibus," which took the wealth of the Ford Foundation, its sponsor, to keep it alive.

Before the end came, the moguls of the programming department met to consider how to make the "Workshop" more "sensational." One think-tanker suggested doing *Aïda* in modern dress with a syncopated score (in a half-hour version!); another proposed doing the story of Primo Carnera, the colorful former heavyweight champion, with Carnera playing himself; another was all for Nostradamus; yet another urged consideration of the story of a man in South Africa who was eaten alive by ants. Surely all of these would have been "sensational," but none could have been done on our budget or in our time allotment.

Speaking of time, I have never forgotten the uselessly consoling wisdom of my unit manager, Charlotte Paley (unrelated to chairman William S.). As the death of the series approached, she observed sadly, "It's too bad about you, Norrie. You seem to think that TV consists of a series of programs of varying lengths interspersed with commercials. In fact—as everybody else knows—it's the other way around: TV consists of a series of commercials interspersed with programs."

To make this short story shorter, CBS took the show off the air after fourteen weeks. And because there was no classy program to which I could be shifted (Hubbell recalled my nose-in-the-air view of soap operas), my resignation was accepted on both sides with regret, and no little relief.

I must say that I found my television days decivilizing. During the weeks devoted to producing those fourteen shows, I never had time to go to the legitimate theatre, to attend a concert, to read anything save "possibles" for the program, not even the morning paper, or to spend a sociable evening with friends not involved with TV.

The demise of the program reinforced my growing conviction that I was not cut out for a career that looked for public acclaim (like high Nielsen ratings) as a measure of success. I'm not sure that I knew what other measure there might be: perhaps one's own satisfaction would have to suffice. But there was no money in that. I was ripe for a reassessment.

11

"Advance from Broadway" (1940–41)

*A*t midpoint back in the 1939–40 Broadway season I was about to turn thirty. It was then, in fact, that the seeds of reassessment were planted. They took a dozen years to reach fruition. I had catapulted through my twenties with considerable speed. But in the fall of 1939 I'd come back from my first St. Louis Municipal Opera season with no Broadway designing jobs lined up. Having always run scared, I anxiously asked myself if my theatrical career was to be but a flash in the pan.

The fact was, I was approaching another exit. From young Harcourt, Brace editors Stanley Young and Chester Kerr came a proposal that I write a second book—this time about the American theatre beyond Broadway. The guns of another August prevented further explorations abroad. Flattered by their interest and having no reason to decline, I agreed to take off that 1939–40 season and reenter the literary world. My Moscow months had whetted my appetite for "investigative journalism" and persuaded me I had a flair for making critical judgments.

Young and Kerr introduced me to David Stevens, director of the Division of Humanities at the Rockefeller Foundation, who agreed to underwrite my research and writing; Stevens in turn passed me along to Barclay Leathem, then executive director of the recently established National Theatre Conference (NTC). Its

sixty-five members would become guides to their informal network of academic and nonprofessional stages across the country.

I sought guidance also from Edith J.R. Isaacs, then editor of
Theatre Arts, and her associate, Rosamond Gilder. They had
influenced the American theatre obliquely and out of all proportion to their visibility. Every year Mrs. Isaacs devoted an issue of
the magazine to "The Tributary Theatre"—it was one of her
enthusiasms. Both Mrs. Isaacs and Miss Gilder had also been
involved, I learned, with the inception of NTC. They encouraged me in my new project.

Shortly before I was to leave New York, in January, I had tea
one afternoon with Mrs. Norman Hapgood. When I returned
from Europe in 1935 she had welcomed me warmly, frequently
gathering friends in her apartment that autumn to hear me wax
eloquent over my Russian experience; after *Moscow Rehearsals*
was published, she redoubled her efforts in my behalf.

Now, over tea, she explained that she had been telling her old
friend Ned Sheldon about my upcoming travels and he had expressed interest and a desire to meet me. She would like to arrange a meeting.

Persons to whom Edward Sheldon's name is meaningful today
are, I suppose, few indeed, but before he died forty years ago he
was a "living legend," one that stretched back another forty years.
Tall, athletic, handsome, talented, he was a golden youth in 1907,
the year he graduated from Harvard, the first product of Professor George Pierce Baker's famous 47 Workshop for playwrights.
The following year, when he was but twenty-two, the reigning
star Minnie Maddern Fiske agreed to appear in his play *Salvation
Nell,* thereby assuring him instant success. He followed it the
following year with *The Nigger* and the next with *The Boss;* in 1912
he wrote *Romance* for Doris Keane, another great star of the day.

Then suddenly, at twenty-nine, he was struck down by an
incredibly virulent and incurable strain of rheumatoid arthritis.
He became immobile, almost literally turning to stone, and lost
his eyesight. His mind, however, was unaffected, and his many
devoted friends formed a procession of visitors to his bedside—
among them, Alexander Woollcott, Margaret Ayer Barnes, Edith
Wharton, Jane Cowl, Robert Benchley, Katharine Cornell and
Guthrie McClintic, and Charles MacArthur and Helen Hayes

(who once told me she never did a play without Sheldon's approval).

For more than twenty years Sheldon had lived in pain and total darkness, lighted only by his own spirit and the ministrations of those who came to read to him their manuscripts, letters they'd received, newspapers, magazines, books. He was one of the best-informed men of his day and certainly one of the most courageous.

My appointment was for five o'clock. The elevator brought me directly into a foyer that looked rather like a doctor's waiting room: a few chairs, some magazines—impersonal but handsome; no one was in sight. I sat down apprehensively. A nurse passed through and smiled. She disappeared behind a pair of double doors. In a few moments the doors opened and she beckoned me into a large room. At its far end stood a plain metal hospital bed, beside it a table and a chair.

As I entered, a voice, firm and vibrant, said, "Come in, Mr. Houghton, and sit here by the bed." I did so. The man lying motionless was wearing a yellow turtleneck sweater. He had a fine, firm, ruddy face, with a mask over his eyes. His hair was iron gray, his shoulders broad and strong-appearing. Below them extended a coverlet, under which his body, arms, and hands seemed to disappear into nothing.

Prepared as I should have been, I was nonetheless terribly shocked. I couldn't think of anything to say. Doubtless Mr. Sheldon was accustomed to that reaction from newcomers, for he took over, talking for five minutes or so, and allowing me to recover my composure. Then he began to ask questions. I talked about Russia, about my work since I returned, about mutual friends in and out of the theatre.

About five-thirty he offered me a glass of sherry and I accepted. In two minutes a nurse appeared with the sherry, summoned as if by mental telepathy. We began to talk about my forthcoming tour. Where was I going? What did I hope to accomplish? I explained that I was off to rediscover the theatre about which Kenneth Macgowan had written in 1926 in his *Footlights Across America.*

Macgowan was an old friend, Sheldon responded. He'd liked

that book, considered him a fine critic, an all-around theatre man.

I hoped to bring his book up to date, I continued, to find out what was going on today in our theatre outside New York. How good, for example, were courses and classes in dramatic art and productions presented on college campuses? For what careers were students being prepared? How satisfactory were facilities and faculties? What relationship did educational theatre bear to the "community theatre" movement? Were such stages of professional caliber? What purposes did they serve? Did the future possibly lie out there rather than on Broadway? I was steamed up by then. I tossed out still more questions. How about children's theatres? Had they any real artistic function or a therapeutic one? Were they preparing children to become future audiences? Was there anything comparable to the workers' theatres in the USSR? To the theatres on their collective farms? I wanted to discover whether the leaders we needed existed in the hinterlands, waiting to be discovered. Changing tack, I wondered what effect Broadway had on the rest of the country—and vice versa.

"What do you mean by Broadway—specifically?" Mr. Sheldon interposed.

"I mean, of course, the commercial theatre in New York," I said. "Right now, it's obviously the home of our best professional stage artists. That's one reason for this trip—to confirm that's so. But there's a lot I've learned to dislike about Broadway too," I added. "I'm impatient at its commercialism, at the waste of talent, at the vicious circle of employment it practices and the unemployment it can't seem to resolve. I'm impatient that it is so inhospitable to experiment, adheres so rigidly to a preset style and technique. I'm impatient that our dreams so seldom come true," I wound up with a rather teenage flourish.

"How long will all this take you?" he asked mildly.

I responded that I expected the traveling I'd laid out to take about seven months, and suddenly I became aware of my surroundings and the passage of time. I looked at my watch; I'd been there an hour. I said I felt I should leave.

Before I departed he offered a bit of advice: Don't expect too much of the stages and the plays I would see. Seek out the people who put these things in motion. They're what matter. Some would doubtless be humbugs, some hard to know, some would meet me more than halfway. Many fine men and women were out there in America. It's they I must remember. Good luck!

I left, crossed to the subway, and headed downtown. I'd expected to be depressed by the encounter. Instead, I was exalted. I thought of Sophocles' line: "Numberless are the world's wonders, but none more wonderful than man." And of Shakespeare's echo: "What a piece of work is a man!"

"Yes," I said to myself. "A man can speak from the tomb; I've just heard him." Edward Sheldon's tomb was his body; his spirit was fire.

2

On the last day of January 1940, I headed westward under the Hudson River, en route to America. The weather encouraged me to move south. At my initial stop, Chapel Hill, North Carolina, I encountered the first of those persons Edward Sheldon told me would make the difference.

At the university there, his alma mater, Paul Green, Pulitzer Prize dramatist, ex-professor of philosophy, ex–Hollywood scenarist, was leading seminars in playwriting. He was also the current president of the National Theatre Conference. His *House of Connelly* had opened the Group Theatre; his outdoor drama, *The Lost Colony*, is still running fifty summers later. Tall, with shaggy black hair and large hands, he looked like a character in one of his plays.

My visit coincided with the annual Carolina Regional Theatre Festival. For two days I was subjected to folk plays—written by some folk, acted by other folk—most of them poor (the plays, not the people, although some of them were poor too). When the festival ended, I had a farewell talk with Green. We sat on his lawn, the incipiently budding woods and fields stretching before us. I was troubled by the festival.

"What good does it do the theatre," I mused, "for all these youngsters to put on plays badly and drag all these audiences to see them? Doesn't it simply turn people against the stage, causing them to say, 'If that's a play, give me a movie any day'? This activity may be fine for people involved—although if they do bad work, I'm not sure—but what has it to do with the theatre?"

Green sat for a moment sucking on a long piece of grass and looking out at the countryside, silent in the noonday Carolina sun. Then he began slowly to unfold his philosophy, which went something like this.

It was true, a lot of that stuff was bad—bad art, bad theatre. He raised his arm toward the field and the edge of the woods. "But look at all those brambles, scrub underbrush, thicket. Most of it grows up a way, struggles along, and dies. The leaves fall off, the stalks droop, they become mold and go back into the ground to fertilize it. Next year, where the soil is a little richer, one of those stalks may grow sturdier, or a seed dropped there may even strengthen into a tree." He ran his hand through his hair.

"A lot of this dramatic activity is like the scrubby underbrush. It doesn't look like much, most of it will die away quickly, but it helps to fertilize the ground. Our soil isn't very rich and we need all the manure we can get. From it someday an oak may grow sturdier, a rose brighter."

In the Bad Lands of North Dakota, at the State Agricultural College in Fargo, I came upon Professor Alfred Arvold, gone now too, like Paul Green. There was his Little Country Theatre, its stage small and poorly equipped. Downstairs in a large room paneled in golden oak was a lending library that contained almost a thousand plays. Fargo was merely Arvold's home base. Most of the year he was in his car, driving to various outposts, holding two- or three-day drama institutes. During the day his audience was almost entirely women; in the evening the men joined them to hear him read plays aloud, instruct them how to produce plays, and encourage them to develop indigenous drama. I've never returned to North Dakota, but I've often wondered what happened after Professor Arvold's mission came to an end.

I traveled from North Dakota to Texas by way of the Pacific Northwest and California. In Pasadena, I found the other face of the Arvold coin. The Pasadena Community Playhouse had been built in 1926. By 1940 it was one of the outstanding theatre establishments in the country, with a staff of seventy-five, a theatre school, and a season of eighty-three productions—new plays, Broadway revivals, and classics intermingling in the repertoire, all performed by local actors and by Hollywood pros temporarily "at liberty." The only resident theatre, to use today's term, comparable to it was the Cleveland Play House, which I had visited the previous spring: it, too, had a school and two stages in operation eight to nine months of the year. Both were, of course, nonprofit, and very impressive, I thought, wondering how many people in New York were even aware of their existence.

In 1940 Abilene was a town of some twenty-five thousand in central west Texas. The sidewalks were filled with the kind of crowd that converges on such towns on Saturday nights all across the country. But here the profusion of ten-gallon hats and mud-caked cowboy boots and the pedestrians' rangy, rolling gait made everything seem different.

At Abilene's hotel I was dining on some excellent Texas beef. As we ate, my guide and friend suggested tentatively that I might like to see a tent show. Of course, it was nothing wonderful, he warned, and might not have anything to do with the kind of theatre I was interested in, but it was all most people had out there. I assured him if that was so, I was certainly interested.

It was December so the itinerant Harvey Sadler Tent Show had moved indoors, to the City Auditorium, which seated fifteen hundred. The evening was almost half over when we arrived, but it didn't matter. Even after we got there people kept coming in and going out, much like a Japanese Kabuki audience. Because all those tent shows were alike, and were performed year after year by the same company, the audience had seen it all before, many times.

Those performances were also called "Toby shows," named for the stock character who appeared in all of them. A cross between Punch and a commedia dell'arte comic, Toby sported a flaming red wig and an equally roseate nose. For part of the evening he wore an antique Prince Albert; for the rest he dressed as a country bumpkin with generously patched overalls and a bandanna. Even if a play's original script contained no Toby character, he could be easily interpolated, for his set dialogue was scant, and subordinate to a good deal of broad pantomime and some extemporaneous gags. When we arrived that evening, Toby was getting tangled up in an exceedingly long telephone cord, as he tried to carry on what he thought was a phone conversation with a character who was, however, standing right behind him and speaking in normal tones. This was good for a lot of laughs.

When the act was over, an orchestra filed into the pit, and a vigorous young man came out to sing in a magenta spotlight; after a verse or two he broke into a tap-dance. He was followed by a sextet of singing cowboys, who offered some traditional cowboy airs, accompanying themselves on guitars and an accordion. Toby then returned and made a speech. He thanked Abilene for its support, made sober references to the world situation, hoped to be back next season, and wished all a Merry Christmas.

The final act was laid outdoors. "Wood wings" of 1905 vintage and a badly painted backdrop depicted a landscape. The light was a flat white. In the face of such a primitive display, what should one do—suspend judgment? I didn't think so.

One could acknowledge its fearful crudity yet admit that it was a good show. There was a liveliness here often lacking on better-lighted stages. Toby was really funny, the cowboy singers' nostalgia was touching, and the audience entered into the performance with zest; indeed, one could almost say they were the best part: farm boys and girls, men with babies in their arms, children ten or twelve years old, aged leathery-skinned grandfathers and grandmothers, all packed to the rafters in eager rows, their faces pink in the reflected glow from the footlights. They had paid ten cents apiece to get in.

Out across the tableland of west Texas, not far from Abilene, stands Albany. In 1940 it had two thousand inhabitants, among them a collegemate of mine, Robert Nail, soft-spoken, with short, curly black hair and sparkling dark eyes. Active in the Intime at Princeton, he had written the best play of my four years. After college he had not gone on to the Yale Drama School or struck out for Broadway like some of us, but had returned to his own turf in the Southwest to continue writing. He had submitted one of his plays to Jed Harris, then at the peak of his fame as a

Broadway producer. An enthusiastic Harris had offered to take an option and invited Nail to New York to discuss some minor changes. Bob had replied gratefully but had said he was really too busy to come. Jed, piqued, had dropped the option. Now that I was in Texas, I decided to pay Nail a visit and find out why he'd had no time for a Broadway producer.

First, he explained, there was the Fandangle, a kind of poetic historical epic based on native lore: Indians, Mexicans, soldiers, settlers, early oil prospectors. Each year Nail wrote a new Fandangle. Preparations began in early spring. The single performance took place in June, in the athletic field behind the high school, with two hundred and fifty in the cast. There was music and dance, parades of covered wagons and horsemen. People rode into Albany from miles around to see it.

"Who trains the dancers?" I asked.

"I do," he replied.

"You're no choreographer," I said.

"I learned how. It wasn't too hard."

"Who makes the costumes?"

"I do—with some of the women to help."

Then, he said, there was the Christmas Nativity play, which he wrote and produced in the local church. Since it seated only two hundred, the play was given ten performances, every one to a capacity audience. That added up to two thousand, which was the entire population of Albany—the only time I've ever heard of one hundred percent of a community attending a play annually.

Besides these two productions, Bob wrote a one-acter or two for the high school to perform in the state drama tournament.

"Then," he added, an amused twinkle in his eyes, "I take quite a bit of time helping cowboys hereabouts with their poems."

As I was leaving Albany, the superintendent of schools said to me, "I don't know what we'd do here if Bob ever went away—but I guess you can see that for yourself."

Nicholas Ray, who later became a prominent film director, worked in those days for the Resettlement Administration in the South. Part of his job was to help people put on plays, and so I went to see him too. He told me that while he was working in

Alabama, he received a letter from students in the white high school of a little town about forty miles south of Birmingham, asking him to come down and help them put on a play. He went and found himself in the heart of the tough Alabama coal mine country. He looked at the youngsters dubiously.

What kind of show did they want to do? he asked them. They didn't rightly know; they'd never done one before.

Had they looked at any play catalogues? They had, but the stuff they read about in them sounded pretty silly. They had an idea, and maybe they could write their own—if he'd help them.

He agreed and asked them what their idea was. Most of them, it appeared, wanted to do a show "that would tell about some of the troubles of the Negras hereabouts," as they put it.

Nick was startled, to say the least: kids at a white high school in the Deep South wanting to write a play about their Negro neighbors! But if that was what they wanted, O.K. They set to work and composed a scenario; around it they improvised dialogue. Together they labored for several weeks.

The time came for the performance. The little hall was packed with a crowd of tough, burly miners and their wives. Most of them had never seen a play. A sleazy curtain hung across one end of the hall to separate them from the stage. The show began and lasted an hour. When the end came, there was a heavy pause. Then someone clapped. Soon the long, low room jammed with hot humanity was reverberating to applause, cheers, whistles. Suddenly someone yelled, "We wanna see it again!"

Nick went back to the youngsters. "Do you want to do it again?" he asked.

"Sure," they said. In ten minutes the performance was repeated. No one had left the hall.

I recall so clearly this series of encounters from my pre–World War II years because the Rockefeller Foundation tour paved the way to a ninety-degree turn in the course of my career. It didn't occur forthwith—the war years intervened; but my exposure to the American theatre lying west of the Hackensack Meadows forced me to look again at my career on Broadway, to see how parochial the place was, to recognize, as I had suggested to Edward Sheldon in 1940, that many of its values were alien to me. My midwestern roots were revived with the infusion of a soil that nourishes as asphalt never can. The unpolluted winds of Dakota and Texas had filled my lungs, and even before I had completed the book recording my hegira, I knew it would be my declaration of independence from the commercial theatre and a call for decentralization of our professional stage. It didn't mean, necessarily, that I would head back to the Corn Belt, or that I would emulate those regional pioneers I've been speaking of. However, "Art has little to do with geography," I earnestly proclaimed, denouncing, while I was at it, the show shops of London, Paris, Berlin, and New York as artificial places that merely pandered to public whim. The verities, I announced, were to be found elsewhere. When pressed as to where, I had few clues. And much later, when the war ended and I was in a position to start over, where did I go? Back to New York and London! My flirtation with Rousseau appeared to be short-lived. Nonetheless, after my foundation-backed tour I was not the same fellow I had been. Alfred Arvold, Bob Nail, and Nick Ray had seen to that. My future would confirm it.

So as the forties began, I wrote and had published *Advance from Broadway*, stating the need for a theatrical Reformation—the money changers must be hurled from the temple—and for a theatrical Renaissance—our medium must rise to its proper place among the other performing arts.

3

We return now from the prewar Corn Belt to postwar Broadway and the reassessment that, after my departure from CBS, I thought it time to make.

Of all the sixty-odd years during which I've been involved in the theatre, first as spectator, then as participant, and again today as spectator, the decade that began in 1945 seems to me in retrospect to have been the richest, the most vigorous and stimulating.

The postwar explosion encompassed the entire professional performing arts scene. On its eve, in 1944, Mayor Fiorello La

Guardia took an active role in establishing the New York City Center of Music and Drama as a true "theatre for the people"; by 1950 it was in full swing. In that decade too, Lincoln Kirstein turned the Ballet Society into the New York City Ballet, which made its home at the City Center until Lincoln Center rose; Lucia Chase started the American Ballet Theatre; and Rudolf Bing arrived from abroad to breathe new life into the Metropolitan Opera.

As for the stage itself, my generation returned from overseas to join hands with our elders in giving birth to a new day. *Oklahoma!* in 1943 was its prelude. The American musical comedy would never be the same, and the first postwar decade confirmed that with *Carousel, Finian's Rainbow, Annie Get Your Gun, South Pacific, Brigadoon, Kiss Me, Kate, Guys and Dolls*—on and on. No decade before or since could compete.

We returning veterans saw the emergence of two dramatists whose talents equaled—indeed, some would say, outshone—those of the prewar generation: I mean, of course, Tennessee Williams and Arthur Miller. Arthur—tall, lanky, Lincolnesque, articulate—I came to know fairly well in that decade, and I admired him greatly. Tennessee, physically and spiritually Miller's opposite, I knew less well but admired equally.

Between them, what a glorious cascade of dramatic writing poured forth in those first years after World War II: *The Glass Menagerie, A Streetcar Named Desire, Summer and Smoke, Death of a Salesman, The Crucible!* Their voices were the voices of our generation. They spoke now fiercely, with rage and regret, now gently, with understanding, affection, and deep compassion. One theme emerged repeatedly: the conflict between reality and illusion. Miller demanded that man embrace truth; Williams recognized the desperate need for illusion to protect sensitive souls. They were joined in that theme by the aging O'Neill, whose *The Iceman Cometh* appeared in that decade, too: he continued to be haunted by the same conflict—pipe dreams versus the unendurable harshness of real life.

All these distinguished works, musical and dramatic, flowered on Broadway, giving the lie, you may claim, to my words of opprobrium. But elsewhere at that time, other forces were at work to make that 1945–55 decade memorable. And they were, I submit, not only reflective of my own dissatisfaction but farther-ranging in their impact.

In Greenwich Village, a ferment comparable to the first years after World War I brought into being New Stages in 1947. In 1948 Kim Stanley, Merle Debuskey, and other pioneers formed Inter-players, presenting Auden and Isherwood's *The Dog Beneath the Skin* and Gertrude Stein's *Yes Is for a Very Young Man*. By the end of the decade (1955), those pioneers had been followed by other downtown adventurers—Julian Beck and Judith Malina, José Quintero and Theodore Mann, T. Edward Hambleton and Norris Houghton. Thus, off Broadway also came into being as part of the explosion. It was a phenomenon directly linked to rising concern about Broadway's financial plight.

"The theatre is an organized calamity," Boris Aronson was quoted as remarking, with "doleful affection." Brooks Atkinson echoed him: "Broadway is economic anarchy. . . . Broadway's showmanship is a local foible rather than a national exploit."

From my travels in 1940–41 I had come to the same conclusion. In *Advance from Broadway* I wrote about labor's "prohibitive wage scales and regulations," and about unemployment: "Five hundred actors at work in mid-season, with more than four thousand unemployed." I asserted that "in order to produce at all, there must be capital, and the theatre depends in large measure on non-Broadway sources for that. These sources provide money in order to make money; [they] own theatres as real estate in order to make money. . . . It is no wonder that the box office becomes the all-important factor."

It gave me, I must admit, rueful satisfaction to find that my youthful trumpeting as a self-proclaimed "minor prophet" was coming to be recognized as accurate. It gave me, naturally, an even greater lift to see that between 1945 and 1955 many thoughtful folk began to take steps to alleviate some of the pain.

Since the early 1930s, the American National Theatre and Academy had been in existence, with a congressional charter, but so far it had accomplished nothing to justify it. Now it began to stir from an Abou Ben Adhem deep dream of peace. Under the benign leadership of Robert E. Sherwood and with the active efforts of its executive director, Robert Breen, ANTA commenced to tackle some of the problems I had harangued about. There was even talk of a "fifty-theatre plan" for America: to create a network of permanent playhouses that could interchange their productions. The idea of not-for-profit theatre as an alternative to commercialism was no longer greeted by derisive hoots.

ANTA's Experimental Theatre has already been cited gratefully in these pages as a catalyst for my *Billy Budd* production. And Theatre Incorporated's shocker of a challenge to Broadway, presenting *Pygmalion* and making the Old Vic's visit a triumph without losing a penny, offered evidence that a nonprofit management could exist alongside the Shuberts et al.

In that first postwar decade there were movements all across the country toward establishing professional but again not-for-profit regional theatres. Halfway through it, Zelda Fichandler was founding the Arena Stage in Washington. In 1947 Nina Vance was starting her Alley Theatre in Houston, which soon became fully professional. In 1952 Herbert Blau and Jules Irving were bringing the Actors' Workshop to life in San Francisco.

Finally, out of the ashes of the Group Theatre of the 1930s, Lee Strasberg, Elia Kazan, Robert Lewis, and Cheryl Crawford brought forth in New York the Actors' Studio, destined to become an internationally renowned training center.

There has never been a decade quite like it in the theatre of the American twentieth century. New York and cities around the nation seemed of a piece in reassessing their credits and their debits, seeking to strengthen the former and reduce the latter. My own commitment to the theatre, after my momentary fling with TV at CBS in 1951–52, fitted well with the temper of these exhilarating times. The forms my recommitment would take constitute the rest of my story.

12

The Phoenix Rises (1953–62)

*O*n the eighteenth of April in 1953 (which Longfellow reminds us is the anniversary of Paul Revere's ride), I joined an acquaintance named T. Edward Hambleton for lunch at The Players in Gramercy Park. The club is housed in the impressive foursquare Victorian mansion that once belonged to Edwin Booth, the greatest American actor of his day. It was a not inappropriate date and place for a couple of men in early middle age to meet and cogitate upon a revolution of sorts in the theatre of their day, and this was what we were doing.

The following morning Hambleton was on the phone. "I've been thinking about our lunch conversation," he pulled himself together to say after a lengthy silence. (His pauses, I was to discover, were as famous as Chekhov's but more prolonged and less pregnant.) "I believe your project is worth doing, but I'm more convinced than ever that you can't do it alone. I think you need me, and I want to get involved."

It was my turn to pause, but more briefly. "I've been working at this for almost a year now," I finally replied. "I admit it takes two to have a baby, but I think one is the right number to give birth to a theatre." I suppose I was jealous of letting him in on my act. I knew perfectly well that theatres—and very successful ones—had been created by two people; Stanislavski and Nemirovich-Danchenko of the Moscow Art Theatre come immediately to mind, Klaw and Erlanger if you'd rather look closer to home.

I didn't really know Hambleton very well. We first crossed paths during the 1940s at the ANTA Experimental Theatre, where we were each involved in separate offbeat enterprises, he with Charles Laughton's portrayal of Brecht's idea of Galileo, I with my young, innocent seaman hanged from the yardarm of HMS *Indomitable* in that poetic tragedy then called *Uniform of Flesh*. T. Edward Hambleton was an impressive figure: a large head and broad face topped a chunky body usually clothed in a mussed Brooks Brothers suit; he regularly wore button-down shirts, as did I. Anyone who had seen us in the Players Club dining room that April day would have taken us for a couple of Ivy League WASPs, which indeed we were—he a forty-one-year-old Yale man, I a Princetonian two years his senior. I liked T. Who could help it? He had such twinkly blue eyes, such an unruly shock of hair, such a broad smile and generous laugh. He resembled a big cuddly stuffed bear, the companion of one's nursery days. But did I dare to go into business with a teddy bear?

Replying on the phone to my claim in support of theatrical parthenogenesis, T. repeated cheerfully, "All right, but I think you'll find you need me." Then he added, not altogether irrelevantly, "I have a station wagon. You said yesterday you were stymied by real estate. I can drive you around town and see whether something can't be found to suit the needs." I accepted his offer, and during the weeks that followed, we drove from abandoned churches in lower Harlem to the derelict shell of a top-floor ballroom impressively known as Beethoven Hall, off the upper Bowery, always in dogged search of a possible building to turn into a theatre. For that was part of what we had been talking about at our Players lunch.

He'd heard I had an idea for a theatre. "Tell me about it. What gave you the idea?"

"I guess I've cherished the notion of having one of my own for as long as I can remember," I began. "When I finally concluded I wanted to be both a stage designer and a director and saw how hard it was to work productively on Broadway, such a place grew more and more desirable. It was *Billy Budd* that caused things to start bubbling to the surface."

I recounted to T. Edward the saga of its production. And I explained that after that experience I had decided I would have to either change my taste in plays or else find another way to exercise it without risking the loss of $100,000 of other people's money every time I produced. T. nodded. I suspect he was thinking of several Broadway oddments he had offered; they had not exactly been financial blockbusters either.

"Let's adjourn to the library upstairs," he suggested. At two o'clock on an April afternoon, we had the place to ourselves, along with the busts and photos of Joseph Jefferson, Otis Skinner, John Barrymore, and other American thespians of earlier generations. When we had settled into comfortable leather chairs, T. ordered me to go on, and I told him that the previous summer in London I had invited an old friend, that fine actress Pamela Brown, to lunch in Soho. "Pamela," I'd said, "we've often talked of doing Middleton's *The Changeling* together. How about coming to New York in the fall and playing that wondrous part of Beatrice-Joanna?"

Obviously that relatively obscure Elizabethan tragedy wouldn't have had a prayer of paying back its investment on Broadway, but that didn't faze me. I had reminded Pamela of T. S. Eliot's dictum that "In the moral essence of tragedy," this play is surpassed by one Elizabethan alone, and that is Shakespeare." And I had pointed out that while *Billy Budd*, too, depicted a profound moral tragedy, I had managed, after all, to raise the capital for it. Why not give gloom and doom a second whirl? Perhaps I would eventually convert Broadway's backers and public to support and relish a diet of highbrow classical sin.

Pamela had replied that she'd like nothing better, but she'd committed herself to join John Gielgud, Paul Scofield, and Eileen Herlie in a short season of repertory—*The Way of the World, Richard II*, and *Venice Preserv'd*—at the Lyric Hammersmith commencing in May, and this would be their contribution to the Coronation. (Odd choices, I thought, especially *Richard II*, to celebrate the launching of QE2.) She would have to be available for rehearsals there in February.

It was then August; I knew that extracting capital from less than eager investors and organizing the production could get under way no earlier than September, which would mean starting rehearsals in November at best and opening not before December. Since a six-week Broadway run just didn't make sense, my dream faded and, much disappointed, Pamela and I parted. Walking along Shaftesbury Avenue after lunch, I said to myself, "Too bad New York hasn't a theatre like the Lyric in Hammersmith, where *our* best actors, like those four, could play a limited season of three great dramas and incur only small losses."

The next day I had had tea in Hampstead with Peggy Ashcroft, in her cozy sitting room with three Sickerts on the walls—one a pink and green portrait of herself looking pensively at the Grand Canal—and a view of fruit trees through the windows. When would she be coming to New York again, I had asked.

"Oh, dear," she had replied, sighing apologetically and looking as though everything were her fault (a way she has). "Not for a long time, I'm afraid." She had reminded me of when she'd last appeared on Broadway, in *Edward, My Son* with Robert Morley: she had insisted on playing for only six weeks in order to get back to her children; that had created a great fuss, because stars were then regularly expected to sign run-of-the-play contracts. "I don't think I could get away with it again." She had sighed once more. "Of course, if only one could go to New York for six weeks or so to do something one longed to do, that would be another matter."

On the bus back from Hampstead I had thought sadly about our Broadway system, which deprived us of the talents of a great actress like Ashcroft and others who might like to play there but had time off from Hollywood or London for no more than a six-week run.

"So you see," I said to T., "by the time I left London, I was meditating on how these things could be brought to pass, and I concluded they couldn't happen on Broadway at all."

T. was now leaning forward. A man of few words, all he said was "Keep going."

I recounted what had happened since. One day in early autumn a young actor friend, Ken Raymond, remarked that he'd recently seen a For Rent sign on New York's old Irving Place Theatre, just above Fourteenth Street. Once a movie house, it apparently had fallen on evil days. I determined to investigate.

It was in many ways a replica of the Lyric Hammersmith—in

capacity (about six hundred), in decor (mid-Victorian, with garlands and cornucopias of fruit and flowers and cherubs in plaster), and in design (two tiers of little boxes at each end of two shallow horseshoe-shaped balconies). In my mind's eye I saw the auditorium repainted white and gold, with crimson carpet and seats. It would lack only crystal chandeliers to remind me of that jewel of a little opera house, the Cuvillier in Munich—my dream playhouse. I went backstage: the facilities weren't exactly up-to-date, but with time and not too much money, I was sure it could work.

The For Rent sign referred me to S. Klein & Co., a rather downmarket Union Square department store (now defunct), which owned the dusty gem abutting its back side. Yes, it was available, and the rent was reasonable. However, having no money at all (a point I did not mention to the Klein folk), I could merely say I would return shortly to negotiate.

I began my pursuit by trying to figure out first how much money would be needed, then where to get it. Creating a budget from imponderables proved exceedingly difficult. For example, what deals could be worked out with theatrical craft unions, who themselves would have no basis for their judgments? But somehow figures were assembled, and after I had received pledges of about sixty thousand dollars from affluent if foolhardy friends, I was confident that finding the balance, whatever it might be, would not prove insuperable. Six weeks later, at the end of November, I returned to Klein's and announced I was ready to sign a lease, only to be told:

"We've taken the theatre off the market. We are going to break through the wall and turn it into a warehouse."

"Oh, no!" I gasped. Was there nothing to be done? Apparently not. I was desolate. Sixty thousand dollars pledged, but no use for it. Three months lost. I shared the news with my lawyer, Arnold Weissberger, who tried to be encouraging. This couldn't be the only workable piece of real estate in New York, he pointed out. I had a good idea—that was what counted. This temporary setback should give me time to develop it, to figure out long-range objectives, and to resolve my budget problems, about which I still seemed a bit vague.

I realized that he was right. Indeed, it was time to make some corrections in course. But though I needed a chart, there was none. In 1952 only two other recent ventures were at all comparable. Four years earlier, Julian Beck and his wife, Judith Malina, an earnest couple with an affinity for modern poets, had found an available cellar in Greenwich Village, wherein they presented Ezra Pound's translation of some esoteric Japanese Noh plays to audiences of twenty; they subsequently moved and by 1952 had produced plays by Kenneth Rexroth, T. S. Eliot's *Sweeney Agonistes*, Auden's *Age of Anxiety*, Jarry's *Ubu Roi*. They called their project—rather superciliously, I thought—the Living Theatre, as though all the rest of us were dead. Theirs was not an example I wished to follow.

The other remotely similar project had been organized by two young men, José Quintero, from Panama, and Theodore Mann, not long out of law school. They had found space just off Sheridan Square that they had converted to a theatre in the round, to be called the Circle in the Square. There they were reviving recent worthwhile plays not commercially successful uptown, like *Summer and Smoke* and *The Iceman Cometh*, with casts of highly talented unknowns. The first part of their approach resembled mine somewhat, but the second, not at all. I wasn't interested in creating a showcase for young talent; my sights were set on the Peggy Ashcrofts and Pamela Browns.

T. Edward interrupted. "I know all about the Living Theatre and the Circle. What's *your* policy?" In response I offered a simile: Broadway today was like a bookstore that stocked only Book-of-the-Month Club selections and the best-sellers on the *New York Times* weekly list. Its proprietor didn't believe there was a public for anything else. But I was rarely attracted to such titles. When I went into a bookshop, I was looking for a cookbook, a play just published or out in a new translation, a travel book, or some classic or near classic I'd never tackled. And the bookstore I talked of had none such to offer. I couldn't believe I was alone in my somewhat offbeat reading tastes. Nor could I believe there weren't other people like me who wanted to expand their theatregoing beyond what the press and the general public had decided was a hit.

"I want a theatre that will fill this vacuum. But I don't believe Broadway can accommodate my tastes. It costs too much. True, there may not be a big enough Broadway public to support me;

there certainly wasn't for *Billy Budd.* But I'm convinced that in all New York are enough people to welcome a small enterprise devoted to revivals of great plays of the past and some new writers whose works don't appeal to the majority. This is no new idea. It was done by Shaw and Granville-Barker at London's Independent Theatre, by Antoine in Paris, by the Irish in Dublin's Abbey."

T. interrupted irritably. "Yes, of course; I know all that. Don't deliver a lecture on theatre history. But they were all focusing on avant-garde playwrights. You don't seem to be looking for them."

"True," I replied. "Perhaps it's because I'm not so much inveighing against Broadway's artistic standards as against its economy. I can't deny that *Our Town* and *Skin of Our Teeth* and *Strange Interlude* and *The Glass Menagerie*—all nontraditional in their time—originated on Broadway, and I can't deny they were hits. But if you check out the scene, you'll find the commercial theatre can't support more than three or four such plays a year. In time past, plays opening to mixed notices and with only 'limited appeal'—de Liagre's production of *Madwoman of Chaillot,* for example—could last for several months. Now they must run for a year or else close on Saturday night. This hit-or-flop pattern is ruining us!" I concluded earnestly. T. nodded. I began to suspect I was working hard merely to convert the converted.

As we drove around Manhattan in T.'s station wagon, house hunting, so to speak, our exchanges grew ever more lively.

"Come for dinner tonight," T. finally suggested after a few weeks. "Afterward we can get out a pad and start writing things down." I accepted with alacrity.

I had met his wife, Merrell, but only casually, around the ANTA Experimental Theatre. A Bennington girl, she was his second wife, his first having died at a tragically young age, leaving him with three young daughters, who were fifteen, thirteen, and twelve when we first met.

I was promptly welcomed into this family circle, largely, I believe, because of Merrell's warmly outgoing personality. She had an emphatic manner of speaking. Younger than T., she had a sense of humor complementary to his, while perhaps somewhat lacking his sublime sense of the ridiculous.

Although the Hambletons enjoyed considerable wealth, the paterfamilias gave few hints of that; he commanded his troops with strong discipline and encouraged them to do most of their shopping at Woolworth's. He himself rarely took a taxi if a bus or subway was available, and he saw to it that the others followed his example. If compelled to hail a cab, he ended the journey with a dime tip to the driver, however long the ride. Clean living, high thinking, and penny-pinching were the order of the day.

Into this household I entered that evening, and by ten-thirty I felt as though I had known them always. My relationship to the Hambleton family has been unique—is unique, for it has continued down the decades. Grounded on congeniality of tastes, interests, and values, it has been tempered by vicissitudes and blessed with humor, and bonded with mutual respect. To be sure, T. and I were painfully conscious of each other's faults: obstinacy, for example, was in my eyes one of his major ones, and sometimes what I might call obtuseness. And, of course, he could have written a chapter on my shortcomings, leading off perhaps with my annoying tendency to finish his sentences for him. Neither was ever the other's "yes man." Our disagreements, however, were honest and usually resolved painlessly.

After that first dinner, T. and I sat down to try to formalize some of the ideas we had been hashing over. (It was plain that I was gradually coming around to his opinion: two heads might, after all, prove better than one.) Certain points now seemed basic. We jotted them down in no particular sequence.

Item: We would situate our theatre away from the Times Square district in order to dramatize geographically that we were not out to compete with Broadway, and to allow us to produce at a fraction of Broadway's overhead.

Item: We would create an ongoing enterprise—"permanent" was the word we used most frequently to distinguish it from the one-shot production setups of Broadway managements. To that end, we hoped to lease a building for more than one year. We would not, however, create a permanent acting company: first, because we felt we couldn't afford it; second, because we believed we could provide better productions by choosing artists with specific talents appropriate to each presentation.

Item: We would present a series of four or five plays for limited engagements of six weeks each, separated by enough time to effect smooth changeovers. We would not perform two or more plays concurrently: that would savor of dreaded and costly "repertory."

Item: We opposed the "star system" and therefore would list casts alphabetically. We would, however, pay Equity minimum salaries; indeed, we had no thought of being nonunion in any department, although we would seek concessions from the theatrical craft unions.

Item: We would try to establish a ticket scale that would be half of Broadway's: seats at a $3.30 top, with some tickets available for a dollar. Accomplishing this would obviously depend on our budget, as determined by our earning potential, which in turn would depend on seating capacity. (So far no luck in house hunting.)

Item: Our management structure would be built along conventional Broadway lines: a limited partnership, in which we would be general partners, our investors limited partners. Our offering would, however, be unique. Instead of seeking separate backing for each production, we would ask people to fund a whole season. If we could produce and break even at one fourth of Broadway's cost, we could offer our partners four properties for the price of one and hope to repay their investment—not a bad deal at all.

During the post–Irving Place, pre-Hambleton days, I had met a newcomer on the New York scene, a tall, broad-shouldered, rather shambling man of about my age, with thinning hair, drawling speech, and ingenuous appearance. Roger L. Stevens had come to Manhattan from Ann Arbor to seek his fortune in real estate and almost at once made headlines by organizing a syndicate that bought the Empire State Building.

Elia Kazan put me on his trail. "You should get together with this fellow Stevens," he advised. "He may be in business, but his real passion is the theatre. I hear he's cooking up a scheme with

Bob Whitehead and Bob Dowling. You and he should have plenty to talk about."

Stevens had an office high in Rockefeller Center, commanding an excellent view of his new skyscraper. He invited me to join him there on occasional Saturday afternoons during the late winter and early spring of 1953, to engage in bull sessions about the state of the theatre. He grew interested in my project and in turn told me about his. He, Whitehead, and Dowling were about to unveil the Producers' Theatre, which then went on to give Broadway some distinguished plays.

Robert Dowling was a powerful Wall Street figure, president of City Investing Company, and like Stevens, he was an ardent theatre buff. Robert Whitehead, a true young professional, I had known for fifteen years. He had already produced *Medea*, starring Judith Anderson, Carson McCullers's *The Member of the Wedding*, and Odets's *Night Music*. His choices reflected excellent taste, good judgment, a commitment to high standards in both artistic and business dealings. He would become one of Broadway's most distinguished entrepreneurs. That trio had potentially the money, power, and brains to remake Broadway.

As I described my plans during those Saturday afternoons, it became evident that given Stevens's wide-ranging mind, I didn't think big enough to suit him. He was inflamed by grand dreams and invigorated by the concoction of huge deals. He did, however, recognize that I had been around twenty years longer than he, and that my smaller dream had its own merit.

One Saturday he said, "Maybe your project and ours could work something out in tandem. You set up your theatre, and when you develop properties with commercial potential, we could incorporate them into our programs and we'd both gain."

I was flattered by this big talk. I also liked Roger. Despite his Choate School background, he was enough of a midwestern hayseed in those early days to speak to the Hoosier in me. As the months passed, he increasingly seemed to me a loner, rather shy and ill at east at public gatherings, inarticulate as a public speaker. Politically he was a liberal, like me, and he liked to cut through red tape. He was the despair of his secretaries because he operated out of his hat, making deals that frequently never got written down. He dialed his own phone calls and often picked up on incoming ones before his staff could head him off. Indeed, there was a rumor, which I began to believe, that two secretaries, one after the other, had had nervous breakdowns because they could never keep track of his whereabouts, let alone what or how many things he was up to.

Roger was about to become an important factor in our lives: backing a whole season of four or five plays for the price of one was to make excellent sense to him. And that, of course, was the last basic point we had formulated, just before our first evening at the Hambletons' apartment on Eighty-sixth Street adjourned.

2

In June, I set our new project aside, if only for a period of weeks, to discharge an obligation I had made the previous winter. It was to Barry Bingham, an old friend whom I had first known as a naval buddy in wartime London. I had been introduced to him then by Lieutenant John Mason Brown, USNR, a native of Louisville, who had explained that Bingham was the owner of both of Louisville's newspapers—the *Courier-Journal* and the *Times*—and one of its radio stations. I found him charming and worldly, with a dazzling smile and a disarming chuckle. He was always to look a dozen years younger than his age, thanks in part to a passion for tennis and whatever else the wealthy enjoy to keep fit and trim, and was a marvel of sartorial splendor. His suits were made by Anderson & Sheppard in Savile Row, his shirts and ties by Turnbull & Asser in Jermyn Street.

Barry had invited me to stage a pageantlike historical drama with music in an open-air theatre in Louisville's Iroquois Park. The reason for perpetrating this gratuitous event on an innocent citizenry was to celebrate the city's 175th birthday. Having had no employment and, consequently, no income since *Billy Budd*, save for a weekly lectureship I held at Columbia, this modest summer job had seemed heaven-sent, and of course I had accepted.

The play, entitled *The Tall Kentuckian*, concerned A. Lincoln, who, as the world knows but has not long remembered, was born in Kentucky, married a Kentucky girl, and had many close associations with Louisville. With such a mighty theme, a score by Norman dello Joio, and a cast of eighty (including eleven children), perhaps the event should have been worth attending. It wasn't. Largely because of the script, which was quite devoid of drama or suspense, but also, I fear, because of my own inexperience in dealing with the eccentricities of outdoor drama, the extravaganza was considerably less than a triumph. However, my friendship with Barry and his wondrous wife, Mary—all of us partners in misery—was more deeply cemented during my stay in Louisville, and that more than compensated for the lavish disappointment. When Barry died, in 1988, I was proud to be asked to serve as one of his pallbearers.

By mid-July, T. and I were back in New York, he from Maryland, I from Kentucky; there were some new real estate leads, the most interesting a vast old movie house on the Lower East Side that had been, but no longer was, showing Spanish-language grade C pictures to handfuls of Puerto Ricans. It was called the Stuyvesant, situated as it was a stone's throw from Peter's grave in the churchyard of St. Mark's-in-the-Bowery, the only landmark to lend an odor of sanctity or historic distinction to the neighborhood.

The owner, Julius Raynes, a lumbering, affable fellow, unlocked the theatre, which had been dark for some time, and showed it to us. "Eleven hundred and eighty seats," he announced proudly. "About seven fifty in the orchestra, four fifty in the balcony." We were taken aback: here was an elephant, while we were in the market for no more than the rajah's howdah. But we inspected it carefully. We looked at it from all angles: a large stage; good sight lines; a broad proscenium, almost thirty feet high; a large orchestra pit; enough backstage space to mount *Don Giovanni;* dressing rooms to accommodate thirty, with showers on every floor.

The auditorium was vaguely Moorish—"Loews' Middle Eastern," someone later dubbed it. Its walls were the color of dung, its floor carpeted with such a thickness of discarded and now resident chewing gum that it would take three men two weeks to scrape it all off.

"It was built for Maurice Schwartz and his New Yiddish Art Theatre in 1926, when the Lower East Side was the hub of the

Jewish arts community," Mr. Raynes reminisced. "That makes it
the next-to-most-recently-built legitimate theatre in New York
today. Only the Ethel Barrymore uptown is newer."

T. and I looked at each other. Was this the end of the search?
Mr. Raynes mentioned a rental price. It sounded reasonable, but
we had to consult our lawyers. Raynes said he was open to
negotiations. We came out into the sunlight, and all shook hands.
"We'll be in touch," we said.

We looked around us. The location was so remote, in character
if not in distance, from the haunts of our Ivy League carriage-
trade friends that it was as if we were about to set up shop in
Gomorrah, which many of them would no doubt think the neighborhood resembled. The Stuyvesant was not ideal, but it had its
points. It was a long way from Broadway, an asset, we felt. It was
workable. Most important, by dint of some simple, not altogether
accurate, arithmetic, we figured that averaging sixty percent of
capacity at a three-dollar top, we could break even and pay off
production costs in six weeks.

There was a hell of a lot of work to be done before this mon-
strosity could be made habitable, and it was already close to
August. T. Edward and I parted again briefly, I to weekend with
Cassie and John Mason Brown at Stonington. On Saturday eve-
ning their telephone rang: T. Edward Hambleton asking for
Norris.

He'd been talking to Roger Stevens, he reported, and had told
him about the Stuyvesant. Roger had said that if T. would put
up $50,000 and I could match it, which Roger thought I could,
considering the pledges I'd already lined up, he (Roger) would
put up an additional $25,000, because in view of the rehabilitation
we'd have to undertake, he didn't think the $100,000 we had been
talking about would be enough. He thought we should settle on
the Stuyvesant. "I told him I'd agree to my fifty thousand," T.
wound up. "So how about it?"

How could I refuse? Wasn't this the culmination of many
months of working and planning and dreaming? "O.K.," I said.

"I'll see you Monday morning," replied T.

Our lawyers moved into high gear, struck a deal with Raynes,
established the 12th Street Theatre Corporation as a holding company to lease the theatre, drew up limited partnership papers. I

started calling in the pledges I'd gathered eight months earlier. By the end of August the $125,000 was present or accounted for. We planned to budget $25,000 for preliminary expenses, including building improvements, then $25,000 for each of four productions.

Early in September, John Houseman hove into view. He was known to me only slightly but was a close friend of T. Edward's. I had great respect for his accomplishment in creating the Mercury Theatre with Orson Welles. A large, balding man with a florid face and sharp little eyes, exuding self-confidence, Jack appeared, in other words, a good deal as he did thirty years later, when he was recognized by millions. We told him of our problems and our hopes. He was full of encouragement, and, in his silken pseudo-British-accented drawl, he made us an offer; he had wanted for some time to stage Shakespeare's unfamiliar and austere tragedy *Coriolanus*, which, he claimed, hadn't been professionally presented in America since 1885. What's more, he'd been working with a young Hollywood actor who was eager to play the title role—Robert Ryan.

I knew Ryan was a big star, but I couldn't imagine him playing a Roman consul who spoke only blank verse. Houseman reassured me. "He'll be sensational, you'll see. And his profile resembles Caesar's on a Roman coin."

Houseman couldn't deliver this package before January, but that was just as well: *Coriolanus* wouldn't really be an ideal opener but would be a humdinger of a second bill. He would fly back to L.A. next day and tell Ryan at once. He congratulated us on our wisdom in accepting his choices, himself as director and Ryan in the title role.

Toward the end of September I returned to Vermont. I had bought my first piece of real estate there seven years earlier: a small house, a barn, and ten acres of land, for two hundred dollars. An abandoned structure on the brink of collapse, it was in the · township of Calais (pronounced Callous), ten miles north of Montpelier, deep in the poverty-stricken spiny ridge of the state.

To reach it, you followed a lane up a hillside overlooking a valley through which a brook splashed and gurgled. The lane ascended through a daisy-dappled upland meadow past my house, then dropped down the other side of the hill to stumble toward Maple Corner. There the country store cum post office stood, opposite a white clapboard schoolhouse and a handful of modest dwellings shaded by elms and maples. That was as far as the unpaved but well-graded county road led in 1947. Beyond it you struck out into the back country, where tranquillity lay.

For twenty summers this was my cherished retreat. The first two or three years were dedicated to upgrading my property. I had electricity installed in order to drive the pump for the artesian well that had to be drilled. I had the house reroofed, a staircase built so I could turn the loft into two bedrooms; I engaged a local lady schoolteacher gifted at wallpapering to cover Masonite partitions, a bricklayer to build a chimney and two fireplaces, a plumber to create a bathroom and install a kitchen sink. Naturally, I myself did the painting inside and out—the latter a Vermont barn red with white trim. By the time I was finished, my snug little house had five rooms and cost about six thousand dollars.

To soften its barrenness, I planted an apple tree, a birch, and a couple of cedars, and set a blue spruce against the brown creosoted wall of the barn. In front of the house I created a garden within old stone retaining walls. Cow bells wakened me in early morning. At dusk a thrush sang from the woods behind the barn. At night, beginning in August, I could see the pulsing glow of the aurora borealis. It was an idyllic hideaway, far, far from Second Avenue.

At Maple Corner that September I encountered John Latouche, whom I had known since his undergraduate days at Columbia twenty years earlier. Subsequently, recognized as something of a prodigy, he wrote the lyrics for a wonderful Broadway musical, *Cabin in the Sky*, starring Ethel Waters, as well as for *Banjo Eyes*, which starred Eddie Cantor, and he collaborated with Duke Ellington on a modern version of *The Beggars' Opera*. Hambleton had produced his *Ballet Ballads* in 1950.

John told me he'd just acquired a house on the far flank of my hill, perhaps a mile away. That weekend I drove over in my jeep and fetched him back for dinner.

"Touche" was a southern charmer. Small, black-haired, and

black-eyed, with a thin but winning smile when pleased and a childish pout when upset, he possessed a devastating wit, which shone through his writing and gingered his conversation. He made friends and admirers easily, and cast them off with equal ease. He abhorred clichés and was never a bore. I, alas, having a mind that is at home with the cliché, must admit to having frequently been uneasy in his company. But I admired his considerable talent and his not inconsiderable skill in getting on in the world.

Over dinner he regaled me with problems concerning a musical called *The Golden Apple,* which he had written to a score by Jerome Moross. He had peddled it during the past months to many reputable Broadway producers. Although admiring its wit and originality, they unanimously turned it down. "Too special for Broadway," they chorused. The more he told me about it, the more I understood why.

"It's the story of Paris and Helen of Troy," he began. "The golden apple was the prize in ancient mythology that Juno, Minerva, and Venus offered Paris in competing for his favor. Of course, it's also about the Trojan War, with Menelaus and Ajax and Achilles, and especially Ulysses, wandering around for ten years, trying to find their way home. As you'll see, I've changed some of their names. But the real clincher"—here he dropped his voice to a whisper, as he often did when excited,—"is that all the action takes place in the state of Washington during the Spanish-American War. Besides, it's actually an opera—only one spoken line in the whole show."

That, I agreed, was indeed a clincher.

"Jerry has written a marvelous score," Touche went on, and in a voice that did no great justice to his composer, he began to sing a cappella excerpts, ending up with "Lazy Afternoon."

"Jerry has worked it all out in sonata form and scored it for twenty-four instruments, but that could be cut to sixteen or eighteen. You've got to see Bill and Jean Eckart's sketches for sets and costumes," he concluded. "You'll adore them. Such imagination! Such style!"

"Hold on," I cried. "You mean the show is all designed, the score orchestrated already?"

"Exactly," he replied. "And Hanya Holm loves it and is ready to do the choreography. It could go into rehearsal in three weeks or sooner, depending on how long it takes to cast."

"And how long it takes to raise the money," I reflected.

"But money will be no problem in the setup you've described," Latouche replied amiably. "It would probably cost two hundred fifty or three hundred thousand on Broadway, but you say you can produce for a quarter of Broadway's figure. You really must do *The Golden Apple.*"

"You certainly do make it sound extraordinary," I said cautiously.

"It *is* extraordinary!" he cried. "You must tell T. Edward right away. I'll get the Eckarts to show you their portfolio, and Jerry and I will audition it for you next week. I'm sure you can raise the money overnight."

I was dubious about that. What Touche had described could never be done on Broadway for a quarter million, I calculated, and we probably couldn't do it for sixty thousand. But even if we could, that was more than double the sum we'd budgeted for each production. Still, I had a hunch we'd be wise to take Touche seriously; there certainly would be no harm in hearing the score and looking at the drawings. I jeeped him back over the hill and agreed to talk again on Monday.

As I lay in bed I thought it over. Obviously, we couldn't and shouldn't open with this musical. But the fact that Broadway managers had turned it down only whetted my appetite. What a coup if we could pull it off! If we could follow a Shakespearean tragedy with a contemporary musical comedy, what a piece of programming!

The Vermont night was nippy. I pulled up another blanket and fell asleep.

In the next few weeks pressures grew rapidly, as we began to realize the horrendously complex job we faced. We resolved to open just before Thanksgiving or as soon thereafter as possible. Thus, we had ten weeks to rehabilitate the Stuyvesant; decide about Latouche's musical, and if affirmatively, figure out where to get the extra money and how to organize its production; line up our executive staff (general manager, press agent, secretarial assistance, technical director); consummate deals with unions; choose an opening play; select a director, a designer, and leading actors for it; and think of a name for the theatre. All these matters had to be dealt with simultaneously. Fortunately, we had been theatrical pros in New York for the better part of twenty years; no one could say we were babes in the woods.

At the end of one afternoon spent at Twelfth Street with building contractors and Broadway designer Donald Oenslager, who had unexpectedly agreed—for friendship's sake and no fee— to oversee the interior redecoration of our dreadnought, T. and I walked uptown, pausing for a beer at Pete's Tavern on Irving Place at Eighteenth Street.

"Let's not stall any longer: let's settle on a name," we agreed.

"We want to have something that has connotations of the past but at the same time is unexpected. Maybe something with an *x* in it," I hazarded.

T. paused, a smile dawning. "How about Phoenix?"

"That's it!" I shouted. In three minutes we had made a decision we never regretted.

Hume Cronyn was an old friend. In 1936 we had worked together in Maxwell Anderson's *High Tor,* in which he had played an amateur bank robber. Subsequently Hume had had the taste and good fortune to woo and win Jessica Tandy, one of the toasts of London's West End. Both T. and I admired the Cronyn's artistry, intelligence, humor. They were exactly the kind of performers we wanted. In early September we began conversations with them about appearing in our opening production for six weeks. What should it be?

On the first Monday in October, with now only eight weeks to go, Hambleton returned from a weekend in Maryland with an idea from Louis Azrael, one of Baltimore's more astute drama critics. T. had asked Azrael for suggestions for an opener. Louis recalled being charmed by a Sidney Howard comedy-fantasy, starring George M. Cohan, which had tried out in Baltimore fourteen years earlier. Mr. Cohan, apparently less charmed than Azrael, had bowed out before the Broadway opening, which then had had to be postponed. That summer of 1939, Howard had died and the Playwrights' Company had quietly shelved the play. "You and Norris should get your hands on it," urged Azrael. "I think it's what you're looking for. It's called *Madam, Will You Walk?*"

We called Harold Freedman, Sidney Howard's agent, and asked to see him at once. He was one of the most powerful behind-the-scenes men of Broadway. Knowing everyone of importance, he could bring writers, producers, stars, and theatre owners together for the benefit of all concerned. Harold immediately gave us a copy of *Madam* with his blessing. The posthumous premiere of a new play by a Pulitzer Prize winner would command considerable attention. The author of *They Knew What They Wanted, Yellow Jack, The Silver Cord,* and other hits of the 1920s and '30s could not be taken lightly. Furthermore, his play captivated us.

We rushed the script to the Cronyns, begging them to read it before going to bed. They called in the morning: they, too, were enthusiastic. Not your conventional drawing room comedy, the play rather reminded me (and perhaps Hume too) of *High Tor*.

Before noon Freedman was on the phone, as was his way. In his very soft voice, hardly audible, he asked: What did we think of it? Had we sent it to the Cronyns? Their reaction? As for himself, he whispered, he'd talked to Robert Sherwood, who, apparently, was an informal literary executor for Howard; Sherwood liked the idea. Harold had also called the author's widow, Polly; she, too, appeared to be favorably disposed toward us, inexperienced producers though we were. All of this had occurred within forty-eight hours.

The week that had started off so propitiously careened along at an accelerating pace. We posed our problems to a joint "fact-finding committee" of the theatrical unions. Although larger than many Broadway playhouses, we were certainly not in the Times Square area. Furthermore, our proposed price scale would take in at maximum less than half the grosses uptown. We wanted to employ Equity actors and union stagehands, scenic artists, and musicians, but, obviously, we couldn't afford them at Broadway scale. What could they do to help? There were no precedents.

They would consult their respective brotherhoods and consider the issues. Perhaps each union should propose its own solution. Eventually that's what happened.

We met with candidates for staff positions. First, we asked Carl Fisher, George Abbott's very capable general manager of *This Is the Army* and other shows, to serve as ours. We lined up an experienced press agent, Sol Jacobson, and Robert Woods, of Theatre Inc., as technical director. Everyone accepted at the minimum salaries their unions would allow. We recruited young Dorothy Blass, who wore loose blouses and pendant brass earrings and who I suspected had gypsy blood, as our executive secretary and general preserver of the peace. She and Bob Woods stayed with us for ten hectic years.

We auditioned *The Golden Apple* and went to the Eckarts' to see their portfolio. Enchanted by these sounds and sights, we began to arrange backers' auditions. We met with our law firm, Paul, Weiss, Rifkind, Wharton and Garrison, and with Roger Stevens to see how we could produce a $75,000 musical (its estimated cost) for $25,000 (our budgetary limit). We discovered that, of course, it couldn't be done, but the impossible can, infrequently, become possible, and so it was with *The Golden Apple.*

We met with the Cronyns to select a director for *Madam, Will You Walk?* and talk about a supporting cast. Norman Lloyd, an alumnus of the Mercury Theatre, was invited to codirect with Hume and to play a role; he accepted. Donald Oenslager had already agreed to design a unit set, which we hoped could be adapted to subsequent productions. (It turned out that it could not.) The rest of the cast was assembled; outstanding among them was Susan Steele, a well-upholstered character actress, who was to play Jessica's Irish aunt. Swathed in chiffon scarves, she made wavering entrances from time to time. During rehearsals we interpreted her wavers as reflecting the Celtic mysticism of her character. It appeared on opening night, however, that the wavering was not part of her characterization but derived from excessive exercise with a bottle in her dressing room. The young producers thus had to face her dismissal, the first painful act of their managerial careers.

3

On December 1, 1953, the Phoenix Theatre opened. This was "the most important event of the theatrical year," wrote John Chapman in his volume *Theatre 54*. What by Broadway standards could almost be described as a glittering audience made its somewhat timorous way down to the Lower East Side of Manhattan, a stone's throw from the Bowery, in those days the city's favorite gathering place for bums and derelicts.

Our backbone supporters included professional colleagues and friends—fifty-three partners in all—who, having been wheedled out of portions of gold, showed up for the opening to demonstrate their support, as well as to satisfy their curiosity concerning this widely heralded nativity. Among them were Howard Lindsay, Russel Crouse, Jo Mielziner, Donald Oenslager, Oscar Hammerstein II, Robert Whitehead, Clinton Wilder, Peggy Wood, Mildred Dunnock, William Inge, Arthur Miller (and their spouses where appropriate).

The opening night audience was, obviously, the first to be treated to Donald Oenslager's face-lift. He had repainted the interior a soft deep beige, slipcovered the orchestra seats in lighter beige with scarlet piping, and carpeted the aisles in red. A handsome red velvet house curtain hung in the proscenium. The downstairs lounge was painted Chinese red, its floor of black and white linoleum tile. The total cost was not much more than ten thousand dollars.

After the performance, Hambleton and Houghton entertained the cast, backers, and special guests in the downstairs lounge. We could not spare money for a Broadway-style celebration at a swank hotel or supper club. Anyhow, by definition the place to hold a housewarming is in your own new home. About midnight someone turned a radio on to full volume, and we listened to the CBS program "Music Till Dawn."

An exciting and new theatrical adventure was born tonight amidst laughter and the hearty applause of twelve hundred enthusiastic people who had stirred from their television sets to see a very witty and provocative play by Sidney Howard.

The evening was exciting in another way, however, because it saw a theatre which had been dark brought to light—brought to life again. . . . When the lights are on at The Phoenix—and you are the only ones who can keep them on—there's theatre magic in abundance to be heard and seen and enjoyed. We tell you all this because there will be no papers tomorrow morning for you to read this in.

That last frightening sentence was true. The Phoenix opened on the eve of the first newspaper strike Manhattan had experienced in more years than any of us could remember. We had no time, let alone money, to take ads on television and radio, and this was before TV stations employed on-the-spot staff critics. The strike lasted two weeks: it meant a blackout on reviews, and no way even to communicate our street address or the box office telephone number.

At the last curtain call on Wednesday, the second night, I emerged from the wings, thanked the audience for their applause, and hoped that they had enjoyed themselves. The play had received rave notices in White Plains, Montclair, Great Neck—even in the *Cleveland Plain Dealer*. But nobody here in town knew about it, because of the strike. We needed their help, I entreated. Would they please spread the word? We didn't want to die aborning. At every performance that week T. and I alternated in making this earnest appeal. On Saturday night every one of our 1,180 seats was sold. What a testimony to the power of word of mouth!

Coriolanus went into rehearsal three weeks later. Robert Ryan's did indeed look like the face on a Roman coin, but to my ears he sounded like an Irish cop from Queens who was taking speech lessons from Frances Robinson-Duff, then a fashionable coach. He was nonetheless a very conscientious and sweet fellow, quite unlike his tough-guy image.

The surprise of the production was the presence of Mildred Natwick as Volumnia, the grim, imperious mother of Coriolanus. She had never played Shakespeare before, but there she was, looking more like a slightly buxom prison matron in gray woolens than the hero's imperious mother. There was a slight edge to her voice, suggesting surprise at finding herself in this "fix." Volumnia—the epitome of a Roman matriarch—was not a role for which she, who had created Noel Coward's hilarious Madame Arcati in *Blithe Spirit* on Broadway, was ideally suited. Millie never essayed Shakespeare again, which was too bad.

Coriolanus rehearsals proceeded in the confident hands of Houseman, whose forte was staging, at which he was quite effective, but whose weakness turned out to be coping with actors' problems, about which he appeared to know very little. Among those actors were Gene Saks, Jerry Stiller, and John Emery.

The play opened in mid-January 1954. Ward Morehouse, in the *New York World-telegram & Sun,* declared it was "one of the finest Shakespearean productions I've seen in a lifetime of playgoing." Business was good enough to warrant extending the run two weeks, thus providing needed extra time for the Twelfth Street novices to cope with the intricacies of their full-scale musical. It took nerve to advance into the heavily mined field of musical theatre, but we had more nerve than sense in those days, and luck was with us. So were Roger Stevens and Alfred de Liagre as coproducers.

Many cooks are needed to stir the broth that becomes a successful musical. While in the evenings T. and I kept watchful eyes on the run of *Coriolanus*, by day we listened to singing rehearsals conducted by musical director Hugh Ross—an unlikely assignment for the conductor of the prestigious New York Schola Cantorum—and watched dance rehearsals presided over by Hanya Holm, and we checked on progress in the scene and costume shops. As producers we were learning the necessity for keeping our heads when all about were losing theirs.

Slowly the pieces began to come together, however, and we knew we had a good show. Our actor-songsters, led by Kaye Ballard, Stephen Douglass, Priscilla Gillette, Portia Nelson, Bibi Osterwald, Jack Whiting—indeed, the whole jubilant ensemble of dancer-singers—were of top quality. When *The Golden Apple* opened on May 11, we were not really surprised by its reception. "A light, gay, charming production . . . the only literate new musical of the season," announced Brooks Atkinson next morning.

In the interests of accuracy, a few nay-sayers must be recorded: Wolcott Gibbs of *The New Yorker*, quoting from Scott Fitzgerald, wrote, "Oh, I like her, except not very much." George Jean Nathan backhanded us with his judgment that the Phoenix "is to be more greatly commended for its ambition than for its achievement." And there was the reaction of Nicholas de Liagre, aged five, attending his first theatre performance, a matinee with his mother and little sister. At one point, he was heard to whisper politely but urgently, "May one vomit?"

The general public accepted the verdict of the *New York Post:* "It is certainly no exaggeration to describe it as the best new musical comedy of the season." And, indeed, the New York Drama Critics' Circle voted *The Golden Apple* the Best New Musical of the 1953–54 season. For six weeks we sold out. Our partners, Stevens and de Liagre, decided it might work on Broadway after all and moved it. So before its first season had come to an end, the Phoenix had a musical on Broadway, at the Alvin Theatre on Fifty-second Street, for fourteen weeks, running simultaneously with Chekhov's *The Seagull* downtown.

In 1954 Montgomery Clift was already a Hollywood superstar. He had just completed *From Here to Eternity*. In late winter Bob Whitehead told us that Clift was in town, working on a version of *The Seagull* with two of his cronies, actor Kevin McCarthy and a mystery woman named Mira Rostova. Bob urged us to check the rumor; if true, the Phoenix would be an ideal place for them. Certainly Clift would be the jewel in our crown; and we had no final production yet scheduled.

Our first season consisted of a series of improvisations. Three months before we opened, not a single production was set. And when we did open, we had no idea how to end the season. This kind of hand-to-mouth operation I do not recommend. It is too rash, too unadvised, too sudden. Save for a beneficent Providence, I can't imagine how we could ever have put together a four-play cycle.

I'd known Monty Clift for fifteen years, since he had played in *Dame Nature,* whose settings I had designed for the Theatre Guild. He was eighteen then—one of the most talented and attractive teenagers to grace the American theatre in my lifetime. We were not close friends in those earlier days, but I knew him well enough to appreciate his sensitivity, his intellectual capacity, unexpected in one so young, and the warmth of his enthusiasms. It was a delight to be in his company and a delight to watch him grow.

After the war we had met often, for he was attracted to the ideas Theatre Inc. stood for, and we had many intense discussions. Then he had gone to California to build a screen career, and his New York friends saw him less and less, or at least this one did.

I called Monty and made a date. He greeted me at his brownstone on East Sixty-first Street with effusive affection, throwing his arms around me, like old times, and led me into a white-walled living room, unexpectedly rather empty and curiously devoid of charm. After a bit I brought up the Phoenix and talked of its mission to provide a chance for artists like himself to do a play that especially attracted them, performing it for a limited run. Monty got the idea at once and confirmed Whitehead's rumor. Mira Rostova, a Russian, was providing a literal translation, which he and Kevin then reworked into dialogue both playable and pliable. "How about doing it with us in May for six weeks?" I asked. He said he must first talk with Kevin and Mira. They had agreed to do it together—as Treplev, Trigorin, and Nina—or not at all. I knew Kevin and considered him capable; of Mira I knew nothing.

"You must meet—you'll love her," Monty cried. "She's terrifically talented, the most marvelous help to me in California. My growth in acting is all due to her. She understands truth." I wanted to ask "What *is* truth?" but refrained. I should perhaps wait and ask Mira.

I cautioned Monty that our salary was Equity's one-hundred-dollar-a-week minimum and billing was alphabetical. He brushed these aside. Did he have a director in mind? I asked. He hesitated, then said if Arthur Miller was available, he'd choose him. I was astonished. As far as I knew, Arthur had directed nothing he hadn't written himself. "But I'm not sure he'd do it," Monty added dubiously. Asked subsequently, Miller declined but offered to stand by to help as needed.

I was determined to like Mira. I invited her and Monty to tea at the Coffee House. We sat before an open fire. She was small, looked much younger than I knew she must be, and seemed rather shy. She wore a becoming little fur toque. I thought perhaps she was pretending to *be* Nina. I wooed her with all the charm I could summon. I talked of my experiences in Moscow, of my association with Stanislavski. She grew livelier as the conversation proceeded. Monty, too, as though taking his cue from her, became more relaxed.

So it transpired that *The Seagull,* with Clift, was announced as the final production of our season. There remained the decision about a director and also the fourth principal—Madame Arkadina.

Study of the play had persuaded me that it was built around four equally important characters, each dominating one act. Treplev, the young writer, is the focus of the first; the spotlight shifts to Trigorin, the established older author, in the second; Treplev's mother, the actress Arkadina, becomes central to the third; and Nina, the "seagull," dominates the fourth. An arbitrary oversimplification of a highly complex drama, I grant, but my point here is that the play requires four equally gifted actors; it's not a vehicle for any one star.

Somewhat diffidently I suggested myself as director and was gratified when Clift approved. Throughout this adventure my relationship with him was an ambiguous one. *The Seagull* was his idea; the theatre was ours. He wanted to do the play; we wanted to have him. He was a Hollywood star, now at the peak of his power, as he was quite aware, and despite his camaraderie and modesty, he knew what he wanted. Therefore, I recognized that if we were to work in harmony, he must be treated with care: I was never to forget he was more valuable to the Phoenix than it was to him. For his part, he recognized the delicacy of my position. From his years on the stage he knew the deference due a director, especially one he had known so long and whose efforts he respected. Almost automatically we became collaborators.

In this spirit we proceeded with casting, I encouraging him to take the initiative, especially with the principal roles. For Arkadina his first choice was Marlene Dietrich. I was startled, to say the least.

"I'm serious," said Monty. "We've become great friends and talked in Hollywood of wanting to work together. Here's the chance: a limited engagement in a great play. Besides," he added, "I think she'd be a wonderful Arkadina. Any objections to my talking to her?"

"None," I said, but when he did, Dietrich's response was for me not altogether unexpected: "Thanks—but no, thanks."

His next candidate was, I thought, brilliant: Stella Adler. She had the temperament, panache, emotional fire, and physical power that the part requires—and just the touch of phoniness too. I believed she understood, better than any of us, how to play Arkadina. We went together to see her, took her a script, knelt at her feet. She was flattered and intrigued, promised to give it serious consideration, but wanted a few days to decide. When she had done so, Stella summoned us, on a memorable afternoon. She was wearing black chiffon and looked a dozen years younger than her age. Her golden hair glittered in the setting sun. After a little vocalizing, she came to the point.

"Darlings," she said, "I want very much to play this part, but I am going to turn you down. I must be honest with you. I haven't been on the stage for ten years. I've become a legend. I'm afraid to take the chance. I'm not even sure I could do it—even memorize the lines."

We protested loudly, but she was adamant. With deep regret we said goodbye to Stella Adler. She never did act again on the American stage, and a legend she remains.

While continuing our search for Arkadina, we proceeded with the rest of the casting. Maureen Stapleton was our choice for Masha, and she accepted. Veteran June Walker agreed to take the role of Paulina. We approached a trio of fine character actors to play the Doctor, the Uncle, and the Estate Manager—George Voskovec, Sam Jaffe, and Will Geer. They, too, agreed, as did young John Fiedler when offered the part of Medvedenko, Masha's schoolteacher suitor/husband.

Finally a casting agent suggested Judith Evelyn for Arkadina. A leading lady since before the war, she'd made a name for herself as Mrs. Manningham in *Angel Street*, opposite Vincent Price.

Judith seemed a sound choice, even though I had some doubts as to whether, not being a "Method" actress, she knew what "truth" was any more than I did. She was then in Hollywood but could return just in time for rehearsals, now only two weeks away. We signed her. At the last minute, her movie required some retakes, delaying her arrival by four or five days. I was loath to start without her, and consequently we didn't begin rehearsals until April 15. The opening had been announced for May 11. We should have postponed, but we didn't.

While waiting for Judith, Monty and I embarked on private sessions at his house to explore various key scenes. During this period I became increasingly aware of his instability. Frequently I arrived to find him in a highly manic state. Once, I rang his bell, he answered the door and at once excused himself elaborately: he was on the telephone to Elizabeth Taylor in California. Their conversation continued for half an hour. He came back, all apologies, offered me a drink, and poured himself a strong slug. I had the feeling it was not his first that day.

I was totally unfamiliar with symptoms of drug abuse. Later, in biographies of Clift, I read that this was what I had been up against. At the time, I attributed his high-strung state to increasing anxiety as we approached rehearsals. After all, a lot was at stake for him: this was his first stage appearance since he had achieved Hollywood stardom. None of us could guess that it was to be his last.

It indeed proved a mistake not to postpone the opening. Three and one half weeks is a ridiculously short time to explore properly the multiple levels and the "subtext" of a Chekhov play and to bring it to performance pitch. Clift, McCarthy, and Rostova had, however, been working together for months, and because so many of the critical scenes involved only them, in duets and trios, I felt safe at first with the reduced schedule. I was wrong.

There was tension from the opening rehearsal. Everyone realized, I think, that we faced a play that we feared we couldn't do justice to in such a short time; most of us being both experienced and perfectionists, we became anxious—and anxiety is just what rehearsals must avoid. Moreover, at first the project's three instigators, feeling a proprietary concern, held themselves somewhat aloof from the rest of the cast.

I had heard rumors from Hollywood that Mira exercised some curious psychological hold over Monty: he seemed incapable of judging his own work without consulting her. At his insistence, I was told, she would sit behind the camera, and at the end of each take Monty would look at her; if she nodded, they would continue; if not, Monty would demand a retake.

Similar carryings-on began to develop early in our rehearsals and became enormously disturbing to me. But on the stage, things were a bit different. Much of the time she couldn't sit behind me—she was in the scene herself, playing opposite him. For the first time, I believe, he began to suspect that she was a better coach than performer and, as a result, began to lose confidence in her. He began to question his own capacities, as well—and mine.

Once, late in rehearsals, we were running the scene in the fourth act after Nina has gone out into the storm. Konstantin stands alone, considering in a brief soliloquy his failure in art and life. Monty turned away and addressed an upstage window, muttering the lines sotto voice, then he sat down at his desk and proceeded methodically to tear up his manuscripts, preparatory to committing suicide. (The stage business is Chekhov's.)

I went up to him after the scene and said quietly, "Monty, I can't hear you. I can't see you. That is the key speech in the scene, the turning point in your action. You can't throw it away."

He knew, he said, but it was a very personal, very private moment. He couldn't bring himself to share it, waving his hand toward the absent spectators.

"But that's an actor's first obligation—to share," I ventured. Well, he'd try, he replied, as if unconvinced.

And after we opened, there were many in the audience who complained that Clift couldn't be heard past the sixth row. "And neither can she." I agreed, but I seemed unable to persuade Monty and Mira that a stage performance should never be a closet experience.

Monty asked me to invite Arthur Miller and Thornton Wilder to run-throughs. They came, but they, too, seemed incapable of helping him. Arthur, for instance, after watching the second act, spoke eloquently and illuminatingly for fifteen minutes about Trigorin's great speech on the agony of being a second-rate writer, but he mentioned Monty's work not at all. All our avenues of communication seemed to be constricting.

At no rehearsal, at no performance I witnessed, however, did Monty appear to be under the influence of alcohol or drugs. He was punctual, well-mannered, and apparently in control. Indeed, what I have just written about his anxiety may partly reflect subconscious or even conscious anxieties of my own.

Ironically, *The Seagull* was the hit it was bound to be. As soon as tickets went on sale, lines formed around the block. It sold out for five weeks, closing in mid-June because an early intense heat wave made our theatre, which lacked air-conditioning, uninhabitable—and also because Monty himself was exhausted and disillusioned.

The notices had been mixed: John Chapman had been full of enthusiasm: ". . . one of the three or four most exciting and most satisfying performances in a year of playgoing." John Mason Brown had been more to the point: "Everyone knows it takes time and a lot of it for a group of actors to master Chekhov. All too plainly the product at the Phoenix has been thrown together in a hurry. . . . The styles of playing are as mixed as the accents of the players." Walter Kerr had written: "Actors pass through. But somehow or other they do not meet, they evoke no mood, they leave nothing lingering behind them." I agreed. *The Seagull* was clearly a disappointment. The first triumphant Phoenix season ended, I thought, with a dying fall.

Despite *The Seagull*, T. and I felt rather pleased. I tried to put my own failure with Chekhov toward the back of my mind, rationalizing that this was my first try at staging anything by that subtly ambiguous Russian, that none of my actors had ever played Chekhov before, and that we had so little time. By June I was also probably much more mentally, physically, and emotionally spent than I realized, having been buoyed up by the nervous excitement of the past nine months. What I had to do was to rest, take stock, and begin again.

I went to Vermont for as much of that summer as possible. I had discovered my hideaway there thanks to Robert Woods. He had already acquired, on the hilltop just above me, another abandoned homestead, his surrounded by sixty-five acres. It looked out as far to the east as the White Mountains of New Hampshire, a thin blue line against the sky on clear days; to the west it faced Mount Hunger and behind it Mount Mansfield.

Jointly we bought a jeep; together we would jounce up and down the lane that connected our adjacent properties, and over to Maple Corner at the end of the day, to collect mail, stock up on victuals, and, before we had telephones, pick up messages from the outside world.

It's time to amplify my words about Bob, who remained my next-door neighbor in Vermont throughout my twenty years there. I've already spoken of him in the context of Theatre Inc. and the Phoenix. When he died in 1978, I lost my oldest and closest friend, a relationship I cherished for almost forty-five years.

We met in June 1934 at a summer theatre in Maine where I was the scenic designer, he by chance my assistant. His name then was Wilbur Wertz. He had recently celebrated his twenty-second birthday, and this was his first professional job. I was on my way to twenty-five, and also, in six weeks, to Europe on my Guggenheim. Wilbur, from South Carolina, had an accent as softly southern as Scarlett O'Hara's, albeit his was in a boyish baritone. Slender and of medium height, he had a quick, rather impish smile and a sense of humor that responded to mine. Wilbur knew more about scenery than I expected and was also a whiz at carpentry, a gift I certainly lacked. I also discovered that he had exceedingly good taste. I considered myself lucky to have him at my right hand. He, in turn, found that he had a boss he liked and respected and did not have to fear.

The six weeks passed like a summer breeze. I caught the State of Maine express down to New York on August 12 and on the fifteenth boarded the SS *Manhattan*. Since I'd not be back for a year, I carried a snapshot of Wilbur in my wallet, for I meant not to forget him.

When I returned to New York, in the late summer of 1935, I found that Actors' Equity had persuaded Wilbur to change his name to Robert Woods. Nothing else had changed, however, and we proceeded to pick up where we had left off. Bob (né Wilbur) and I shared an apartment for the next three years, until he went off to Ridgefield to join the Michael Chekhov Theatre Studio.

Our brief years together in New York were tumultuous. Beneath Bobby's southern drawl lay a violent temper, which manifested itself in throwing things. Since I had learned that the best defense is a good offense, I threw things back. So it was that we managed to keep our apartment uncluttered by breakables, they being destroyed almost as soon as they were replaced.

In those days I was designing scenery for Beckhard flops (not by intent but by misfortune). When the plays closed on Saturday nights, the management went off with the most desirable props; the designer usually got his choice of what remained, before the production was carried away to Cain's Warehouse, the graveyard of now useless scenery. Because several of the plays called for period rooms, I was able to make one or two decent hauls.

I garnered a particularly rich collection from a flop called *Wife Insurance;* it starred Ilka Chase, who should have known better. I chose the furnishings with my own apartment's color scheme in mind, for from the first I sensed the play would not last long. At season's end I read in *Stage* that the one-set interior of *Wife Insurance* had been voted "Worst Scenery of the Year." I think it was the puce walls and white corduroy-covered furniture that did it. The latter, however, looked quite good in my living room, I always thought.

Now, in the summer of 1954, we sat on Bob's hilltop or my lawn after the dinners we frequently shared, looking at the stars and reminiscing—not about the old days but about the Phoenix season just ended and what lessons were to be learned from it.

Since Bob's forte was the backstage operation he commanded, we discussed, for example, Oenslager's unit set. It was intended to serve every need: an inner portal flanked by proscenium doors, movable flat pieces of scenery upstage that could be plugged or opened to accommodate windows, doors, fireplaces, as required—à la Jacques Copeau. The scheme worked more or less acceptably for *Madam, Will You Walk?* and very effectively for *Coriolanus* but not for *The Golden Apple,* and it was too severely stylized for the realistic environment that Chekhov needs. The unit set was to be abandoned after a couple of further tries.

We wondered whether it would be a good idea to change designers from play to play, to allow the same diversity that changing directors and actors provided. And with new productions coming up every six weeks, how about a permanent stage managerial staff? Perhaps we also should add a casting director and a "dramaturg," or literary consultant. Such momentous matters we debated under the aurora borealis.

4

Despite transportation problems between Calais and New York, I returned to the city for two or three days each week, usually to rendezvous with Hambleton. Our relationship was unusual. No document of any kind bound us; we never set down job descriptions. Many people were subsequently to think that T. was the administrator, I the artistic leader. Indeed, Stuart W. Little wrote of us in his book *Off Broadway: The Prophetic Theatre*, "the partnership was to prove remarkably stable, trusting and cheerful, in some respects without parallel in the modern theatre," and then went on to say that "Houghton took priority in artistic matters, Hambleton in business matters."

The fact is, we were inextricably bound up in both "matters." Finances necessarily affected artistic decisions and vice versa. We gave ourselves no titles at first because we had no wish to differentiate between our roles. We shared all responsibilities, artistic and administrative. We *were* the Phoenix Theatre.

Subsequently, when our corporate structure changed, we became managing directors. By common consent we developed a mutual veto: only if both of us were in favor of a project did we undertake it. It was only because our judgments and our tastes were so closely compatible that we kept things "stable, trusting and cheerful." A mere marriage of convenience it never was.

As summer wound down, two things were of paramount importance: to put our financial house in order and to decide on at least the first two or three productions of the new season. Financially we were not in too bad shape: of our original $125,000 we still had $85,000 in the bank. What to do with the money was of greater importance.

On the whole, so far we had done what we had said we wanted to do: we'd demonstrated an interest in both classics and new works, given opportunities to distinguished actors to perform, not for lucre but for love, maintained a $3.30 top, and drawn audiences of sharp-witted flies who thought we had produced a pretty good batch of honey. But we were experienced enough to know we could neither rest on our laurels nor hope to hit an artistic jackpot regularly.

In our second season, we once again seemed to develop our program mostly by improvisation; we continued to be drawn to diversity. We started off by presenting the world premiere of *Sing Me No Lullaby*, a comedy with serious overtones by a young American, Robert Ardrey, who would gain subsequent fame through his socioanthropological works, *African Genesis* and *Territorial Imperative*. *Sing Me No Lullaby*, although graced by the presence of Richard Kiley and Beatrice Straight, didn't, alas, have a sweet enough refrain. Indeed, *Daily News* readers were disconsolately advised: "Jes' go see it, honey chile, and you don't need no lullaby." We closed after three weeks, a brave but not very cheerful start.

Having been dazzled by the success of *The Golden Apple*, Hambleton and Houghton were not averse to trying another musical. So our next offering was *Sandhog*, about the men who built tunnels under rivers. They had been the heroes of a short story by Theodore Dreiser, "St. Columba and the River." Waldo Salt adapted it into the book for a musical, with a score supplied by Earl Robinson. It was brought to us by Howard Da Silva and Arnold Perl, who owned the rights but, at least partly because they were victims of the McCarthy witch hunts, were unable to generate a production on their own. We agreed to present it "by special arrangement" with them and have Da Silva direct.

If you were hunting for an offbeat musical, *Sandhog* was the perfect animal. Take its settings alone: half the action took place above ground in the tenements, streets, and parks of lower New York in the 1880s, the other half in the first tunnel being built under the Hudson River.

We asked designer Howard Bay to reconcile the two images.

He succeeded only partially. There was no contrast between light and dark—it was always murky, both above and below ground. Possibly, too, Da Silva overly stressed the proletarian struggle he saw as underpinning the action, and thereby added to the sense of darkness. An unreconstructed leftist of the Union Square vintage, he was also a fine artist, and the production had its champions. For, its politics aside, *Sandhog* presented a fascinating juxtaposition of roughhouse and lyricism, owing in large part to a mellifluous score, set against the Irish boisterousness of its male characters, who were figuratively and literally on the brink of being engulfed.

As early as the middle of our second season, the huge size of our theatre became a matter of concern. There were a number of offbeat, even avant-garde, projects we wanted to develop, but with such theatre fare twelve hundred seats were too many to expect to fill eight times a week. Thus we came up with a series of "Sideshows" for single Monday nights when our house was dark.

That rarely seen Jacobean tragedy of John Webster, *The White Devil*, directed by Jack Landau, with nineteen characters and seven sets, we presented on a bare stage in modern dress, on a budget of fifty dollars. It was a tempest of an evening, ending with cheers that shook the chandelier. We repeated it the following Monday to a sold-out house. I wished that we had tried *The Changeling* too.

For Stravinsky's "music drama" *L'Histoire du Soldat*, our next Sideshow, we put together a company that included Erich Leinsdorf as conductor, an orchestral ensemble of seven headed by Alexander Schneider, Franchot Tone as the Narrator, Paul Draper dancing the part of the Soldier, Edward Caton as the Devil, and Janice Rule as the Princess—truly an elite ensemble. In all, our second season, counting Sideshows and major productions, brought nine offerings to the Phoenix stage.

Others were less impressed with our accomplishments than we. A number began to ask, "What are those boys trying to do?" I attempted to answer them in a *New York Times* Sunday piece. (The paper was very generous to us with space, I must say.)

If the Phoenix doesn't seem to have any easily discernible policy or platform, it is, I suppose, because Hambleton and I are not platform types. We both seem to be catholic in our tastes and we believe the stage has many potentials and many functions, no one of which seems to us all-important nor yet unimportant.

I was much given to pompous generalities in those days.

As a practical matter, we didn't want to do only classics, because that might have drawn us away from our contemporaries. Nor could we even think of becoming addicted solely to current works, because we knew that we could not compete against Broadway for the most stageworthy new scripts, and we certainly didn't know enough about music and dance to make ours a full-fledged lyric theatre. Finally, and frankly, we enjoyed what we'd done, and if others thought us too idiosyncratic or wanted us to conform to their ideas of how to run a theatre, our response was to suggest they start their own. Dozens and dozens did so almost at once and in the years that followed. All we had wanted to do was open a door; we didn't expect it to be a Pandora's box.

A preseason Sideshow, a two-week run of Marcel Marceau's one-man show, ushered in the Phoenix's 1955–56 stanza. Like the majority of New Yorkers, T. and I had never heard of that extraordinary artist until, in a reversal of roles, *Times* critic Brooks Atkinson brought him to our attention. Brooks knew about the great French mime, who was then in Canada, and shared his discovery, urging us to book him at once, sight unseen. Ever cautious, T. Edward flew to Montreal and came away joining in Atkinson's enthusiasm.

Marceau was, of course, triumphant. Every seat was sold after the second performance, and the Phoenix moved him to the Barrymore Theatre uptown for another fortnight. We now claimed we were international impresarios—Twelfth Street Huroks.

"Tony Guthrie sends his regards and says to tell you he's heard you're doing *Six Characters in Search of an Author,* and if you would like him to direct, he'd be delighted to do so."

This unexpected message was borne to us by Michael Langham, just appointed successor to Tyrone Guthrie as artistic director of the Stratford Shakespearean Festival of Canada. He stopped at the Phoenix office one October morning in 1955, our third season, not as Guthrie's emissary but just to get acquainted.

We had been having troubles with the Pirandello play, and Guthrie may have heard about them. The preceding spring we'd invited Fredric March and Florence Eldridge to appear in it in the fall. They were intrigued, so we proceeded to set rehearsal schedules and engaged Albert Marre to direct. September, however, brought for us disappointing news: Freddie had been offered a Hollywood movie, and since his Phoenix salary would have totaled six hundred dollars, he really couldn't afford to turn down a sixty-thousand-dollar picture offer. Obviously, and sadly, we had to let him go. Soon thereafter came the second blow: Marre withdrew to take over direction of Enid Bagnold's *The Chalk Garden,* in trouble on its pre-Broadway tour. That a director of Guthrie's international stature offered to take Marre's place was incredibly good luck.

We had heard that Guthrie was to be in New York that autumn to restage his London production of *The Matchmaker* for David Merrick on Broadway. What we didn't know was that the premiere had to be delayed by a few weeks. To Tony the prospect of even brief idleness was intolerable; so why not offer his services in behalf of a play he knew and loved?

I had met him a couple of times before. In the founding days of Theatre Inc., he had appeared at Beatrice Straight's house one afternoon to delight and inspire our original board with tales of Lillian Baylis and her aunt, Emma Cons, and their Old Vic's early days. He always seemed present when some new stage project was aborning or some old one was in trouble.

In London a year later, in 1946, I had been initiated into the Guthries' exotic ménage, a small flat inexplicably situated deep in the Inns of Court, where he, Judith, his handsome, chain-smoking wife, and I spent a hilarious evening among the cats and piles of unwashed crockery, opening tins of salmon and drinking tea and alternating it with gin.

When Dr. Guthrie appeared on any scene, things began to

hum, and so they did on lower Second Avenue. Our first problem was finding an acceptable text. Tony had arrived with his own version, but the Pirandello estate in Rome felt it was far too free an adaptation and would have none of it; through Marre we ourselves were committed to a Brattle Theatre version arranged by Michael Wager. The matter was resolved by wedding the Wager version to Guthrie's, which was forthwith done to the satisfaction, somewhat surprisingly, of all.

Next came the challenge of casting. Big-name actors per se had no great attraction for Guthrie. He would much prefer a talented youngster whom he could mold or an obscure colleague to an established star. Consequently, for our Phoenix production he assembled a company that contained several "good" names but no "big" ones.

Because Guthrie was then needed by *The Matchmaker* company in Philadelphia, the first week's rehearsals of *Six Characters* had to be conducted without him. I was to serve as his surrogate, and anxious to please, I had asked him how he wished me to proceed.

"I leave that to you, dear boy," he said, adding, "Don't spend too much time reading. Just start in and put the cast on their feet. Don't worry about blocking the moves; just push them around as you please. It can easily be changed. After all, I'll be back at the end of the week. They should have the first act memorized by then, maybe the second as well."

On Sunday Guthrie was free to return for the day to check the week's work. The call was for two o'clock. He allowed the first act to proceed uninterruptedly for about fifteen minutes. Then he clapped his hands.

"Thank you very much," he said. "Now let's go back to the beginning and start again."

With torrential force and whirlwind speed, line readings and pieces of business began to pour out of him. Up and down the aisles he raced, onto and off the stage he leapt, all six feet four of him—his bedroom slippers flapping (he favored them or tennis sneakers when working), his fingers snapping, his arms waving, his voice crackling—pausing only now and then to take a sip from the thermos Judith held out to him, whether of tea or gin

I never was sure. After five hours—at about seven o'clock—he suggested to the actors that perhaps it was time to break for supper.

"Oh, no!" they cried. "Don't let's stop! Can't somebody just bring in some sandwiches and coffee?"

This was done; it was the only time I have ever seen a cast so caught up in their work that they literally refused to take a break. At midnight—after ten hours—the rehearsal ended, long past proper Equity quitting time but still with nobody having demurred. Of course, much that he created that day was later altered; that was also part of Tony's working method. But the production's style was established, the comedy, which he felt essential to the Pirandello piece, firmly laid out. Actors learned that day what pace he demanded and what vocal power. "I can't stand most American actors," he once remarked, "because they have no breath."

The ensuing three weeks were glorious. Our staff worked harder than ever; by example, Tony made people want to work. At all times he was in command, ordering—but with infinite tact and his rich sense of humor always in evidence—the lighting setups, costume details, the sound of music. He even found time to write an article for the Sunday paper.

He knew how to execute every stage effect he demanded, and his wildly theatrical production was full of them: how to make the Six Characters appear out of nowhere; how to turn the Boy into a sawdust dummy; how to make Madame Pace dissolve in a puff of smoke; how to make the Stepdaughter disappear before our very eyes with a blood-curdling shriek, as she raced toward the footlights, like the railroad engine bearing down on Anna Karenina in a Moscow Art production.

Not all the critics and Pirandellists loved what Guthrie irreverently did to their sacred modern classic. "Where's the philosophy?" they asked. This has often been asked of his productions. But we at the Phoenix adored his work—and him—and could hardly wait to woo him back.

Six Characters was followed by a revival of Strindberg's two short plays, *Miss Julie* and *The Stronger*. James Daly, Ruth Ford, and Viveca Lindfors constituted the entire speaking cast. *The Stronger* is really a monologue addressed across a café table by one woman (Ford) to her silent companion (Lindfors). Ruth was an exotic tropical bird of an actress, with a voice to match; Viveca responded to her with enigmatic smiles, sighs, frowns, and twitches, and naturally stole at least fifty percent of the scene.

My most vivid recollection of *Miss Julie* is of anguished cries from the other actors over Viveca's inability (or unwillingness) to follow any fixed staging. When they expected her up center, she was down left; when they moved into position for a scene before the stove down right, she was elsewhere, and they had to search the stage until they found her standing behind the sofa. She justified this hide-and-seek by claiming it added freshness to each performance; for the others it added unexpected hazards that reduced their concentration.

Never mind: Walter Kerr wrote in the *Herald Tribune* of this "stinging revival": "it isn't likely we'll get such gripping Strindberg again." Our stinging revival ran only thirty-three performances. Perhaps the audiences felt they were the ones being stung.

By the third season's end, the Phoenix had chalked up fifteen productions of various styles, kinds, and lengths, perhaps too much of a muchness so early in our life as a theatre. But we did it, I think, because—whether or not we recognized our aim at the time—we wanted to create a microcosm of Broadway under one roof, to suggest the diversity to be found by visiting fifteen uptown playhouses, while not actually imitating any of them.

The summer of 1956 gave evidence that the name of the Phoenix was becoming widely known. In July, being in Yugoslavia visiting a classmate, Heath Bowman, I attended the annual festival of performing arts in Dubrovnik. I flew there from Belgrade on a two-engine plane, the only kind the Dubrovnik airport could accommodate, and then only after the cows had been herded off the runway while we impatiently circled overhead.

Once in that port city, one of the most beautiful in the world, I was treated as a VIP, invited to be the guest of honor at a party where every critic and artist in sight was dragged over to meet the American who had founded the Phoenix Theatre in New York. Ah, how sweet is international fame, especially for one yet to savor its domestic variety. I was taken on a tour of the city walls, with a photographer snapping me at every turn, or so it seemed. I sat in the best seat at an evening of chamber music played in the courtyard of a Baroque palace, at a production of *Hamlet* performed at a castle on a precipice high above the Adriatic Sea, at a street-corner play presented in commedia dell'arte style, and at a symphonic concert given in a Romanesque church.

You might say that celebrity in a small town in Yugoslavia doesn't qualify as "international fame," but if Cannes, Salzburg, or Edinburgh are not on your itinerary, Dubrovnik will do. How could I not be proud that after only three years the Phoenix was being hailed in the Balkans?

When I returned home, T. Edward added a climactic touch, showing me a letter from a theatre group in Tokyo. With an outpouring of deference, they asked if we would allow them to change the name of their theatre to ours—the Phoenix. Of course we said yes. On three subsequent trips to Tokyo, I never encountered anyone who had ever heard of it. *Sic transit!*

W e began our fourth season with a flourish—Shaw's monumental *Saint Joan.* I had been overwhelmed by Katharine Cornell's production twenty years before. Now came our chance. In 1954 the Irish actress Siobhan McKenna, having decided her native Gaelic was limiting her career, had left Dublin to appear as Joan at the Arts Theatre Club in London. Her performance was widely hailed; the production moved to the West End and earned her the *Evening Standard* Award. The next season she made her Broadway debut in *The Chalk Garden* opposite Gladys Cooper. Again acclaim. Miss McKenna cherished the dream to play *Saint Joan* in New York, but alas, she had no takers.

Brooks Atkinson was largely responsible for this. He had seen and panned her London performance. For as long as I can remember, such has been the power of the drama critic of the *New York Times* that a nod or a shake of that head—be it on the shoulders of a forty-five-year-old or a seventy-year-old, a ninny or a sage—can make or break almost any Broadway play. With a bad *Times* notice in the offing, who would dare risk the fortune in financing that *Saint Joan* would require?

The Phoenix managing directors would—well, on Twelfth Street it wasn't exactly a fortune; and weren't they in business to accommodate a talented actress hungry for opportunity? They had seen McKenna's Miss Madrigal in *The Chalk Garden* and admired it. So they invited her to play Joan and, of course, she accepted.

Everything turned out much as we had anticipated. Atkinson was reserved in his praise; the public was captivated. My own response to the McKenna interpretation was wholeheartedly favorable. I agreed with Atkinson and others that her performance was short on mysticism, a quality not stressed by Shaw, and closer to earth, which I liked. McKenna's honesty held me from beginning to end. Her slender body, close-cropped hair, magical Irish lilt, and forthright stance—feet apart, arms akimbo—struck me as very much what Shaw would have wanted, and would have preferred to Cornell's romantic, gracious, and decorative heroine.

5

Shortly after Christmas, 1957, I entered my office, to be told that a stranger waited to see me. He introduced himself as a federal marshal and handed me a subpoena to appear thirty days thence before the House Un-American Activities Committee.

It may seem derelict of me that in recalling the years between 1952 and 1957 I have so far made almost no mention of the deep shadow that McCarthyism cast across the entertainment world at that time. I somehow imagined it would never touch me—even though few prominent persons in government or in literature and the arts who had evidenced sympathy for liberal causes during the 1930s or thereafter were safe from the evil forces let loose by the senator from Wisconsin.

In fact, those were the most shameful years through which the Republic has passed in my lifetime. When Joseph McCarthy was finally broken by the Senate's censure in 1954, we thought the nightmare was at last over. We were wrong. The next year the Phoenix was hit.

Few who lived through that time will forget the pernicious, poison-pen publications, *Red Channels* and *Counterattack*. On the flimsiest of evidence, honorable men and women, like Margaret Webster and Cheryl Crawford, were denounced because they had once been members of the Anti-Fascist Refugee Committee or the Council for Soviet-American Friendship or had given twenty-five dollars to aid Loyalist forces in Spain in the thirties. When they could make no direct charge, the witch hunters employed guilt by association and innuendo to devastating effect. That was how they attacked the Phoenix, during the summer after our second season.

What about Hambleton and Houghton, they asked, the latter in particular? Hadn't he been to Russia twice in the thirties? (It didn't fit into their scenario that I had also been there during my wartime naval service, and had even been awarded a Commendation Ribbon for Yalta.) And John Houseman—hadn't he worked for the subversive Federal Theatre in the thirties and associated with dubious persons in Hollywood? And John Latouche—hadn't he written the words to "Ballad for Americans," which had been made famous by Paul Robeson's recording of it, and didn't everybody know Robeson was a Commie? And hadn't its score been written by Earl Robinson, another one? As for Robinson and Salt's *Sandhog*, that was a red stain from start to finish. So the word went out: Don't let those smooth Ivy League types fool you. Their whole enterprise smells of sedition. Nip this so-called Phoenix Theatre in the bud and prove your own true patriotism! We managing directors were troubled—of course we were troubled; but we went ahead knowing that our hearts were pure and our actions always honorable. What followed was the season of Pirandello, Strindberg, and Turgenev, hardly a radical lineup.

Only a handful of our supporters withdrew their help. Among them, however, was Mrs. Vincent Astor, and that made a difference. The previous May she had cochaired with Richard Rodgers a benefit luncheon to launch our first subscription season. But when *Red Channels* upbraided her for her naïveté in supporting a couple of traitors and urged its horrified readers to write to her in care of *Newsweek* (which her husband owned), Mrs. Astor backed away from us. I feared it might be our death blow and was profoundly upset at what seemed both an action totally alien to Brooke's character and a betrayal of a long friendship. I subsequently came to understand the difficulty of her position at the time—married only recently to Astor, she was burdened with all the unaccustomed responsibilities that entailed and doubtless felt insecure in her new role. Nevertheless, her defection caused a breach that healed only after Vincent's death four years later.

Eustace Seligman was a senior partner of that upright and sanctified Wall Street law firm Sullivan and Cromwell. I had known the Seligmans for a number of years. Indeed, he was an original limited partner in the Phoenix. After I received the subpoena, I went to him seeking legal advice. He held out his hand in support, and I grasped it tightly.

"You have nothing to fear," said Eustace. "I'll turn you over to one of our bright junior partners. Do whatever he says." That bright young man said he'd like to read *Moscow Rehearsals*. I brought him a copy and then went home to bed with the worst cold I've ever contracted, totally psychosomatic I'm sure.

During those troubling weeks before my committee appearance, I also went to see Henry Allen Moe at the Guggenheim Foundation. I thought that he could perhaps give me advice or, better yet, a letter saying I wouldn't ever have gone to Russia if it hadn't been for him! Of course, he declined.

"Just tell them the circumstances under which you went. You'll be under oath, so they'll be bound to accept your word." Then he added, in effect: "Norris, there is something about our Fellows which unites them all. . . . Be they in the arts or letters or science or scholarship, our grantees are men and women who are creative, instinctively opposed to the status quo. Often that's reflected in their political thinking. . . . Why, if I had to write a letter for every Fellow who got into trouble with the government these days, I'd have no time to run the foundation. You should feel honored by this summons. We're proud of you!"

On the morning of February 7, 1957, I felt unexpectedly calm. I donned a 1950s Princeton outfit—white button-down shirt, black knit tie—polished my shoes, and went down to Foley Square. When my name was called I entered the hearing room. Two or three congressmen were seated behind a table; their counsel, a smooth-appearing fellow, ushered me to a chair. The first question startled me.

"Mr. Houghton, have you ever heard of the Manhattan School of Music?" Although confused by this unexpected tack, I replied that of course I had. What did I know about it? Only what I had read, I said in effect. The subject was dropped. Then: "Have you ever heard of a book called *Moscow Rehearsals?*"

"Yes, I wrote it."

"What is it about?" This was a question I expected.

Quoting its subtitle, I replied, "It is a study of methods of production in the Soviet theatre." I was asked to amplify and did so. It was apparent that no one in the room had read the book. That was not surprising. I was accustomed to rooms in which nobody had.

Changing the subject, counsel asked, "Did you ever hear of the Phoenix Theatre?"

"Yes, I founded it." (There seemed no point in mentioning Hambleton.)

"Suppose you tell us about it." This was a subject I could wax eloquent upon, and maybe win a few new subscribers in the process. But after several minutes I was cut short.

"Are you acquainted with Zero Mostel? With John Latouche? With Howard Da Silva? Jane Hoffman? Earl Robinson?"

"Yes. I am."

"Under what circumstances?"

"They have all worked at the Phoenix."

"Why did you employ them?

"Because we believed our job was to put on the best possible productions, and to do so, we engaged the best possible talent."

"Didn't you inquire into their political affiliations?"

"Never. It didn't occur to us that that was any of our business. We wanted them for their ability, not for their politics."

There was a pause. "Thank you; that will be all." As I rose, one of the congressmen said, "By the way, Mr. Houghton, before you leave, let me ask, are you or have you ever been a member of the Communist Party?"

"No, I am not nor have I ever been," I replied, and made a virtuous exit. It was noon when I got back to the office. "Let's go to Luchow's and have lunch," said T. When we got there he said, "Let me buy you a drink." That meant it was a very special occasion.

During the following summer (1957) we altered the basic structure of our enterprise. With four seasons behind us, every one ending in the red, the Phoenix seemed unlikely ever to prove a get-rich-quick scheme. Indeed, the net loss for the year just ended had for the first time passed the $100,000 mark. Much of it had to be met by general partner Hambleton. Our attorney, John Wharton, advised that this must not continue, lest T. get into serious trouble with the IRS. He proposed that the "profitmaking" partnership be dissolved and replaced by a not-for-profit corporation.

I pricked up my ears. "I have just such a corporation," I announced, and explained that when Theatre Incorporated had ceased production in 1950, its lawyer, Milton Rose, had insisted that it not be dissolved and that a caretaker committee of its board be appointed to ensure that annual reports would be filed with the IRS. In that way, Rose had said, the charter of Theatre Inc. would remain alive, and someday when one of us wanted to use it for a purpose consonant with its educational and cultural provisions, its tax-exempt status would be intact.

This had been done, I explained, by the caretaker committee, which I, as current president of Theatre Inc., now headed. Since the aims of the Phoenix were much the same as those of Theatre Inc., why shouldn't I propose to the committee that it take over the Phoenix as one of its projects? With neither T. nor John finding objection to this, I proceeded to convene the committee, which then agreed that the charter, originally granted to the Chekhov Studio, could be invoked. We had only to create a board of directors and seek contributions as a charitable institution. We named Roger Stevens as first president and John Wharton as chairman of the board. T. and I modestly put ourselves up as vice presidents.

As for fund-raising, that was much harder then than now. The National Endowment for the Arts lay five years ahead. No New York State Council on the Arts existed. The managing directors called on various foundation executives, who told us, "You're ahead of your time." All we could do was to go on seeking support from our original backers, now as tax-exempt contributors instead of investors, and hope that T. wouldn't run out of funds. Most of the partners sighed but dug deeper into their pockets.

While the Phoenix Theatre's structure was reorganized, it did not yet have a new season. Early the previous June, Tony Guthrie had been in New York en route to Stratford, Ontario, and we had enjoyed a bibulous reunion. During an hour or so of gin-and-tonics, Tony had said he would be delighted to direct our next season's opener. What were we planning? We had countered by asking what he would like to do. Neither he nor we had been prepared to say, but now it was up to us to take the initiative.

We made several suggestions; none appealed to him. Finally, in late July, with time shortening, we sent him a copy of a fresh adaptation of Schiller's early-nineteenth-century tragedy *Mary Stuart.*

"Ah ha!" cried he. "This is it! Come up to Stratford at once, and let's get moving."

On the lawn of his little house in Stratford, we discussed the play, details of production, schedule, casting. Critical was the selection of the two actresses to play the queens, Mary and Elizabeth. Our choice for the former was Irene Worth, whom we tracked down in London. At first, over the transatlantic phone, she thought we were asking her to appear in Arizona. When we assured her that our Phoenix was in Manhattan, she accepted. Our first choice for Elizabeth was Judith Anderson. We called her in California. She expressed interest, but when she heard our salary scale she turned us down—the only actor who ever refused us on those grounds. Our second, somewhat hesitant choice was Eva Le Gallienne. Eva was unpredictable; it was rumored, perhaps falsely, that she'd become a difficult actress to work with. And being a director herself, would she, we wondered, willingly put herself in Guthrie's hands? The only way to find out was to talk it over with her. This we did, and all agreed it would work.

Once more Tyrone Guthrie blew on our ashes and the Phoenix rose up higher than ever. *Mary Stuart* was one of our most colorful and satisfying productions. Guthrie, a master of grand operatic effects, pulled out all the stops. Donald Oenslager and Alvin Colt, our designers, met his challenge, providing magnificent sets and costumes. Irene, in black throughout until her final death scene, when she was robed in white, and Eva, in gold, with copper-colored hair, were both triumphant. They gave Guthrie the larger-than-life dimension he sought.

Even though our ideology scorned the idea, it was good to have a hit again. The play sold out for eight weeks, with the reviewers tossing their caps and hairpieces in the air: "The Phoenix has restored the theatre to high estate," cried the *Daily Mirror;* "This is big-time all the way," said the *Journal-American.*

Some people of consequence journeyed to Twelfth Street for the first time. One such was that grand old English actress Constance Collier, who had played in her time opposite both John and Lionel Barrymore. She was an ample woman, trailing clouds of glory, by that time fashioned by her seamstress and her milliner. With a friend, the actress Dorothy Stickney, she taxied to a matinee of *Mary Stuart.* After the performance she swept backstage to embrace her old friend Eva and her new friend Irene. Her famous voice echoed through the dressing room corridors. Dorothy, a lady of lesser years—Miss Collier was in her eighties—hailed a taxi for them as the latter sailed forth from the stage door. At Twenty-third Street she sank back in the seat and expired. What a magnificent way to die, I thought—on your way uptown from a Phoenix matinee!

If the double bill of *The Chairs* and *The Lesson,* which introduced Eugene Ionesco to our Phoenix audience, was no sellout, it was a production we were proud of. Two years before, Beckett's *Waiting for Godot* had had a brief premiere run on Broadway. When I saw it there, I had said to myself, "We should have done this at the Phoenix."

The European avant-garde theatre of the postwar generation, led by Beckett and Ionesco, was, of course, grounded in the existential philosophy of Jean-Paul Sartre, who based his texts on Kierkegaard. This movement, which came to be loosely (and not in every case accurately) dubbed the Theatre of the Absurd, was probably the first wave of change in both the form and the substance of the world's stage after 1945. In those upbeat years most

American theatregoers were not inclined to embrace a philosophy of hopelessness, and even in New York it took a long time before people learned what Existentialism was all about.

Nevertheless, the Phoenix should have been quicker to perceive its significance and more hospitable to receive it. Admittedly, Hambleton and I were temperamentally tone-deaf to that particular European message. We were really staunch artistic conservatives, I guess, at best still back with Georg Kaiser, Karel Capek, and those other Expressionists who throve after World War I—just one war behind. Besides, we were both good churchgoing Protestants, and we had no wish to truck with the folks who went around shouting "God is dead!" So we missed the boat, which set sail with Alan Schneider at the helm and headed for smaller off-Broadway harbors.

But when those Ionesco plays came our way, paradoxically we both fell in love with them. To the extent that they were hilarious nonsense, we embraced them totally. That their absurdity was a mask for nihilistic despair only slightly dampened our enthusiasm, certainly not enough to deter us. *The Lesson*, a delectable piece of buffoonery, had a Grand Guignol twist at its end. *The Chairs* possessed more thematic substance, but its bleakness was hidden behind eccentric whimsicality. It concerns an old couple in their nineties preparing for a meeting with invisible guests, to whom the man is to deliver his ultimate message to mankind. He has arranged for an orator to speak in his behalf. When the still invisible guests have arrived and all is ready, the couple jump from the window to their death, confident that their mission in life is fulfilled. The Orator, a deaf-mute, mumbles incoherently as the curtain comes down.

I am reminded now of one of the on-duty firemen standing backstage, as they often do, watching the show from the wings, who remarked at the end of one performance, "It's a lousy, rainy night, but it's the first time I've ever seen a whole cast, except these three, fail to show!"

As noteworthy as the duo of Ionesco plays was New York's introduction to Joan Plowright. Small, bright-eyed, and all innocence as the teenaged pupil in *The Lesson*, incredibly wispy as the nonagenarian wife of the equally crumbling Eli Wallach in *The Chairs*, Miss Plowright captivated everyone. It was quite a coup to have wooed her successfully to our stage from the Royal Court in London for a twenty-two-performance run in Tony Richardson's impeccable production. But we knew in advance that she would have to leave before most theatregoers would become aware of her presence, for she was committed to join Laurence Olivier in *The Entertainer* on West Forty-fifth Street. (And, of course, shortly afterward she became Lady Olivier.)

Whenever Tyrone Guthrie was in New York, we spent a lot of time talking about the Phoenix's future. Tony was among those, along with Brooks Atkinson, who hammered away at the managing directors to create an "image" for their theatre. Our zigzag course seemed willful and capricious, whisking from nineteenth-century tragedy to Restoration comedy, from the Jacobeans to Ionesco, from musicals to Sideshow; it added up to no definable personality and to our critics revealed an absence of policy.

"Even more important to the continuing development of a theatre than its repertoire," they argued, "is a permanent body of artists. You have developed no acting company; you change directors from play to play—hence you have no identity, no coherent style."

This situation, not only true but looked upon by me as a virtue, justified by economic necessity, was, I now kept being told, leading us into a wilderness. It was ironic. For years an ardent exponent of permanent companies, which frequently developed unique styles, I had been forced to abandon the idea, but only because in the late 1950s the cost of maintaining a professional company was inarguably prohibitive.

Finally, however, I admitted that I should be the last person in town to hold out against a permanent company, and one evening T. and I invited to his apartment about a dozen actors whom we hoped to interest in forming a Phoenix ensemble. I'm not sure, a quarter century later, exactly who was present. I'd like to think that among them were Maureen Stapleton, Julie Harris, Mildred Dunnock, E. G. Marshall, Karl Malden, Geraldine Fitzgerald, Fritz Weaver, the Cronyns, Mildred Natwick, and Beatrice Straight. They were roughly of our generation, brought up in the same theatrical environment, and they had all at one time or another professed enthusiasm for repertory.

The evening was revealing. All recited their confessions of faith, admitting they had not done what they ought to have done, had done what they ought not to have done. But when they rose from their penitential knees, they turned practical. How much income could they count on? After all, they had children in private schools, places in the country to maintain. How long a commitment would be required? What freedom would they have to move out of and back into the company? What parts might they get in what plays? Who would direct?

We had no answers: this was only an exploratory session. But we certainly found out the questions. Mildred Dunnock, for example, spoke with fervor. She longed to be part of such a company; she would accept tiny supporting roles, provided she could play her dream part—Christine in *Mourning Becomes Electra.*

To prove we were serious, we followed through on that offer. T. invited O'Neill's widow, Carlotta, to tea. She floated in, swathed in veils, looking like Lady Manners in *The Jewel in the Crown.* We knew she held all the cards. Mrs. O'Neill had done some homework, and she knew about the Phoenix, Hambleton, and Houghton, and she would consider a revival there, but only under one condition: José Quintero, whose off-Broadway production of *The Iceman Cometh* had sparked an O'Neill revival, must direct. So we approached José. He would be delighted to stage the nine-act trilogy, he said, but when we proposed Mildred Dunnock to play Christine, he shouted, "With Millie? All wrong! Never!" We were back to square one.

During that summer of 1958 I meditated on some way to provide coherence to our repertoire, to provide an overall theme. I came up with a desperate notion: a series of plays written by winners of the Nobel Prize for Literature. Eliminating O'Neill as too obvious, I came up with Eliot's *The Family Reunion,* Shaw's *Arms and the Man,* Pirandello's *As You Desire Me,* Camus's *Les Justes (The Just Assassins),* and a fifth play, to be chosen from the works of Nobel laureates Hauptmann, Yeats, and Maeterlinck. I thought it a challenging season—the cream of modern drama—and after I persuaded T., we announced it.

It did not catch fire: it seemed the idea of a Nobel season was pretentious and boring, even to hear about. Nevertheless, we manfully started off with *The Family Reunion.* For me it was a landmark of sorts: I designed the scenery—only the third time I'd made a creative contribution to a Phoenix production since directing *The Seagull.* (The second was scenery for *The Makropoulos Secret* in 1957.) It also marked our first association with director Stuart Vaughan, who was soon to become the company's artistic director. Stuart did a creditable job, with the help of a pair of distinguished older actresses, Lillian Gish and Florence Reed, and of a relative youngster, Fritz Weaver, who was on his way to the top.

The good ladies, especially Miss Reed, had not the ghost of an idea, I'm sure, of what T. S. Eliot was up to in his mystical rewrite of Aeschylus' *Oresteia,* but they resolutely mastered their lines. I told the cast Alec Guinness's anecdote about the first reading of *The Cocktail Party:* Before it began, E. Martin Browne, its director, introduced the famous poet; everyone seized pencil and paper to record any illuminating remarks he might make, for the play's meanings were elusive. Mr. Eliot rose and said, "There are two stresses and one caesura in every line, but you'll have to find them out for yourselves," and sat down.

Our struggles with Eliot were rewarded by a nod from Walter Kerr. "It seems to me," he wrote in the *Herald Tribune,* "that the Phoenix has performed a considerable public service in arranging an earnest, beautifully spoken, genuinely distinguished production of an extraordinarily difficult piece of work."

Walter meant well; nonetheless, he sent a message: a play that performs a "public service," is "earnest" and a "difficult piece of work," is nothing your average New York theatregoer wants to spend an evening with. Leave that to the universities and the Germans.

So few were the takers that our Nobel-Prize-winner idea went down to defeat after thirty-three performances.

It was Roger Stevens who again delayed the Phoenix's descent into ashes. He held the dramatic rights to Graham Greene's *The*

Power and the Glory, as adapted by Denis Cannan and Pierre Bast, but having no immediate plans to present it, he offered the play to us. Deeply stirred by the drama, we accepted enthusiastically. Stuart Vaughan again directed, and again Fritz Weaver was brilliant, in the principal role of a dissolute Mexican priest struggling to uphold his faith.

"The Power and the Glory is well named," wrote Brooks Atkinson. "It is the most engrossing and the noblest play the Phoenix has put on in recent years. . . . It is wonderful acting in a wonderful play that fills the Phoenix with power and glory." With that kind of rave in the *Times,* one would have thought we would sell out for a long run. Sadly, the play, which opened in early December, had by mid-February run out of gas.

Without enough money to complete the season, the Phoenix lay in ashes, but not for long. In mid-May it soared again, with a new captain, a new crew, and a new set of funders—eighty-three of them—who hoped to share in the profits from a $125,000 investment. The captain was veteran director George Abbott, while the crew was headed by Carol Burnett in her first big role; her unique, boisterous clowning won the hearts of all and fame for herself. The ship was christened *Once Upon a Mattress.* It cruised for over a year, leaving thousands happy and the backers satisfied.

Actually, it was not a bona fide Phoenix production. Mary Rodgers, Richard Rodger's daughter, learning of our predicament, proposed that the theatre play host to a musical based on the fairy tale "The Princess and the Pea," for which she had written the score, Marshall Barer the lyrics and, with Jay Thompson and Dean Fuller, the book. They had worked on it the previous summer at a Pocono resort and were ready to go into production as soon as they found a house. William and Jean Eckart, the designer team, proposed to coproduce with us; we agreed. Our principal coup, however, was in getting George Abbott, who was already past seventy—in his prime of life—to direct. The show—funny, offbeat, charming—ran for 216 performances before moving uptown.

6

Since 1948 I had been leading a double life. On Saturday mornings from September to June I subwayed to Morningside Heights to lecture at Columbia University on modern drama. This paid the rent—no more—but it also allowed me to keep one foot inside the academic door, which I looked upon as a fire exit should the life of the stage ever get too hot.

In 1954 I transferred to Barnard College, across the street, became an adjunct professor, and so encountered another adjunct professor, teaching creative writing, Frederica Barach, attractive and erudite, a few years older than I. One day she said, "Norrie, I'm much interested in Vassar, you know." I didn't know, but I soon discovered she was chairman of its board of trustees. "Do you think you might ever consider going up there one or two days a week, as you've been going to Barnard?"

After a pause, I heard myself say I didn't think that would be very practical, considering the distance and time factors and my responsibilities in town. No, I thought the only way it would make sense would be to teach on a full-time basis.

"Do you mean you'd think of that?"

I pulled back. Had I made an unconscious slip? "I don't know," was all I said.

She pursued: would I mind if she told Sarah Blanding of our brief conversation?

"I guess not." I was responding in monosyllables now. What had I been thinking of? Soon I received a call from President Blanding: she was coming to New York the next week. Would I have tea with her at the Cosmopolitan Club? I accepted.

During the intervening days I pondered the situation. The current Phoenix season had certainly been disappointing: indeed, three plays hardly formed a season. Stuart Vaughan and the company he was assembling had effected no miracles. It looked then as though *Once Upon a Mattress* was headed for success, but whether it was or not, I myself had little to do with that. And not only was the Phoenix once again broke (we had lost $150,000 in 1958–59)—so was I. Hambleton and I had agreed to accept salaries of ten thousand dollars apiece. By each midseason our corporate exchequer had been pretty well depleted. Faced with the alternatives of paying our creditors or paying ourselves, we made the honorable choice—and thus drew salaries for only the first half of each season. My tiny savings were dwindling, for it was barely possible to live in Manhattan on ten thousand a year, let alone five.

Actually, my financial plight bothered me less than other factors. I had dreamed of having my own theatre, as I told T. when first we talked, for the chance it would provide to exercise whatever talents I had as a designer and director and to enlarge them in a propitious environment under my own control. The Phoenix had presented fifty-six productions, if you counted the Sideshows. I had directed one and designed but two.

I had contained my frustration pretty well. After all, I used to think, to establish a theatre in New York City and help guide its steps is a creative act of considerable magnitude in itself. But unlike T. Edward's, my ambition was not really to be a theatrical producer. I had been doing that as a means to an end, and as the years passed and the frustration grew more acute, I began to fear my own skills were deteriorating.

Furthermore, although the Phoenix's financial insecurity may not have been in itself my chief concern, for a long time I had been troubled by the fact that we had not won the support of a broad, loyal audience, come what may (which is to say, whether we were praised or panned by the press); nor, after our initial success, had we remained the darling of the critics, which would at least have enabled us to say, "To hell with the general public. People who *know* appreciate us." I considered the twenty-six major productions presented to date; nine had possibly paid for themselves, the other seventeen certainly had not—admittedly a better percentage than on Broadway but hardly any reason to ring bells. "But hold on!" I said to myself. I was judging the Phoenix in the context of Broadway. So was the public, and so were the reviewers.

Here was the problem. T. and I were operating on a double standard: We wanted our shows to pay off; to that end, we invited first-string critics to review our work, and they, in turn, applied their uptown criteria, which, when the results were favorable to us, we then advertised to generate audiences. But paradoxically, we continued to act as if we were an art theatre, by maintaining our low ticket scale, limiting our runs (true, top talent wouldn't come to us otherwise), and continuing to select plays commercial managers wouldn't touch, from *Coriolanus* and *The Golden Apple* down to T. S. Eliot's verse tragedy and *The Power and the Glory*. We wanted the best of two worlds. But we couldn't have them, and I didn't know what to do.

In this frame of mind I went to see President Blanding. I liked her immediately. She was direct, and I felt confident I could trust her. Not stylish, her graying hair pulled tightly back, she would never have won a best-dressed-woman award. But the deep crinkles around her mouth and eyes conveyed humor and understanding. She told me, as she wafted the smoke of cigarette after cigarette my way, about the state of the drama department at Vassar, why she would like me aboard, and what she could offer.

"Maybe one year—to see how it works. Think it over, and let's talk again soon." She had hooked me.

At The Players a few days later, I exposed to T. my state of mind. I laid bare my personal financial anxieties. I couldn't afford to go on as before. I said I had no interest in returning to Broadway: that would be a betrayal of him, of myself, and of all the Phoenix stood for. Besides, the heat of our frying pan was as nothing compared to the fires of commercialism. No, for me the only way out led into the vales of academe. While I had never heard of anyone going into teaching in order to improve his financial condition, I could think of no other solution. I told him about Vassar and Sarah Blanding's offer.

After a pause, T. responded. He recognized my problem but was not prepared to accept my departure from the Phoenix. He had a counterproposal: that he himself guarantee my full salary for the year ahead or until such time as the Phoenix could afford to. I rejected this out of hand. "If you pay my salary," I said, in effect, "we are no longer partners. I shall be working for you, and that, you must agree, is a situation neither of us really wants. Eventually it could lead to tensions that haven't occurred so far but might very well emerge from a different relationship."

I then said there was an aspect other than the financial: I told him the first five Phoenix years had been the most exciting of my life, the exuberance of those days unforgettable. I had gloried in

our successes, and I had had him to share and ease with philosophical good humor the pain of our failures. But lately, I explained,
I felt some of this gratification slipping away from me.

I had been deeply troubled, for one thing, by a recent Sunday
article by Brooks Atkinson in the *Times*, which said in part:

> With a record of so many interesting plays, the Phoenix is
> justified in wondering why it has not captivated the imagi-
> nation of the public. As an institution, the Phoenix has not
> really been exciting . . . the managing co-directors have not
> been able to give the Phoenix a personality or point of view
> . . . nothing cumulative has happened to develop a Phoenix
> point of view.

In other words, he had at last "gone public" with the concern
he had voiced to us privately over the past two or three years.
Coming when it did, his piece was a severe body blow, but in my
present state of mind, I was prepared to accept his judgment.

I had of course suffered other blows in my life and had always
had the resilience to recover, but frequently that had taken a good
deal of time. T. Edward was—or appeared to be—fortunate in his
disposition. He could ignore slings and arrows or snap back to
reacquire his balance more rapidly than I. While we were both
basically optimists, his was a more consistent and dogged optimism than any I'd ever known.

Concluding our conversation, I said I thought I should take a
year's leave to find a new lease on life. The Vassar invitation
would make that possible. I would not, of course, resign as vice
president of Theatre Inc. or from the board of directors. In a year
we could review the situation. Meanwhile, I would become an
adjunct professor of drama and a guest director of the Vassar
Experimental Theatre. Reluctantly T. acquiesced. And so it came
to pass.

During the academic year from September 1959 to June 1960,
I kept in close touch with the Phoenix but assumed no responsibilities. When the year ended, I did not return to Second Avenue
or to Vassar either. Instead, I headed for Moscow, on another
Guggenheim, to gather material for a "postscript" to *Moscow*

Rehearsals and to deliver a series of lectures on American theatre under the U.S.-USSR cultural exchange program.

My most memorable address was given under the auspices of the All-Union Society for the Dissemination of Political and Scientific Knowledge. That I spoke about neither politics nor science didn't seem to matter. About a thousand people jammed the historic Central Lecture Hall of Moscow's Polytechnical Museum—some had to sit on windowsills or in the aisles—to hear my lecture and to ask such surprising questions as whether Eva Le Gallienne was still performing at the Phoenix.

From Moscow I went on to Kitzbühel, where I worked on and completed *Return Engagement,* my follow-up book on Soviet theatre. The final three months of my travels saw me in fifteen countries on a special mission for the State Department. I had been asked to serve as a sort of advance man for a touring company, headed by Helen Hayes, that State was soon to send forth into the world.

I have three vivid memories of that last whirlwind trip. In Oslo, my official host was the Cultural Affairs officer of the American embassy, Paul Child, who was quick to invite me to dinner at his home the day I arrived. I happily accepted, even though I didn't know the meal would be prepared by his wife, Julia. At that time she had neither a cookbook nor a television appearance to her credit, but I'll never forget the delicious New England boiled dinner she served that evening—to remind me of home. The Childs and I have been friends ever since.

In Vienna, I called upon H. Freeman Matthews, then our ambassador to Austria, and we reminisced about those tense and exciting days when we had both watched history being made at the Yalta Conference fifteen years earlier.

And, finally, I remember a moment in Brussels that gave me, like a splash of cold water in the face, a reminder of the reality that awaited. The woman who headed the National Theatre of Belgium had recently returned from a cross-country trip in the United States, visiting dozens of residential, community, and college theatres—examining the "advance from Broadway" for herself. "I've never seen so many people involved in the theatre in any country as in yours, and everyone was so dissatisfied with what they were doing," she remarked, and I can still hear her words.

Back in New York, to which I returned in May 1961, the Phoenix was winding up its season with a then record-breaking run of *Hamlet,* Donald Madden playing the Dane (101 performances versus John Barrymore's 100). I rushed to see it and was jubilant. Not only was Donald a superb and sensitive young Prince; the whole production was exhilarating. By this time Stuart Vaughan had forged a Phoenix acting company of fine young actors, variously numbering between sixteen and twenty-two.

I learned, however, that Stuart would not be returning in the fall. He had received a Ford Foundation grant to spend a year abroad; inevitably the company he had worked hard to form would fall apart, for no successor would be prepared—understandably—to take over someone else's team. (The Ford giveth and the Ford taketh away!)

Another crisis loomed for my doughty colleague Hambleton. Although he had produced no fatted calf to celebrate this Prodigal's return, he had graciously assented when I asked him if I could rejoin him as co–managing director.

At the top of my summer agenda was to move the Phoenix from Twelfth Street. A new image could never be created as long as we were constrained by that huge playhouse. T., I discovered, was not as hard to win over as I had feared. During my absence he had come independently to the same conclusion: we must escape from our financial albatross. So we went house hunting again and discovered an attractive three-hundred-seat theatre on East Seventy-fourth Street. We grabbed it and were installed before Labor Day.

In a "L'Envoi" message to our Twelfth Street subscribers, we wrote in August:

> It's been the scene of all our triumphs and our traumas since we first began. But we've developed a conflict of loyalties: between a building and an idea. After a while we seemed to be looking for plays to fit a building. That was obviously the

wrong way around! We decided ideas come first. So we have looked for a theatre to fit the plays—and we've found it. To be ourselves we had to become different.

So we said farewell to Twelfth Street and Second Avenue, and in September 1961 opened in new quarters. Our first triumph there was Arthur Kopit's hilarious spoof on the Theatre of the Absurd, *Oh Dad, Poor Dad, Mamma's Hung You in the Closet and I'm Feelin' So Sad*, written while its precocious author was still a Harvard undergraduate. Now in his twenties, he was tall, attractive, and bumptious, very sure of himself, and rightly so.

Under our roof, however, he had to share honors with Jerome Robbins, who, at our urging, made his debut as director of a straight play. It's been a great loss to our American nonmusical theatre that Jerry, a born virtuoso, has chosen to devote himself single-mindedly to a career in dance. He has as instinctive a mastery of theatrical as of balletic wizardry. And nothing ever took place on the Phoenix stage—and I include the Guthrie productions—to top *Oh Dad* in wit and style.

Robbins approached his assignment with diffidence and care, as though testing the waters before plunging in. Once immersed, however, he swam with complete assurance. He told the Eckarts exactly what he wanted the scenery to provide; he paid close attention to every detail of the costume designs of Patricia Zipprodt, a tall, gangling mass of enthusiasm, uncombed hair, and youthful talent, and made sure that the apparel revealed the characters. As for the cast, with unerring instinct he chose Jo Van Fleet to play Madame Rosepettle and surrounded her with a Hungarian, Sandor Szabo, to play her admirer; two youngsters, Barbara Harris out of Chicago's Second City, and Austin Pendleton out of nowhere (it was his debut), to play her antagonists; and a half-dozen more or less Latin-looking youths to play bellhops in the Caribbean hotel where the shenanigans occurred.

Jerry was very demanding: stage business and the actors' timing and movements had to be executed with precision—that was the choreographer at work. In his mind's eye he could visualize the props, and he sent the prop man out to find exact replicas of his fantasies. The result was a production in which all elements, from the jokes to the tank of piranhas, were meticulously orchestrated into a dazzling fugue. It all paid off handsomely, artistically and financially.

Again we were beholden to Roger Stevens, who had taken an option on the unknown author's piece but, sensing it would work best in a small house, had turned it over to us. When it became a success, we debated whether to move it to Broadway or keep it on Seventy-fourth Street. It remained in our new home, where it ran for thirteen months. During the summer Hermione Gingold succeeded Van Fleet as Rosepettle. One of our elderly patrons, A. Thornton Wilson (a descendant on his mother's side from Commodore Vanderbilt), was so delighted with both ladies that he saw it thirty-seven times!

7

During the late winter of 1961–62 I faced another personal crisis when, one evening, Sarah Blanding telephoned from Vassar. Mary Virginia Heinlein, chairman of the drama department for nineteen years, had just died. Her successor had to be appointed quickly. I was the first choice. Would I return, this time as a full professor, with tenure at the end of three years, to be chairman of the department and to direct the legendary Vassar Experimental Theatre?

I was torn. I seemed to be replaying that scene from the spring of my Princeton senior year when I had had to decide between a graduate fellowship and a theatre job. Then I had turned my back on academia, and I never regretted the decision.

I thought about this as I weighed the invitation from Vassar. Suddenly I perceived something else about myself: I had developed a pattern of entrances and exits. After just about becoming established as a scene designer, I had decided I'd never be as good as Robert Edmond Jones, and besides, I had more to say than could be expressed in visual terms. So I had set my sights on becoming a director, only to conclude, after a handful of successes, that Broadway would not be a congenial environment for me and it was time to be an off-Broadway producer. Now here I was, after a decade, considering another exit-entrance: Though this step would mean a truly major break, maybe I could fulfill myself more satisfyingly on a college campus than in New York theatrical management.

From time to time I used to tell friends I was a soi-disant arsonist. I was never happier than when lighting a fire. But when the blaze began to burn brightly, I lost interest and looked about for another fire to light.

Once a friend replied, "Don't flatter yourself by claiming such gaudy criminal instincts. Arsonists want to destroy. That's not you. Why don't you recognize you are a spiritual descendant of the trailblazers who opened up the West? When the wagon trains caught up with them, they jumped on their horses and moved on to clear another trail."

I liked that metaphor better; but though it was certainly more flattering than arson, I wasn't sure it applied to me. Now, as unexpected circumstances arose, challenging me to set forth again, my character, I thought, might justly be interpreted as Olivier once claimed he interpreted Hamlet's: "A man who could not make up his mind." Or perhaps I am just one of that vast company who want to eat their cake and have it too. In any case, I journeyed up to Poughkeepsie.

"Sarah," I said, "I'm much tempted by your offer. If I accept, remember you're not getting much of a scholar. Unlike most full professors, I have earned only an A.B. degree. What you'd get would be a theatre professional. If I were an academician, you would expect me to continue my scholarly studies. Under the circumstances, I would want you to let me continue to justify my professional standing. Otherwise you'll have made a bad bargain."

"Of course," Sarah replied instantly. "That's why you are valuable to me." Then she added, with an innocent air, that all she wanted was for me to agree to live in Poughkeepsie and go to New York, not the other way around.

So it came to pass that I remained co–managing director of the Phoenix Theatre and also held a professorship at Vassar College, a hundred miles away. T. Edward, by now accustomed to my mutability, approved the arrangement. He had become used to running the show on his own, although he did like company— and I thought rather needed it.

For the next three years I divided my time between Pough-keepsie and New York. Obviously, my work at the Phoenix was significantly curtailed, but on my personal agenda for the theatre during this time were two unusual plays, both Russian in origin.

The first, a Soviet fairy-story comedy, ostensibly for children, called *The Dragon,* was in fact a parable for adults. Written in 1944 (the playwright, Yevgenny Shvarts, died in 1958 and received enormous posthumous popularity in Russia by 1960), the play contained all sorts of satiric parallels with the events and figures of recent Soviet history.

I designed the sets for *The Dragon,* using as my inspiration the pink and orange extravaganzas of prerevolutionary Bakst, Benois, and Soudeikine. Patricia Zipprodt did the costumes and created a ten-foot-tall dragon with three heads; Joseph Anthony deftly directed, wedding the animation of a fairy tale to the common sense of perceptive political commentary. But unlike Moscow, New York was not impressed, and our embodiment of *The Dragon* was buried about four weeks after it was unveiled, in April 1963.

The second Russian play was a stage adaptation by Erwin Piscator of Tolstoy's *War and Peace,* which I had seen performed by the Bristol Old Vic in London in 1961. It took us more than three years and association with another company to bring our production into being, but for me it was worth the wait and the struggle.

The "other company" was the Association of Producing Artists (APA), whose founding director was the talented, wittily sardonic, and somewhat eccentric Ellis Rabb, a beanpole who wrapped himself in woolen scarves and affected a rather drawling voice. His APA, after working out of town for two years, had made an introductory sortie into Manhattan off Broadway. We approached him with *War and Peace,* and the ultimate result was a series of four plays from the APA repertoire produced at the Phoenix in the 1963–64 season and the opening of the Piscator drama, a complex play with a large cast, in December 1964.

When finally presented, the joint APA/Phoenix production of *War and Peace* spectacularly fulfilled our hopes. It confirmed Rabb's great directorial flair, and it also introduced to Phoenix audiences the remarkably gifted Rosemary Harris. The APA's greatest single asset, she could bring to any role the voice, age, emotional power, and style that it required, whether it be tragical, comical, historical, or pastoral. In my opinion, Rosemary Harris was—and remains—one of the great actresses of her generation. She also happens to be endowed with charm, humor, intelligence, radiance. As Ira Gershwin asked, "Who can ask for anything more?"

The action of the play unfolded on two levels. On the higher one was played out the world-shaking conflict between Napoleon and the Tsar, and here the two rulers appeared, banners were unfurled, and trumpets resounded. On the downstage lower level, the personal family tragedy, with Rosemary playing Natasha and Donald Moffatt her fiancé, Andrei, came into focus. Knitting the two worlds together was a Narrator in dinner jacket, who introduced characters, encapsulated the exposition, and occasionally intervened by stepping into a scene as a minor character.

The most arresting *jeu de théâtre* was the battle of Borodino. It was fought on a giant pegboard tilted toward the audience, the opposing armies represented by outsize lead soldiers. The river and its valley were spread forth as if viewed from a mountain peak—villages and churches in miniature, puffs of smoke emerging from the holes of the pegboard. The Narrator presided, describing the swings in the tide of battle and using a croupier's stick to remove a regiment of hussars or a brigade of cavalry after they were destroyed in the swirling action. Never have I seen a battle scene more imaginatively or grippingly mounted on a stage.

I think of *War and Peace* as my legacy to the Phoenix. I actually had no direct hand in the production—the triumph was Ellis's and the APA's—but behind it all stood Hambleton and Houghton, and it was the latter who had introduced the play to the former. And I use the word "legacy" quite deliberately, because I was departing.

I came to realize after three years that it was impossible for me to hold two full-time jobs and do full justice to either. So in 1964, for the second time in five years, I submitted my resignation as co–managing director. This time it was for keeps. While I remained on the board for a while and continued as a vice president of Theatre Incorporated, for the next sixteen years I went to the Phoenix only as a member of the audience.

To be sure, my labors in the educational world would not remove me totally from the theatre. The latter would continue to be my preoccupation; but now my focus would be upon the next generation, with whom I would strive to share what I'd learned during the past thirty-odd years. A teacher, I believe, must be something of a missionary to succeed. He must have faith in his message, visions to inspirit him. My father's brother journeyed to China as a medical missionary in 1906; my mother's sister to Chile as a Methodist missionary in 1917. I guess that zeal runs in my blood.

As I sit at my desk years later, I wonder why the idea of the Phoenix held me in such a powerful grip, only to release me, relatively speaking, so soon? And why did T. Edward Hambleton pursue it for another twenty years after I left, lending his hand at the Phoenix to young dramatists like Marsha Norman and Wendy Wasserstein, and to neophyte actresses Meryl Streep, Glenn Close, Mary Beth Hurt?

T.'s pursuit I can't really explain, except to suggest that it derived from blind belief in the rightness of a cause, from the bulldog streak that tends to inhabit the sons of Eli Yale who have strong jaws, from a conviction that turned into an obsession. If I recognize a missionary zeal in myself, I see in T. Edward the stern qualities of a defender of the faith.

For me the idea of the Phoenix derived from everything that had preceded it, from the moment I had made a commitment to the theatre at twenty-one, or even before. By the age of forty-two I felt I was ready to perform a major feat for which I had been preparing myself all along, a feat that would pull together my beliefs, my experiences, and my dreams. In retrospect, the whole enterprise seems to have been inevitable. It was my mission.

More interesting is why I abandoned it. Am I perhaps someone in thrall to illusion, who cannot cope with reality? History as well as the pages of dramatic literature are full of such persons. From Ronald Reagan in the real world to Willy Loman in the imagination of Arthur Miller, we have beheld such men; from Emmeline

Pankhurst to Blanche DuBois, we have beheld such women. I hesitate to place myself in their company. But I recognize in them all a stubborn resistance to facing life's hard facts, and I recognize that quality in myself.

The Phoenix was my dream. I worked strenuously to make it come true, and it did—up to a point. But because, I think, there must be a counterbalance somewhere in my nature, I came to perceive, almost against my will, that the dream *was* only a dream and could not survive the forces of reality—the financial obligations, the insufficient public support, the pressures of the marketplace, my own limitations. Instinctively I recognized the need either to forsake the dream or to face a future that would find me hanging on, embittered and disillusioned. If I couldn't create to my own satisfaction the theatre I sought, I had to alter course and abandon my dream. To some that may seem fainthearted; to me it seems an awakening to truth. I regret it, but I am not ashamed of it.

As for the Phoenix—the reality, not my dream—it did, I believe, perform remarkable services during a remarkable life. To a substantial degree it changed the way the theatre operated in New York City. It succeeded in making stage folk and the general public realize that there were other stages and other reasons to produce than Broadway's, and other motivations than commercialism. It stood as a signpost pointing the way toward a new land: "off Broadway." Hundreds of folk who have never heard of the Phoenix or seen a single one of its productions today earnestly seek the fulfillment of *their* dreams in playhouses away from Times Square—indeed, in lofts, garages, converted movie houses, and churches uptown and down. Together those playhouses offer the diversity of delights that the Phoenix sought to provide in itself.

I can claim, too, that the Phoenix played a role, perhaps unrecognized, in altering the theatrical pattern of the nation. Since 1953, a vast number of resident theatres, almost all of them noncommercial, have arisen in conscious or unconscious emulation of off Broadway. The Guthrie in Minneapolis, the Mark Taper Forum in Los Angeles, and the Actors Theatre in Louisville are only three of fifty times that number, not a few with Phoenix graduates at the helm, that can claim heir rights to the traditions of Twelfth Street and Second Avenue. The leaders of these theatres have been missionaries too. Their begetters have a lot to be proud of.

13

Theatre to a New Generation (1962–67)

Long before I took up my position at Vassar, the missionary zeal I've referred to as one requisite to successful teaching used to sweep over me recurrently, especially when my cash flow was at a minimum. The first time was shortly after publication of *Moscow Rehearsals*, in 1936. I was invited by the Finch School to share my knowledge of theatrical history with the young ladies it was "finishing." Having had no experience with finishing schools, I eyed them with suspicion, troubled by the educational implications in the idea of preparing for adult life by being "finished."

However, since an early-morning hour two days a week shouldn't interfere with serious practice of my major profession and I needed the money, I accepted. The girls I taught had charming manners and responded warmly to my instruction. After all, at twenty-six, although no Adonis, I was eager, and reasonably personable, and only six or eight years their senior. One pretty, round-faced young thing with a rich Texas accent found theatre history mesmerizing. She regularly arrived ahead of time and took a seat at the seminar table directly to my left. There she quickly fell into a trance, her chin cupped in her hand, her wondering eyes never wandering from my face, as she feasted on the crumbs of learning I dropped before her. Had my response been more encouraging and her parents receptive, I could perhaps have ended both my theatrical and my academic careers there and then and returned with her to Houston—or wherever she dwelt—to live my life in idle luxury, but my heart was not in it. Instead, I stayed on at Finch for three years, until I received my Rockefeller grant, which effectively ended my first engagement as an educator.

My next encounter with academia came two years later. It was heralded in the spring of 1941, as I was completing *Advance From Broadway,* by an invitation from my old mentor Dean Christian Gauss at Princeton. The university had recently established a "Creative Arts Program," had enlisted composer Roger Sessions, poet and critic Allen Tate, and sculptor Joseph Davis as artists in residence. Dean Gauss proposed that I join the program the following September, my duties to include teaching an undergraduate drama course, staging the Triangle Club's annual musical, acting as an informal adviser to the Theatre Intime and undergraduate dramatists, and running the McCarter Theatre. So ten years after graduation Princeton again beckoned, and this time I followed.

Unlike Finch, this was a full-time commitment. Why did I take it on? When I had left New York in 1939, I had every intention of returning to pick up my career as a Broadway stage designer after I'd fulfilled my obligation to my publishers. But enchanted by my own siren song about the theatre's decentralization and having made a strong case against commercialism—one that I deeply believed in—in *Advance from Broadway,* could I feel comfortable in Times Square? Furthermore, persistently drawn to academia, I had grown wistful from time to time, during the travels just completed, for what I saw, perhaps erroneously, as the security and serenity of the cloister. Then, too, Dean Gauss summoned me in May to talk about his offer—May, when Princeton is at its most enticing: dogwood, wisteria, azaleas, soft green lawns.

What's more, that spring before Pearl Harbor many of us felt a draft on our necks; almost certainly there were storms ahead. A safe haven, if only briefly, seemed attractive. "Going back, going back to Nassau Hall" is a favorite Princeton song, and if Dean Gauss wanted me, I was ready to "go back," even if it didn't mean going forward. Less than three months into the academic

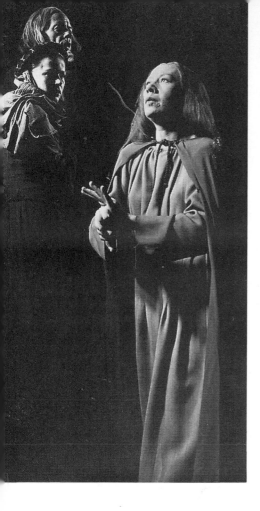

From Theatre Inc.'s production of *Macbeth*, 1948: Flora Robson in the sleepwalking scene, Michael Redgrave in the apparition scene.

The final scene of *Billy Budd*, 1951: (far left) Dennis King as Captain Vere and (upper center, in the rigging) Charles Nolte as Billy.

With Gertrude Lawrence and her daughter, Pamela, at the circus, 1946.

Producer-director Houghton at CBS-TV, 1952.

First Attraction 1953 Season

JESSICA
TANDY

HUME
CRONYN

in SIDNEY HOWARD'S COMEDY

"MADAM, WILL YOU WALK"

PHOENIX THEATRE 189 Second Avenue
December 1 thru January 10

Evenings Including Sundays Matinees Saturday and Sunday (No Performance Monday)

At lunch launching the Phoenix Theatre's first subscription drive, 1955: (left to right) Montgomery Clift, Nancy Walker and husband David Craig, Mrs. Vincent Astor.

Announcement of the Phoenix Theatre's first production, 1953.

Hambleton and Houghton watching a rehearsal of a Phoenix production, sometime between 1953 and 1961.

Scenes from Chekhov's *The Seagull*, 1954: (left to right) June Walker, Maureen Stapleton, Will Geer, Judith Evelyn, Kevin McCarthy, George Voskovec; Judith Evelyn and Montgomery Clift.

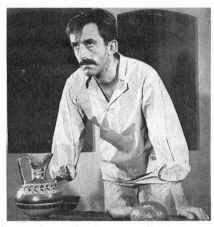

Poster for Ionesco's *The Chairs* and *The Lesson*, 1958.

Fritz Weaver in *The Power and the Glory*, 1959.

Siobhan McKenna in Shaw's *St. Joan*, 1956.

Eva Le Gallienne, Irene Worth, and Douglas Campbell in Schiller's *Mary Stuart*, 1957.

LIFE

BROADWAY'S MOST
IMAGINATIVE SEASON

KAYE BALLARD
IN 'GOLDEN APPLE'

20 CENTS
MAY 24, 1954

REG. U. S. PAT. OFF.

Cover girl
Kaye Ballard
as Helen in
The Golden Apple,
1954.

The marquee of the Phoenix Theatre, on Second Avenue and Twelfth Street, during the run of
The Golden Apple, in which Paris (Jonathan Lucas) carries Helen off in his balloon as Menelaus
(Dean Michener) vows vengeance.

Lillian Gish in T.S. Eliot's *The Family Reunion*, 1958.

June Havoc in Farquhar's *The Beaux Stratagem*, 1959.

Barbara Harris and Austin Pendleton in Arthur Kopit's *Oh Dad, Poor Dad, Mamma's Hung You in the Closet and I'm Feelin' So Sad*, 1962.

Joe Bova as the Prince and Carol Burnett as his fiancée, Princess Winifred, in *Once Upon a Mattress*, 1959.

Lecturing on contemporary American theatre in the hall of Moscow's Polytechnical Museum to an audience of 1000 Soviets, 1960.

Kim Eui Kyung of I.T.I. (center) and Houghton (third from right) pose with cast of a Korean mask-drama, Seoul, 1966.

Professor Houghton presides over a Vassar seminar, 1965.

In the dean's office at SUNY Purchase, 1975.

Theatre "A," the "Opera House," of the Purchase Performing Arts Center, designed by Edward Larrabee Barnes.

Celebrating my arrival at three-score-and-ten, New York, December, 1979: David Rockefeller, Jr., serenading; the "birthday boy" (center) with his first cousin, Mary Houghton Boorman, and her husband, Howard.

The Phoenix founders, Hambleton and Houghton, who enjoyed the last laugh!

year, we were at war. My appointment ended in June 1942; six months later I was commissioned a lieutenant, junior grade, in the U.S. Naval Reserve.

I'll not claim Shakespeare was solely responsible for my next appointment—to Columbia's faculty in 1948, but I do suspect that if I had not directed a critically well received *Macbeth* on Broadway that spring, the invitation might not have been forthcoming. In any event, a small band of Columbia professors, including the distinguished Elizabethan scholar Oscar J. Campbell, approached me with an invitation to take over the course in modern drama at Columbia's School of General Studies from which Richard Lockridge, then drama critic of the *New York Sun,* was retiring.

Macbeth had claimed my attention for close to a year; now, to balance my theatrical activity, I was eager to reestablish a connection with the academic world. I realized also that a part-time appointment would serve as a fiscal anchor to windward, and its timing—Saturday mornings from ten to twelve—was not likely to interfere with any rehearsal or managerial schedule. Finally, fired again with missionary zeal, I liked the idea of once more talking with students about my faith.

I continued to trek to Morningside Heights for a decade. In 1954, after six years of Saturday mornings, a trio of powerful women—Millicent McIntosh, Mrs. Ogden Reid, and Mrs. Richard Rodgers, president, board chairman, and trustee, respectively, of Barnard College—lured me across the street with an offer of an adjunct professorship and directorship of their new Minor Lathem Experimental Theatre. It might have been a full-time appointment, but because the Phoenix Theatre was rising simultaneously, once again I had time to teach only one course. At Barnard I did, however, sneak in a production of my old love *The Changeling,* and I discovered an unknown but arresting young actor, Peter Falk, to play the male lead.

When the time came to say "Hail" to Vassar and "Farewell" to Barnard, I felt I was experienced enough to deal with what lay ahead. But life has a curious way of obliging us to make decisions, only to find that they lead to just the opposite of what we anticipated. I thought I'd be a Teacher, perhaps ultimately a Guru.

Instead, the half decade I entered in 1962 provided *me*, much more than my students, with an education.

First, as departmental chairman I discovered that my working life was so filled with managerial functions that I had little time for the reflection and meditation I'd imagined were the life's blood of academia. I seemed to have no more time for selective reading, for instance, than during the previous hectic decade. But a lack of opportunity for intellectual growth was for me offset by the gradual recognition that I had a flair for educational planning.

Second, during that half decade I not only remained devoted to the stage, if at a distance; I also found time to make an entrance into the world of public affairs.

Third, I came to realize how much I needed travel to sustain me. Though much of it was theatre-related, its ramifications extended in many directions.

Finally, in the Hudson Valley I began a more or less unconscious self-evaluation, one that had little do with my professorial life but much to do with my persona. I learned, for instance, that I was by no means the intellectual wizard that one expects in a Phi Beta Kappa whose Princeton diploma carries the phrase *summa cum laude.*

In my undergraduate days I had never had a Vassar girlfriend. Although many of my friends did, generally without complaints, the Vassar students I met seemed formidable and inclined to be bossy; besides they were apt to be better dancers than I—not too hard to accomplish—and they "knew their way around," which put me at a double disadvantage. My prom dates came from Bryn Mawr, Goucher, and the Abbott School in Boston. I found the Bryn Mawr girl more intellectual than any Vassar candidates I knew, the others danced no better than I, and all of them were equally pretty. Naturally, no Vassar girl ever invited me up to a Poughkeepsie dance.

In 1962, the young women seemed a little less formidable than the girls had in 1931. The self-confidence I'd found so intimidating in their mothers' generation had been replaced by self-centeredness (a preview of the "me generation," perhaps), but these girls also appeared more vulnerable—or maybe it was only that I felt less so. The Vietnam years of student revolt lay ahead; so, too, did the drug culture that was to claim so many of the young. Looking

89933445888

back at them from the perspective of the nineties, I see the girls innocent to a degree certainly not evident at the time. They were even biddable, perhaps because "women's lib" had not yet arrived.

Some of those who fancied themselves actresses put on the airs they thought appropriate, but those who *were* talented had no time for that—they worked very hard. I hesitate so many years later to single out any by name, but I mention a few because they made a particular impression on me. Etain O'Malley, who was the niece of both Mrs. John D. Rockefeller 3rd and Mrs. John P. Marquand, suffered from the insecurity common to many talented artists. (Interesting that so many of the untalented never have doubts.) An exotic-looking young lady, today Etain is a good working professional actress. Susan Kaslow, a petite brunette, gave a mature and lyrical performance as Natalia Petrovna in our production of Turgenev's *A Month in the Country*. And Beth Bowden, a tall, statuesque blonde, seemingly unaware of how lovely-looking she was, shone as Katherine of Aragon in *The Royal Gambit*.

I omit mention of would-be dramatists because it was hard to judge their gifts: most of the students in my playwriting seminar were incapable of producing any sustained piece of dramatic writing that exceeded eleven pages.

Conversely, and as usual, the hardest-working of all the students were the "techies." Outstanding among them, not only because she was the tallest and strongest, was Elizabeth Villard. A capable and conscientious stagehand, she had her eye on becoming a director and in due time joined the Vassar faculty to teach acting and directing. One of Liz's backstage cohorts was Marjorie Kellogg, a mouse to Liz's lion, who, after a graduate stint at Yale, went on to become a busy and accomplished set designer in New York—both on and off Broadway. I regret that Vassar's recent stars, Jane Fonda and Meryl Streep, never crossed my Vassar path, Jane being before my time, Meryl after.

Sadly, during my five-year tenure the drama majors were not a flamingly talented lot. Young women with real ability and strong stage ambition weren't apt to come to Vassar. They headed for schools with professional training programs, admission to which usually required competitive auditions. At Vassar, any student who wanted to major in drama at the end of her sophomore year was free to do so, one of the cherished privileges of a liberal arts college.

The faculty at Vassar, an institution with strong traditions of academic excellence, would not countenance any curricular reorganization that might endanger the school's humanistic image. And I was in sympathy with them. The product of a Princeton liberal arts program that was equally disdainful toward awarding academic credit for frivolous activities in the performing arts, I posed no threat to those members of the Vassar faculty who viewed with alarm the arrival of a professional to chair the drama department. I had no desire to turn my bailiwick into a professional school.

That didn't mean that I had no convictions or plans. If we were allowing students to major in drama, I believed we had to give them their money's worth. The courses we offered and the effort we required had to match the demands of the classics or chemistry or history departments. Given the nature of theatre, this translated into theory supported by practice. In order to graduate, drama majors had not only to complete courses in the history and literature of the theatre but to earn performance or production credits as well. We may not have been a professional school, but we insisted that professional standards be the goals to strive toward.

During the summer before I started at Vassar full-time, I reviewed what I knew about the drama program from my part-time appointment. Various problems emerged, most serious the familiar one of quantity versus quality, as it applied to the production schedule. At the Phoenix in 1955–56, we had presented fifteen shows. In her last year at Vassar, my predecessor had scheduled fourteen—all the major ones directed by herself. Our total had included Marceau and a multiplicity of Sideshows; hers had included their rough equivalents: student-directed productions running for two or three performances each. I have speculated about whether the Phoenix didn't overextend itself, and I would have posed the same question to Miss Heinlein if her premature demise, perhaps hastened by the overload, had not prevented me.

Statistics, I grant, prove nothing in matters of art; nonetheless, they may imply flaws and imbalances. The Vassar students and the three faculty men who could act met themselves coming offstage as they went on for the next play. In consequence, no one really had time to learn *how* to act. I know that "learning through doing" is a popular maxim in academic environments, including Princeton, where the blind often lead the blind. What it really encourages, however, is an emphasis on *product* at the expense of *process.* Anyone who measures thespian talent by proficiency in learning lines does not know what acting is all about. There is considerably more to it than a foolproof memory. Consider Laurette Taylor and Gertrude Lawrence and Ina Claire: none of them was ever quite sure of the next line, but it mattered not a whit.

Thus, at our first faculty meeting I told my colleagues that it was important to do fewer things better; that I believed their production work load was impeding their efficiency; that students were being presented to the public before knowing anything about acting; and that, consequently, the Experimental Theatre would henceforth do only three major productions a season, with none of us staging more than one.

To make sure that process was upgraded, I determined to expose students to professional performers who knew that product resulted from it. The first to be invited in 1963 was Mildred Dunnock. Everyone knew her to be a superb actress (as Linda Loman, for example); her students discovered her equal preeminence in the classroom. Furthermore, while she epitomized professionalism at its highest, she was also a strong exponent of a liberal education.

During one of her master classes, after two students had finished a scene from *Mourning Becomes Electra,* Millie rushed forward and embraced them.

"What wonderful work!" she cried. Turning to the class, she said, "Did you see how beautifully they played to each other?" On and on she marveled. When the class ended, one of these two girls—a junior—asked her if she really meant what she had said. Dunnock reassured her: of course she did—every word.

"What would you think, then, if I left Vassar at the end of the term to try my luck in New York?"

"Darling," Millie fired back at once, her voice vibrating with passion, "you mean you'd throw over these past three years, not finish your education? Don't think of it! You must realize that the richness of your performance as an actress depends upon the richness of yourself as a human being. To deprive yourself of the next year of college would reduce by that much what you bring to the stage. Finish Vassar—of course—then think about a career." She was stating the whole case for a humanistic approach to the arts.

Millie Dunnock was so successful that following her I brought in a series of other fine professionals—actresses, directors, choreographers, voice coaches. In Millie's wake came Anne Revere: since *The Children's Hour* in the 1930s, I had—to risk the pun—revered her. The search for truth in acting was her constant goal, and to her students she imparted the basic lesson that truth is more important than "effects." But since technique cannot be disparaged, I next called in Dorothy Sands, a comedienne in the high classical sense, who balanced the class's diet by demonstrating how to get laughs just by raising an eyebrow.

Janet Reed and Elizabeth Smith appeared twice a week, the former to teach classes in movement, the latter, in speech. Janet had been an early star of the New York City Ballet. Elizabeth Smith reflected another kind of glamour. Fresh from London, she had been trained by the great Elsie Fogarty, at whose feet Gielgud, Olivier, and other knights had also knelt. Elizabeth seemed to put Vassar in touch with them all.

Our drama majors included some, like Liz Villard, who thought they'd like to be directors. To demonstrate to them what directing was all about—and to explain something more about acting to the others—I asked Joseph Anthony and Milton Katselas to become visiting directors. Before the former staged *The Dragon* at the Phoenix, he had directed a string of Broadway hits, among them *The Lark, The Most Happy Fella,* and *Mary, Mary,* and in Hollywood such movies as *The Rainmaker* and *The Matchmaker.* Equally important, Joe was also a superb and experienced teacher, one who loved teaching because he loved young people. Also, having studied and then taught at Tamara Daykarhanova's School for the Stage since the 1930s, Joe was able to expose his students to Russian-inspired acting methods. Milton Katselas, a handsome thirty-two-year-old Greek, had made his name in New York by directing Edward Albee's *The Zoo Story* and *Call Me by My Rightful Name*. The Vassar students deserved a respite from middle-aged artists, and Milton offered some sex appeal.

Thus was our aviary enlivened by these varicolored transient birds of paradise. They also served to challenge the regular faculty, who, although still young, had Ph.D.s and had been in residence for almost a decade. By mentioning the talented but unscholarly first, I certainly do not mean to minimize the contribution of the resident staff. Indeed, I admit that, with only an A.B. to my name, I felt rather daunted by a trio of "doctors." They included Dr. William Rothwell, with his Ph.D. from Yale; Dr. Evert Sprinchorn, his from Columbia; Dr. Seabury Quinn, his from Harvard. They formed a motley group. Rothwell had a penchant for motorcycles and leather jackets by day, white tie and tails for the occasional evening of dancing. Sprinchorn was a specialist in Strindberg and Ibsen, about whom he was constantly publishing books and monographs. Quinn, who nicely exemplified the absentminded professor, once took his convertible Volkswagen to a car wash and forgot to put the top up and close the windows. When his auto came out, the canvas top was nowhere to be seen, which didn't perturb Quinn, since he, at least, hadn't disappeared!

Our fourth faculty member, scene designer and technician Tadeusz Gesek, had an M.F.A. from Yale. He was a second-generation Pole, who devoted his spare time to wooing and winning the young assistant alumnae director of the college. His colleagues—Benedicks all—looked on somewhat enviously.

In academia, it usually takes about three years to produce an innovation—that is, to discuss a matter exhaustively, to come up with a new idea, and to find the money to implement it. My second problem related to academic planning was male acting support; I solved it in only two years, though I'm not sure how much time had passed since all-girl casts had dazzled Vassar audiences. The fact is that male casting was "in" by the time I arrived, but it was accomplished pretty much catch-as-catch-can: flattery was used to lure stagestruck faculty, like Gordon Post, professor of history; strong-arm tactics to coerce friends and husbands; and sly intrigue to tempt young-men-about-town. But the result of such maneuvering did not satisfy me. Most of our actors were, at best, no more than willing amateurs who did little to improve our production standards or provide real support to our students. Too often and quite unintentionally, the men damaged overall morale by absences from critical rehearsals when they conflicted with jobs, seminars, or lodge meetings.

I proposed creating a small, paid, young men's acting company in residence, recruited from recent graduates of reputable theatre schools like Yale, Carnegie Mellon, and Goodman. Miss Blanding approved, subsidy was found, and twenty-seven candidates from nineteen institutions applied, allowing us to choose six top-notch men for a year's residency.

A third problem, this one allied to academic planning, concerned facilities. Vassar's Avery Theatre, which also housed the classics department and its museum, had been converted forty or fifty years earlier from an indoor riding ring. But as the department's enrollment rose, theatre space became inadequate. Six months after arriving, I wrote a proposal for a new wing to Avery, "to provide us with a small flexible laboratory theatre, that would give us, through double duty, additional rehearsal space, plus increased dressing rooms and office space." If the college did nothing, I indicated, we would find ourselves losing out in the competition for students to colleges whose stage facilities were vastly more inviting than our antique riding ring. "Furthermore, we [the faculty] shall find ourselves unable to grow in our work; when that happens, Vassar will lose not only students but those teachers for whom growth is essential to their well-being."

Vassar got the message and chose John Johansen as architect. His drawings provided for just what we needed. A year later everything was set to go forward, but all the money was not yet in hand. When I left Vassar a year or so after that, the situation was unchanged. And as of today that new wing has never been built.

My last and perhaps most challenging problem: I seemed unable to restore to Vassar's Experimental Theatre the excitement of the twenties and early thirties, when its inspired founding director, Hallie Flanagan, was at the helm. Since that time it had never truly justified the word "experimental."

Were the times that different? Were the 1920s and '30s more open to artistic experiment than the early '60s? Was academic theatre now so accustomed to purveying "noncommercial" fare that there was no longer any peculiar excitement in offering plays by Giraudoux, Genet, Farquhar, Strindberg; Pirandello's *Liola; The Trojan Women, Everyman,* and *Pericles, Prince of Tyre?* (These were among the dishes served up during my tenure.) Perhaps a new definition of "experimental" was needed for a new generation, but if so I never discovered it.

We did attempt one "experiment" that, I believe, deserved the name, a staged version of Ingmar Bergman's film *Smiles of a Summer Night.* We found its text in a collection of his screen-plays. Everyone has seen stage plays turned into movies, often quite effectively, but in 1965 I couldn't recall ever having seen a movie turned into a play. (It was eight years later that Stephen Sondheim, Hugh Wheeler, and Harold Prince transformed this same work into the musical *A Little Night Music.*)

I had journeyed to Sweden a few years earlier to woo Bergman into directing a play for the Phoenix, a contemporary Swedish work by Hjalmar Bergman (no relation), which he had staged successfully during his artistic directorship at Stockholm's Royal Dramatic Theatre. Told that he never answered letters, I flew to Stockholm, where Hjalmar Bergman's widow led me to Svensk Filmindustri. There we waited twenty minutes before a slight, youthful-looking chap, in worn corduroys and a cardigan sweater, burst into the reception room. I took him for a stage manager come to fetch us to the master. It was, of course, the master himself, who, apologizing for the delay, led the way into his cubbyhole of an office.

An hour's talk ensued. Bergman was all charm and humor, with no mystical veils evident, but though we laughed a lot, I came away empty-handed. He could not consider our invitation for at least a couple of years: he had a Mozart opera to direct in Switzerland, with another film to follow. Besides, he wasn't sure the play the Phoenix proposed was one he'd want to make his debut with in America. We, of course, would have been glad to present *Little Red Riding Hood* if he'd so wished. But he wasn't certain, if it came to that, that he wanted to make an American debut—ever. And after more than a quarter century, he never has directed a play specifically for a U.S. stage.

If Bergman wouldn't come to the Phoenix, I proposed now to collaborate with him in absentia—provided he would grant me the rights. Kay Brown, the legendary literary agent, was his American representative. In response to her persuasive powers, Bergman cabled his approval and wished us well. Just possibly he recalled my regret when we parted in Stockholm and was making amends for refusing the Phoenix a few years before.

My intent at Vassar was to offer in stage terms as close an approximation of the original movie as possible, in order for us to experience firsthand what makes a film *not* a play and vice versa. Viewed as an educational experiment, the project successfully realized its objective. Using a gauze scrim downstage, two proscenium doors opening onto small side stages, and a deep apron in front, designer Gesek made it possible to achieve the seamless action and rhythms so essential to cinema; in effect, action unfolded by means of stage equivalents to a film's dissolves.

Because Bergman's dialogue was so good, vividly revealing character motivations and reactions, we were almost persuaded that our experiment would succeed in broader terms, that a fine film *could* make a good stage play. But when the production finally came together, it was a theatrical disaster. Basic ingredients were missing: the encompassing environment, the camera's close-up eye, the visual images that reveal, sustain, and interpret the script's critical moments. Take but one example: the dinner party scene—and never mind identifying the characters—as set down in Bergman's text:

> Fredrik drinks, and a mist comes over his eyes. He tries to brush it away, but it remains.
>
> Henrik's glass stands full and untouched in front of him. He stares at it as if hypnotized. Then he grips it, brings it to his mouth, but changes his mind and puts it down again.
>
> The old lady dips a small, bony finger into her glass and allows it to be colored by the wine. She licks her finger like a cat.

Then Henrik drinks, emptying the whole glass and putting it down so violently that he cracks its fragile stem.

FREDRIK: Watch what you're doing.

HENRIK: Watch what *you're* doing yourself.

Henrik flares up; his eyes flash and his mouth trembles. He has turned absolutely white. Petra runs forward and tries to wipe up the red stain which grows and swells across the white tablecloth.

Only nine words of dialogue are used, but thanks to the camera's close-ups and the editing, the moment's dramatic significance is recorded in a way the stage could never fully reveal. What chance that those in the back rows of an auditorium could see that mist over Fredrik's eyes, Henrik's trembling mouth, the old lady's bony finger, the red stain spreading on the tablecloth? Although the Vassar audience left the theatre dissatisfied and baffled, we were glad we'd undertaken the experiment. Certainly, it failed—it was bound to—but the Experimental Theatre in this instance lived up to its name.

14

The Vision Enlarged (1962–67)

*I*n the late winter of 1965, I received my first invitation to travel abroad since coming to Vassar. The West German government invited me to make a three-and-a-half-week tour of its principal theatrical centers. I accepted, as always grateful for the chance to travel at other people's expense. My fellow travelers were Robert Schnitzer, professor of theatre at the University of Michigan, and Robert Chapman, by then professor of English at Harvard and director of its Loeb Theatre.

At Princeton, Chapman had acquired fame as president of the Triangle Club and balanced that by enacting Hamlet in the Theatre Intime with such emotional power, thought, and good diction that audiences were transfixed—all this while he was only a sophomore. He retains his Danish-princely look and courtly manners, has honed his wit to rapier sharpness, can consign Ophelias to nunneries with a glance and outroister Guildensterns until dawn—but he has never acted since.

For three and a half weeks we whirled our way through a titanic Teutonic itinerary: from Bonn and adjacent Cologne to Düsseldorf, with side trips to Recklinghausen and Solingen, small steel-mill cities in the Ruhr, which none of us had ever heard of before, each with a newly built sleek steel and glass playhouse of which the inhabitants were properly proud; to Hamburg for five days, Munich and Berlin for six each. Most days were alike:

official Rathaus luncheons with welcoming toasts and effortful responses, receptions, inspection tours of theatre buildings, sightseeing tours of cities, performances of operas (eleven of them), ballets, plays (nine), and a concert of the Berlin Philharmonic in its then just-finished hall (which looks like the TWA terminal at Kennedy Airport). On June 20 we flew home.

I used to dream about those days. Chapman and I are always running, with Schnitzer and our guides slowly gaining on us. We are whisking through stage doors, watching revolving stages go round faster and faster. Then we find ourselves in light booths that resemble airplane cockpits, with tiny red and yellow bulbs flashing, as electronics wizards take futuristic lightboards through their computerized paces.

In my dream I relive our visit to the Bavarian State Opera in Munich for a performance of *Tristan and Isolde,* sung in the dark. (That part of the dream is accurate—Wolfgang Wagner, the director, apparently considered it an indignity to his forefather to reveal the performers to the naked eye, since they might distract from the music.) Now we are being escorted to a reception room behind the *Intendant*'s box for bottle after bottle of German champagne. Then the dream shifts: we are having supper afterward in a restaurant across the street; suddenly Birgit Nilsson sweeps in and sits down beside us, happily recovered from the "Liebestod," and indeed, if anything, looking the better for her exertion. Just as I am about to kiss her hand, the dream fades and I awake. But the dream is still clear, for the experience was actually very like that.

The tour was my first visit to Germany. I was most impressed by the architectural and technological virtuosity of its stages. Many theatres had been destroyed by Allied bombings, and the Germans, who care deeply about music and drama, gave high priority to rebuilding them. Occasionally, an opera house was lovingly restored to an approximation of its original nineteenth-century state; more frequently, architects started from scratch, making innovations in both form and function. With unparalleled sorcery they developed new stage technology surpassing that of the other countries of both Eastern and Western Europe.

The Germans of the mid-sixties also boasted directors and designers who could make the most of the new facilities and equipment. But their plays and players, I felt, did not measure up to the technological wonders that surrounded them. I saw few extraordinary acting performances; I saw few plays that stirred me deeply.

The newly installed telephone rang at my Vermont farmhouse. "Norris, Porter McCray here. Might you be free next spring to go to Korea?" It was the voice of the director of the JDR 3rd Fund in New York—the personal foundation of John D. Rockefeller 3rd, as distinguished from the Rockefeller Brothers Fund.

This was Labor Day weekend, 1965. Next spring was a little far off, I replied, but in any case, the answer had to be no. I'd missed this year's commencement, having been in Germany, and a department chairman shouldn't miss two in a row. "But why do you ask?"

Because, he explained, he'd hoped to interest me in going to Seoul on a mission for the fund, and he now proposed that we meet anyhow. Porter, an old friend, was a slightly rotund fellow of about my age with dimples and a whimsical smile. His courtly manners and soft Virginia accent concealed both his mastery of executive detail and an incongruously ribald sense of humor. This was his story:

In the early 1960s, Mr. Yoo Chi-jin, South Korea's senior dramatist, decided to build a theatre center in Seoul and turned to Mr. Rockefeller for help in realizing his dream.

"He was very persuasive, was Yoo," said Porter, adding, "You must remember when I say 'Yoo' I mean *him,* not *you.* " Mr. Rockefeller agreed to a small grant—perhaps $25,000—as encouragement. Yoo soon learned it was but seed money: it was nowhere near enough to build an arts center. With admirable persistence, however, he amassed the needed capital, among other devices by selling his own house and moving his family into the basement of the rising structure.

It proved to be quite acceptable a plant, inspired by the theatre at the State University of Iowa, which impressed Yoo when he had visited the campus to see his son, who was enrolled there. The Seoul facility contained a large thrust stage and a small adjacent laboratory theatre. To celebrate the opening of the center, Yoo wrote a new play, *So Flows the Han,* and he filled out the rest of his first season with translations of *Death of a Salesman, Hamlet, Porgy and Bess, Long Day's Journey into Night,* and *Romeo and Juliet.*

It must have come as a surprise only to Yoo that the drama lovers of Seoul were discomfited by this unfamiliar repertoire and showed it by staying away, leaving him, at season's end, still more deeply in debt. His advisers (among whom, I suspect, was his wife, surely by then weary of subterranean housekeeping) persuaded Yoo to do what proprietors of failing theatrical real estate have so often done: turn the place into a movie palace. As for the lab theatre, it became a marriage parlor. And as a result, after two years, Yoo had recouped his losses. Remembering his faraway friend in New York, he then wrote to Mr. Rockefeller, asking for renewed assistance to underwrite a resumption of theatrical programming.

Now, Mr. Rockefeller had never fancied himself an absentee backer of a Seoul movie house, let alone a Korean marriage parlor. Still, his fund was not noted for walking away from projects it had in part helped to create.

"Here's where you come in," McCray announced. The fund needed someone to go and investigate the situation. Would Yoo be able to pull his project together? Were there talented younger people the fund should pay attention to? What did the arts community think of Yoo's project now? And, most basic, did the Korean stage deserve serious attention? "We need an expert, for none of us at the fund feels capable in this field."

I was intrigued, but I told Porter I feared I was miscast. Certainly no expert on Far Eastern stages, I had seen none farther from home than Mott Street. And with no standards for comparison, how could I make a judgment? They'd make me an expert, persisted McCray. If I could ascertain where in Asia the best stage work was being done, they'd send me there to acquire some basis for an informed evaluation.

How many years did he expect this to take? I wondered. McCray had said Yoo was already passing his prime, and I would be, too, pretty soon. I could learn enough in a summer, responded

Porter airily; they weren't looking for a scholarly examination. If a scholar was not needed, perhaps I was less miscast than I had first feared, and I agreed to consider the fund's request.

I did and learned that since China was then off limits, the countries other than Korea that I had to visit were Japan and India. There didn't seem to be much dramatic theatre elsewhere. Porter immediately approved my itinerary.

"But," I remarked, "if I head for East Asia and then go to India, I'll be more than halfway round the world." Remembering how the Rockefellers prize a dime, I added, "Wouldn't it be cheaper to send me all the way around the world?"

"The budget is based on that," he replied.

So the week after Vassar's 1966 commencement, off to Asia I went, first to Tokyo, where the next day I boarded a plane for Seoul. At the foot of its ramp, the Japanese stewardess cried, "Have a good fright!"

As I stepped off the plane in Seoul, I knew at once I was in for a culture shock that would gain momentum as I circumnavigated the globe: from Korea back to Japan, thence to Hong Kong, Thailand, Cambodia, India, and Nepal, over the Khyber Pass to Afghanistan, through Iran and Lebanon, and onto familiar ground at last in Athens.

In most places, scenery competes for my attention with people, but I could concentrate on the latter in Seoul, which is not the most beautiful of Asian cities. Mr. Yoo, a fairly square, large man in his sixties, was quite hospitable. He conducted me through his drama center, showed me the marriage parlor, took me to dinner with his wife (not in their basement), and spent hours talking of his plans.

At an elaborate banquet arranged by the Korean Center of UNESCO's International Theatre Institute, the professor from Vassar met many of the country's drama professors, each of whom offered a presentation copy of his latest work—in Korean and usually unillustrated.

I attended such theatrical productions as were available, including an ancient, traditional mask-dance drama that was performed in an open field, the accustomed environment since time im-memorial. In a shabby playhouse, the so-called National Theatre, I witnessed probably the worst Shakespearean production I've ever seen: *The Merry Wives of Windsor,* played in Korean with awestruck solemnity by actors garbed in what purported to be Elizabethan costume but was, in fact, a ragbag from many centuries and lands. The cast clearly found nothing merry about the wives—nor did the audience, none of whom, myself included, cracked a smile.

After a couple of weeks in Korea I flew back to Japan, where the scenery is more vivid and the people less sweet. The Japanese stage has incredible fecundity. Paralleling the mask-dance dramas of Korea are the well-known Kabuki and the highly sophisticated Noh plays, so esoteric that even my Japanese interpreter slept through much of the one I attended. In Japan, I was coming to a new understanding of what Meierhold had been driving at in his "theatre theatrical" of the 1930s.

My schedule included meetings with prominent playwrights and directors, smiling and eager, and with actors young and old. I attended contemporary plays and musicals, both foreign and domestic, including the currently popular British musical *Half a Sixpence,* the famed Bunraku puppets, an all-girl musical. In Yokohama, I saw a play by Yukio Mishima, *The Marquise de Sade,* the first time I had ever been made aware of the Marquis's matrimonial life.

It was Mishima whom I was, understandably, most eager to meet. In the West he was regarded as Japan's great contemporary man of letters, and for some years he had been spoken of as a potential Nobel Prize winner in Literature. An erstwhile editor of mine, Frank Taylor, had written alerting Mishima to my imminent arrival, so he was prepared for my call and responded by proposing that we meet at my hotel the followinmg evening.

Punctually at ten he knocked. I welcomed a slender, lithe, rather short young man with deep-set, sparkling eyes. His movements were rapid; so was his speech. His English was impeccable. Our exploratory conversation was mostly about the theatre and New York, where he had been not long before. He said, after about an hour, that he was on his way to a party. Would I like to come along? He wouldn't stay long, he explained, but if I was enjoying myself, he'd see that I was driven home. I accepted, and off we drove in his little car.

At the party there were about twenty guests, all of whom rose when we entered. Most of them were good-looking young men, and I subsequently wondered if they might have been members of his "private army." Everyone had been awaiting Mishima's arrival before running a movie. We all sat on the floor, looking up at the screen, he in a corner with one of his favorites. When the lights came up, like Cinderella he was gone.

Having been prepared, I was not disturbed. I'd learned that his daily life was lived upside down: he slept from 8 A.M. until 4 P.M., when he rose, mingled with his wife and children, conducted business with his secretary and pleasure with the world at large until midnight, at which witching hour he disappeared and spent the rest of the night at his writing desk, secure from all distractions.

The memory of that single brief encounter with one of Asia's most arresting figures acquired added significance with the shocking news, not long after, of his inconceivable suicide—hara-kiri committed on a public balcony before a crowd of political followers, gathered to express their (and his) disillusionment with the changing values of modern-day Japan. How I wish that I'd been allowed to nurture the seeds of a potential friendship, planted on that Tokyo evening, and to have penetrated, perhaps only a little way, into the mystery of his life and the enigma of his death.

B angkok was my next destination after a weekend in Hong Kong. The old Oriental Hotel, on the bank of the broad, muddy Chao Phraya River, would house me for the next few nights. I found on arrival a neatly typed note: "In connection with a telegram received from Mr. Porter McCray, Princess Chumbhot will be pleased to receive Mr. Houghton at luncheon on Tuesday, July 19th, 1966 at 12:00 o'clock. Please confirm."

Now, the Princess Chumbhot of Nagor Svarga was the widow of a grandson of king Chulalongkorn, the king in *The King and I.* Having formed my impression of Siam's royal family from that musical, I was eager to discover what was in store. The car sent to fetch me stopped before the private entrance of a rambling single-story house (actually five houses joined by covered walkways). There I was ushered into a sunny living room, filled with chintz-clad furniture, that might have been on Long Island. Several guests were already there, everyone in Western garb and speaking perfect English. My hostess, a Siamese princess in her own right, was of less than medium height and more than medium appeal, with a lively, pretty face framed by slightly graying hair.

During lunch Princess Chumbhot expressed her regret that Thailand had no dramatic theatre. Dancing and music were its only performing arts. But if I would come to lunch again tomorrow, she said, she'd show me something afterward that might interest me.

One doesn't decline a royal invitation, so I returned the next day, and once luncheon was over we drove to a nearby movie house. After watching ten minutes or so of what we would call a Western, she took my arm and rose.

"Come along," the princess whispered. We walked up the aisle and climbed a flight of stairs into a small room adjacent to the projection booth. The wall facing the screen was of heavy glass. Against it stood a long, narrow table at which sat half a dozen men and women, talking loudly, even occasionally shouting angrily. They kept their eyes glued to the screen as they spoke.

What I was being shown was a silent film with a live sound track, being dubbed before my eyes. These six were providing the voices for all the characters, synchronizing the dialogue to the lips of the performers. After we watched for twenty minutes, she led me out, explaining as we left that while all the films shown in Thailand were made there, the Thai motion picture industry was poor and primitive and could not afford sound equipment. Besides, a single sound track would be useless, because Thailand had so many dialects that audiences in Chiang Mai in the north, for example, wouldn't understand dialogue spoken in the south and vice versa, multiplied several times over. Consequently, for each film one text was written and then spoken by different casts, thus dubbing it in different dialects for the different provinces.

I am not writing a travelogue, but there is one sightseeing

experience I particularly want to record, because so few have had the chance to share it.

A two-engine plane transported me from Bangkok to Phnom Penh in Cambodia, where I took another plane to Angkor. I was to view on that Rockefeller trip many breathtaking wonders—the giant Buddha at Kamakura, the Taj Mahal, the ancient Persian city of Persepolis, the massive Roman ruins of Baalbek; and later, on self-subsidized trips, the pyramids and tombs of the Nile valley, the Mayan ruins in Yucatán. Angkor Wat overwhelms them all.

There I wandered for hours, tracing stone bas-reliefs of warriors, men on horseback and on elephants, princes and slaves, oarsmen and spearmen, priests and Buddhas, bullocks and rams, fishes and birds, bees, fronds, fruit, flowers—an incomparable cosmological tapestry. Giant three-dimensional figures included guardians: the high gods Shiva and Vishnu, lions rampant, two and three times life-size, supple female forms with pleated draperies. A great, overarching plan binds the remarkably well preserved ruin, encompassing staircases, temples, monuments, towers, canals and basins, bridges and causeways, everywhere the elaborate embroidery wrought in stone nine hundred years ago.

Surrounding Angkor Wat is the silent mystery of the jungle, pushing toward it like waves of a sea, pressing to reembrace everything that modern man has extracted and reclaimed from nature's centuries-long, stifling grasp.

Nancy Hanks had given me the name of an old friend of hers in Kathmandu. As I stepped onto the tarmac, a youngish woman in brogues moved forward from a little group of welcomers.

"You must be Professor Houghton, and I'm Elizabeth Hawley," she said, offering me a firm handshake. This attractive, cheerful woman, a stringer for Time-Life in Nepal, whisked me through customs, drove into town in her Volkswagen, and deposited me at the Hotel Annapurna, a structure three stories high with, supposedly, a view of the Himalayas that stretches across the horizon. I interject "supposedly" because what I viewed from the hotel were green foothills that looked like Vermont. I was there in monsoon season, when the greatest peaks are blanketed in clouds, and the only time I saw Everest, Kanchenjunga, Annapurna, was when my departing Fokker Friendship climbed above the cloud cover: suddenly there they were—awesomely high above us.

Liz Hawley guided me about the strange city of Kathmandu, explaining the great eyes on temple roofs, and drove me through vivid green valleys to Patan and other nearby villages. The social highlight of my stay was a cocktail-buffet that Liz gave to introduce me to local literati. She invited twenty, and save for a few folk from our embassy and missions, most bore unpronounceable names.

My favorites were Mr. and Mrs. Bal Krishna Sama; he was the dean of poets and playwrights in this tiny hidden kingdom. After everyone had arrived and the hostess had delivered a few introductory words, the aging Mr. Sama, who spoke somewhat halting English, rose to welcome me. He was the only theatre man present, he pointed out. His remarks were rather extended, for he clearly enjoyed ventilating his English. He concluded by reciting some of his own poetry—in his native tongue, of course.

Perched on the arm of his wife's chair, I was acutely aware that in a loud whisper she was prompting him, line by line, a beat ahead of him, rather as though she were in a prompter's box at the opera, and also beating time with her forefinger. Since linguistic limitations prevented me from appreciating the verses, I was content to focus on this joint conjugal activity.

Encouraged by the polite applause that rewarded his lengthy recitation, Mr. Sama announced that, to honor the Western guest, his encore would be a soliloquy from *Hamlet,* in English: "O, what a rogue and peasant slave am I!" complete with gestures. When he concluded, I hastily rose to thank him for his kindness, and before he could open his mouth again, Liz, by announcing that the bar and buffet were now open, managed to wake everybody up. But I recall old Mr. Sama's contribution as a touching moment—a hand extended to me across the mountains and the seas.

In late August I returned home on the *United States,* to allow myself time to compose my Korean report to the JDR 3rd Fund. In it I had to single out Yoo Chi-jin himself, the fund's petitioner, as the chief source of the difficulties faced by the Korean Drama

Center. Egocentric, arrogant, and stubborn, he refused to work with other, younger creative people. But I saw a future for the Center only in a collective approach that brought together many groups from Korea's hard-pressed theatrical community. Achieving such a "union" was a dubious prospect, I acknowledged; nevertheless, it was the only one that justified even modest and judicious support from the fund.

A week after I arrived home, I attended the academic year's first Vassar faculty meeting. Responding to a colleague who asked how I had spent my summer, I said I'd enrolled in an eleven-week course in geography and discovered that the world is round and rather small.

2

On a Saturday afternoon in October 1962, shortly after the beginning of the school year, I drove my Volkswagen through the autumnal Berkshire countryside to the Phillips Academy at Andover, Massachusetts, there to attend the third Dartmouth Conference, so called because the first had been held at that college. These were nongovernmental Soviet-American meetings organized by Norman Cousins, then editor of the *Saturday Review,* and Philip E. Mosely, then director of studies at the Council on Foreign Relations. For seven days some two dozen prominent American and Soviet "private citizens" were to join in informal talks about critical issues between our countries.

The cast was high-powered. The Americans at the 1962 conference included burly young Professor Paul Doty and his somewhat older Harvard colleague Professor Louis B. Sohn, Max Millikin of MIT, and Margaret Mead, then at Columbia bearing her shepherd's crook; as well as such other prominent figures as Thomas Coughran, executive vice president of the Bank of America; Robert Meyner, former governor of New Jersey; and Herman Steinkraus, a former president of the U.S. Chamber of Commerce. The Russian contingent was led by the secretary of the prestigious USSR Academy of Sciences; and Yuri Zhukov (the only one I had encountered before, in Moscow), a senior political commentator of *Pravda.* Of the others, I was particularly pleased to meet Boris Polevoi, the novelist, a tousled, lively, casual fellow, and a career cosmonaut who was the only woman on the Russian team.

The official agenda was formidable. It began: "1. The role of the United Nations in strengthening international peace and cooperation . . . through the rule of law . . ." and ended: "5. Improving Soviet-American relations in the fields of economic, scientific and cultural relations." Without the words "and cultural" in item 5, there would have been no reason for me, or for Boris Polevoi, to be present. As it was, I listened carefully, mostly via simultaneous translation, and tended to keep my mouth shut, except during the hours of socializing. Actually, these relaxed times, over cocktails and at meals, were important to the conference.

Twenty-four strong, we forgathered at the Andover Inn late on that balmy Saturday afternoon. After a get-acquainted cocktail hour, at which my ability to speak small-talk Russian proved passable, we had dinner, with numerous toasts to peace and friendship, as guests of the headmaster of Andover. The next morning we met in the academy's oak-paneled Trustees Room to consider our ponderous agenda.

On Monday afternoon we were told that dinner would be served thirty minutes earlier because President Kennedy was to make an important address to the nation at seven o'clock. We Americans would assemble in a parlor with TV, where those Russians who were bilingual were invited to join us; the others would meet with simultaneous translators in the Trustees Room.

On the hour, the President came on the air to announce the Cuban missile crisis. It was, as everyone who lived through it recalls, the most serious confrontation between the superpowers that had—or yet has—occurred. When the President ended his message, "The Star-Spangled Banner" came over the set loud and clear. We Americans, naturally, rose, while those Russians who had listened with us slipped out of the room to join their colleagues.

What lay ahead, what our government's options were, how Khrushchev and the Russians would react—all this we discussed from many angles for about an hour. Then we pulled ourselves together and moved to the Trustees Room to face the other conferees. I looked about me. The Russians with whom I had just been joking at dinner looked concerned but calm. I wondered how I would feel if I had been in Russia, six thousand miles from home, when such a diplomatic explosion occurred. Were our friends fearful? I wondered. If the situation deteriorated quickly, might they not find themselves interned—or, at the least, participants in an unanticipated incident?

It was nine o'clock when the Soviet chairman (it being his turn to preside) finally called the meeting to order. Quite simply he presented their position. They had telephoned Moscow for instructions and had been told to determine their own course of action. They had agreed among themselves that a decision to disband was for us to make. They were here as our guests. If unwelcome, they would leave; if we wished them to remain, they would do so. Norman Cousins responded that we had not considered the matter and asked for a show of hands. "How many in favor of continuing the meeting?" Every American's hand went up.

Nevertheless, though it may have been my imagination, thereafter the tone of the proceedings seemed to alter. The very purpose of a conference such as this was being tested by the events we heard about over the airwaves during each recess. We were gathered together to seek ways for Russians and Americans to understand one another better and so to lessen international tensions. But the tensions outside our meeting room grew each day, and events were overtaking and outstripping our discussions.

Most interesting was the way the delegates individually seemed to draw closer, as we watched world events unfold far from our retreat. We became increasingly aware of our fraternity, even while developments seemed to be inexorably pulling us apart. As we pursued our agenda, the role of the UN, for instance, seemed to gain in importance; disarmament took on new urgency, and, in the end, even substantial improvements in the area of cultural relations acquired a greater significance than, I daresay, had originally been assumed. At the close, young Spartan Beglov, representative of the Novesti Press Agency, gave me his card. "Be sure to let me know when next you come to Moscow," he said. Thus, as the initial anxiety subsided somewhat, the 1962 Dartmouth Conference came to a close on a hopeful note.

As we parted, I'm sure we all felt we had shared a uniquely

critical experience. At Andover, during a time that held the most dire threat, we Americans and Russians, albeit unofficially, had talked things over for seven days and nights. We left with an enhanced sense of sober responsibility. That week I had for the most part put the theatre out of my mind altogether, and Vassar had seemed remote. A world drama was being enacted that was considerably more engrossing than any I had ever seen onstage, and I had been privileged to occupy a spectacularly good seat.

3

That summer, I had crossed the Hudson to lunch one Sunday with Claude and August Heckscher in their seventeenth-century Dutch stone house in Stone Ridge. That lunch was destined to change my life in some ways; at least it propelled me into a new world, one with dimensions considerably larger than those of Vassar or of any other world I had previously inhabited, including the Phoenix.

After lunch, my host drew me aside. The Twentieth Century Fund—of which Heckscher was then director—was about to join forces with the Rockefeller Brothers Fund to examine the state of the performing arts in America. His foundation would focus on economic problems. The RBF would engage in a broader study of general policy.

Economics was not up my alley, Augie knew, but he thought I could be of value to the RBF, whose study would be a successor to a series of public panel reports that had been issued between 1958 and 1961 and then collected and published in one thick volume, *Prospects for America*.

I recalled the work vaguely and knew that Augie had made some contribution to it. His somewhat pontifical phraseology, uttered in a high voice and with a slight stutter that makes it sound less pompous, is one of the things that endears him to me, along with his appearance—then lean, austere, with bright blue eyes, a shock of gray hair not yet turned white, and today, a goatee that makes him look like Pantalone in the commedia dell'arte drawings of Callot. At that time, Augie and I had known each other for twenty years, and I had always been a little in awe of him. That he was then serving as special consultant on the arts to President Kennedy only made him seem more awesome.

If I wished, he'd tell Nancy Hanks of my interest, he offered. Did I know her? . . . Well, never mind, he added, explaining that she had succeeded Henry Kissinger as project director of the *Prospects for America* studies. The RBF had set up an ongoing office called the Special Studies Project, and she was still its director. John Rockefeller was chairman of its new Arts Planning Committee. I'd like Nancy, he assured me, and he thought she'd like me. That's the way my entry into a new world began.

It was in November, weeks after the Dartmouth Conference, when Miss Hanks telephoned. In a voice with a warm Texas drawl, she said cheerfully, "August Heckscher thinks we should get acquainted." We made a date, and I appeared at her office in Rockefeller Center a week later.

I liked Nancy Hanks at once—everybody did. She was then in her mid-thirties. Of medium height, though she seemed taller, she had what nineteenth-century novelists called 'laughing eyes" and was quick to laugh at a witticism even if she didn't come up with many herself. She was totally unselfconscious and totally self-confident, and when she chose she could charm the birds out of the trees. Of course, I wanted to work with her.

She outlined the project. A panel of about thirty distinguished citizens would meet in five or six two-day sessions over six or seven months, study the testimony of expert witnesses, read background papers on the state of the arts, discuss all the angles, and finally issue their report.

Starting from the assumption that "today the performing arts are in trouble," as John D. Rockefeller 3rd would put it in his foreword to the eventual report, the panel would concentrate on music, dance, opera, and theatre, and would "identify the impediments to their greater welfare and to their wider enjoyment."

Although I was aware of Rockefeller's interest in the fine arts, I had not theretofore associated him with the performing ones. I wondered whether Lincoln Center, in whose creation he had been a prime mover, might have sparked his somewhat belated realization that "the performing arts are in trouble"? I'd certainly been aware of that for decades.

I did not again meet with Nancy Hanks until the following

February, when she proposed that I write a background paper on the off-Broadway theatre, which I did. There followed several meetings in March, at which I was introduced to various administrators of the fund. I began to sniff like a camel to see how I could best get my nose further under their tent. They seemed to welcome my intervention, for it was soon proposed that I coordinate all theatre papers, of which six had already been commissioned and another three were under consideration.

Meanwhile, Rockefeller's inner planning committee was lining up the panel membership—a balanced group of thirty people from business, labor, and the professions and from academic and arts institutions—and formulating the panel's agenda. As part of this phase, I recall a Rockefeller Center meeting in early June that brought together a small cross-section of off-Broadway theatre leaders to discuss with RBF executives their struggles and their goals. Among them were Julian Beck and his wife, Judith Malina, of the Living Theatre, producers Warren Enters, David Ross, and Theodore Mann of the Circle in the Square. Dana Creel, director of the RBF, presided, and flanking him were Nancy Hanks, Stephen Benedict of the fund, and, to my surprise, John D. Rockefeller himself. I was "the rapporteur."

After a delicious Cantonese lunch, served in a circular dining room, we moved to the conference room, where each guest described his or her theatre company: its aims and aspirations, its problems (focusing particularly on costs), its institutional development and support, and its relationship to Broadway and the American theatre as a whole.

The session lasted well into the afternoon. One by one, the guests excused themselves to return to work, until only Beck and Malina, JDR 3rd, one or two staffers, and I remained. There was a confrontation for you! I loved it. The Becks, ardent anarchist-pacifists, had recently been jailed for the twelfth time, for failure to pay taxes to the IRS and for various acts of civil disobedience. They had gone off proudly, being champions of radicalism in the good old Union Square sense.

They were also radicals of the theatre: theirs, for example, were among the first productions to feature full frontal nudity, which enjoyed an exultant but passing vogue in the 1960s. I'm not sure how much, if anything, JDR 3rd already knew of their background, but that afternoon he found out a good deal about them and their philosophy. He was a good listener, and the Becks, not at all shy, stayed on for a half hour. Soft-spoken, intense, and eloquent, they tried hard to convert JDR 3rd to the path of anarchy, but I fear they failed.

In mid-November 1963, the Rockefeller Brothers Fund Panel on the Performing Arts assembled for its first plenary session. Around a huge table were assembled the thirty members, with John D. Rockefeller 3rd and August Heckscher sitting together in the center of one long side. The staff and representatives of the two funds sat along the walls. I was reminded of the conference setup at Yalta.

Most of the members were strangers to me, though I knew that they all had some supportive interest in the performing arts, mostly in symphony orchestras. It was as large and high-powered a group of distinguished Americans as I'd ever had the privilege of sitting on the periphery of, let alone having drinks and dinner with. But after the conclusion of the second day's session I took Nancy Hanks aside.

I didn't think I belonged there, I said earnestly. Here we were talking about the performing arts in America without a single artist present. These were sterling men and women, I granted, but they were all amateurs. Where, I asked, were the Leonard Bernsteins, the George Balanchines and Martha Grahams, the Helen Hayeses and Rudolf Bings? How could we talk of the future of the American performing arts without them?

Nancy interrupted, saying that I didn't seem to grasp the point of this exercise. Of course "the pros" weren't there. It was no news that Leonard Bernstein was in favor of music or that Martha Graham believed in dance and Helen Hayes in theatre. But it *was* news that John D. Rockefeller was in favor of music and dance and theatre, that great business leaders like Stanley Marcus of Neiman-Marcus, and Harold Zellerbach of Crown Zellerbach, and James Oates of Equitable Life, and Devereux Josephs of New York Life, and all the others were concerned about the health of the performing arts.

I must wait, Nancy continued. The artists would be heard

from soon enough. The first purpose of this panel was to *educate* the movers and shakers, civic leaders around the country, and then to *convert* them. When converted, they would become missionaries themselves, in turn to convert their communities and indeed the nation. "The performing arts in America don't lack for great artists; what they need is *these* people's help."

Nancy converted me. Though I still felt out of place, I withdrew my proposal to quit. The ideas and intentions she outlined to me are clearly reflected in John Rockefeller's foreword to *The Performing Arts: Problems and Prospects:*

> ... From the beginning, the panel had particularly in mind a study that would be useful to those responsible for the direction and management of performing arts institutions. We also wanted to be helpful to foundation and corporate executives who are considering support for the arts. We hoped, too, that the study might be of value to local, state, and federal officials as the arts become increasingly important to the well-being and happiness of the people. And finally, we wished to serve private citizens who are working to enhance the quality of life in their communities.

So that was it. Our work was intended to bring into being massive financial support for the performing arts. It was certainly a job that needed doing. As a participant in this effort, I, who had previously worked only for my own institution, found my horizons greatly expanded. (Incidentally, years later Nancy confided that she had not herself initially wanted to be the panel's project director. She had no background in the arts and hadn't been very interested in them! This from the woman who subsequently became a truly great chairman of the National Endowment for the Arts.)

The Rockefeller Panel held four more two-day meetings, conferring for more than sixty hours in all. Early formality gradually gave way to relaxed give-and-take on a first-name basis. I even began to find myself feeling comfortable with John Rockefeller, not an easy task. At first, when encountering in an RCA Building elevator that tall, slightly stooped figure, his sandy hair beginning to gray, I could think of nothing to do but offer a wan smile. But as the months passed, I concluded he was perhaps even shyer than I. Certainly his unfailing courtesy and sincerity broke down my insecurity and went a long way toward offsetting his lack of humor.

As Nancy had assured me, before long professionals from the performing arts fields were invited to participate, and they enlivened our sessions considerably. All accepted our premise that "the arts are in trouble" and answered the panel's questions as best they could.

From my field came Harold Clurman, one of the founders of the Group Theatre; Alfred de Liagre, Jr., Broadway director and producer; Richard Barr, whose current production, *Who's Afraid of Virginia Woolf?*, was known to even the most philistine panelist; and Elmer Rice, distinguished dramatist.

Music, dance, and opera were represented by Herbert Graf, of the Metropolitan Opera; Julius Rudel, of the New York City Opera; composer Samuel Barber; violinist Isaac Stern; Peter Mennin, the president of Juilliard; John Martin, dance critic of the *New York Times;* and youthful Alvin Ailey and Paul Taylor, founders of fledgling dance companies.

Figures from the political world included John V. Lindsay, then congressman from New York, and Terry Sanford, then governor of North Carolina. Other invited participants included Henry B. Cabot, president of the Boston Symphony; William Baumol and William Bowen, consultants to the Twentieth Century Fund, who reported on its parallel study; George Buckingham from Standard Oil of New Jersey, who spoke about corporate support for the arts. It should be evident that in their background and experience, most of our witnesses were associated with institutions. The panel had early concluded that it did not have the capacity or the mandate to deal with individual creative artists and that the cause it was pleading was that of nonprofit arts institutions.

After the last panel session adjourned in June, Nancy asked whether I could spend some summer vacation time helping to write the first draft of the report. I agreed and spent six weeks doing that in an office on the thirty-fourth floor of the Sperry Rand building.

The key chapters of *The Performing Arts: Problems and Prospects* were the five addressed to financial support. I took on an introductory chapter, "The Performing Arts—Today and Tomorrow," and later ones concerned with organization and management of arts institutions, the university's role, and the broad challenge of "building greater appreciation" of the performing arts—a vital subject on which I could expatiate with enthusiasm. One day during those weeks, Nancy told me I had been promoted to full membership on the panel. The camel had gotten under the tent! She never explained how it came about, and I've never discovered.

The finished document appeared with considerable fanfare in March 1965. The press hailed the job, and I am certain that Tom Kramer was right when he wrote retrospectively in *Performance-Management Magazine,* twenty years later, that *"Problems and Prospects* permanently altered the face of the performing arts in America. . . . The report brought, first, an unprecedented sense of urgency about the importance of the performing arts to the nation's well-being . . . its recommendations paved the way for a far-reaching expansion of activity in theatre, dance and music, changed the pattern of public and private support for the arts. . . ."

Could as much be said for its effect on Houghton? Speaking also from the perspective of twenty years, I believe *Problems and Prospects* altered my face too. It put my previous thirty years' work in the theatre into a new perspective. It illumined especially some of the Phoenix's problems. It led me to think more deeply about theatre vis-à-vis the other performing media. It also gave me an opportunity to take my place as an equal among men and women whom I had heretofore assumed to be my superiors. It helped to uproot from my psyche a deep-seated insecurity, for it led me to believe that I, too, was a mover and shaker in the area of public affairs. I doubt that the change was noticed by anyone but me.

4

After the Phoenix decade, its joys and disappointments played out pretty much in the public eye, I had been ready for a change of pace, slower, more reflective, less crisis-ridden. As it turned out, the five years at Vassar were largely endurable because, ironically, I found ways to keep my life moving at a pace just as fast, hectic, and eventful as before. I had been too long in the theatre to be altogether happy consorting with my drama faculty quartet, with college-age young ladies, and with fellow senior faculty, who generally exhibited no overwhelming compulsion to consort with me and, indeed, often seemed to consider me an outsider.

However, it was not really the faculty that led me to seek out those "extracurricular activities" that I needed to keep my batteries charged. Eventually, I was forced to recognize that the fault was not in my stars but in myself: the contemplative life of the mind ill-suited my disposition, and despite all my protestations, I was still a compulsive activist.

It has been satisfying to record those activities I have called extracurricular: the Dartmouth conference and the Rockefeller Brothers Fund's panel report, the weeks in Germany in 1965, and my JDR 3rd trip around the world. They were linked by a common thread—my experience in the theatre, and in one way or another, with the exception of Andover, they were extensions of that experience, or at least threw new light upon it. Still, at that time, at the heart of all, lay Vassar and my life in the Hudson Valley. Wherever I turned up during those five years, I identified myself as a Vassar professor of drama. My livelihood came from the college, my first loyalty was to her, and my home as in her Dutchess County.

Indeed, the Hudson Valley deserves some attention here, for it provided as significant a learning experience as the campus or the conferences or the travel.

Back in the spring of 1962, shortly after the *New York Times* announced my Phoenix departure and my Vassar appointment, I dined one evening at the New York apartment of Mrs. Vincent Astor. Since we had first met twenty years earlier, I had grown very fond of her, in spite of the Phoenix episode that had so distressed me. Her gaiety is irrepressible; she possesses great charm; her eyes sparkle as they respond to the ridiculous. But she is not frivolous; far from it: she has intense intellectual curiosity, is an omnivorous reader, and is herself the author of several books.

Where was I going to live at Vassar? Brooke Astor asked, being always interested in other people's domestic arrangements. When I replied that I had no idea, she offered to help: there was a tiny, seventeenth-century Dutch stone house, unoccupied, on the Astor estate at Rhinebeck, twenty miles north of Poughkeepsie. She suggested that I go up and look at the Pond Cottage, and if it suited me, she'd be happy to have me live in it.

So on a mid-May morning I drove up to Rhinebeck, where, on its outskirts, I saw a small sign on low stone gateposts: "Ferncliff." There I turned in, passed through apple orchards and rolling green pastures where Black Angus cattle punctuated the prospect. After about a mile, the driveway crossed the River Road, a narrow public highway linking many of the great estates on the east bank of the Hudson above Hyde Park, which there bisected the Astor property.

It was another mile to the Pond Cottage, which stood on a point surrounded on three sides by water. Entering through a tiny foyer, I found a small living room, dining room, and newly equipped kitchen; upstairs, two bedrooms and bath.

On my return I called Mrs. Astor and gratefully accepted.

Brooke herself spent only weekends at Rhinebeck in spring and fall. Thus, she was in Maine when I moved in in August, and it was a month before she appeared at Ferncliff with her dachshunds and her housemaids. The original Astor mansion having been demolished years before, her residence was now the former "sports palast," designed by Stanford White in 1903. Its facade looked somewhat like a small replica of Baltimore's Union Station, except that it was only one story high. Behind and at right angles to it was the huge glass-enclosed structure that gave the place its name: it housed tennis and squash courts, dressing rooms, and a spectators' gallery. A broad open balcony to the south and west commanded a sweeping view of the Hudson.

I attended my first gathering at Brooke's in mid-October. It was a Sunday luncheon for about twenty, and we assembled for cocktails on that south gallery. The river sparkled in the noonday sun. Shortly before lunch was announced, the butler sought out Adlai Stevenson, a weekend guest at Ferncliff, who happened to be standing near me. "Pardon me, Governor, there is a telephone call for you from the White House."

Stevenson, then our ambassador to the United Nations, excused himself; lunch was delayed for fifteen minutes until he returned. We had just finished the first course when the butler reappeared. "I'm sorry, sir, but the White House is calling again." This time Stevenson never reappeared.

When the lunch party broke up, he was standing at the front door, all apologies, to say goodbye to the guests. His weekend at Ferncliff had been abruptly terminated by a summons to an urgent conference with President Kennedy. A White House helicopter would be landing on the front lawn in twenty minutes to carry him to his rendezvous. He was sorry to have caused such inconvenience. Later I would associate this incident with the Cuban missile crisis, which broke out the following week.

For two years I was to live in the midst of this bastion of the American patrician establishment—the estates of the Livingstons, Aldriches, Roosevelts, Ryans, Vanderbilts, and Astors—the Hudson Valley. To be sure, Poughkeepsie provided a rather different environment, but Vassar, after all, was as much a stronghold of the academic establishment as Ferncliff was of the social. And when Mrs. Astor gave up her estate, after my second year, and I moved into a faculty house adjacent to the campus, I happily maintained my links to my erstwhile neighbors up the river.

To Brooke I was further indebted for putting me in the care, so to speak, of Mrs. Lytle Hull. "Keep an eye on Norris, Helen," she said, when she left to spend the winter in Manhattan.

Helen Huntington was Vincent Astor's first wife. She had reigned over Ferncliff for twenty-five years. When they were divorced and she married Lytle Hull, she built a beautiful house on her family's property in Staatsburg, about five miles down the river. There she still lived, now a widow, when I arrived in the Hudson Valley.

We had never met before, but I recalled seeing her at a white-tie Philharmonic benefit thirty years earlier: the shy way she spoke, welcoming the guests in a high, halting voice; her pale pink satin ball gown, her lovely head crowned by the upsweep of a golden coiffure.

In 1962 Mrs. Hull was in her early seventies. On occasion, she would still don a pale pink satin ball gown; her hair, now almost white, she still wore in the soft upsweep I recalled. Despite a problem of balance, she held herself slenderly erect. She was a *grande dame* in the fullest sense of the term.

After Brooke departed, Mrs. Hull frequently invited me to a weekend meal, until, one day, she proposed that I call her whenever I'd like to come to Staatsburg, for the chances were twenty to one that she'd have a place for me at her table. I was enormously pleased. Gradually and cautiously we became good friends.

Because of Helen's devotion to the performing arts, especially music, she gathered around her many artists—such as Yehudi Menuhin, Nathan Milstein, Rudolf Firkusny, and their wives—and patrons of the arts. But the majority of her guests were quite different. If one was curious to know what the establishment had been like between the wars, one had only to become a habitué of Helen's drawing room, where the atmosphere was uncompetitive and relaxed but always more than a touch formal. The older people shared memories of days *before* World War I, and almost everyone had grown up together and still lived in the Hudson Valley. For the most part Helen's old friends were WASPs and—although the ghost of Franklin Delano Roosevelt loomed large in the environs of Hyde Park (his was the first signature in her Staatsburg guestbook)—conservative Republicans. Many of them bore famous names, had inherited fortunes, and were associated with great cultural and philanthropic institutions, but I thought they generally possessed little imagination, little intellectual curiosity, and indeed little interest in the world outside their own. Their conversation concerned family and friends, who were referred to only by first names. Genealogy was the one subject on which they were authorities.

They looked upon me and, I believe, tolerated me as a curiosity in their midst. I could talk about the theatre and education—even religion and politics after a couple of whiskeys—but these were subjects with which they seemed only vaguely familiar or, at least, about which they had not thought very much or very recently.

The day after Helen's last Christmas, in 1975, I went to Staatsburg to stay for a couple of days. Rudolf and Tatiana Firkusny, who lived just up the road, dined with us, and when, after dinner,

Rudolf learned it was my birthday, he bounded across the drawing room, sat down at the piano, and serenaded me with "Happy
Birthday" in thundering chords, then improvised an intricate
fugue around the nursery tune. It was a great send-off for the year
ahead.

But that was the year Helen Hull died. Her death left me
deeply saddened. She had given me a surer sense of the world
around me and its infinite variety; a surer sense, too, that I could
eventually find a place in *her* world, should I decide that it was
where I wanted to be.

As I entered my fifth Vassar year, I began to feel that recurring
need to look for the exit. It was as if I lacked air. I had instituted
a number of changes in the drama department, and I sensed that
if I immediately proposed others, some might suspect I was out
to grab more than my share of the college lucre for my program.
The previous year, the powerful Faculty Curriculum Committee
had intimated that adding more courses requiring more faculty—
and thus more money—might lead to the professionalization of
the drama program, and this they opposed.

In early November, I went to Nancy Hanks for advice. She
asked if I remembered Abbott Kaplan from the panel and if I
knew that Samuel Gould (also a panel member) was now chancellor of the State University of New York. I nodded.

Did I also know that Sam had just recommended to the SUNY
trustees that Abbott be appointed president of the new college for
the arts being created in Westchester? No, I knew nothing of
this—it had not yet been in the newspapers. Nancy, deep in the
cultural establishment, always had such knowledge before almost
everyone else.

She added some details about SUNY's as yet unannounced
plan to build a four-year college in Purchase. It would be a
double-header: a liberal arts college allied to a professional school
of the arts. Said Nancy, "Abbott's fire is going to be the biggest
I've heard about in this neck of the woods in a long time. Why
don't you get in touch?"

I wrote to Dr. Kaplan at UCLA and received a cordial response. He would be coming east shortly after Christmas, and

we would talk. We met at breakfast—on Friday the thirteenth. After two hours of discussion, he invited me, then and there, to join the Purchase experiment as a professor and dean of theatre arts. In February, I accepted Dr. Kaplan's invitation. It had all occurred in less than three months.

After receiving formal confirmation of my appointment, I resigned from Vassar, effective as of the end of the academic year. In mid-June, I made my exit from Dutchess County and began to prepare for my entrance into Westchester, there to help gather kindling for Abbott's fire.

15

The Purchase Challenge (1967–80)

"Do tell me," she urged warmly, as I sat down opposite the settee on which she was ensconced, "what you are doing these days. I'm told you have been in the theatre."

"That's true," I replied, "but for the past eight years I've been the dean of theatre arts at one of the colleges of the State University of New York."

"Do tell me more," she encouraged, her bright blue eyes lighting up as though she could hardly wait to hear.

"I wonder whether you are aware, Your Majesty, that my university is the largest institution of higher learning in the world—as of 1975, 185,000 students on sixty-nine campuses."

"Good heavens!" she exclaimed.

I had addressed her as "Your Majesty" because my vis-à-vis, so eager for information was Elizabeth, the Queen Mother of England. Our chat (should I call it an audience?) was occurring on a late-August afternoon in a small castle in Scotland overlooking the North Sea. Responding to her queries, I continued to brief her, with growing enthusiasm.

My college—one of the sixty-nine—had been established, I told her, only eight years before, in 1967. When completed, it was to consist of two parts: a four-year liberal arts college and a professional conservatory of the visual and performing arts. We had been mandated to develop innovative approaches to the teaching of the humanities and the social and natural sciences, and to formulate model programs in music, dance, theatre, film, and the visual arts. One of our first jobs, I explained, had been— and I thought the metaphor appropriate to the moment—to invent a formula for a perfect martini of an education, determining the best proportion of academic vermouth to artistic gin. "Naturally, we've never succeeded," I admitted.

Our campus was being built on five hundred acres, at an estimated cost of $150 million, and it would encompass the finest teaching facilities in all those fields. Moreover, in the School of the Arts, for example, the faculty was drawn from the best professional artists available, and New York City being but twenty-five miles away, it was not hard to engage them, if only on a part-time basis. Our standards of admission had been carefully set to bring us the most talented students in the arts and the brightest in the liberal arts.

The Queen Mother, still appearing to hang on my every word, interrupted. She wanted to know how one identifies talent in the young, a very perceptive and difficult question.

While one couldn't be sure, I replied, our selection procedure required auditions by all aspiring musicians, actors, and dancers, and submission of portfolios or film clips by painters, sculptors, graphic artists, and filmmakers. We conducted searching interviews with applicants and evaluated their school records. Generally, though, we had to be guided by instinct. The hardest to judge were applicants who wished to study stage direction: How could they demonstrate their talent without actors to direct?

Her Majesty, responding at once, asked how we dealt with that. But I was spared having to tackle her question by a light tap on the shoulder from her equerry, who wished to introduce another guest. I had, of course, fallen for the "Queen Mum," but I didn't mind returning to the sideboard to steady my nerves. Now let me backtrack a bit.

I'd arrived from Edinburgh that morning to help celebrate the birthday of my hostess, Dixie Miller, who was from Columbus, Ohio, and was a Vassar graduate I had first met at Alumnae

Council meetings in Poughkeepsie. She and her husband (now deceased) had a few years before bought a Victorian Gothic castle at Keiss, only about a dozen miles from the Castle of Mey, the Queen Mother's present summer home in northern Scotland. The Millers had met her during their first summer at Keiss. She had actually invited herself over one Sunday afternoon—to welcome her new neighbors from America—and they had been good friends ever since.

"The Queen Mother is coming for birthday drinks today," Dixie announced to her three other houseguests and me. "But don't be upset. She's really very simple. It will be just like any ordinary small cocktail party."

It was like no ordinary cocktail party *I* had ever attended. True, it was small—only five couples from the local gentry, we four houseguests, the Queen, her lady-in-waiting and equerry, Dixie and her daughter. There was no staff in evidence: Gordon Kinder, the other male guest, and I tended bar and served drinks; Dixie and daughter Blythe passed canapés. But of course that was only after the royal party had arrived.

The locals knew that though they had to show up before the Queen, they could not be served until she appeared. Happily for the thirsty Scots, she was punctual. A few moments before her arrival, I noticed, with some panic, that Dixie had disappeared. But, it turned out, this too was protocol: royalty doesn't ring the bell; the host must be at the door to greet them. I thought of Lady Macbeth and how she kept Duncan waiting, a menacing sign, as he and his retinue, cooling their heels, had to talk about birds.

The Queen didn't really sweep in; she walked in quite modestly, dressed in a simple silk flower-print summer dress; though her pearls and single diamond clip were certainly real. In any case, it was not her diamond that dazzled but her extraordinarily sweet smile and the frank eyes that looked directly into mine as she held out her hand.

Bartenders Kinder and Houghton at once repaired to the sideboard, mixed the royal martini (straight up), presented it to Her Majesty (who pronounced it perfect), and then began to serve the others.

Alas, I never managed to pursue our interrupted conversation about SUNY Purchase, for after an hour—longer than I had expected her to stay—the Queen Mother rose, saying she was sorry to leave but she had guests coming for dinner. She was sorry, too, that there would be no other chance to meet that week, because, she said, "I leave tomorrow for Balmoral to visit my daughter and her children." The remark was made so casually that one almost forgot that she was referring to the Queen of England, the Prince of Wales, and the other heirs to the throne.

If there had been more time, here are some other things I might have told the Queen Mother about Purchase.

I approached my new job in 1967 with considerable excitement and some trepidation. To be in at the beginning of such an endeavor offered all sorts of unforeseen challenges and opportunities. The opening of the college had been scheduled for 1970, but the first students didn't actually arrive until 1972, and even then facilities were only partially completed.

Our largely unstated goal was to turn out young Renaissance men and women: those enrolled in the college were to master a humanistic or scientific education and be exposed to at least one major art form; those in the arts were to achieve performance-level mastery in their chosen field and to acquire a general education. That goal was crucial to the president, Abbott Kaplan, to Chancellor Gould, even to the governor, Nelson Rockefeller, whose "baby" we were told Purchase was. We would find that there weren't enough hours in the school day nor days in the school year for our students to accomplish what we had dreamed for them. But we would continue to chase our objective like a pack of hounds.

"Innovation" was the watchword of our mandate: our purpose was not to organize just another college. And, indeed, the very idea of a Janus-like institution was, to say the least, innovative.

Ever since Stanislavski had exhorted me thirty years before that success in art derives from overturning the status quo, I had sought to practice his teaching. In creating Theatre Inc. and the Phoenix Theatre, I'd attempted to devise innovative substitute approaches for Broadway's entrenched commercialism. Now Purchase provided an equally challenging opportunity to change the ways of traditional education.

There were four areas toward which we had to direct our attention: first (chronologically), facilities planning, for buildings take the most time to generate; second (but more important), the kind of education we would offer; third, the human equation of faculty recruitment and organization and student selection; fourth, how to realize our objectives. Other, more intangible but signally important matters also required thought and discussion: the tone and style of the institution, its position in a world of changing social and political mores.

2

Early in the spring of 1967 I journeyed into Manhattan for conferences with President Kaplan, Edward Larrabee Barnes, the site planner and principal architect, and Gibson Danes, the only other early appointee, who was leaving Yale in June to become our dean of visual arts. We were told by Albany in effect, "You fellows have five hundred acres in Westchester County and $150 million. Come back in three years with a college. Draw on what you've learned about education, about what you think the world may be like in forty years, what you would like it to be like. Don't try to come up with the maximum; come up with the optimum."

One gray, windy day in late March, we gathered at Purchase to look over our acreage. Our leader was not very prepossessing; he was of medium height, and as he walked, his somewhat hunched shoulders made him look smaller than he was. There was a whiff of the rabbinical about Dr. Kaplan. His speech was slow, and occasionally he would pontificate in a sort of singsong.

Barnes, one of America's most highly respected architects, was, on the other hand, a one-hundred-percent Ivy League WASP. Then fifty-two, he looked like a bright graduate student—slender, with a shock of unruly hair that fell across his forehead—and exhibited an outgoing personality. My biggest conflicts would be with him, for under his disarming exterior lay an iron will and a stubborn adherence to aesthetic convictions that were frequently at odds with mine.

Barnes led us about a quarter of a mile across bleak, brown fields to a spot that, he announced, was the highest point of land on the estate. Here he proposed to center the campus. Feeling like Moses surveying the Promised Land, I looked around and saw gently rolling fields and pastures, beyond which lay woodland not yet in bud. We seemed to be standing on a slightly elevated plateau, and I fancied I could see the thin gray line of Long Island Sound off to the south.

Barnes had been engaged as architect even before Kaplan had been appointed president. So he had already had more than six months to think about and work on the project. Now he began to unfold his basic scheme. While he conceived of the college in contemporary terms, he was inspired by medieval Italian hill towns and eighteenth-century New England villages, all of which were built around a central piazza or a square or a green. At one end of the site, where the church or cathedral traditionally stood, he'd place the Performing Arts Center (PAC); in the middle of the square, the library, most of its stacks underground; at the far end, the gym. Along the sides of the piazza he planned to place classroom and lab buildings, studios, dormitories, dining halls, student centers, an art museum. These, like buildings flanking medieval piazzas, would be interconnected by arcades, which would be separated from one another by narrow streets fanning out from the center. As the campus grew, it would expand down those streets, as towns do, until it reached the surrounding greenbelt of woods.

I thought this a sound conception and was very supportive (although, liking daylight, I was a little dubious about the subterranean library). It turned out, however, that because the same material was used for all buildings—brick that would be called dun-colored (a hue that to me suggested dried dung but that my dictionary identifies as "grayish brown")—and because so many of the walls were unrelieved by windows, the campus on completion seemed to me a cross between Fort Knox and the state penitentiary at Attica. Admittedly, nature and time have since softened the initial dreary effect.

I joined the project full-time in August 1967. A week later I found myself charged with writing the "Program" for the Performing Arts Center, and soon after William Bales, the dean of dance,

Danes, and I began planning our instructional buildings. Albany had wisely decided that those who were to design the buildings and those who were to use them should work hand in hand. Actually, of course, our efforts should have preceded those of the architect. But I soon discovered that the procedural pace of the Barnes staff and the State Construction Fund, which was charged with building our campus, made the Supreme Court's justices seem like hares, so we planners caught up pretty quickly. Indeed, by the end of the first year (1968) I, for one, had run out of ideas!

An early bird on the job, I had a chance to select my own office space in the mansion that became our administration building. Modestly I chose what had been a large second-story bedroom, with fireplace and adjacent bath, that looked south over a sweeping lawn. When my secretary arrived, however, she and I were surprised to discover that she would have to occupy the bath. Plumbing fixtures were soon replaced by her desk and file cabinets, and though pleased she was so close by, I regretted losing my bit of luxury.

In that "bedroom" I worked for the next eight years, and there that August, under the guidance of Norman Taylor, director of facilities planning, I started developing the PAC Program. Summer turned into autumn, autumn into winter, and still we labored on what seemed a Sisyphean task, involving so much backing and filling, so many imponderables. A word of explanation of the so-called Program seems appropriate here. It was like a gigantic shopping list drawn up by a client to enumerate his wishes. In this instance, however, the college was not technically the client—the State Construction Fund was. It was this agency that had commissioned the architect—who was responsible to it and not to the college—and controlled the money. We were rather like tenants, but because, theoretically, we were supposed to be satisfied too, we had to specify exactly what we wanted.

It was fearsome to assume responsibility for writing a program that involved $30 million and roughly 320,000 square feet of space, every square foot of which had to be justified and accounted for. At the age of fifty-seven, I felt like a boy sent out to do a man's job, knowing that if I omitted anything, I ran the risk of being told, "But you did not *ask* for that."

I had heard, for example, of one recently built theatre that, when completed, was found not to have a box office. I recalled Philadelphia's old Forrest Theatre: dressing rooms having been forgotten in the design, space for them had to be commandeered in a building on the other side of a back alley, across which for decades actors scampered in all weathers. I knew of yet another playhouse in which the public lavatories had been inadvertently omitted. I prayed I'd not be guilt of a similar oversight.

Our talks with Ed Barnes that summer concerned the number of theatres the Arts Center would have, their respective seating capacities, the character of their stages, and the spatial relationships of one to another. We all agreed fairly quickly that four theatre could best fulfill our needs.

We designated the largest space "Theatre A," referring to it also as the "opera house," for it would have a seating capacity of approximately 1,500, a proscenium arch the width of the Metropolitan's, dressing rooms sufficient for 100 performers, and an orchestra pit that could hold 100 musicians.

"B" was the code name for the principal drama theatre, with a capacity of 750, though, as plans developed, this could be expanded or contracted as necessary. The audience would face the stage head-on, but the performing area would be flexible: with two hydraulic apron stages, acting space could be thrust forward deeply into the auditorium or remain at its 50-foot depth behind a curtain.

From my recent trip to Japan, I had the idea of runways on both sides of the auditorium leading to the stage, much like Kabuki's *hanamichi*. They could be used for entrances, exits, and even entire scenes, and would permit actors to surround the audience on three sides. Above these runways, upper *hanamichis* would extend to the stage from the balcony level and provide space for surprise entrances and antiphonal effects.

"Theatre C," seating approximately 500, was to be the principal recital hall for music and dance and therefore was outside my area of responsibility.

But with "Theatre D" I was determined to dream, to be truly innovative. So far we had planned two theatres—"A" and "C"—that were traditional nineteenth-century proscenium playhouses and one—"B"—that was partially so. While they were ideal for the conventional staging of operas, ballets, and realistic plays with realistic interiors, we were supposed to be building for the twenty-first century, and I refused to believe that the picture-frame stage would remain standard forever. I was convinced that we needed one theatre that took an imaginative leap into the future.

On a visit to Expo '67 in Montreal, I had marveled at the Eastman Kodak exhibit, wherein one was surrounded by visual images on a seamless ribbon of 360 degrees. That was, of course, a totally optical experience, but it carried broad theatrical implications. Stereophonic sound was already being used in some cinemas and legitimate theatres and widely in homes. We no longer sat like the Victor dog, listening to "His Master's Voice" from a single horn, but were enveloped in sound coming from all sides. Why could we not create a theatrical space that *visually* embraced the spectators too?

It meant, I envisioned, creating a circular space with a flat floor, no fixed seats or stage space, beneath a dome—a sort of planetarium, wherein a large disk might rise hydraulically to provide a central acting area when desired. Audience and performers would be bound together in the expanse under that dome: colorless, suffused with light, or with still or moving images projected upon it. In *Hamlet*'s opening scene on the battlement, for instance, when Bernardo and Marcellus look up at the stars, they are usually twinkling on a sky drop behind the actors, and if the spectators look up, they see the auditorium's crystal chandelier. In the theatre of my imagination, we would all be enclosed under the same night sky. Total theatre calls for that kind of total environment.

I consulted with an outstanding Broadway lighting technician, Jean Rosenthal, and she agreed that what I proposed would create a spectacular breakthrough in theatre design. Perhaps I should also have asked to have a great theatre experimentalist, like the Czech Josef Svoboda, come over to help refine the idea. For the fact was that Barnes did not share Rosenthal's enthusiasm. Acoustically, the theatre would not work, he believed, and aesthetically it would be at odds with surrounding buildings. I fought for months to have my idea developed, and I admit that, at some expense and labor, Ed did provide a mock-up, but I eventually lost my case. I was reminded that I wasn't going to live forever, and if something were to be built that I could make work, there was no certainty that those who followed me could or would want to use it.

"What makes you think that fifty years hence people will want *any* of the kinds of theatre we've grown up with?" I'd retort.

What I should have as an experimental theatre, the others insisted, was a black box much like that at Harvard's Loeb and other art centers, which would give me ample opportunities to play with space.

"But if everybody else has one, that prevents it, ipso facto, from being an experiment," I said. "Besides, I've seen that kind of black box of a theatre for thirty years—first in Moscow in the nineteen thirties and in Seattle in the forties. We're at the sixties and should be looking toward decades ahead. To provide three proscenium theatres and a black box is to look hopelessly backward."

But those were what Barnes wanted to build, and those were what he built. "Houghton's Folly," as they nicknamed my dream house in Albany, was disapproved by the Construction Fund, thus killing my first proposed innovation.

From the beginning there was the usual running battle between planners and architects over form versus function. The planners' fervent desire was to ensure that the PAC worked; the architect's was to create buildings that from without and within were aesthetically pleasing. By nature, I am predisposed to be on the side of aesthetics, but in this instance I leaned heavily toward the concerns of function. I was disgruntled that areas exposed to public view—lobbies, grand staircases, and the like—received more tender loving care, and money, than did those areas related to educational purposes—that is, the actual process of mounting works of theatre, music, dance, by and for Purchase students, for whom I believed the PAC was intended. The struggle ended, of course, in a variety of compromises, which, as usual, satisfied none of us completely.

My immersion in facilities planning in no way deterred me from joining in the equally or perhaps even more important matter of academic planning. It headed the agenda of the weekly Wednesday-morning staff meetings that the president began in September of 1967. By then our planning group had been augmented by the appointment of Frank Wadsworth as academic vice president and head of the College of Letters and Science; Robert Evans as director of the library; Bryan Robertson, imported from London, as director of the art museum; as well as a director of business affairs pro tem. Nevertheless, yawning gaps still marked our table of organization: not yet on board were a vice president for the arts and deans for the three divisions of the College of Letters and Science and for music.

The heaviest burden that autumn fell upon Dr. Wadsworth, the liberal arts' principal representative among the planners. Thrice over a Princetonian, he had bachelor's, master's, and doctoral degrees all from Old Nassau. He was there long after my time, but from our first meeting I felt a strong bond between us. I would say he looked like an intellectual, if I were sure there is such a look. In any case, he knew his own worth but coupled that with innate modesty.

"Next Wednesday I think we had better turn our attention to the master plan," said Abbott Kaplan to the six of us during one of our first staff meetings in his office, the handsome, wood-paneled library of our white neocolonial mansion. We were to continue to do this for the next ten months, preparing our first contribution to the quadrennial rite of drafting SUNY's massive master plan. Our portion of this document would outline how we planned to implement the basic "Guidelines" set down for us by Albany in 1966–67.

Many jolly Wednesday mornings were spent, for example, discussing whether we should possibly require five years of study for B.F.A. degrees rather than four, or whether the first—or possibly the last—year of the traditional four should be given exclusively to fulfilling liberal arts requirements, with the other three years devoted to conservatory training.

Among other issues discussed: the college calendar—semester, trimester, four quarters; the importance of academic advisers; restrictions, if any, on choosing double majors (for those students who might want to put our "Renaissance man" principles into practice); how closely to follow the "core curriculum" idea that Henry Rosovsky had recently introduced to Harvard; team teaching in interdisciplinary introductory freshman-year courses; and the merits of pass/fail grading, especially for artists.

3

"I'm still undecided about film," President Kaplan had remarked at a meeting with Dean Danes and me the previous spring.

"You mean whether it's here to stay?" I asked.

"I mean where it belongs."

"Belongs?" asked Danes in some confusion.

"Should motion pictures, like still photography, be considered one of the visual arts, or," Abbott asked, turning to me, "should they be dealt with as an extension of theatre?"

Don't think I argued that morning in favor of an enlargement of my turf. "Why not make it a division by itself?" I suggested, "In budgetary terms, isn't it going to overwhelm theatre arts *or* visual arts if it's a part of either. Think of the costs of installing and equipping sound stages, lights, cameras, all that," I added, not really knowing what I was talking about. "Besides, won't we soon be embarking into television? We can't avoid it, can we? And taken together, those mass media—TV and movies—would surely make a separate division."

I don't remember all the ins and outs of this discussion, but I do know its outcome: a man who had never handled a camera larger than a Kodak Brownie, who went to the movies at most once a month, who had never worked a day in Hollywood, who had never directed a movie, or edited one, who had never written a film script or performed on a sound stage—that man perforce was to add "and Film" to his decanal title.

"Well, I'll certainly need guidance," I announced.

I received it unexpectedly from an old friend closely associated with the Museum of Modern Art who urged me to get in touch with Willard Van Dyke, the director of MOMA's Film Collection. So I went to see Van Dyke, who, though in his early sixties, seemed a young man: his handshake was firm, his eyes bright, his smile almost roguish. He spoke and moved rapidly. I told him of my plight and asked for his advice and assistance, admitting that I knew too little to know what advice and assistance I needed.

Willard agreed that I had a big job on my hands; he thought he could help and would be glad to try. "What a challenge!" he added.

The first thing I should do, he told me, was to attend the Robert Flaherty Film Seminar at Arden House in Harriman, New York, in early September. Did I know anything about it? I replied proudly that I knew about *Man of Aran* and that I even used to encounter Flaherty at the Coffee House. He was a stocky old white-haired Irishman, and I thought he was dead.

"He is," said Willard, "but he started annual summer get-togethers of filmmakers before he died, and since then my wife, Barbara, and I have kept them going." I should spend three or four days there, he advised; it would be good for me to meet some important young filmmakers—and some old ones too.

I went to the seminar and proceeded to be astonished. Everyone there—about thirty in all—seemed to have brought a suitcase full of her or his latest work, which everyone else was prepared to watch. Short films and long (ten, twenty, fifty minutes, an hour), documentaries, experimental works—they were all critiqued after the viewings, with Willard leading the discussion periods. While I would go to bed about one, exhausted, the filmmakers stayed at it until three or four every morning—viewing and talking, talking and viewing. They were passionate about cinema, the younger the more intense. I marveled at their total dedication, and their lack of humor, which was also pretty much total. Even their cartoon shorts occasioned the most serious deliberation. Worn out but impressed, I left Arden House after three days.

Next Willard encouraged me to go to Montreal to see people at the National Film Board of Canada, who were doing remarkable work. When I returned, he suggested I cultivate Haig Manoogian and George Stoney, who could tell me about NYU's burgeoning film school. I cultivated them, and they blossomed for me. Haig, a black-haired young Armenian, offered me invaluable gratis advice about film facilities. Another "Program," for the theatre and film instructional building, would have to be written soon, and Willard recommended that as formal consultant for motion picture facilities I commission Ernest Rose of Temple University.

At some point Willard decided I had to venture beyond the academic film world: "Go call on Jonas Mekas. He created the

Cinematheque Center. He'll broaden your horizons. He's one of the most imaginative avant-garde filmmakers we have. You'll find him in Greenwich Village."

I spent an afternoon with Mekas, a small, soft-spoken artist. He was barefoot and garbed in something that looked vaguely like lounging pajamas, though it was not at all chic. He may have been thirty—or fifty. A true futurist, he spoke hesitantly, like one feeling his way, as he opened up vistas of what cinema might be like someday.

Years later, in 1970, when it came time to make initial key faculty appointments, I asked Willard for help in finding the best candidate to head our film program. I had drawn up a short list, which we reviewed, with Willard expressing strong prejudices about various people. Finally he said, "There's something I haven't told you. I'm retiring from the museum at the end of next year. Perhaps you'd like to add my name to your list."

"Why haven't you told me?" I cried. "There'll be no list. The search ends here." It was not hard to persuade President Kaplan. Willard led the Film Program of the division from 1972 until 1977 and, in an emeritus capacity, was still working part-time when I retired in 1980.

There have never been adequate facilities for film at Purchase, for our instructional building was never built. Moreover, to establish and maintain a film program takes lots of money, and Albany never supplied enough. But Willard knew where gold was buried and how to get it. Always a great prospector, he became committed to education, and the film program would have starved to death before the age of five if by his own means he hadn't found outside support. He died in the spring of 1986, in his eightieth year.

As Willard Van Dyke was in filmmaking, so Joseph Anthony, actor, stage and film director, and teacher, became my tower of strength in developing the acting program. For about twenty years, we had been encountering each other at dozens of theatre-related panels and meetings and at the parties of mutual stage friends. Finally came *The Dragon* at the Phoenix, when we worked together for the first time, he directing, I designing, and, after that, his stint as a guest lecturer at Vassar. By that time we knew we were on the same wavelength.

When, during the summer of 1969, I initially talked with Joe about the Purchase acting program, he was in his mid-fifties, tall and shaggy-haired. From our discussions on long afternoons beside his Westchester pool, it was clear that he had become as disenchanted as I with Broadway and the New York theatrical world. Perhaps it was a matter of recognizing that fame and fortune, both of which he had acquired in good measure, were not enough. At any rate, he showed growing interest in the job I faced and the plans I was so nebulously forming.

The roles he was to play varied: he started as a sounding board; he advanced to being a contributor, making suggestions, pointing out discrepancies in my logic, enriching my ideas with his own, helping me crystallize some of my dreams and exploding others. He nagged, he disputed, he cheered me on. Unafraid of innovation, he was a true man of the theatre, whose standards were as high as anyone's I've known and to whom God had given imagination and talent. Eventually he became my closest and most valued accomplice.

After a couple of years of gentle suasion, Joe committed himself to Purchase, and the two of us set out to draft our plan for an actor training program that would be the heart of the Theatre Arts Division. It became my second innovative contribution to the planning of our "innovative college."

Joe and I agreed that each year a single master teacher—a mentor—would be chosen to preside over actors' training during their first two years. He or she would participate in auditions for admission, become individual adviser to each of the thirty-odd students who were accepted, and thereafter act successively as gardener—planting, watering, and tending—as tutor, as guide, and as director. Since the mentors would endue their students with their own philosophies and techniques, for each entering class the grounding would differ as the mentors differed.

At the end of the first two years, however, the juniors would be released from the potentially stifling hold of their mentor, who would be succeeded by a series of masters: visiting directors brought to Purchase to lead their apprentices through various new exercises and whole productions, all designed to expand, and even perhaps contradict, the basic style imposed by the mentor.

Thus, the first two "cloistered" years devoted to "process" would be followed by two years devoted to "product" (echoes of Vassar), to performances that would expose students to a variety of acting approaches and that would round out their preparation for the multifaceted world of the practical professional stage. Though strongly grounded in their mentor's work, they should now be flexible enough to do whatever might be asked of them.

I invented a metaphor to describe our approach to actor training. Instead of building a pyramid, with a broad base of experience, derived from exposure to many techniques, which would be narrowed down over the years to a single technique, the pyramid's apex, we would cultivate a tree: its seed, planted by the mentor, would grow until its stem became a trunk from which many branches could spring forth in many directions. Joe and I preferred this living and expanding image to that of the static pyramid, just as we felt that movement from the one to the many was more organic and inspiriting than contraction from the many to the one.

Unlike my idea for a theatre, my actor training program continued while I was at Purchase. My third innovation was, I still believe, my boldest one. In late 1966, a feature article by Howard Taubman announcing the establishment of Purchase had appeared in the *New York Times*. I was much struck by its final paragraph: ". . . They have a chance to create a model center within a university for the training of professional artists. All that remains will be to find ways to employ the talent they train. We are back to a national problem."

It *was* a national problem—and one that continues to trouble all honest theatre educators: were we—are we—preparing young people for nonexistent careers? I wondered then how I would feel handing out diplomas with a shake of the hand while mouthing, "Good luck—hope you find a job," and knowing that at least a third of the graduating class, talented though they might be, would be pushed off the road to their dreams.

The article inspired an idea that took shape two years later: why not graduate whole theatre companies ourselves? Repertory groups had occasionally been part of my early theatrical experience—first in the University Players and then subsequently in my exposure to nothing but repertory companies during my months in Moscow.

There I had also been impressed by the program of the Central Theatre Technicum, whose students, after training together for four years, went forth as an ensemble to Omsk or Tomsk, to Minsk or Pinsk, to become a resident theatre company. If the Russians could do it, why couldn't we? A need existed in America in 1967 and 1968, which had been touched upon as a "long term goal" in the Rockefeller Brothers Fund Panel report on the performing arts: "permanent theatre companies," one for every "metropolitan area with population over 500,000." In those days, at the rate art centers were going up across the land, many with nothing to put in them, it looked as if that RBF objective might soon be realized in terms of buildings. But from where would come the companies to give those structures life?

At a staff meeting one Wednesday morning I presented my plan. I was suggesting a way not only to solve a national problem—what to do about empty art centers—but also to solve a Purchase problem—how to find jobs for our graduates. I proposed that after putting twenty or twenty-five actors and a few directors, designers, and technicians through a four-year training program, we should invite those who wished to go forward together to commit themselves to two more years of practical service to the theatre.

The first year after graduation would begin with a summer of preparation and rehearsal on campus. In the autumn they would embark on a two-part, twenty-two-week tour of SUNY campuses. It seemed safe to estimate that a third of the sixty-nine would welcome the company for a week to play in repertory and offer campus workshops. After a Christmas break and a six-week refresher period back at Purchase, the troupe would resume its tour and after five months "on the road" would have gained invaluable performing experience.

For the sixth year the group would return to Purchase as a professional repertory company in residence. Perhaps it could even perform in New York briefly at some off-Broadway house. At the end of that last year it would be ready to go forth to its

Omsk or Tomsk, and Purchase would try to help find it a home. Whether or not a continuing relationship endured, "their experience of working together," I pointed out, "would have provided a richness and variety of artistic endeavor such as few stage neophytes could have acquired."

My colleagues endorsed my plan with unexpected enthusiasm. Bales thought it could work with dance companies; the music dean considered the possibility of creating quartets and chamber ensembles made up of Purchase graduates.

It must be noted that John Houseman, then head of the new theatre division of the Juilliard School, came up independently with much the same idea. Because his entering class preceded Purchase's by a couple of years, he was able to implement his plan in 1974, and the Acting Company he then created still exists a decade and a half later. The basic difference between our concepts was that I wanted to graduate an *entire company* each year; as its name implies, his was limited to actors, and only one troupe was established, with subsequent generations of Juilliard graduates feeding into it as older actors moved on. My plan was more grandiose—too much so, I now conclude.

The idea of graduating companies became the center of divisional planning. Entering freshmen would be referred to as "members" of a "company," not as "students" in a "class." They would be selected partly to create a balanced ensemble—that is, a more or less equal number of men and women. Among them I hoped to find two or three with directing potential, but if none emerged, students transferring to Purchase in upper-division years would be chosen for their directorial talent.

4

Weaving in and out of these theatrical matters were the threads that the planning staff sought to fashion into a pattern for the college as a whole. By 1970, all seven deans had been appointed, and our Wednesday conferences began to look like the Congress of Vienna. The last arts administrator to be hired was Michael Hammond, the dean of music, our one Rhodes Scholar and our in-house example of a Renaissance man: having begun his career as a physiologist, he subsequently shifted his attention to music.

Joining us was also John Straus, vice president for the arts, who, until the post was formally filled, doubled as vice president for administration. Among us he was quite special. The scion of a great New York merchant family, he was the grandson of Isidore Straus, the head of R. H. Macy & Co. until, with his wife, he went down with the *Titanic*. Graduating from Harvard as an art history major, John had assumed his place in the family business, but his temperament was, I suspect, unsuited to Herald Square, for he was in love with the arts and happily accepted Dr. Kaplan's call.

Often our staff meetings were monumentally dull. My greatest solace lay with Academic Vice President Frank Wadsworth, next to whom I would try to sit in order to exchange critical asides. Both of us were dedicated to a common objective: to fight for elitism—boldly, we even used the word. Acknowledging that Purchase was part of a tax-supported state university, we accepted words like "populism" and "egalitarianism," but we wanted to create an institution to serve the brightest young men and women we could find and to provide them with the richest all-around education possible. What a couple of snobs we were! We wouldn't admit it, except perhaps to ourselves, but in the vast complex that was SUNY we secretly hoped to establish a little Princeton.

I never knew just where the president stood on this issue. Dr. Kaplan had a fierce desire to make Purchase special, and he was vigorous in his demands for excellence. But that drive was not quite the same thing as elitism. And Abbott was a dyed-in-the-wool populist. He had grown up in Springfield, Massachusetts, in modest circumstances. His background was in labor relations. Only later, at UCLA, had his interest in the arts burgeoned, under the tutelage of John Houseman, who persuaded Dr. Kaplan to give a campus home to a theatre group he had just organized. His interest kindled, Dr. Kaplan not long after became chairman of the California Arts Commission. But his principal job at UCLA had been as director of its vast university extension program, which embraced some thirty-five thousand people— certainly a "populist" kind of enterprise.

Purchase was to be a residential college, with but a small percentage of Westchester residents admitted as "day students." High on our agenda, therefore, were questions of life style, parietal rules, sleeping and eating accommodations, and recreational and sports activities. Remember, we were discussing these matters in the period between 1967 and 1972, the years of the Vietnam War and a social revolution largely sparked by college youth. The students to whom I'd said goodbye at Vassar in 1967 bore little resemblance to those I would welcome to Purchase a brief five years later.

Time and *Newsweek* were full of sensational dispatches and unsettling pictures of college presidents being carted down stairs in wheelbarrows, official files being ransacked, and sit-ins taking over academic offices. In cloisters thick with clouds of marijuana smoke, those employed to administer were summoned to listen to "non-negotiable demands." In our still quiet ivory tower, the more wary, like me, trembled in anticipation of the arrival of the "flower children."

Flowers and all, their health and happiness had to be of prime concern to us. We would be stuck with them and they would be stuck with us in a place that was in the middle of a teenage nowhere—ten miles from any movie house, from but one bar and grill, from any snack shop, and indeed from any kind of shop. It looked, too, as though our faculty wouldn't be around to offer aid and comfort, for real estate in the Purchase-Greenwich-Rye neighborhood was prohibitively expensive, and our colleagues would have to depart at dusk to less costly retreats. What was more, we expected that few resident students would have cars to carry them in and out of our wilderness. These were all matters with widespread potential to ignite student strikes and demonstrations. How to anticipate and defuse incendiary situations became urgent problems we had to address.

On a cloudless late afternoon in early October 1969, we held our first Event, a ground-breaking ceremony. Governor Rockefeller came by helicopter. Chancellor Gould arrived with some key SUNY figures, Ed Barnes (of course), and Philip Johnson, architect of the building for which ground was being broken. And what was that building? Not the library, not a laboratory or a classroom facility, nor yet a dormitory. It was the Roy Neuberger Art Museum. First things first on our campus.

Unfortunately, this propitious event was not followed by other rapid achievements. Intermittent budget freezes—recessional reflexes, you might say—slowed our progress, delaying the recruitment of key staff and faculty and postponing the acquisition of vital equipment. What principally held us up, though, was what seemed the snail's pace of building construction; critical facilities like dormitories and dining rooms, classroom buildings and the library, fell, one by one, behind their target dates.

The postponements became so perennial that one friend in New York finally remarked, "Norris, I begin to think you may well be the only dean I've ever heard of to reach retirement without ever having to confront any faculty or students to be dean of!"

So the planning staff, too, slowed down a bit, while bulldozers, concrete mixers, and structural-steel workers wreaked havoc on our acres; during spring months the place was a sea of mud. Our opening date was twice postponed. The only thing to do was to find other activities to keep us occupied. I wrote and had another book published, *The Exploding Stage*, twice taught seminars at Yale, made a return trip to the USSR, participated in a Salzburg Seminar, and assumed leadership of the National Theatre Conference and, subsequently, of the American Council for the Arts in Education.

Early on, Abbott had made it clear that if at all possible, senior administrators were to live within a reasonably accessible distance from the campus. So in the spring of 1968 I went house hunting. Nothing affordable could be found in or near Purchase, but in late May I discovered what I sought in Chappaqua, twenty miles away.

Everyone, I suppose, develops his own priorities. Low on my list are items high on others': automobiles, appliances, clothes. I've never owned any vehicle larger than a subcompact. I've managed without a color TV, Cuisinart, VCR, or hi-fi, even an electric knife. As for clothes, from the frugalities of my childhood I learned that clothes do not necessarily make the man, that a flashy wardrobe may dazzle but not automatically impress, so I never elevated haberdashery to top priority.

After setting aside funds to support my old age—pressing ever closer until now I'm in it—I have dedicated my savings to my priorities: enhancing my environment, travel and more travel, and the enjoyment of food, drink, and friends.

My find was a beautifully restored seven-room pre-Revolutionary farmhouse, set in the midst of three acres, looking across a sloping expanse of lawn down to a duck pond. The planting had been particularly well done: azaleas, lilacs, rhododendrons, and laurel all blossomed in late spring, after two pink magnolias and several hundred daffodils had stopped blooming.

Our entering class enjoyed the unexpected privilege of attending two SUNY units at once. Since by opening day, in September 1972 no dormitory at Purchase was habitable, students repaired in the evening to the SUNY Maritime College, under the shadow of the Whitestone Bridge in the Bronx. After breakfast the wandering tribe, several hundred strong, were bused to Purchase, where they had lunch, only to be bused back to the Bronx in time for dinner. During the few months that this arrangement was in effect, the Maritime cadets who weathered life with the dancers, actors, fiddlers, and filmmakers, all the worldly young men and women of Purchase, were, we heard, corrupted almost beyond recall.

Purchase, once the apple of Rockefeller's and Gould's eyes, certainly got off to an inauspicious start. Acting classes, for example, took place in the estate's spacious four-car garage, which, with some "temporary" adjustments, served not badly for two years. But Rockefeller, soon to be Vice President of the United States, now had other things on his mind, and the chancellor had resigned and fled to Florida to pamper his heart. As for the students, there was remarkably little grousing; as time passed and that first class reached their senior year, there was even misty-eyed talk about the "good old days." Indeed, a fraternal bond seemed to be forged among the survivors of that frontier era.

Since none of the PAC theatres or its shops were operative before 1974, we could offer no public performances for almost two years. That didn't matter to Joe Anthony or me, because, believing in "process first, product afterward," we weren't preparing for audiences anyway. The delay in theatre construction did, however, persuade me not to set up the program in stage design and technical production until the second year.

Finally, the first company presented at the end of its second year the inaugural production in "Theatre D," the black box against which I had fought so hard. Anthony chose Arthur Schnitzler's sophisticated comedy *La Ronde*, to give our unsophisticated students a whiff of the sensualities of pre–World War I Vienna. The play didn't really show off Theatre D to best advantage. It remained for guest director Alan Schneider to do that in 1975, with a brilliant production of *Marat/Sade*, in which he used to startling effect the theatre's light grids and the runways that hug its four walls. I had to admit, if only to myself, that "D" wasn't a total disaster after all.

5

Abbott Kaplan had decided at the beginning that he wished his first deans of the arts to be senior people in their fields. His rationale was threefold: he preferred the experience that comes with age; he thought that "headliners" were likely to attract the brightest young faculty more readily than vice versa; and he felt it essential from the start that Purchase have built-in prestige to command immediate respect and attention.

For me this policy did not turn out to be as smart as it had seemed in 1967. At that time we had all assumed the college would be in full swing by 1970, and I, five years from administrators' mandatory retirement age, would be able to shepherd the first student generation through its collective life and start on the second. But with the delays, I was to graduate a year before my first class.

As my decanal retirement year of 1975 loomed, I felt I must accelerate my pace, particularly with regard to graduating whole theatre companies. Our first would be ready in '76, with enough actors and technicians to form a reasonably balanced troupe. By then they would have worked with their mentor, Joseph Anthony; with two others from the acting faculty, George Morrison and Kay Carney; and with five guest directors.

"Y ou've told me you want to get to know your new chancellor, Ernest Boyer, better," said Richard Leach, calling from Saratoga one snowy day during the winter of the company's third year. "Well, the Boyers are driving up from Albany to dinner next Saturday night, so I think you'd better come too." Dick and Katherine Leach were fast friends of some thirty years' standing. I accepted forthwith.

After dinner we sat before the fire. The chancellor took charge: "Tell me, Norrie, about your idea of graduating theatre companies." Twenty minutes later I concluded my pitch. "I like it," said Boyer. "How much is it going to cost? And where are you going to get the money?"

I said I thought the project could be launched for fifty thousand dollars, adding, "I hoped I could get half of it from you." The chancellor nodded. "I think I can find it," was the way he phrased his reply. We shook hands on it, and the Boyers went out into the snowy night. I was exultant.

At that point I faced one last semester in the upstairs bedroom-office I'd occupied for almost eight years. Each entering class had been briefed about the "company" plan. and I had watched with pleasure as each group of disparate students had slowly come together as a team. Now I was quick to tell the senior company about the chancellor's support and to explain that, after eight years, my sabbatical was overdue and I would be away for the next fall term, while my successor was being selected. I would return and remain a professor until my academic tenure expired, in five years. But when my sabbatical was over, my only concern would be to see the first company launched.

In my absence Joe Anthony would stand in for me. Meanwhile, each student should finally decide whether he or she wanted to be part of the long-awaited enterprise or go it alone. I urged those who chose the former to set up a small steering committee to run what was, after all, to be *their* theatre. Although Joe and I stood ready to offer artistic counsel and managerial support, I expected them, like their forerunners, the University Players, to take charge. I had created one theatre, the Phoenix; at sixty-five I didn't plan to start another. I wished them Godspeed.

I returned to Purchase from my sabbatical semester freed of all administrative responsibilities save for launching the first company. I was in for a shock at my first meeting with the students. It turned out that they had not selected a steering committee during my five-month absence: they couldn't agree on any three, four, or five classmates they were willing to trust! Factions had developed, personal jealousies had emerged, the rapport that had held them together had dissolved. Their most talented actor had decided to go it alone; others followed his lead. The rest were shaken and downhearted, suspicious, blaming each other for what had or had not occurred.

Several, however, blamed both Joe Anthony and me for wanting to push them into the water, to sink or swim, while we sat on the bank. They seemed to feel we could not expect them to start a theatre on their own: they needed us, and we were deserting them by not leaving Purchase to go along with them. (It was useless to tell them that joining them had never been intended and was, in fact, impossible: we both had continuing contractual obligations to SUNY.) Furthermore, two or three charged, it had never been their idea to form a company; it had been mine. And after four years they were fed up with being told what was good for them: it was time to take their future into their own hands and for each to stand on his own. I realized that I was the one who had been naive, thinking I could play Svengali to their thirty Trilbys. We had all been miscast in our roles.

What had gone wrong? I believe the problem was primarily that while Purchase's arts training was technically undergraduate, what we were offering, in its intensity and concentration, really consisted of graduate work. If the company had been composed of graduate students, the outcome might have been different. Our undergraduates were too immature, too unprepared professionally, to cope with the creation of a theatre, and I had not taken that sufficiently into account. So my third contribution to the creation of our "innovative college" foundered. No subsequent class has ever undertaken to become a company.

For that earlier light of mine that had failed—the theatre to be built for the future—I was considered an impractical dreamer.

Perhaps the same could be said of me because of the theatre company that never materialized. Still another of my bubbles burst at a divisional faculty meeting toward the end of my tenure as professor: I sat quietly while new, younger members pricked at my cherished "mentor" system, wanting to turn our actor training program into one that would resemble those they had known elsewhere. In my experience, familiarity seldom breeds contempt, but rather breeds contentment. So Purchase succeeded in losing yet another claim to being "innovative."

SUNY Purchase was conceived as a dream. Its planners spent five years in pursuit of their Grail and wore themselves out in the search. Then they learned about reality and, one by one, shed their dreams, or left the college. Purchase, they tell me, is not as dreamy a place today.

Except in summers only recently past. Then for a few weeks it burst into glory. The Performing Arts Center fulfilled itself from 1981 to 1989, spreading before the public an extraordinary international array of music, opera, dance, and drama. Sophisticated art lovers gathered in theatres we once called "A," "B," "C," and "D," to hear string quartets and to see strikingly original stagings of Mozart opera, to watch foreign acting companies and dance troupes, all the kinds of performances we had dreamed of: "Summerfare" the festival was called.

How did it come about? Shamefully, not through the beneficence of Albany, where SUNY has lived in an apparently chronic state of indigence, but because the chief of Pepsico, Donald Kendall, in his world headquarters across the street from the college, decided he should do something for the community. I've written and talked a good deal about corporate funding for the arts, but I doubt that Mr. Kendall has ever read anything I've written, and he has certainly never heard my harangues. Nevertheless, Pepsico's "Summerfare" provided, in the years since my retirement, the fulfillment of one of my private dreams for Purchase. Now this corporate support has come to an end and the future seems clouded.

"Summerfare" took money and imagination, more than SUNY could summon—and it took time, more than this emeritus dean approaching the end of his academic tenure had at his disposal. Still, to me it seems disgraceful that the college couldn't have initiated this festival, that SUNY had to yield the honor to an enlightened corporate executive, and that it was not integrated into the college's educational objectives. Obviously, Don Quixote speaks out of loyalty to his dream. He should by now bow to reality and just be grateful for the chance to have enjoyed for a time his illusions.

16

Culmination: From One Art to Many (1972–80)

The American Council for the Arts in Education (ACAE) is an organization of organizations. Back in 1956, when it began to take shape, its constituents numbered some forty thousand teachers. Its genesis was an informal group of gregarious arts education leaders who headed huge organizations like the Music Educators National Conference, the National Art Educators Association, the American Educational Theatre Association. They enjoyed bemoaning their plight and sought consolation from one another. At first they designated themselves, rather impressively, the National Council of the Arts in Education; their purpose has always been to represent the rank and file in their respective fields.

Somewhere along the way the council started to hold annual conferences, at which delegates shared experiences, delivered and listened to papers, and consistently discussed how badly off they were. In doing so, they set out to prove the truth of two old adages—that misery loves company and, with a view toward ameliorating their situation, in union there is strength. As it happened, for a long time they found only the first to be true, and in their weakness they took refuge in collective inebriation, returning home to face familiar and long-standing frustrations: their subjects still not fully accepted into the curriculum and their programs the first to suffer when budgets were cut. For the truth that did not have to be proved was that the arts were generally considered "frills," and as such as easily dispensed with in classrooms and on campuses as they were for the most part in American life.

By its sixth annual conference, in 1967, the organization had changed its name to the *American* Council for the Arts in Education and had grown to a membership of thirty, representing seventeen organizations of educators and academic leaders in every field of the fine and performing arts and at every level, from the first grade through graduate school—all concerned with both critical and creative practice in their respective areas. And a change was in the air.

Barnaby Keeney, the president of Brown University, had recently become the first chairman of the National Endowment for the Humanities, established by Congress in 1965, and at the ACAE's 1967 conference he delivered the keynote address. Explaining the role of the NEH and the equally new National Endowment for the Arts, he spoke sympathetically but warned:

> One hears today a great deal about the financial plight of the arts in this country. . . . If the arts outside of education become bankrupt, the art inside [it] will suffer terribly. Yet, in your program I do not see a section on achieving excellence in art education through money—a subject that is fully as important as academic accreditation [high on that summer's agenda], and one to which I personally feel you should devote considerable attention.

The incoming president of the ACAE, Joseph C. Sloane, a former president of the constituent College Art Association, chairman of the art department at the University of North Carolina at Chapel Hill, and my Princeton classmate, rose to Keeney's challenge. Agreeing with the endowment's chairman—that money, the necessary evil, was also needed for the achievement of excellence in art education—he later called upon Dr. Keeney, invited him to put his money where his values were, and emerged with a grant of $300,000 over the ensuing three years.

The ACAE was thunderstruck. They immediately organized a conference, held at Wingspread in Wisconsin, to consider how

to spend their windfall. Then they rented an office, hired a director and staff, and charged them with bringing into being a program dubbed "Arts/Worth." Its aim was to launch a public campaign for the arts in education, to persuade everyone that
mattered—legislators, state boards of education, college and university administrators and trustees, school superintendents and
principals, and parents of children—that the arts are just as basic
as the basics—that is, the three Rs.

As educators are apt to do, the ACAE staff spent three years
in endless discussion and fact-finding about their gigantic task,
issuing opinion surveys, monographs, reports. By then the $300,-
000 was gone and Norris Houghton, who had become a council
member-at-large only three years before, was elected president.
It was 1973, when I was still a dean at Purchase.

Sloane's baby, Arts/Worth, although noble in concept, was
almost impossible to bring to maturity. I thought it would take
a multimillion-dollar campaign to convince the nation's taxpayers
that the arts belonged at the center of an education, not at its
periphery. Moreover, the ACAE was the only organization that
represented all the arts in education, and therein lay one of its
chief weaknesses. Its constituency was so broad—from musicolo-
gists to puppeteers, from Chicano tots learning about finger
painting in ghetto storefronts to advanced scholars studying ancient texts in air-conditioned carrels—that it faced an insur-
mountable challenge in trying to speak with a common voice.
The member organizations, each preoccupied with its own problems, lacked peripheral vision. Naively, I hoped to energize their
sense of "strength through unity."

So a few months after my induction, I wrote a recommendation to my colleagues on the council and to the presidents of its
constituent organizations. "Our common concern," I noted,

is to strengthen our position in the educational hierarchy,
acquire more money to support our work, more and better
teachers, more chances to develop innovative programs, acquire greater knowledge of what is going on in the national
scene. Most of these objectives require adequate funding. I
see this as a national, very public concern, but one that
strikes *us* where we live.

And my proposal? The Rockefeller Brothers Fund panel report, *The Performing Arts: Problems and Prospects*, had made a deep impression on me. By throwing an intense spotlight on a national problem, it had succeeded in its objective of altering public attitudes toward the arts and how they should be funded. My own RBF experience now led me to the conclusion that a solution to the ACAE's problems lay in a parallel approach.

With my letter I enclosed this proposal:

> Create a public panel of distinguished and objective citizens which, after study, would issue a widely disseminated report on the "problems and prospects" that face our fields. Through the work of such a panel, not only might we achieve the objectives of Arts/Worth, with a relatively small expenditure of funds, but also find an instrument to "bring us together."

The membership of the ACAE endorsed the proposal at its next annual meeting and returned to their jobs, leaving their dewy-eyed president to make the proposal a reality. My first thought was, not surprisingly, to get in touch with Nancy Hanks. Now chairman of the National Endowment for the Arts, she, if anyone, knew the ropes where panels were concerned. We had not talked since she assumed office. I went to Washington to consult her in early November 1973—Election Day, in fact.

"Come in, Norrie," she cried cheerily, ushering me into her sanctum. "We'll lunch right here. And here come the martinis!" She lowered her voice conspiratorially. "It's the first time I've ever served a drink here."

In our days at RBF, we had enjoyed the custom of lunching on Election Day, when, because bars were closed for as long as the polls were open (as is still the case), she'd brewed cocktails in her Special Studies office, it also being closed for business. (I've since heard that not only was this the first time she served them at the NEA offices—it was the last.)

When I finished my presentation, she said, "It's a great idea. It must be done, and you must do it."

While I hoped the panel report could be completed before my tenure as president expired, in 1975, and I estimated it would cost around $75,000, she thought I was wrong on both accounts: the report could not be done in two years and certainly not for that figure. It would take at least six months just to get organized, find a project director, and put together a staff. Then I'd first have to find the proper panel chairman (I knew that on a national level I had neither the name nor the prestige to assume the post myself) and recruit panelists, which couldn't be done overnight. Meanwhile, I'd have to determine how much the entire project was likely to cost. Indeed, I'd need $25,000 just to find that out. Clearly, she concluded, I'd be lucky if the panel was in business a year from now.

"I'll tell you what I'll do," she offered. From some contingency funds she could draw on for small grants, she would put up $12,500 if we could raise an equal amount. This would prove, if nothing else, that she was all for my proposal.

I left her office aglow from her vote of confidence. In six months the $12,500 was raised, a project director was selected on the basis of her work in the Bureau of Educational and Cultural Affairs of the State Department in Washington—Margaret Howard, a handsome, chicly dressed brunette in her early forties, who exuded organized efficiency—and four or five key staff people were recruited. But we still had no panel chairman.

My first choice was Frank Stanton, a member of the RBF arts panel. Now retired as president of CBS, he was serving as chairman of the American Red Cross, and in his contemporary, white-walled office, high above Fifth Avenue, I found him as dapper and forceful as ever. His eyes seemed never without a twinkle. Although he was much interested in the arts in education and the idea of the panel report, and was impressed by Nancy Hanks's support, he turned me down when I asked him to be chairman: he was currently heading a public commission working to reorganize the USIS/USIA and to rethink their relationship to the State Department.

He'd be glad to serve on my panel, however, and had a suggestion for its chairman—James Michener, who, Dr. Stanton assured me, was a deeply conscientious and concerned citizen. He urged me to get in touch with Michener at his home in Bucks County, Pennsylvania, but before calling, I checked with Hanks, who enthusiastically approved.

Three days later, the celebrated author, wearing a plaid wool lumberjack's shirt and a reserved smile, took me to lunch at a country inn near New Hope.

Michener was surprised that Nancy had recommended him: she should know, he claimed, he wasn't cut out to be a chairman. He didn't have the kind of initiative or drive that leadership required. But he'd like to serve on the panel—if I'd accept him. I did. Then he declared, "I'll tell you the man I think you should get for the job—Frank Stanton!"

When, without delay, I reported this Alphonse/Gaston routine to Nancy, she had another suggestion. "I've been thinking that David Rockefeller, Jr., would be a good candidate. Do you know him?"

I said we'd met only once, at Tanglewood, when he was the Boston Symphony's assistant manager.

"David is a very bright and likable young man," Nancy said. "At the moment he's running a newspaper in Boston called *The Real Paper*, somewhat like New York's *Village Voice*. But that's not really up his alley, and I'm sure he's open to suggestions. He has no desire to follow his father into the Chase Bank, nor to follow up his Harvard law degree. If you could interest him, he'd work very hard; in fact, the more I think about it, the better I like the idea. He's ready for the national scene; it would be good for both of you."

I talked to Kathryn Bloom, director of the Arts in Education program in his uncle's JDR 3rd Fund, and she agreed with Nancy. So the following week I went to Boston to see David, a rather hulking young man of thirty-two, with a fair complexion, ginger-colored hair, and the Rockefeller nose. Slightly reserved, but with a quick smile, he was wearing an exuberant necktie of orange, aquamarine, and white swirls. This was but one of a large and startling collection he sported in those days—to set him apart from others of his clan, I judged. It was of a piece with his refusal to dwell among them in New York—he lived in Cambridge and came to Manhattan as seldom as possible. (David is the eldest son of the youngest son of John D. Rockefeller, Jr.)

Over lunch I told my story. Rockefeller asked all the right questions and finally announced that he'd like to have a few days to think it over. We met on a Monday. On Thursday night he called to say he'd be in New York the next morning and to ask if I could join him for breakfast at the Biltmore. I could. His tie was yellow and red. "I'll do it," he said.

So began an association with David Rockefeller, Jr., that would become almost as close as my earlier relationship with T. Edward Hambleton. It was of briefer duration, of course, and there was, too, a generational gap, about which he was probably more sensitive than I. After all, I was five years older than his father. Nonetheless, we established a warm rapport.

Like T. Edward, David was blessed with lightness of wit and ebullience of humor, qualities he must have inherited from his Irish mother, born Margaret McGrath, for both are in short supply among the Rockefeller clan, or at least among those I have known.

Only six more weeks remained of 1974; before 1975 ended, I would have completed my tenure as president of the ACAE. I was behind schedule, just as Nancy Hanks had foreseen. But David's presence reassured me. Having committed himself, he would, I had no doubt, see the project through: that is a Rockefeller characteristic and one key to the success of their dynasty. We agreed on the priorities—recruitment of a panel and the acquisition of funding sources were of the highest but equal importance—and vigorously we tackled them both.

With a Rockefeller aboard, fund-raising became vastly easier. The National Endowment for the Arts pledged $125,000; the Rockefeller Brothers Fund and the U.S. Office of Education joined hands with the NEA in making a grant of $70,000 each. That, however, was just half the sum eventually required. Fortunately, corporate and other foundation funding was soon forthcoming. David and I were determined that support be nationwide, and it was, due to his entrée into the offices of corporate executives and foundation decisionmakers throughout the country.

David had equal access to the kinds of men and women we wished to recruit for panel membership. It was agreed from the start that with one exception—myself—arts educators would be excluded, on the same grounds that Balanchine, Bernstein, Graham, and Hayes had been excluded from the RBF panel. The case for the arts in education must be put before the American people by concerned, prominent citizens who had no axes to grind.

In any case, the panel had been created by and was eventually to speak for the American Council for the Arts in Education, whose president was the panel's vice chairman—and that should suffice. However, since neither professional artists nor non–arts educators were precluded from serving, our panel was to embrace Lorin Hollander, the concert pianist; Ray Eames, the artist, designer, filmmaker, and wife of Charles Eames; Melissa Hayden, the ballerina; Francis Keppel, the former Harvard dean and U.S. Commissioner of Education; Thomas P. Bergin, dean of continuing education at Notre Dame; John B. Davis, Jr., who during our study resigned as superintendent of schools of Minneapolis to become president of Macalester College; Glenn T. Seaborg, professor of chemistry at Berkeley, but more widely known as the former chairman of the U.S. Atomic Energy Commission and a Nobel Prize winner; and Donald M. Carroll, Jr., the former commissioner for basic education in Pennsylvania. They constituted the artists who were not educators and the educators who were not artists.

David and I met at least once a week to refine our objectives and, with the help of a small advisory committee, to develop our priorities. The panel, we decided, should place major emphasis on children (K through 12); on schools rather than on community arts activities, "because," as David claimed, "that is where most young people are"; and on encouraging public funding rather than private. The "target group" for our arts education effort would be acknowledged amateurs rather than those gifted students who aimed to become professionals, but the learning experience we hoped to foster would emphasize participation rather than observation.

2

The panel's first meeting was held on June 27, 1975, in New York City. Again, as in 1963, a Rockefeller presided. I sat beside him. The other members sat around the table in alphabetical order, starting from David's right. The staff sat, as staffs always do, along the wall.

Looking around at the panelists, I speculated as to what their various contributions might be. My friends among them included Barry Bingham, chairman of the *Courier-Journal* (Louisville); Jay Iselin, president of WNET (New York); Elizabeth McCormack, adviser to the Rockefeller Family Fund; James Michener and Frank Stanton. I knew I could count on them. Far less known to me were Peggy Cooper, a young black woman from Washington, levelheaded and articulate, who was the founder of the Duke Ellington School of the Arts in Washington, D.C., and now held an important position with the Post-Newsweek stations; Edward Hamilton, who had the forceful manner that befitted a former deputy mayor of New York City (under John Lindsay); and, particularly, Patsy Mink, Hawaii's representative in Congress, who sat on the powerful House Committee on Education and Labor. She began as an enigma but proved to be a combination of good old American pragmatism and idealism.

The panel endorsed the priorities David had set—they could hardly have done otherwise—and agreed to a meeting schedule that was roughly modeled on JDR 3rd's: five two-to-three-day sessions, about two months apart, with the next meeting to be held at the Rockefeller estate in Pocantico Hills in September.

David then unveiled our plan to "go on the road," as we say in the theatre, so that the panel might observe how the arts were actually being taught and learned in selected cities across the country. On-site visits would provide evidence of how in general the arts fared in elementary and secondary school environments, and how, more specifically, certain procedures like "open classrooms" worked. Along the way we would invite testimony from concerned citizens: art teachers, community leaders, officials of national organizations, and federal agencies. We would devote part of each day to closed sessions at which we would review and discuss the lessons we ourselves were learning.

So we journeyed to Memphis in December, to Los Angeles in February 1976, and to Minneapolis in June. What did we learn during our travels? In Los Angeles, we talked with John Goodlad, then dean of the Graduate School of Education at UCLA and the author of *Dynamics of Educational Change*, who told us that "although among young students art ranks at the top in regard to their *satisfaction,* when they are asked to rate subjects as to which is most *important,* the arts are placed near the bottom."

The panel pondered this afterward: if children like arts best, who persuades them they are least important? Their parents? Their teachers? Their peers? The media?

Howard Gardner, codirector of Project Zero at Harvard Graduate School of Education, explained to me and other less knowledgeable panel members the difference between the "cognitive" and the "affective" lobes of the brain, and how American education had long been fixated on cognition and suspicious of the realm of the senses—that is, imagination, intuition, feeling. Too much learning he said, was geared merely to memorization of facts. Gardner gave us increased understanding of the implications in the rather swinging title David Rockefeller had come up with for our report: *Coming to Our Senses.*

We heard the reminiscences of two eminent black women who were pioneers in arts and education: Katherine Dunham from St. Louis, teacher of dance and head of her own world-renowned company; and Elma Lewis, the eloquent founder of a well-known school of the arts in Boston. In Los Angeles, our project received the enthusiastic endorsement of Norman Lear, producer of the famed "All in the Family" and other television series. Michael Tilson Thomas, articulate young conductor of the Buffalo Philharmonic, came to Tarrytown to talk with us, as did John Culkin, director of the Center for Understanding Media at New York's New School. It was Culkin who brightened one meeting with an anecdote about his visit to an elementary school where he had been invited to address the pupils.

"I asked them how many of them considered themselves media-minded. A dozen raised their hands. I asked one of them what he meant by 'media-minded.' He said, 'Well, I'm not too smart and I'm not too stupid. I guess I'm just 'media-minded.' "

Without question, from all that we observed and heard, the panel became strikingly aware of the reefs and shoals and cross-currents through which American education wound its uneasy course in trying to accommodate the arts into its mainstream.

Perhaps it lay in David's informal style of presiding, perhaps in the personalities of the members, but we seemed a more flexible, however disputations, group than JDR 3rd's panel of the 1960s. We enjoyed more laughter, felt more relish in making discoveries, and displayed more fervor. This may have been simply because of the panel's size and composition: while we were but twenty-five, the earlier group numbered thirty, among whom were three women, one black, and a majority of senior corporate executives and elderly philanthropists. Our panel included seven women, two blacks, one person of Hispanic origin—and no "captains of industry."

It was at our Memphis meeting that John B. Davis first made an observation that was a key to our study: "When we look at the arts, we are looking at much more than the arts: we are looking at what a concerned society should be doing to improve the basic human condition."

We agreed that we were indeed considering a more sweeping issue than arts in education: one that enhanced the quality of life in America.

The panel, now formally named the Panel on the Arts, Education and Americans, held its last session at the beginning of October 1976, at Pocantico Hills, once again in "The Playhouse." I had earlier thought: How appropriate for me, for I had naturally assumed it was a small theatre. Now I knew that it was instead a rambling, informal building, not unlike Ferncliff's "sports palast," that boasted a swimming pool, indoor squash courts, a billiard room, and a huge living room, its walls hung with full-length portraits of Mr. and Mrs. John D. Rockefeller, Jr., and their six sons and daughters, all now looking down upon our deliberations.

We carefully studied every page of the rough draft of the panel report, which had been written during the summer of the Bicentennial. Particular attention was paid to the report's opening Summary Statement:

> This Panel reaffirms the conviction of our founding fathers as expressed by Benjamin Franklin, that "nothing can more effectively contribute to the cultivation of a country . . . than a proper education of youth."

In this Panel's view "proper education" consists equally of four things:

1. The acquisition of knowledge, skills, and the power to reason.
2. The development of critical faculties and moral judgment.
3. The cultivation of *creative potential.* [My italics added.]
4. The promotion of self-knowledge and effective interaction with others.

To deprive individuals of any one of these is to deny them their opportunity to lead a full and balanced life. . . .

The arts are a function of life itself, and the process of making art—both creative and recreative—can give insight to all other areas of learning. The arts help people understand themselves in historical, cultural, and aesthetic terms; they provide people with broader choices about their environment and influence the way they do their work and live their lives. Since artistic expression is also truly basic to the individual's intellectual development, it must be included as a component of all education.

Ninety-seven "Recommendations" followed—two more, as some wag remarked, than Martin Luther had nailed to the portal of the church at Wittenberg!—grouped under fifteen different headings. It was astonishing that only one recommendation elicited as many as three dissents (a fact duly footnoted): "That a Secretary for Education be added to the Cabinet." And this, ironically, was one of the first of our recommendations to be acted upon affirmatively.

"Publication is not of itself meaningful," I had written to the ACAE trustees in 1973,

if the report simply joins the great library of foundation-sponsored studies that accumulate dust on the shelves of a few specialists and scholars in the field. This panel report is clearly a means to an end: the support of our increased role for the arts in education throughout the nation.

Therefore, the publication, promotion, dissemination, diffusion of the panel's recommendations are of the utmost importance. Not only must the report be issued in paperback and in large quantities; its appearance must be heralded in the press and mass media, through reviews of its contents in newspapers, national magazines, on the air, with press conferences and interviews.

And thanks to David Rockefeller, Jr., that was what happened. The report's official publication date was May 24, 1977. On that day we were in Washington, for David had persuaded Congressman John Brademas, chairman of the House Select Subcommittee on Education, that our work was worthy of a joint congressional hearing. Seldom has a specialized book been heralded with more fanfare than *Coming to Our Senses: The Significance of the Arts for American Education.* It was introduced at a press conference at the Watergate Hotel, which was followed by a reception and luncheon in the handsome Diplomatic Reception Rooms of the State Department. To this we invited 125 distinguished guests, who represented a good cross-section of Washington's cultural establishment, as well as national organizations like Actors' Equity, the ACAE, and the Urban League.

After lunch, we all crossed the street for the day's principal meeting, held at the National Academy of Science—a nice juxtaposition, we thought—where we were joined by another two hundred people. The program consisted of a dozen panelists presenting, in three informal mini-colloquiums, the outstanding themes of *Coming to Our Senses:* "The World of Learning," "The Arts Are Basic," and "People Are the Key." Interspersed among these sessions were short documentary films and an animated cartoon or two. At four o'clock, Joan Mondale, wife of the Vice President, delivered the principal address of the day, "Arts and Education: A Personal Perspective." In conclusion, David Rockefeller, Jr., offered his final "Charge," in which he urged the gathering to join him as he pledged his continuing support for the arts in education.

(That "Charge" he fulfilled over the next eight years: Arts, Education and Americans continued as the name of a nonprofit corporation we—(David as chairman, and I as vice president—

formed to promote the report and to follow through on its recommendations. The corporation became an advocacy organization for the arts in education, sponsoring regional conferences, establishing a resource library, and publishing monographs and newsletters for its constituents. They, interestingly enough, came in large measure from the grass roots—classroom teachers and their supervisors who had been fired up by our report to accept new challenges, confident at last that they were not alone.)

At ten the next morning, a substantial number of our panelists assembled at the Rayburn Office Building for the Joint Congressional Hearing on "The Arts Are Fundamental to Learning." Congressman Brademas presided, and in attendance were Senators Claiborne Pell and Jacob Javits, and Representatives Carl Perkins and Cec Heftel. The session lasted over two hours: eight panelists testified. They were joined by a surprise witness—Pearl Bailey, who began by saying, "Sunday I went to Georgetown University to deliver the commencement speech and got a degree. Isn't that something?

"It is nice to have a common cause," she went on, speaking off the cuff. "I bet you this is the first time you have seen a long table like this filled with people with a common love. That is because of the arts. Music, singing, dancing, everything to me is an art. Life is an art. God is art." When she finished, after ten minutes, everyone in the hearing room responded with spontaneous applause.

I felt that warmth again as I listened to Congressman Brademas sum up at the end of the session:

"My own judgment, and I'm sure Senator Pell would not disagree, is that your report, *Coming to Our Senses*, will prove to be one of the most significant studies of a crucial national issue that has yet been produced. . . . What you have done *is* absolutely critical, pointing to the indispensable role of the arts in the human experience and therefore in the learning experience."

At that moment the thirty years of my life in the theatre seemed as remote as my childhood. Now, in art—in its broadest sense—and education, my post-Phoenix years seemed to have reached their culmination. I felt that I had helped to bring some light—and heat—into the world of learning, and my work as a missionary was almost done.

Curtain Speech

*O*n that spring day in Washing-
ton, the Brademas plaudits for *Coming to Our Senses* may have
banished from memory my years in the theatre, but that proved
only temporary. As it has been since 1917, when I was first smitten, the stage continues to be the centerpiece of my life. So to it
I return to compose this postlude for my theatrical Diamond
Jubilee.

In the beginning—1917, a very long time ago—I was, naturally,
a spectator. My memories of *Chu Chin Chow* and *The Taming of
the Shrew* are today hauntingly elusive. But what these shows
unquestionably did was to introduce me to a world of action,
music, dance, color, excitement, and fun, and to engender my
subsequent ardor for the stage in all its diversity.

Growing up in Middle America, I was dependent on "the
road" for providing those feasts of fine acting: George Arliss,
Nazimova, Maude Adams, Walter Hampden, Minnie Maddern
Fiske, even John Drew; of great plays—*Cyrano de Bergerac, Tre-
lawny of the Wells, The Rivals*—and enchanting musicals—*The
Student Prince, Babes in Toyland, HMS Pinafore.* My early stage
experience was also enriched by the local resident stock company
of Stuart Walker, which had the peculiar attraction of allowing
the leading man and woman, the ingenue, the juvenile, and the
character actors to become familiar and beloved figures in our

midst. And when I advanced from spectator to professional participant, it was in a stock company, the University Players, that I first found my place.

Then, thanks to the Guggenheim Foundation, I was again cast as a spectator, and fell in love with the Russian stage. I was thrilled by its diversity, its color, its action, and, unexpectedly, the artistic strength that derived from the counterparts of what I'd grown up with: actors working together, not exactly in stock companies but in repertory theatres, whose member artists were familiar to—indeed, beloved by—Soviet playgoers and who remained together for decades.

So when I returned from Russia I could trace a clear line from Indianapolis via Cape Cod to Moscow. But now I had to build a career and earn a living on Broadway, though not forgetting the permanent resident company idea. Broadway was glamorous, challenging, and for me—lucky enough to be rarely unemployed—rewarding: not financially but in giving me the chance to do what I wanted to do.

Stage folk—actors, playwrights, directors, designers, backstage technicians, producers (at least in those days)—formed a closely knit community, almost a fraternity. We rejoiced in each other's successes, commiserated about the flops. Sure, Broadway was "show business," not an art colony, but it was astonishing how often art poked its head up, for these stage folk were creative, gifted professionals.

They were also, however, a collection of individuals, each concerned for himself or herself. And the system that prevailed dictated that in a ten-year period, seasons between 1932 and 1942, I worked on fifteen productions for ten different managements.

The Broadway I came back to after the war began to change. The Group had dissolved, but its influence lingered on through individuals such as Harold Clurman, Lee Strasberg, Robert Lewis, and Stella and Luther Adler. Like me, they had been influenced by Stanislavski, and they wanted to lift the level of acting by the study and practice of his teachings. In consequence and nourished by the G.I. Bill, the Actors' Studio and more classes and schools than I can recall sprang up.

Allied to that was another new phenomenon that became noticeable as the postwar seasons passed: more and more young theatre professionals held college degrees. In 1932, when we University Players had hit New York with ours, we were in a small minority. By 1952, enough university and college departments of drama had been created across the country to feed the theatre hunger for new talent and to overpopulate Times Square.

Finally, and maybe inevitably, there grew to be a quite pronounced difference on Broadway between commercialism and professionalism, which, I think, can be traced to a difference in basic motivation. Pros, in the sense that I mean, are forever amateurs—they're in the theatre because they love it. Others are in it as a means of growing rich and famous, as a stepping-stone to more glittering rewards: they're commercial.

I reached a turning point in my theatre outlook and priorities when I went forth to discover America, traveling some nineteen thousand miles to look at seventy theatres in thirty states. The experience made it painfully evident that if there was little commercialism outside New York, there was little professionalism as well. The virtual demise of "the road" and of resident stock companies, largely caused by the Depression, meant that nine out of every ten students on the campuses I visited had never seen a professionally performed theatre piece.

Shocked and troubled, I now began to have a vision. While the alternative to Broadway's commercialism could not be found in the rest of the country, it seemed to me that the potential for something better was there, ready to be awakened and to assert itself. It took twenty years before resident professional companies began to emerge, but when they did I was astonished at my prophetic gift and gratified no end. Today those stages may be numbered in the hundreds and their annual attendance in seven figures.

After the war I returned to New York, but to work at *Theatre Arts*, not *Variety*; to reenter Broadway through an unheard-of door, a professional but not-for-profit institution that I helped to form, Theatre Incorporated. I made my directing debut in London with *Macbeth*, for the nonprofit arm of a commercial management. I was having my cake and eating it, working professionally but released from the pressures of commercialism.

But, inevitably, heeding the advice of my own 1941 book, *Advance from Broadway*, I moved from Forty-second Street to

Twelfth Street, and by establishing the Phoenix, with T. Edward Hambleton, lit one of the biggest fires in the New York theatre in that first postwar decade. Attracted by the blaze, others decided to bypass Broadway too, and off Broadway became a "movement," with a glow visible on horizons all across the country.

With this decentralization almost automatically came broad acceptance of the idea of nonprofit theatre. Gone were the days when T. and I had to persuade people that the stage was just as worthy of tax-exempt support as orchestras, ballet and opera companies, museums and libraries; that theatre, in other words, was an integral part of American culture's mainstream. Today, in cities from San Diego, Los Angeles, and Seattle, to Denver, Houston, Louisville, Minneapolis, and Chicago, to Boston, Providence, Washington, and Baltimore, with many others along the way, nonprofit theatres thrive, and contribute—with London—many of Broadway's most important and, ironically, commercial offerings.

So far in this "Curtain Speech" I've reviewed my roles as spectator and participant in theatre. But there is another part I played for quite a long run—missionary, in the guise of teacher. In earlier years, teaching served as both a safety net under the risks of stage unemployment and an opportunity to reinvigorate my knowledge. But as I grew older, my principal aim was to convert succeeding generations to the gospel of my own faith in theatre.

This missionary zeal was also ignited by my work on the Rockefeller Panel on the Performing Arts and the later Panel on the Arts in Education. But the briefest, the most recent, and perhaps the most spectacular of my gospel-spreading efforts occurred in 1984, when I spent five weeks in China as a guest of the government. Most of that time found me in Shanghai, at its Theatre Institute, where I delivered a series of sixteen three-hour lectures on Western theatre, especially our own, to students and faculties of acting, design, playwriting, and stage history, and to members of Shanghai's professional theatrical community. But I also made a short lecture tour, to Beijing for a week, with one-night stands in Hangzhou and Nanjing. My uncle, Henry

Houghton, who went to China as a medical missionary in 1906 and remained, off and on, about forty years, would have been pleased. I know I was.

Do you remember the ambiguous Fortune Teller in Wilder's *The Skin of Our Teeth?* "I tell the future. Nothing easier . . . but who can tell the past, eh? Nobody. Your youth—where did it go? It slipped away while you were asleep. . . . You're like our friends, Mr. and Mrs. Antrobus; you lie awake trying to know your past. What did it mean? What was it trying to say to you?"

I must admit I've been doing just that—trying to know my past—ever since I commenced this journey in memories. And, strictly speaking, the future should have no place in such an expedition backward in time. But the longer I live, the more interested I become in speculating on what I'm going to miss. So let me indulge in some conjecture about the good and the bad. The bad first.

I see no evidence that the materialism that began to burgeon in our society at midcentury will soon abate. The Reagan years gave it tremendous encouragement. Greed grew like plantain, and Americans now seem insatiable in their interest in the subject of Money—my money, your money, "other people's money" (the title of a recent play). As we enter the last decade of the century, billionaires dominate the tabloids, while conglomerates, arbitrageurs, hostile takeovers, "S&L" scandals, and colossal bankruptcies claim the headlines of the *New York Times* and the *Washington Post.*

The effect of materialism on our culture, our values, our social responses, and our political health is everywhere visible. Anyone concerned with activities in and sustenance of the arts—whatever the form may be—is forced to grapple with these consequences. The commercial Broadway theatre has "gone about as fur as it c'n go," to paraphrase *Oklahoma!* The not-for-profit theatres, which for a while have looked like the wave of the future, now face the most serious questions of where their subvention will come from. Federal and state support grows ever more precarious; private sources are being pressed by the increasing needs of education, health care—drug addiction, AIDS—the environment, and the campaign against poverty and homelessness, all urgent and proper—indeed, basic—demands that the government appears not to have enough billions to meet. How then can the private sector be expected to cover the deficits of ever more costly cultural institutions?

But "the arts *are* basic," we said in *Coming to Our Senses,* and of course I believe that. So let's take a second look, and let's not join the "money majority." Let's not assume that only increased outlays can guarantee a higher degree of excellence in our fields. Sometimes just the opposite is true. *The Golden Apple* had greater taste, charm, imagination, and wit than *Kismet,* which opened during the same season and cost ten times as much. And the Phoenix musical certainly had more of those qualities than that multimillion-dollar spectacle of unparalleled opulence and idiocy, *The Phantom of the Opera.*

Now, as I approach a valedictory of good cheer, let's think about *Driving Miss Daisy.* No marvels of staging, no "effects," just a couple of incandescent actors in a simple drama that speaks to our hearts and minds. It wins the Pulitzer Prize. Its low-budget film version receives nine Academy Award nominations and garners four Oscars. The play enters the third year of its run in New York. The movie sells out from coast to coast. Money was *not* a deciding factor in the success of this work.

In *The Exploding Stage,* I also managed to close on an optimistic note. To quote myself:

> There can be as profound emotional catharsis in a mass performed in a prison cell as in a basilica [how could I have said that? I've never been in a prison cell], as much excitement in watching two small boys dancing on a street corner as in seeing the Royal Ballet perform at the opera house. It is not a question of scale but of intensity. . . . Some of the most memorable theatre events I have ever witnessed have taken place in tiny lofts. The miracle was that the loft only strengthened the intensity.

Do I sound like a minimalist? Don't misunderstand—I love spectacle. How could I not, with *Chu Chin Chow, The Miracle,* my own Christmas pageants, and Princeton Triangle shows still strong in my memory? I've learned, however, in the almost three quarters of a century since I was first bedazzled by it, that splendor is not necessarily synonymous with beauty, that sometimes the mightiest pipe organ cannot match the power of the still, small voice.

Index